"We Can
Always
Call Them
Bulgarians"

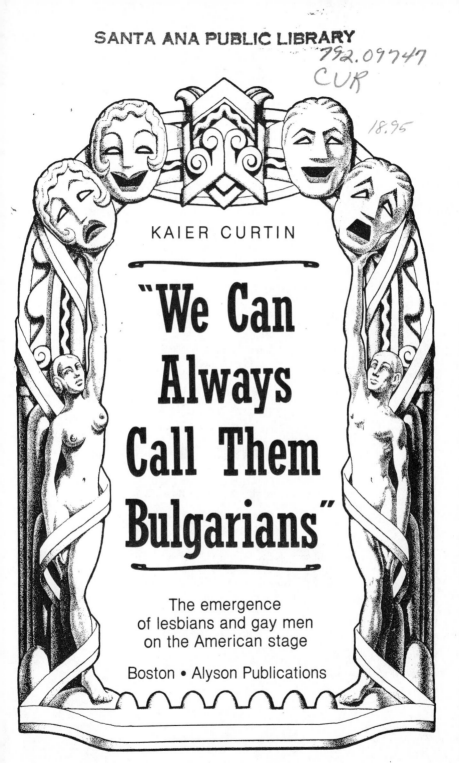

KAIER CURTIN

"We Can Always Call Them Bulgarians"

The emergence
of lesbians and gay men
on the American stage

Boston • Alyson Publications

Alyson Publications, Inc.
40 Plympton Street
Boston, Massachusetts 02118
Distributed in England by GMP Publishers,
PO Box 247, London, N15 6RW.

First edition, April, 1987

Library of Congress Cataloging-in-Publication Data

Curtin, Kaier.
"We can always call them Bulgarians".

Bibliograpy: p.
Includes index.
1. Theater — New York (N.Y.) — History — 20th century.
2. Homosexuals in literature. 3. Drama — History and
criticism. I. Title.
PN2277.N5C87 1986 792'.09747'1 86-17288
ISBN 0-932870-36-8

first printing

CONTENTS

LIST OF ILLUSTRATIONS

"We Can
Always
Call Them
Bulgarians"

INTRODUCTION

A Crime Not to Be
Dramatized Among Christians

In 1896, for the first time on the American stage, an audience in New York City saw two actresses passionately hugging and kissing; during the intermission immediately afterwards, seven ushers rushed down the aisles to offer ice water to any patron on the verge of fainting. Three decades later, the law descended on the first Broadway plays that dared to deal with lesbian love. In the 1920s, the dramatization of such a traditionally taboo subject was still intolerable to powerful religious and political pressure groups — even in cosmopolitan Manhattan.

One drama critic warned theatergoers that they would next have to look at the lesbians' "pale brethren" in Broadway plays; "then," he predicted, "it will all be over."[1] In 1927 the first play to introduce gay male characters to Broadway's legitimate theaters was scheduled to open. Theater owners, however, refused to rent the producer a stage. New York state legislators took further action to prevent the predicted moral breakdown in American society by passing a law prohibiting plays "depicting or dealing with, the subject of sex degeneracy, or sex perversion."[2] Despite such legal restrictions, over the next four decades New York theatergoers saw more than a hundred Broadway shows featuring gay or lesbian roles. It was not until the 1970s that self-identified lesbians and gay men began to emerge from their invisible status within the American social structure. Half a century before, their fictitious, dramatic counterparts completed that traumatic giant step on the boards of Broadway.

Two dozen of these "illegal" plays were produced during the most repressive era in American theater history, from the 1920s well into the 1940s. During this period, several shows were closed in police night-stick raids, and performers, playwrights and producers were arrested and threatened with imprisonment. Still, a number of plays with gay themes proved to be among the most commercially successful and critically acclaimed dramas of their theatrical seasons.

In the United States, it was not the gay liberation of the '70s, but rather the stage liberation of the '30s and '40s, which ended the legal restrictions on Broadway's portrayal of gay people. Civil libertarians joined activists within the theater to insist that the First Amendment right of free speech, which had already been granted to print media, be extended to the American stage. Even homophobic George Jean Nathan, the celebrated drama critic, raised his voice in support of the liberation of the New York stage. In 1938, Nathan argued that:

> The sons of swish may not *in facie curiae* constitute an endearing picture, it takes no heated argument with the bartender to prove. But in a world drama that has freely presented almost every other form of abnormal and perverted humanity, most often without objection, they may — if treated objectively and without cheap sensationalism — be allowed their clinical place.[3]

Trio, a drama about the breakup of a lesbian relationship, finally reached Broadway in 1945 despite formidable and much-publicized opposition. Bedlam broke out during the curtain calls on opening night. "I looked for them to tear down the marquee and do a snake dance up on the street in frenzied triumph," reported Burton Rascoe in the *World-Telegram.* Doubting that the play itself had elicited such enthusiasm, he concluded that "this demonstration was the natural reaction of Americans against any threat of official censorship — against any form of regimentation."[4]

Official censorship of the English-language stage had long been practiced in England, where the Lord Chamberlain's Office was empowered under the Theatres Licensing Act of 1737 to decide what was appropriate entertainment for the British public. Such "offensive personalities"[5] as lesbians and gay men were not seen on the British public stage until the Licensing Act was liberalized by Parliament in 1968. Before that time, only production companies with subscription-list memberships were able to perform plays not approved by the government censor. In the 1920s, therefore, during legally limited engagements, London playgoers were able to see gay male characters on the private stages of little theaters for the first time in over three and a half centuries.

Anyone convicted of sodomy in Elizabethan England could be hanged. It is hardly surprising then that the marked gay sensibility of William Shakespeare is less apparent in his works for the public theater than in his private love sonnets. But this penalty of death, seemed not to have intimidated Shakespeare's contemporary, Christopher Marlowe. According to theatre historian Frederick Howe, Marlowe's *Edward II* is "the only play in English literature that treats homosexual love as a grand passion and a fit subject for tragedy."[6]

There were, to be sure, references to gays before Marlowe. Historian William H. Hoffman points out: "In *The Killing of Abel* of the fourteenth century and among the earliest mystery plays written in English, there are obscene puns about Cain's behavior with Abel, the Devil and his 'boye' Garcia."[7] Marlowe, nevertheless, was the first dramatist to write plays with overtly gay characters for the English-language public theater; that Marlowe did so during the reign of Elizabeth I is astonishing. British scholar Alan Bray states in *Homosexuality in Renaissance England:* "If there was one characteristic of homosexuality which must have influenced behavior more than any other, then that is the revulsion and hostility which homosexuality aroused."[8]

The horrifying and historically accurate mode of execution of the gay king in Marlowe's *Edward II* may have made a subject "not to be mentioned among Christians" not only tolerable but also satisfying to Elizabethan audiences. A red-hot poker shoved up Edward's rectum hardly seems appropriate punishment for dereliction of the king's royal duties; it does, however, illustrate the Elizabethan attitude toward homosexuality. A popular poem of the period, which sadistically described the dying agony of Sodom and Gomorrah, further illustrates that attitude. The poet, according to Bray, "was a spokesman for a culture in which homosexuality was a loathsome and evil thing: the horror of the sodomites' deaths was in his eyes a fitting counterpart to the horror of their lives."[9]

Marlowe is quoted by an intimate as having said, "All they that love not Tobacco and Boies were fools," and that "St. John the Evangelist was bedfellow to Christ."[10] He must also have shocked some of his audiences with scenes just as outrageous. In *Edward II,* for example, the king openly declares his love for two of his favorites at court. In *The Massacre of Paris,* King Henry III of France is shown indulging himself with his minions. And in *Dido, Queen of Carthage,* Jupiter is seen holding Ganymede, his catamite, on his lap. *Dido* was acted, incredibly enough, by the Children of the Chapel Royal.

Performances of *Edward II* seem to have been rare after its premiere in 1593. Although done once for Jacobean audiences, there is no record of any other productions, either at colleges or in public theaters, for the next 286 years. In 1903, Granville Barker played the title role in a production by the Elizabethan Stage Society at Oxford. But it wasn't until 1958 that an American audience saw a professional performance in an off-Broadway theater in Greenwich Village. Director John Houseman's City Center Acting Company gave *Edward II* its Broadway premiere during the 1974–75 theatrical season. "With the fading of sexual inhibitions of our contemporary stage, it has become possible to realize a production,"[11] Houseman said almost four centuries after the tragedy was first performed.

While Marlowe penned four plays with gay characters, there is only one passing reference to an overtly gay sexual relationship in all of William Shakespeare's work. In *Troilus and Cressida,* Thersites, a deformed and scurrilous Greek, accuses Achilles and Patrocles of being lovers, as Homer had suggested in the *Iliad.* Thersites taunts Patrocles by calling Achilles his "masculine whore." The commander neither denies the charge nor mentions the matter to Achilles in later scenes.

In recent years a number of theater historians, along with critics, scholars, psychologists, psychoanalysts, poets and players, have identified other plays by Shakespeare that contain sexually ambiguous male characters. Some scholarly analyses of *Othello,* for example, suggest that Iago is a covert gay.[12] According to another scholar, not only is Hamlet gay, but so was Shakespeare.[13] Samuel Taylor Coleridge described the king in *Richard II* as having an "intensely woman-like love for those immediately around him."[14] W.H. Auden called King Leontes in *The Winter's Tale* "a typical case of repressed jealousy brought on by repressed homosexuality."[15] Actor Ian McInery, who played Mercutio in Franco Zeffirelli's film version of *Romeo and Juliet,* said, "In order to justify the role, I had to play it with a deep attachment to Romeo. That's the only way Mercutio makes any sense."[16]

In a 1934 analysis of *The Merchant of Venice,* Thomas Arthur Ross was the first to ever suggest that the title character is sad because he is gay: "Antonio is homosexually in love with Bassanio. Shakespeare regards continent homosexuality as noble and admirable and therefore he shows Antonio in Act V as the most noble character in the play."[17]

In addition to Ross, a number of other scholars have identified Antonio as an "unconscious homosexual."[18] At the beginning of the play, he laments "In sooth, I know not why I am so sad." If Antonio was not aware that his attraction to Bassanio is sexual, *New York Times* critic Clive Barnes was. In a 1970 review of the play, Barnes identified Antonio as an apparent "homosexual,"[19] as if such an interpretation of the role was indisputedly clear. It has even been suggested that "Antonio's melancholy, or depression. . . is Shakespeare's own,"[20] since such a state of mind is evident in the playwright's *Sonnets.*

It is rather ironic that in 1752, the first known professional company to perform in America selected *The Merchant of Venice* as their premiere production. Had that audience in Williamsburg, Virginia, recognized in the play what now seems so apparent to scholars and critics, the acting company might have been run out of town. Even 165 years later, when Mae West tried to introduce more readily recognizable gay male characters to the American stage, police intimidation forced the pre-Broadway show to close during its out-of-town tryout.

Except for two plays, English-language audiences saw neither overt gay roles such as Marlowe introduced, nor covert gay ones such as Shakespeare contrived, until the turn of the twentieth century. Both exceptions were comedies: Sir John Vanburgh's *The Relapse,* produced in 1692, and Oscar Wilde's *The Importance of Being Earnest,* produced in 1895.

Scott Giantvalley of the University of Southern California

describes the gay characer who appears in *The Relapse:*

> There is a mock homosexual seduction scene, in which Coupler, "a Matchmaker," puts the make on Young Fashion, who promptly exclaims, "Stand off, old Sodom!" But since he does need the older man's skills at intrigue, he finally allows the matchmaker a couple of kisses at the end of the scene. The author hardly intends his audience to be on Coupler's side in this comic conflict between homosexual and heterosexual, but unlike so many homosexual characters in 20th century drama, Coupler is no figure of pity or scorn or villainy, and certainly not sick or criminal — the only problem is that he's "got the wrong man," not unlike many Restoration comedy heterosexual characters, whose sexual excesses are often misdirected.[21]

Critic Eric Bentley, when asked for the most significant piece of gay theater to date, replied, *"The Importance of Being Earnest,* because it is by Oscar Wilde (and his best play)."[22] Wilde's work marked the first appearance in English dramatic literature since the Elizabethans of characters who seem to be sexually involved with their own gender. "To the bisexual man," critic Mary McCarthy wrote in 1963, "it was perhaps deliciously comic that a man should have one name, the tamest in English, for trips and 'lost weekends.'"[23] In Wilde's Victorian comedy of manners about two young bachelors, Jack invents a fictitious personality living in London, an imaginary brother named Ernest, whose name and reprobate lifestyle he adopts during his frequent trips to the city. Algernon, the other young bachelor, also invents an imaginary friend, Bunbury, whom he visits frequently in country. Algernon calls these visits to his friend "bunburying." Such trips, of course, were actually taken by the bachelors to "sow their wild oats."

Algy and Jack are very much enamored of two lovely young ladies, whom they succeed in wooing. Their sexual preferences, both close to and away from home, would seem to be heterosexual. The 1895 comedy met with great success during its initial engagement and in countless revivals since; still, critic McCarthy complains that the audience "is pointedly left out of the fun," because "the joke about the name Ernest is doubtless a private one."[24]

Since she made no mention of the name Bunbury in her critique, McCarthy herself may have been left out of the fun by failing to recognize Wilde's bawdy humor in devising a name that contains a slang expression for the buttocks. In 1881, W.S. Gilbert had fun with the same slang expression when he called the fleshy poet in his comic opera, *Patience,* Bunthorne. Oscar Wilde, of course, was the poet being satirized, and fourteen years later, he toyed with the same first syllable. Had the Lord Chamberlain's office understood what Algernon meant by "bunburying," the comedy would hardly have been licensed for public production in Victorian England.

America, unlike Great Britain, had no pre-production censorship by a government official, although certain private citizens wanted to decide what the public could read in books or see on stage. Chief among these moral censors was Anthony Comstock, a spinsterish drygoods salesman whose I.Q., according to one of his critics, "would almost certainly not have rated him above the age of twelve."[25] In 1873, Comstock founded the New York Society for the Suppression of Vice, which he headed until 1915. Under his direction, the Watch and Ward Society was organized in Boston. In a number of widely publicized attacks on publishers and theatrical producers, Comstock called upon the police to suppress books and plays that he believed would tend to corrupt public morality.

In February of 1900, New York police closed *Sapho,* a drama about a Parisian prostitute who had modeled for a statue of the lesbian poetess Sappho. As the curtain descended, audiences were shocked to see a woman carried by her lover through a bedroom door. Newspaper editor William Randolph Hearst protested, "We expect the police to forbid on stage what they would forbid in streets and low resorts."[26] *Sapho* reopened when a jury acquitted Olga Nethersole of giving an indecent performance in the title role.

In 1905 the Manhattan police, egged on by Comstock, closed George Bernard Shaw's *Mrs. Warren's Profession* because it dealt with a seemingly respectable woman who operated a brothel. In 1913, *Damaged Goods,* a play about a syphilitic young man, caused a furor but was not shut down. By 1921 there was talk of state censorship of the Broadway stage when Al Woods produced *The Demi-Virgin.* The mildly risque play became a hit after the producer obtained an injunction to prevent the license commissioner from closing the show.

The Society for the Suppression of Vice was headed by John S. Sumner after Anthony Comstock's death. Sumner spearheaded the drive against gay and lesbian characters when they were introduced to Broadway theatergoers in the 1920s. Joining him were publisher

Hearst, a few politicians, much of the clergy, and several of New York's most prestigious drama critics.

Curiously enough, female impersonators, who had been familiar for many years to American theatergoers in minstrel shows, vaudeville skits, Broadway follies and even serious dramas, seemed to have no connection in the public consciousness with an abhorrence of lesbians and gay men. Charles Pierce, a professional imitator of famous actresses, observed that, "until the nightclub came along in the '30s, 'homo' was not inevitably attached to female impersonation."[27] Ziegfeld Follies star Bert Savoy, as well as other vaudeville entertainers, often did comic or campy impersonations of women. Julian Eltinge, on the other hand, was considered a serious artist, playing female roles in straight dramas and musical comedies. He was so successful, in fact, that he was able to build his own theater in 1912.

Even though Eltinge was held in the highest public regard and female impersonators in vaudeville were warmly received, actors who portrayed men wearing female attire in Mae West's 1928 Broadway play *Pleasure Man* were arrested by police and spat upon by onlookers as they were led from the stagedoor to the paddy wagons. There was no mistaking from their performances, with dialogue supplied by West, that the actors in *Pleasure Man* were portraying sexual deviants. Theater historian Graham Jackson reminds us:

> Gay theatre has a longer history than the gay novel — but not nearly so fertile a one. From the very beginning, innuendo has been the chief means of conveying homosexual themes to the theatre audience ... The public, the majority of the theatregoers, have always insisted upon special protection from anything unpleasant. As many playwrights, directors and producers learned the hard way, one cannot always do on a stage what one could do without censure in a novel. The stage presentation packing a more immediate and less intellectual punch. *[sic]*[28]

English novelist and playwright Elizabeth Inchwald (1753–1831) said that the novelist "lives in a land of liberty, whilst the dramatic writer exists but under a despotic government,"[29] an observation that held true of the English-language theater until the second half of the twentieth century.

According to a study by Dr. Jim Lewis, there were no novels with overt gay male characters before the 1930s.[30] In 1896, however, the first American drama with a gay character was published. Written by Chicago-born novelist, Henry Blake Fuller (1857–1929), the eleven-page playlet *At Saint Judas's* is included in a collection of twelve very brief one-act dramas under the title *The Puppet-Booth*. Despite the collection's title, the playlets do not seem suited for puppet production. When one considers the work's brevity and the elaborate scenery prescribed for its performance, *At Saint Judas's* may be a "closet drama" meant to be read rather than played. As a result, it did not receive a professional performance during the author's lifetime,[31] and there is no record of any production since his death in 1929.

Fuller, eulogized by fellow novelist and playwright Thornton Wilder as his "friend and teacher,"[32] wrote this tragedy — which concerns a gay bachelor — when he was twenty-nine and himself a bachelor . Set in the sacristy of the church of St. Judas, the dialogue is interrupted throughout by Latin chants and comments from symbolic figures who come to life in eight stained-glass windows. In the foreground, a bridegroom and his best man, both in uniform, are readying themselves for the wedding ceremony. The distressed best man tells of first learning of the planned nuptials when the bridegroom talked in his sleep, his friend's pillow next to his own. He then confesses:

> The Best Man. . . . *(He places his hand upon the other's shoulder.)* If she were to come, I should not let her have you. She shall not have you. Nobody shall have you.
> The Bridegroom. What is your meaning, Oliver?
> The Best Man. I shall not let you go. Our friendship has been too long; too close, too intimate. It shall not be destroyed; it shall not be broken. No one shall come between us.[33]

Revolted at his friend's passionate affection, the bridegroom rages:

> The Bridegroom. You are not fit to live. You are not fit to die, but die you shall. I shall not kill you. You shall kill yourself. You shall do it now, and I shall see you do it, you have no other road to redemption.[34]

The play's final scene reveals the body of a man in a pool of blood.

The lesbian as a character does not exist in English-language dramatic literature until the third decade of this century. Still, such characterizations appeared in both English-language novels and in Broadway plays a whole decade before gay male characters were to be found either in such books or on the American stage. When lesbian roles were introduced to New York theatergoers in the 1920s, in translations from Yiddish and French, apparently many in the audiences did not recognize them as such. That may have been a significant factor in the toleration seemingly accorded them before gay male characterizations were allowed in theatrical productions. However, when more sophisticated theatergoers, such as the critics, did recognize lesbian characters, they often reacted with rage and horror.

A Florida Enchantment, the first play in which young actresses were seen in one another's arms, "hugging ... passionately and kissing ... with paroxysmal delight,"[35] had nothing to do with lesbians at all. A.C. Gunter, "the shopgirl's favorite novelist,"[36] had based the farce on one of his most popular penny novels. The play premiered at the Park Theatre in April 1896 and was seen again that autumn in a three-week engagement at Hoyt's Theatre. A silent-film version starring Sidney Drew was released by the Vitagraph Company in the summer of 1914. Neither the novel nor the movie version had the effect on people that the staged performances did. After only one scene, a reviewer reported, "the management very considerately arranges to have seven boys walk smartly around the audience with ice water."[37] Another reviewer wrote: "It was nauseous ... disgusting. It will insist upon being recollected as the most singular of all the offenses that have been committed upon our stage."[38]

The *New York Dramatic Mirror* provides us with this plot summary of the play which so unsettled theatergoers before the turn of the century:

> A young girl becomes possessed of a few magical seeds that confer a change of sex upon any individual who swallows one of them. The maiden courageously swallows a seed, and finds herself a young man ... Thus transmogrified, the young girl obtains revenge on a faithless lover by paying court to a pretty widow. Her former devices to play parts in contrary sexes constitutes the body of the play.[39]

From another reviewer we know that the plot of *A Florida Enchantment,* which he called "a most audacious one," also involves "the transformation of a very masculine and persistent love-making physician into a timid and somewhat hysterical female."[40] "The change from manhood to womanhood is so mortifying and disappointing," according to another critic, "that his pleadings to be changed back into a man are complied with."[41] On the other hand, the young woman — now a man — has a marvelous time flirting and romping about. The *Dramatic Mirror* reported, "Mr. Gunter took pains to announce that his primary reason in perpetuating the play was to show that in a measure men have a better time than women amid the social environment of our present civilization."[42]

If one accepts the comedy's farcical premise that no less than four magical sex changes take place, then it is not a woman who falls in love with a woman, but rather a man who does so. A.C. Gunter wrote the first play about transsexuals, male as well as female. *A Florida Enchantment* does not, therefore, relate to the emergence of gay and lesbian characters on the American stage any more than does George Axelrod's 1959 Broadway hit *Goodbye Charlie*. In that comedy the title character, a notorious womanizer, is reincarnated in the body of a beautiful woman. In both plays, a physical change in sex diffused the charge of same-sex romance.

That the author of *A Florida Enchantment* "took pains" in 1896 to dissociate his farce from any suggestion that it had to do with sexual deviation may have had something to do with the trial of Oscar Wilde. Just a year before Gunter's comedy was produced, Wilde was publicly humiliated and imprisoned as a convicted sodomite. The entrenched homophobia of the English-speaking people that surfaced in the wake of Wilde's trial could not but have intimidated any British or American writer, no matter what his or her sexual predilection, who dared to even touch upon the plight of the despised minority. Consequently, when gay and lesbian roles were finally introduced to the American stage in the 1920s, none of their creators were identified as being gay. W. Somerset Maugham, Noel Coward, and other famous authors dared not risk public exposure or popular rejection by identifying themselves with gay themes.

Late in his career, Maugham told his nephew:

> Why do you suppose that Noel or I have never stuck our personal predilections down the public's throats? Because we know it would outrage them. Believe me, I know what I'm talking about. Don't put your head in a noose ... [43]

While his reference to hanging was not, of course, meant to be taken literally, it is a reminder that not until 1861 — just thirteen years before Maugham's birth — did England discontinue the penalty of death by hanging for men convicted of sexual activity with other men.

Notes

1. Fragment of an untitled, undated newspaper article in file folder MWEZ n.c. 6901, New York City Public Library, Lincoln Center.
2. Jonathan Katz, *Gay American History* (New York: Thomas Y. Crowell Company, 1976), p. 90.
3. George Jean Nathan, untitled, undated magazine article from unknown publication in Oscar Wilde file, Lincoln Center.
4. Burton Rascoe, "'Trio' Is Good But Fails Buildup As Sensational," *New York World Telegram,* 30 December 1944.
5. Phyllis Hartnoll, ed. *The Oxford Companion To The Theatre* (London: Oxford University Press, 1967), p.248.
6. Frederick Howe, "Homosexuality In English Drama," *Advocate,* 23 February 1977.
7. William Hoffman, ed. *Gay Plays: The First Collection* (New York: Avon Books, 1979), p. xiv.
8. Alan Bray, *Homosexuality in Renaissance England* (London: Gay Men's Press, 1982), p. 58.
9. *Ibid.,* p. 59.
10. Paul Kocher, *Christopher Marlowe* (New York: Rusell and Rusell, 1962), p. 209.
11. Gerald Pinciss, *Christopher Marlowe* (New York, Frederick Ungar Publishing Co., 1975), p. 110.
12. Marvin Rosenberg, *The Masks of Othello: The Search For The Identity of Othello, Iago and Desdemona by Three Centuries of Actors and Critics* (Berkeley and Los Angeles: University of California Press, 1961), p. 175-184; Martin Wangh, "Othello: The Tragedy of Iago," *Psychoanalytic Quarterly,* (XIX, 1950), pp. 202-212.
13. E. E. Krapf, "Shylock and Antonio: A Psychoanalytic Study of Shakespeare and Anti-Semitism," *Psychoanalytic Review,* (XLIII, 1955), pp. 113-130.
14. Paul M. Cubeta, ed. *Twentieth Century Interpretations of Richard II,* (Englewood Cliffs, N.J.: Prentice Hall, Inc., 1971), p. 60.
15. W. H. Auden, "The Alienated City: Reflections on 'Othello'" *Encounter,* (August, 1961), p. 11.
16. Ian McInery, private conversation, New York City, 4 November 1981.
17. Thomas Arthur Ross, "A Note On The Merchant of Venice," *British Journal of Medical Psychology,* (XIV, 1934), pp. 301-311.
18. E. E. Karpf, "Shylock and Antonio: A Psychoanalytic Study of Shakespeare and Anti-Semitism," *Psychoanalytic Review,* (XLII, 1955), pp. 113-130; Graham Midgley, "The Merchant of Venice: A Reconsideration," *Essays in Criticism,* (X, 1960): cited by Norman N. Holland, *Psychoanalysis and Shakespeare* (New York: McGraw-Hill Book Co., 1964), p. 238; W.I.D. Scott, *Shakespeare Melancholics* (London: Mills and Boon, Ltd., 1962), Ch. 3, as cited by Holland.
19. Clive Barnes, "Theatre: Another Look at 'Merchant'" *New York Times,* 10 June 1970.
20. Karpf, pp. 113-130.
21. Scott Giantvalley, Dept. of English, University of Southern California, private correspondence, 5 July 1977.
22. Terry Helbing, "Rogues' Gallery," *Christopher Street,* (June, 1978), p. 18.
23. Mary McCarthy, "The Unimportance of Being Oscar Wilde," *Mary McCarthy's Theatre Chronicles* (New York: Farrar, Straus & Company), p. 106.
24. *Ibid.,* p. 106.
25. Ernest Sutherland Bates, "Comstock Stalks," *Scribner's Magazine,* (April, 1930), p. 362.
26. Abe Laufe, *The Wicked Stage: A History of Theatre Censorship and Harassment in the United States* (New York: Frederick Ungar Publishing Co., 1978), p. 25.
27. Frederick Howe, "An Exploration of the History of Female Impersonators," *Advocate,* (5 October 1977).

28. Graham Jackson, "The Theatre of Implication," *Canadian Theatre Review* (Fall, 1976), p. 34.

29. L.W. Connoly, *The Censorship of English Drama 1737-1824 (San Marino, California: The Huntington Library, 1976), p. 11.*

30. Jim Levin, *"Butterflies, Pansies, Twilight Men and Strange Brothers: The American Male Homosexual Novel Between the Wars,"* Gai Saber (New York: Gay Academic Union, 1978), p. 244.

31. Constance M. Griffin, *Henry Blake Fuller: A Critical Biography* (Philadelphia: University of Pennsylvania Press, 1939), p. 49.

32. Anna Morgan, ed. *Tributes to Henry B. Fuller In Whose Minds and Hearts He Will Always Live* (n.c.: Ralph Fletcher Seymour Publisher, 1920), p. 106.

33. Henry B. Fuller, *The Puppet-Booth: Twelve Plays* (New York: The Century Co., 1896), p. 96.

34. *Ibid.,* p.98.

35. Untitled review of *A Florida Enchantment,* dated 12 October 1896, from unknown New York newspaper on file, Lincoln Center.

36. Fragment from another review in *A Florida Enchantment* file.

37. Fragment from another review in file cited above.

38. Fragment from another review in file cited above.

39. "At Hoyt's Theatre A Comedy in 4 Acts by Archibald Clavering Gunter," *New York Dramatic Mirror,* 17 October 1896.

40. Fragment from another review in file cited above.

41. Fragment from another review in file cited above.

42. *New York Dramatic Mirror,* 17 October 1896.

43. Robin Maugham, *Somerset and All The Maughams,* (New York: The New American Library, 1966), p. 201.

1

The First Lesbian Character
Ever Seen on an English-language Stage

Despite the social, sexual and cultural revolutions that followed World
War I, British and American playwrights were restrained from including gay and lesbian roles in their work. Although such characters
were known to Continental theatergoers during the same period, they
were legally prohibited in English-language theater productions.
Eugene O'Neill would wait until 1928 before introducing a gay
character in *Strange Interlude,* and then so circumspectly that Broadway critics seemed not to recognize it. Banned from any public stage,
Prisoners of War, by J.R. Ackerley, could only be seen in a limited
engagement in 1925 at a private membership playhouse in London;
another decade passed before an American producer was bold enough
to bring that drama about a gay infatuation to New York.

It is not surprising, then, that the first lesbian character seen on
the New York stage was introduced by a playwright far removed from
the English-speaking world. Even before World War I, plays done in
the Yiddish theater, according to one of its greatest stars, Maurice
Schwartz, "were more forthright, earthy and robust in the treatment
of sex than were plays seen on Broadway."[1] And so it was that
Sholom Asch — whose novels in translation eventually won him international popularity among both Jewish and non-Jewish readers —
gave New Yorkers their first play with a lesbian love scene.

Sholom Asch was only twenty-one when he wrote the shocking play which "aroused heated debate"[2] and "created bitter dispute on both sides of the Atlantic,"[3] among both liberal and more conservative Yiddish-speaking audiences. Asch became the first Yiddish dramatist whose plays established an international reputation outside the Jewish world. In 1907 Max Reinhardt gave Asch's *Gott fun Nekoma* its first German-language production at the Deutsches theater in Berlin. By the end of the next decade, after being translated into a dozen languages, it had played throughout Germany, as well as in Russia, Austria, Poland, Holland, Norway, Sweden, and Italy. *Gott fun Nekoma* had been seen for seventeen years in productions at New York's Yiddish theaters. It ran into trouble only after it was translated into English as *The God of Vengeance* and moved from the Provincetown Theater in Greenwich Village to the Apollo Theater along Broadway's Great White Way.

The God of Vengeance is set in a Jewish house of prostitution in a provincial town in Poland. The proprietor naively believes he can raise a teenage daughter untouched by the sensuality of the brothel he operates in the cellar of his home, only one floor below the family's living quarters. To insure that his closely protected daughter marries a respectable, middle-class scholar (instead of following in the footsteps of her mother, an ex-prostitute) the father buys a Torah scroll for his home. He expects the Pentateuch to protect the girl and placate the vengeful God of the Old Testament.

Once the problem has been presented early in the first act, the outcome is predictable. The surprise comes in the person of a young prostitute who sneaks upstairs to visit the daughter. Instead of being lured below by a male patron or male procurer, the young girl becomes involved in her own home with the prostitute — a possibility that never occurred to her overprotective father. As the curtain descends on Act One, the two young women, locked in an embrace, passionately kiss.

In Act Two, Rivkele, the daughter sneaks out of her bedroom while her parents sleep to join Manke, the prostitute, for a frolic outside in the warm May rain. Barefoot and dripping wet, Rivkele and Manke come into the basement bagnio, wrapped together in a wet shawl. Manke proceeds to seduce the young girl in a frank and sensual scene of lesbian lovemaking, the like of which has never been repeated

Two of these actresses, Dorothee Nolan and Virginia MacFayden (not identifiable), played lovers in the first production in the English language of a drama with lesbian characters. The whole cast of The God of Vengeance, *including famed Viennese stage star Rudolph Schildkraut who was making his English-language debut, was arrested in 1922.*

in a Broadway play. As they snuggle closely on the sofa, Manke fondles Rivkele's breast and washes her face in the girl's loose hair. After combing it in the manner of a Jewish bride, the prostitute tells Rivkele:

> *Manke.* ... you're my bride and I'm your bridegroom. We embrace. *(She puts her arms around her.)* We're pressed together, and we kiss very quietly, like this. *(They kiss.)* We blush, we're so embarrassed. It's good, isn't it, Rivkele?
> *Rivkele.* Yes, Manke, it is.
> *Manke (lowers her voice, whispering in her ear).* And then we go to sleep in the same bed. No one sees us, no one knows, just the two of us, like this. *(She presses Rivkele to her.)* Would you like to sleep the whole night through with me, Rivkele, in the same bed?
> *Rivkele (embracing her).* I would, I would.
> *Manke.* Come, come.
> *Rivkele (whispering).* I'm afraid of my father. He may get up.[4]

The proprietor's daughter runs off with Manke to spend the night with her in the house another prostitute shares with a procurer. As Act Two comes to a close, the enraged father discovers too late that his daughter has escaped from the bedroom in which he had locked her.

In the final act, the procurer returns Rivkele to her home after her mother has paid him handsomely. "Are you still a chaste Jewish girl?" the distraught father shouts repeatedly at his frightened daughter. After a night of lesbian lovemaking, Rivkele is unsure of the answer: "I don't know!"[5] she replies. Enraged at her evasiveness, the proprietor brutally drags his daughter by the hair to place Rivkele among his prostitutes in the brothel below. As he does so, the embittered father instructs an astonished, matchmaking rabbi who has witnessed the climactic scene to take away the Torah scroll that has failed to protect his daughter from the vengeful God of Israel.

It may be difficult for many modern, secular readers and theatergoers to relate to the predominantly religious motif and the melodrama of *The God of Vengeance.* According to one authority on Yiddish literature, the drama has "retained merely antiquarian interest"[6] since World War II wherever it has been produced. Asch's delicately erotic lesbian love scene from *The God of Vengeance,* nevertheless, is surprisingly modern in its candor and insight into the dynamics of sexual seduction.

Dr. Isaac Goldberg, who translated Asch's drama from Yiddish into English in 1918, observed that "When Ash *[sic]* wishes to deal with sex as sex he is not afraid to handle the subject with all the poetry and power at his command."[7] Although Asch had been venturous enough to introduce the subject of lesbian love in 1907, it was not until 1922 that an American, a woman, dared to produce *The God of Vengeance* for English-speaking audiences. This was four years after Dr. Goldberg's English translation had been published in Boston.

Because of its subject matter, the setting, and the fact that the protagonist turns against his religion at the end, *The God of Vengeance* was predictably attacked as being scandalous and sacrilegious by certain critics and playgoers when it was first produced in Yiddish.[8] Asch felt no need to reply to such a criticism until an American court had judged it obscene and immoral.

After its English-language premiere the playwright wrote:

> I was not concerned whether I wrote a moral or immoral play. What I wanted to write was an artistic play and a true one. In the seventeen years it has been before the public, this is the first time I have had to defend it...

As to the scenes between Manke and Rivkele, on every European stage, especially in Russia, they were the most poetic of all, and the critics in those countries appreciated this poetic view. This love between the two girls is not only an erotic one. It is the unconscious mother love of which they are deprived. The action portrays the love of the woman-mother, who is Manke, for the woman-child, who is Rivkele, rather than the sensuous, inverted love of one woman for another. In this particular scene, I also wanted to bring out the innocent, longing for sin, and the sinful, dream of purity. Manke, overweighted with sin, loves the clean soul of Rivkele, and Rivkele, the innocent girl, longs to stay near the door of such a woman as Manke and listen within.[9]

Two little-known actresses portrayed the lesbian characters in *The God of Vengeance,* which starred Rudolph Schildkraut, who had directed himself in the Reinhardt world premiere in Berlin. Schildkraut agreed to make his English-language debut as the proprietor of the house of prostitution in the Greenwich Village production at the Provincetown Theatre, a small theater off Washington Square.

Produced by play-broker Alice Kauser, Schildkraut's American debut was called a "superb performance which hushed his audience and held it breathless."[10] Another critic wrote:

Last evening at the Provincetown Theatre his performance stirred one of those outbursts of violent approbation more common to Grand Opera histrionism and football games than to displays of impersonification without music. They were still cheering when we left.[11]

Backstage, John Barrymore, who had electrified Broadway the month before with his Hamlet, knelt dramatically before Schildkraut to kiss his hand.

Those who read Burns Mantle's review of the play in the *Daily News* could have had no idea that *The God of Vengeance* was the first play to introduce lesbian characters to English-language audiences.[12] Mantle, like most of the New York critics, failed to make any mention whatsoever of the lesbian motif. In like manner, the critic for the *Evening Telegram,* defending the sketchiness of his review, explained, "The terrible details need not be recorded here, They are almost too terrible to look upon in the theatre."[13] The *Morning Telegraph* observed that "despite the fact a story or an episode may be 'true to life,'; even a reproduction of life, it seems to us that there are some themes that have no place on the stage."[14] Just as evasive was the *Globe* critic who made no reference to the lesbian love scene other than to note that, among the prostitutes, there was "one of even more irregular and nasty habits."[15] Finally, the critic for the *New York Sun* mentioned "two episodes such as we have never before seen on the stage"[16] without identifying them any further.

From the inconclusive evidence available today, it is impossible to tell exactly how much of the rather brief lesbian love scenes actually appeared in its first English-language presentation. According to Alice Kauser, the producer, cuts were made in *The God of Vengeance* "to defer [to] the sensitive people who do not care to listen to passages spoken in public although those very passages could possibly have no offense when read."[17]

Alexander Woollcott, who reviewed the drama for the *New York Herald,* seems to have been familiar with Asch's script as it was seen abroad and in Yiddish-language productions in America. Woollcott noticed that the two "scenes of amorous inversion" had been "severely shortened."[18]

Even with cuts, Heywood Broun of the *World* understood that "the play deals frankly with the perversion of a young girl." Disgusted at what he saw, Broun complained that "the scene between the young girl and the harlot in the father's establishment made us a little sick ... The American stage has not yet achieved absolute frankness in dealing with the more traditional vices. We can afford to wait until that fight has been won before venturing into decadence."[19]

The critic for the *New York Evening Post,* like Broun, fully understood that "the girl falls victim to a lesbian." He also observed that "despite the fact that certain pathological phases of life are not suited for the stage, those in Sholom Asch's *The God of Vengeance* were more or less absorbing."[20] Percy Hammond of the *Tribune* commented, "Propinquity to the Polish Jezebels influences her to odd aspirations, the nature of which it unbecomes us to suspect. At any rate she is carried away by one of her parent's dubious saleswomen."[21] A woman reviewing *The God of Vengeance* — perhaps the only woman to do so for a national publication — was more candid than most of the male critics in appraising the personality and the plight of the brothel owner's daughter. "Her inverted curiosity makes her the easy victim of her sex," wrote Maida Castellum, "and she escapes with Manke, a lesbian companion, to her predestined fate."[22]

Although *New York Times* critic John Corbin made no mention of lesbianism in his review, he may have had that in mind when he made a pessimisitic prediction about the play's chances of survival: "It is not likely to achieve popularity, unless Greenwich Village should develop an appetite for the seamy side of life beyond anything it has yet displayed."[23] Asch's drama, it turned out, appealed to a wider audience than that within walking distance of the drafty avant-garde playhouse. In fact, the demand for seats during its run at the Provincetown was such that Attorney Harry Weinberger, who took over production from Alice Kauser, first moved it to the larger Greenwich Village Theatre and then, to attract bigger audiences, to Broadway: it opened at the Apollo Theatre on Forty-second Street on February 19, 1923.

Greenwich Village, particularly after World War I, had become New York City's Left Bank, hospitable not only to the so-called bohemians, but also to the underground gay community. Audiences supporting the experimental little theaters in the Village were composed, in large part, of anti-establishment, avant-garde intellectuals, writers and artists. As a result, newspaper critics would only come to the Provincetown Theatre to see a production with a star as prestigious as Rudolph Schildkraut. Booming Broadway kept the watchdogs of public morality so occupied in 1922, they did not concern themselves with tacky little showcases in the Village.

Because Asch's drama had already been reviewed when it premiered in December, none of the critics went for a second look when it opened on Broadway in February. Newspaper columnists pointedly ignored the production, as well as its star. Even in those rare editorials or news items which either damned or defended the production, *The God of Vengeance* was often not mentioned by name.

One magazine review, however, indicates that the lesbian seduction scene was still in the show after it moved to the Apollo Theater. English-born Arthur Hornblow, critic for *Theater Magazine,* fumed:

> The progress of this translation from the Yiddish from a Washington Square theatre to the august sanctity of a 42nd Street house is ascribable, alas, not so much to its merits as to its dirt. A more foul and unpleasant spectacle has never been seen in New York ... Mr. Asch's drama deals fundamentally with the vengeful god of Judea.
> ...The Jewish god is a horribly cruel one in this instance. He

thwarts the father's purpose by having his pure young daughter fall into the clutches of Lesbians and the audience is treated to a nightgown scene in which the women make overtures to each other which go so far beyond the pale of what is permissible that I can only voice my astonishment at the authorities allowing a thing of this sort to be continued before heterosexual audiences, comprised of individuals young and old who go to the theatre to be entertained and without any conception of what they may be asked to witness. It is really a bit thick. There may be a place for such dramas on the stage but their audiences must be known as intelligent and incorruptible and not the immature, easily influenced individuals to whom *The God of Vengeance* might do grievous damage.[24]

Although Hornblow recognized the implications of the nightgown scene, at least one member of the cast did not. Morris Carnovsky, veteran actor and one of the few surviving members of the original Provincetown Theater production, could not remember any mention of lesbians during rehearsals. Carnovsky recalled:

No such thing even occurred to me until some reviewers mentioned it. I would recognize such a thing today, but at the time it seemed to me just a sensitive little scene, very subtly done, in which the prostitute offered to help the daughter, if I remember correctly, run away from home. Of course I was very young as this was my first acting job in New York.[25]

If a young man in the cast of *The God of Vengeance* was unable to recognize the women's relationship for what it was, it is likely that, in 1922, a considerable portion of the audiences, as well as some of the critics, were just as naive. Manke's attention to Rivkele might have seemed a ploy not to physically seduce her — a possibility inconceivable to many — but rather to lure her to a life of prostitution as a male procurer might have done. Producer-director Herman Shumlin, who had seen the show at the Apollo Theater, recalled:

I had no idea that the scene in which the two women fondle one another — and I do remember it — had anything to do with sexual perversion which would have shocked and puzzled me in 1923. Women in America were often openly and physically affectionate with one another even in public. Sisters, schoolgirls, matrons, mothers and daughters would touch, kiss, hug and hold hands. So the scene seemed familiar to me. American men rarely touched except to briskly shake hands.[26]

A visiting reviewer from the *Baltimore Sun* wrote: "One may say in passing that there are those who like to read into the friendship of the two girls something more than appears on the surface, but this is scarcely borne out by the dialogue in the third act.''[27]

In his autobiography *My Father and I,* stage and film star Joseph Schildkraut remembered this about the plot of the play in which his celebrated father, Rudolph Schildkraut, had starred: ''The girl is seduced by a prostitute in her father's brothel, is paired off with one of the customers, and runs away from home in search of glamour and excitement.'' [28] Thirty-six years after the fact, Schildkraut's memory of his father's show may have been impaired; on the other hand, it may have been that, sometime during the run of *The God of Vengeance,* a line or two of dialogue had been added to both the second and third acts suggesting that Manke had turned Rivkele over to a male customer, an ending less unsettling to audiences and drama critics alike.

Schildkraut would have readers of his memoirs believe that lesbianism was a false charge brought against Asch's drama. The actor contends:

> To bolster their accusations the ''moralists'' presented as witness a policeman who testified that the girls in the brothel scene had performed in the nude — which was an outright lie; that the daughter and the prostitute were ''openly flaunting their lesbian relationships'' — another lie.[29]

Joseph Schildkraut blamed the Society for the Suppression of Vice for lodging a complaint against *The God of Vengeance* which denounced the drama as ''obscene, indecent, disgusting, and tending to corruption of the morals of youth.''[30] In the 1920s these private citizens, with private funding, monitored the New York stage as if they were government censors. With new playwrights like Eugene O'Neill and veterans like W. Somerset Maugham writing on such subjects as sex, religion, politics, and economics, the society was kept very busy.

Rain, a play based on one of Maugham's short stories, told of a married preacher's repressed sexual infatuation with a prostitute. Starring Jeanne Eagles, it became the biggest hit of the 1922–23 Broadway season. During that same season *Loyalties* by John Galsworthy examined anti-Semitism in English high society; *Why Not?* questioned existing divorce laws; and both Bernard Shaw's *The Devil's Disciple* and Elmer Rice's *The Adding Machine* criticized the establishment.

Despite the failure in the early twenties of the national prohibition against the sale and consumption of alcoholic beverages, American public opinion continued to be as restrictive throughout that decade as some playwrights dared to be progressive. During its Greenwich Village run, for example, *The God of Vengeance* was closed twice for brief periods when the producers were charged with operating without a license and violating the law prohibiting Sunday performances. After its move to Broadway, certain citizens demanded, and won, criminal court action against the play. But it was not the predominantly Protestant Society for the Suppression of Vice on whom the *Jewish Daily Record* placed the blame:

> The entire pogrom on Sholom Asch's *The God of Vengeance* comes from Dr. Silverman, the rabbi of Temple Emanuel. It was he who brought the charges to the District Attorney ...
> Behind Rabbi Silverman are American Jews, who are up to date with their suits and dresses, but not with their understanding. They belong to the generation which believes that the highest duty of literature is to hide the truth.[31]

Sholom Asch had this reaction to the hostility American Jews were directing at this play:

> *God of Vengeance* is not a typically "Jewish Play." A "Jewish Play" is a play where Jews are especially characterized for the benefit of the Gentiles. I am not such a "Jewish" writer ...
> Jews do not need to clear themselves before anyone. They are as good and as bad as any race.[32]

Rabbi Silverman, one of the most outspoken religious leaders in Manhattan, was among those who demanded throughout the 1920s that the Broadway stage be purged of plays with sexual settings or situations, most especially those relating to any sort of deviations. He took particular exception to Asch's drama in which all of the characters in the brothel, including the lesbians, were Jewish. Coming from Europe, the Jewish actor Rudolph Schildkraut could not have had the same sort of reservations. Instead of vilification, *The God of Vengeance* had met with enthusiastic receptions in many capitals on the Continent.

During the play's run, Chief Magistrate McAdoo, in an obvious reference to *The God of Vengeance,* was quoted as saying:

If you attack a book or play you only advertise it to the class of people who want that sort of thing. In the last few days I was asked to begin what would have turned out to be a long dilatory proceeding against a play, and I am convinced that the theater people themselves were behind the movement to advertise their thoroughly nasty, rotten production.[33]

Even some supporters and admirers of *The God of Vengeance* thought it best not to identify the play in print. A lengthy *New York American* editorial defending freedom of expression on the Broadway stage, for example, never once mentioned the title of Asch's play. The editorial, in part, read:

Here, now, is a play on Broadway charged with being "immoral." It has been in print and on the stage all over Europe and in this super-sensitive city for seventeen years. Suddenly some dramatic tea-tester discovers a poisonous flavor in this histrionic brew. Hosts of respectable persons see the play. Apparently none the worse for their experience. Yet the senseless censors, having by request begun to condemn, continue condemnatory.

The present writer has seen the play in question. He finds it *terribly* moral. Believes that no one who sees this play can escape a thrill of terror because of the inescapable "moral" — the inevitable working out of the law of compensation. And yet the officially censorious find immo-rality — mainly because they can and do ...

Freedom of expression, liberty of action, exercise of choice in doing or avoiding — which is the very essence of morality — all that gives significance to the democratic experience and evolving humanity.

All this is involved in censorship and in the effort of well-meaning but misguided minorities to guide the really superior majority with their benevolent despotism.[34]

It is surprising that such an editorial attacking the self-appointed public censors would have appeared in any daily paper during the decade; it is nothing less than astonishing that it should have been printed in one of William Randolph Hearst's publications. Four years later, the homophobic publisher would pen an editorial damning another lesbian love drama and calling for a censorship law to keep such productions off the New York stage.

The God of Vengeance would probably have completed its run undisturbed if it had remained in Greenwich Village. It was easy enough for the middle-class Manhattan establishment to ignore a show running in the bohemian milieu of the Village. It was something

quite different when it was being done in the mainstream of Broadway
— particularly when it was a popular success. "It packed them in,"[35]
the *Times* reported, after Asch's drama opened at the Apollo. The
newspaper continued to run ads for the play for another two weeks. In
the meantime a Grand Jury went about surreptitiously investigating
The God of Vengeance without consulting those involved with the
production. For that reason, the playscript, which differed from the
published text, was not available to the District Attorney and was not
taken into consideration by the Grand Jury.

On March 6, 1923, during the Tuesday night performance, detec-
tives appeared backstage at the Apollo Theater to inform theater-
owner Michael Selwyn, producer Harry Weinberger, and twelve actors
in the cast that they had been indicted by a Grand Jury. The fourteen
were charged with violation of the Penal Code which "defines the
crime of presenting an obscene, indecent, immoral and impure theatrical production."[36] According to the *Times*:

> Between the second and third act a detective informed Harry
> Weinberger of the indictment.
> The play continued without interruption, Mr. Weinberger having
> requested the detectives not to molest the players before the end of the
> performance because of their temperaments.[37]

No summonses were issued and no formal arrests made. The
fourteen simply agreed to appear voluntarily the next morning before
the judge presiding in General Sessions. When they did, the defend-
ants were officially arrested. All pleaded not guilty to the charge, paid
$300 bail,[38] and were back at the theater in time to give a matinee per-
formance. The *American* reported:

> Inspection of the indictment revealed that the Rev. Joseph Silver-
> man, Rabbi of the fashionable synagogue, Temple Emanuel, on Fifth
> Avenue, was one of the witnesses to testify as to the immorality of the
> play.[39]

"Most of the complaints were alleged to have said that the play was
anti-Semitic,"[40] the *Times* noted. Yet racially offensive material was
not a consideration that the Grand Jury could have acted upon: the
penal code violation concerned only the presentation of an "impure
theatrical production." The arrests of Rudolph Schildkraut and the
cast of *The God of Vengeance* did not make the front page of any of

the New York dailies. Instead, they were briefly noted — in those papers that reported them — inside, and then without the photographs that usually accompany events involving theatrical personalities. In the brief plot summary, which was included in some of the news reports of the Grand Jury's indictment, no mention was made of the plot's pivotal lesbian seduction.

In one of the few editorials to comment directly on the indictment, the *Herald* congratulated the Grand Jury for keeping a watchful eye on the city's theatrical fare. The editorial went on to note:

> This country particularly demands that its literature, its stage and its art be kept clean as American opinion has maintained them. It will not do to defend impure plays or books with the statement that they have been tolerated in this or that country of Europe. The Continental standards are not ours.[41]

The God of Vengeance was no longer being performed when the case finally went to a jury — more than two months after the producer, theater owner, and cast members had been arrested. Although the trial itself was largely ignored by the press, the guilty verdict made front-page news in most of the important New York dailies. The Assistant District Attorney said that in his thirty years as a playgoer, he had never seen a more salacious performance than *The God of Vengeance.*[42] The producer, Attorney Harry Weinberger, had argued his own defense, citing questionable material in the Bible and Shakespeare as being more shocking than anything in Asch's drama. The jury felt otherwise. Rudolph Schildkraut was at home ill the day of the verdict, and the *World* ran a page-one photo of him under the caption "He May Go To Jail."[43]

Schildkraut and Weinberger were both fined $200 and the cast given suspended sentences. Judge McIntyre, obviously pleased, announced that the verdict would have a wholesome effect on the theatrical profession, adding that "the time had come when the drama must be purified."[44] The last case ending in a similar conviction had occurred thirty years before when a judge, not a jury, decided that a play called *Orange Blossoms* was immoral. The conviction of those involved in the production of *The God of Vengeance* marked the first time that an American jury had found performers guilty of presenting immoral public entertainment. It was hardly a coincidence that Asch's drama marked the debut of a lesbian character in an English-language dramatic presentation.

The *World* quoted a number of theatrical personalities who were just as pleased as Judge McIntyre by the conviction. Theater-owner Lee Shubert said, "No salacious play should be produced on the American stage. Anything that tends to lower the standard of public morals should never be produced."[45] Arthur Hopkins, who had directed John Barrymore in *Hamlet* that same season, contended that, "The best way to avoid obnoxious censorship is to enforce existing laws. If *The God of Vengeance* violated the recognized law, the decision reached today will prove a good thing for the American stage."[46]

Like Hopkins, an editorial writer for the *New York Times* pointed out how much better it was to have a jury decide that a play was immoral than an official comparable to the English censor. The *Times* editorial continued, "It is a wholesome thing for all to know that there is a Penal Code to which painters and writers and playwrights and actors and theatrical managers must pay due regard."[47]

With the single exception of Heywood Broun, the New York drama critics were curiously silent about the jury's decision. Broun, who admittedly did not appreciate Asch's work, and who had even been made "a little sick"[48] by watching the lesbian love scene, could not understand why it should have been made a legal issue. Broun wrote:

> We want to know specifically and precisely just what harm has been done to the community by the production of *The God of Vengeance*. The nature of the play was fully discussed after the first night. People who went thereafter wanted to be shocked. Very probably they were. What of it?[49]

Constantin Stanislavsky — who had brought the Moscow Art Theatre to New York for its first appearance in 1923 — could not comprehend why *The God of Vengeance* should have been judged immoral by an American jury. Noting that it had been presented without protest throughout Russia during the days of the Czar, Stanislavsky added, "Russia in those days had a very rigid censorship."[50]

The guilty conviction of those involved with the production of *The God of Vengeance* was eventually overturned by the Court of Appeals, which held that in such a trial for breaking the Penal Code "the manuscript of a play must be allowed in evidence and anyone who has seen it [the show] at any time must be permitted to testify."[51] This opinion has stood as a protection to all plays since 1923.

We can be certain that at least one drastic cut was made in the Provincetown Theatre production. Reviews in both the *Times* and the *Sun* mentioned that during the last moments of the play, the bawdy-house operator drives his wife and wayward daughter from his establishment. Certainly this conclusion is less shocking than the original in which the enraged father drags his daughter down into the bordello-basement to offer her as a prostitute to his patrons. A review in *Theater Magazine,* however, indicates that the lesbian seduction scene was, in large part, still in the show when it played on Broadway.[52]

The fate of a father being punished for operating a brothel by a vengeful god seemed to some critics — if not to the Grand Jury — to argue for the moral merits of Asch's drama. "Its moral is the familiar maxim, 'as ye sow, so shall ye reap,'"[53] concluded the *Sun*. Another critic defended the play as "so important an example of the way in which the stage can most properly be used as a pulpit — for no sermon is more vivid."[54] A columnist enthused, "No better sermon can be preached from Synagogue or Church than can be heard at the Apollo Theatre,"[55] and Mary Garden, the famous opera star and respectable maiden lady, declared that "*The God of Vengeance* was the most moral play in New York."[56]

Although some members of the press who were covering the trial made reference to prostitution as the drama's subject matter, not one made mention of the play's lesbian motif. In 1923, the subject was simply unmentionable as far as newspaper reporters were concerned. Still, at their trial, no other aspect of Asch's play was as damaging to the producer and his cast as the charge of presenting lesbian characters on stage.

Three years after Broadway audiences had had their first look at lesbians in love, a drama critic referred to it as "a brief flash in *The God of Vengeance* — a flare up that was soon snuffed out by the courts."[57] That "brief flash" referred to the brevity of the erotic scenes, not to the duration of the drama's engagement. In fact, the play had been running for two months in little theaters in Greenwich Village before moving to Broadway for another two-month engagement. It then moved to a theater in the Bronx before returning to reopen in one of the small playhouses, where it had first been seen by

New York audiences. In all, *The God of Vengeance* was performed 133 times before it closed.[58]

Such a long run is all the more impressive considering that two of New York's most important newspapers turned down advertisements for the show. After Burns Mantle of the *News* saw the play in Greenwich Village, the paper not only refused to run ads, but also ceased coverage of the court proceedings against it. The *Times* stopped running ads the day after everyone connected with the show had been arrested — before they had even been tried. That ordeal, gloated critic Burns Mantle, "put the fear of the law in the hearts of several other producers given to taking chances with plays of questionable character."[59]

Like most popular plays produced in the prolific 1922–23 New York season, when 190 shows were mounted,[60] *The God of Vengeance* passed into theater history and, despite its notoriety, was quickly forgotten. Four years after its close, few reviewers reporting on the far more sensational opening of *The Captive* seemed aware that Sholom Asch had been the first to present lesbian characters on the English-speaking stage.

The God of Vengeance is still considered by some critics to be the greatest drama of the Yiddish theater.[61] The play's effects on the Yiddish and the Broadway theaters, however, were quite different. Despite negative reactions from the more conservative elements in the Jewish community, Asch's sensational and seamy drama started a vogue in Yiddish theater. Managers and stars began searching for scripts, if not about lesbians, certainly about prostitutes. Broadway, on the other hand, was intimidated by the police arrests and the court convictions. As a result, producers avoided plays about women outside the pale of middle-class morality.

The drama was banned by the author himself during the Nazi Holocaust of the 1940s. In the two preceding decades, however, a number of Yiddish productions had been seen in the United States without provoking police raids. In 1974, when the English-language version was revived for the first time since it had served as a vehicle for Rudolph Schildkraut, *The God of Vengeance* caused no discernible stir in an off-off Broadway production by the Jewish Repertory Company. The Society for the Suppression of Vice had, by then, long been defunct. Nightstick censorship of the Broadway stage, like Prohibition, was no longer a viable tool of public suppression.

Notes

1. David S. Lifson, *The Yiddish Theatre in America* (New York: Thomas Yoseloff, 1965), p. 93.
2. Sol Liptzin, *The Flowering of Yiddish Literature* (New York: Thomas Yoseloff, 1930), p. 188.
3. A. A. Boback, *The Story of Yiddish Literature* (New York: Yiddish Scientific Institute, American Branch, 1940), p. 217.
4. Joseph C. Landis, trans. and ed., *The Great Jewish Plays* (New York, Horizon Press, 1966), pp. 98-99.
5. *Ibid,* p. 111.
6. Liptzin, p. 188.
7. Sholom Asch, *The God of Vengeance;* Issac Goldberg, trans. (Boston, Stratford Co. Publishers, 1918), p. xi.
8. Liptzin, p. 92.
9. Program for the Broadway production of *The God of Vengeance* in 1923 at the Apollo Theatre, Lincoln Center, pp. 17-18.
10. Alexander Woollcott, "The Reviewing Stand," *New York Herald,* 21 December 1922.
11. Percy Hammond, "The Theatres," *New York Tribune,* 20 December 1922.
12. Burns Mantle, "Father In Double Role Gets Ovation," *New York Daily News,* 21 December 1922.
13. "The Elder Schildkraut in a Devastating Play," *New York Evening Telegram,* 20 December 1922.
14. "Truth," *New York Morning Telegraph,* 21 December 1922.
15. Kenneth MacGowan, "The New Play," *New York Globe,* 20 December 1922.
16. "Rudolph Schildkraut Stars In God of Vengeance," *New York Sun,* 20 December 1922.
17. Program for the Broadway production, p. 6.
18. *New York Herald,* 21 December 1922.
19. Heywood Broun, "The New Play," *New York World,* 20 December 1922.
20. "The Play," *New York Evening Post,* 20 December 1922.
21. *New York Tribune,* 20 December 1922.
22. Maida Castellum, "The Stage," *New York Times,* 20 December 1922.
23. John Corbin, "The Play," *New York Times,* 20 December 1922.
24. Arthur Hornblow, "Mr. Hornblow Goes To The Play," *Theatre Magazine,* April 1923, p. 68.
25. Morris Carnovsky, interview by telephone, 15 August 1977.
26. Herman Shumlin, interview, New York City, 4 March 1979.
27. Program for the Broadway production, p.14.
28. Joseph Schildkraut, *My Father and I,* as told to Leo Lania (New York: The Viking Press, 1959), p. 181.
29. *Ibid.*
30. *Ibid.*
31. Program for the Broadway production, p. 18.
32. *Ibid.*
33. "Morals Critic No Court, Says M'Adoo," *New York American,* 13 March 1923.
34. "Oh, For Sense For Censors!" (editorial), *New York American,* 26 March 1923.
35. "News and Gossip Of The Rialto," *New York Times,* 25 February 1923.

36. "14 Indictments Follow Probe of New Play," *New York American,* 7 March 1923.
37. " 'God of Vengeance' Cast Is Indicted," *New York Times,* 7 March 1923.
38. " 'God of Vengeance' Brings 14 Arrests," *New York American,* 8 March 1923.
39. *Ibid.*
40. *New York Times,* 7 March 1923.
41. "Plays That Cross The Line," (editorial), *New York Herald,* 8 March 1923.
42. " 'God of Vengeance' Players Convicted," *New York Times,* 24 May 1923.
43. " 'God of Vengeance' Immoral: 11 Actors in Play Convicted," *New York World,* 25 May 1923.
44. *New York Times,* 24 May 1923.
45. *New York World,* 24 May 1923.
46. *Ibid.*
47. "Better Than Censorship," (editorial), *New York Times,* 25 May 1923.
48. Heywood Broun, "The Play," *New York World,* 20 December 1922.
49. Heywood Broun, "It Seems To Me," *New York World,* 25 May 1923.
50. Program for the Broadway production, p. 15.
51. Harry Weinberger, "Provincetown And The Law," (typewritten article with notations), in file "Censorship: U. S. Stage, 1920," Lincoln Center.
52. *Theatre Magazine,* April 1923, p. 68.
53. *New York Sun,* 20 December 1922.
54. Program for the Broadway production, p. 14.
55. *Ibid.,* p. 16.
56. *Ibid.,* p. 13
57. Frank Vreeland, "The Marble Bride," *New York Evening Telegram,* 30 September 1926.
58. Burns Mantle, ed., *The Best Plays of 1922-23,* (Boston: Small, Maynard & Company, 1923), p. 584.
59. *Ibid.,* p. 11.
60. *Ibid.,* p. vii.
61. *Encyclopedia Britannica* (14th edition), XXII, p. 892.

2

They Said It with Violets in 1926

After the 1926 Broadway premiere of *The Captive* at the Empire Theater, a newspaper critic announced: "Lesbian love walked out onto a New York stage for the first time last night."[1] The report was erroneous, of course. Most other critics were similarly mistaken. *The God of Vengeance* had introduced that unmentionable subject to Greenwich Village theatergoers in 1922, four years before *The Captive* unsettled Broadway audiences. And, of course, the New York Yiddish theaters had been reviving Sholom Asch's drama ever since 1905.

In Broadway's busiest decade, the 1920s, *The Captive* had not only the most anxiously anticipated opening in memory, but also a closing that made front-page headlines in almost every New York paper. As a result, it became the most notorious, most highly publicized drama in American theater history.

Many theatergoers, even some critics, failed to recognize the erotic female relationship in *The God of Vengeance*. Four years later, there were still theatergoers who were unable to recognize the lesbian infatuation that is the very core of the dramatic conflict in *The Captive*. Even though all of the critics understood, many could not bring themselves to clearly identify what the play was about. With the use of euphemistic and evasive language, they were as discreet in the daily press as the playwright himself had been on stage.

One critic felt that, even in 1926, some of the seemingly sophisticated readers of the show business publication *Variety* were unaware
of American's unrecognized minority. The reporter confided to that
publication's less-knowledgeable readers:

> Ladies of this character are commonly referred to as Lesbians.
> Greenwich Village is full of them, but it is not a matter for household
> discussion or even mention. There are millions of women, sedate in
> nature, who never heard of a Lesbian, much less believing that such
> people exist. And many men, too.[2]

Word of the Parisian premiere of Edouard Bourdet's *La Prisonnière* — which American theatergoers would come to know as *The
Captive* — became common gossip in the drama critics' circle.
Reviewers were well aware of the nature of the play months before it
opened on Broadway. Because of its shocking subject matter, some
reporters began preparing New Yorkers for the arrival of the English-
language production. Occasional news items indicated that the Parisian import would be a lesbian love drama. By the time *The Captive*
was closed in 1927 — after a sensational police raid — there was really
no denying its nature. Reports of the night-stick raid were carried in
newspapers throughout the United States and Europe. Historian
Frederick Lewis Allen noted: "*The Captive*... revealed to thousands
of innocents the fact that the world contained such a phenomenon as
homosexuality."[3]

A month before that start of the 1926–27 theatrical season, New
Yorkers read in the *Morning Telegraph* about producer-director
Gilbert Miller's plans to bring Bourdet's *The Captive* to Broadway.
"Rumors are about that women's organizations and ministerial asso-
ciations may try to halt the production or emasculate it, basing their
actions on reports of persons with the reforming complex who have
seen the play in Paris."[4] On his way back from France, after having
seen the original Parisian production, Miller was "flatly told by Mrs.
Henry R. Loomis that she intended to use all her influence as former
president of the Colonial Dames of America to prevent such an af-
front to American womanhood as would be involved in the unmolested production of this unsavory drama."[5]

The *New York Evening Post* reported apprehension in other
quarters:

The town's busybodies had it that M. Bourdet had written stuff unfit for the American ears and suggested calling the police. No less a sage than Mr. Al Woods [the well-known, very successful theatrical producer] predicted that if Mr. Miller lifted the Empire curtains upon *La Prisonnaire" [sic]* he would be taken forthwith to play the title part in Ludlow Street [where a city jail was located].[6]

A number of misinformed critics tried to placate theatergoers who expected to be traumatized by *The Captive*. Questionable characters, bits of dialogue, even whole scenes were rumored to have been cut from the original Parisian script. "No," protested Bourdet. "It is given exactly as it is being shown in Paris — the only difference being that the words are spoken in your tongue."[7]

Like Yiddish dramas of the same period, Continental dramas were often more candid in their treatment of sexual matters than English-language plays. *La Prisonnière* was written for the theater in Paris, a city far more sophisticated and sexually liberated than either London or New York, especially after World War I.[8] Said one New York critic: "Our native dramatists have, up to this point, evaded such an issue. It was for M. Bourdet to blaze the trail."[9]

Bourdet was not only most discreet in his references to the delicate subject matter; he was also skillful in his dramaturgy. As a result, Bourdet's work was hailed, almost unanimously, as a serious and subtle study of a subject most critics found to be a "loathsome possibility ... horrible in its implications, terrible to contemplate."[10]

Psychological analyses of sexually shocking or titillating situations were Bourdet's forte. A one-time administrator of the Comédie Française, the playwright tried not to overstep the boundaries of French dramatic propriety. His work was never considered salacious, even when his subject matter was scandalous. Bourdet was faulted — if not censored — in France for failing to include a more emphatic moral point of view in his plays.

One day in Paris, after rereading Sappho's lesbian love poems, Bourdet told an interviewer about a man he had met who seemed very unhappy:

> He was a man distinctly troubled about something; but he never mentioned it to me, whatever it was. I merely conceived the idea that perhaps he was tortured by his wife's failings. For all I know, his sorrow may have been the results of an erring son — but the thought gave me the idea for *La Prisonnière*.[11]

Humphrey Bogart had encouraged his wife, stage star Helen Menken, to accept the role of a married woman pursued by a persistent lesbian admirer in the 1926 Broadway sensation, The Captive. *Menken's chalk-white makeup, apparent even in this photo, provoked critical gibes. The actress used it to indicate the character's terror at being captivated by another woman's allure.*

The Captive deals with Irene De Montcel, an evasive, perturbed young woman whose father insists that she join the family on his new assignment with the Foreign Service in Rome. Desperate to remain in Paris, Irene pretends to be interested in Jacques, a suitor favored by her father. She persuades the young bachelor to aid her in this deception.

If her father believed the couple were involved in a courtship leading to marriage, Irene reasons, she could stay on in Paris. She cannot be sure, however, that Jacques will lie on her behalf. He goes into another room to be questioned about his intentions by her father. As the curtain comes down on the first act, Irene touches the corsage of violets she has been wearing and lifts the phone to make a call. The audience does not know the identity of the person she is so eager to talk to as the curtain descends.

Act Two takes place in Jacques's apartment one month later. Jacques, it turns out, did support Irene's lie. His mistress has come to announce that she is ending their six-month relationship. Jacques, however, is more interested in his next visitor, Monsieur d'Aiguines, an old school chum. D'Aiguines is a married man reputedly involved with Irene, who spends most of her time visiting the d'Aiguines' home. The gentleman denies being Irene's lover and even resents being mistaken for her good friend. After much difficulty, d'Aiguines admits that Irene has been phoning and visiting his residence because of an intimate emotional involvement with his wife. D'Aiguines then warns his friend to avoid Irene.

D'Aiguines. . . . it is not only a man who can be dangerous to a woman, . . . in some cases it can be another woman.[12]

The distraught husband tells Jacques that his hair has turned gray at thirty-five because he has married a lesbian. Euphemistically he refers to lesbians as "shadows,"[13] mysterious and menacing since they threaten the sanctity of the male-dominated household.:

D'Aiguines. . . . They must be shunned, let alone . . . We don't know anything about it. We can't begin to know what it is. It's mysterious — terrible! Under cover of friendship a woman can enter any household, whenever and however she pleases — at any hour of the day — she can poison and pillage everything before a man whose home she destroys is even aware what's happening to him. When finally he realizes things it's too late — he is alone! Alone in the face of a secret alliance of two human beings who understand one another because they're alive, because they're of the same sex. Because they're of a different planet than he, the stranger, the enemy![14]

After this damning tirade, surprisingly enough, d'Aiguines compliments his Austrian-born wife:

D'Aiguines. She has all the feminine allurements, every one. As soon as one is near her, one feels — how shall I say it — a sort of deep charm. Not only I feel it. Everyone feels it. I really believe that she is the most harmonious being that has ever breathed . . . I worship her.[15]

D'Aiguines has no intention of leaving his wife of eight years, he claims, because he could not live without her. Remembering that Irene has been miserably unhappy of late, Jacques asks his old school chum why she should be suffering so:

D'Aiguines. I don't know. *(Rises.)* You don't suppose I'm confided in, do you? She is suffering as the weak always do, struggling with the stronger nature until they give in.[16]

Before departing, d'Aiguines again warns Jacques to have nothing more to do with Irene even though he might still love her:

D'Aiguines. . . . remember — she can never belong to you no matter how you try. They're not for us.[17]

Jacques's fourth visitor is Irene herself, since her younger sister had come earlier to report on Irene's unhappiness. Even before Irene is aware that Jacques knows about Madame d'Aiguines, she pleads:

Irene. Protect me! Shield me! . . . I know I must seem crazy. Well, I am crazy! You have to treat me like a crazy person — a sick person—[18]

Distressed, she tells Jacques that she is in imminent danger because Madame d'Aiguines has invited her to go on a cruise.

Irene. . . . and I mustn't go. I don't want to go — if I do, it's all over. I'd be lost.[19]

After Jacques confronts her with her secret involvement, Irene confides in him for the first time.

Irene. You see, there are times in which I can see clearly, such as now, when I am sane and free to use my own mind . . . But there are other times, when I can't, when I don't know what I'm doing. It's like — a prison to which I must return captive, despite myself. I'm — I'm —

Jacques. Fascinated?
Irene. Yes![20]

Believing that Jacques can cure her fascination with another woman, Irene offers herself to him. Ignoring d'Aiguines's warnings, Jacques attempts to kiss her on the mouth. When she looks up at him, the longing on his face forces her to turn away. Crestfallen, he lets her go.

> *Irene.* No, no — forgive me! *(This time it is she who offers her lips to him. Then, her nerves giving way, she lets her head fall on his shoulder, struggling with herself a moment and breaks into tears.)* ... No, no! — pay no attention! — It doesn't mean anything ... It's all over! You will keep me with you always?
> *Jacques.* I'll try.[21]

The final act of *The Captive* takes place in Jacques's drawing room. Eleven months have passed since his marriage to Irene, months the couple has spent mostly traveling. During this time, Irene has been doing everything in her power to be a dutiful wife and homemaker. Jacques, however, is clearly dissatisfied with the mechanical lovemaking of a woman who submits to him but is unable to return his passion. This puzzles Irene, who is not unhappy in the relationship. To test her, Jacques invites his ex-mistress to their home to return the love letters she had requested. As expected, Irene is utterly without jealousy. In fact, she tells Jacques that returning the lady's compromising letters is only fair. As he waits to receive his guest, Irene goes out to visit an interior decorator's shop.

Jacques's ex-mistress does not want to resume their affair as he would have it. She struggles against being hurt again by the man she loves, almost as fiercely as Irene had struggled against her involvement with Madame d'Aiguines. With one kiss, the lady's passion is rekindled. Her resistance collapses and the couple plan to see each other again.

Soon after his mistress's departure, Jacques's wife returns. Disconcerted, Irene begs him again to take her away from Paris. It turns out that she has seen Madame d'Aiguines again for the first time since Irene's engagement to Jacques. They had met quite by accident in the decorator's shop. Irene confesses that during the past year Madame, whose husband has left her, has attempted to correspond with her. Irene, however, has been returning the letters unopened. On one occasion, Madame d'Aiguines had begged Irene to visit her during a serious illness; even then Irene had refused. But now, to ensure her complete recovery, Madame d'Aiguines's doctor has ordered her to go to Switzerland. At the risk of losing her life, she refuses to go unless she can effect a reconciliation with Irene.

Coolly and civilly, Jacques tells Irene he is through helping her. As he leaves his wife alone in the study, a box of violets arrives from the florist. Irene crushes the violets to her bosom and flees the room with her hat and coat. Jacques returns in time to hear the front door slam. As the curtain falls, he tells a servant that, like his wife, he too will be going out.

For the second time in the history of the theater, the sound of a young wife slamming the door as she leaves her husband had an unnerving effect on many critics and audiences. Although the climax of Henrik Ibsen's *A Doll's House* had provoked hostile reactions throughout the Western world, Bourdet's lesbian love drama seemed to enrage only some New Yorkers. Its reception in Europe was far more cordial and appreciative.

La Prisonnière, starring Madame Sylvie, was first produced at the Théâtre Femina in Paris in March 1926. It was instantly hailed by French critics as one of the great masterpieces of dramatic writing. The *New York Telegraph* informed its readers: "It has been likened to a Greek tragedy, and even compared by critics to that sacred cow of French classics, Racine's *Phèdre.*"[22] One American critic, however, reported that at its French premiere, "even Paris sat up and gasped."[23]

La Prisonnière's acclaim was soon duplicated in Berlin and Vienna by Max Reinhardt, who had premiered Asch's *God of Vengeance.* "Even in a Reinhardt production," another American critic contended, "the play was too strong for the stomach of Berlin."[24] Nevertheless, it broke attendance records in the German capital with its one hundredth performance and was still playing a month before the Broadway production was forced to close.[25] No play in recent years had had so many simultaneous presentations as *La Prisonnière,* which could be seen during the same theatrical season in Paris, Brussels, Berlin, Vienna, Holland, and Switzerland. The play had been rejected by the Lord Chamberlain in London and was banned in Budapest, the single instance of censorship on the Continent.

As a result of the success of *The Captive,* French florists experienced a devastating drop in the violet market.[26] The same thing happened in those sections of America familiar with the drama's lesbian
love notoriety.[27] The *Brooklyn Citizen* entitled its review "They Say It
With Violets,"[28] and Alexander Woollcott labelled his critique, "The
Message of Violets."[29]

Bourdet was familiar with Sappho's lesbian love poems. In one
Sappho mentions that she and her lover had worn "violet tiaras"[30]
when they were happy together. Thus Bourdet selected violets as a
symbol for lesbian love. As a result, many women refused to buy the
flower, or even wear the color.[31] In fact, decades after the origin of
this prejudice had been forgotten, one was careful — at least in certain
sophisticated or theatrical circles in Europe and America — not to
give unintended offense by sending a corsage of violets.

When Bourdet visited New York to see Arthur Hornblow, Jr.'s
translation of *La Prisonnière,* the thirty-eight-year-old playwright
confided in an interview:

> I have never made a study of the sort of woman discussed. They are
> something entirely out of a man's knowledge and always will be. I have
> not attempted to do a portrait.
>
> Instead, I imagined I was writing the story of man's great sorrow. It
> was a Calvary I was showing, with a man and not a woman on the
> cross.[32]

To another American reporter, Bourdet said:

> I do not believe such a situation as I present it is an exceptional one
> — else why the vogue for the play?... You've seen it; you know that I
> present it from the man's viewpoint, being a man. I do not know how it
> would be handled from the women's angle...
>
> But I am aware of this; a playwright must not be the judge of his
> character. He should not be for or against the character but he may
> show the disastrous consequences of a character's actions...
>
> It was not for me to absolve or blame anyone. And yet, I can see no
> result except good from the presentation of my play, for while it reveals
> a given course of action, it casts no glamour over unnatural acts.[33]

At least one American critic concurred with Bourdet's French
detractors. The reviewer for the *Bronx Home News* protested that the
drama "points no moral and, indeed, it has none to offer. The play
serves no apparent purpose and it would have been better if it had not

been written.''[34] This reaction was not shared by most American critics. J. Brooks Atkinson of the *Times,* for example, commended rather than faulted Bourdet because the "play approaches its subject matter objectively.''[35] Apparently that was something Atkinson himself could not do. In his review of *The Captive,* he referred to the older lesbian as "the festered one,''[36] who was involved in a "twisted relationship''[37] with a younger woman, caught up in a "warped infatuation.''[38] While Bourdet, in an interview, called lesbian love "an unnatural act" just as Sholom Asch had called it "sinful," it is to their credit that they avoided passing judgment on their lesbian characters.

The Captive was produced and directed by Gilbert Miller for the Charles Frohman Company. The Famous Players Lasky, a Hollywood motion picture company, had owned and operated the Broadway production company since Frohman's death. According to reports from the West Coast, *The Captive* caused a serious split between Adolph Zukor, president of the film company, and Jesse Lasky, its first vice-president:

> ...it is *The Captive* that is said to have put Zukor and Lasky at daggers' points... Lasky ... commanded Gilbert Miller, ... to produce the play last August over the protest of Zukor, who is said to have regarded it as "obscene and unworthy of presentation on the American stage." As a result bad feeling is said to have resulted between the two film executives, which culminated in an open split on Wednesday when the play was raided.[39]

The Captive also destroyed the twenty-five-year business relationship between the Charles Frohman production company and Abraham L. Erlanger, who controlled the largest chain of playhouses in the nation. Because of his objections to producing a lesbian love drama on the Broadway stage, Erlanger refused to lease Miller a theater. Miller then approached the Shubert brothers, who operated a rival theatrical chain. They agreed to rent him their Empire Theater. Its thousand seats made it too big for an intimate drama. Because of the sensational box office receipts, however, the second balcony had to be opened for the first time since Maude Adams had played in *Peter Pan.*

It was with varying degrees of trepidation that the first-night audience took their seats at the highly-publicized American premiere of *The Captive* on September 29, 1926. Critic Percy Hammond reported: "Appalling rumors had been brought from Paris by shy American tourists that *La Prisonnière* dealt with dreadful sex-specters, the nature of which is customarily discussed in nervous whispers."[40] *The Captive* was unquestionably the most exciting entry of the 1926–27 season. One critic wrote about opening night: "The play rose into the Empire Theater last night upon a transatlantic tidal wave."[41] The gilt-edged, first-night audience included New York's playboy mayor Jimmy Walker; theatrical stars Billie Burke, Otis Skinner, and Ruth Gordon; studio boss Adolph Zukor; film star Norma Talmadge; playwright Anita Loos; and Broadway star Eva Le Gallienne, who that very season had started her famous Civic Repertory Theater.

The reviewer for *Vanity Fair* magazine reported:

> A new motif has crept insidiously onto the American stage and as a consequence one of the darker secrets of sex has been exposed to the multitudes ... Never once does the author present his thesis in the open; it remains an intangible complication. It is developed entirely by suggestion, which might lend itself to other interpretations, were not rumors of the play's evil implications flying thick and fast about town.[42]

Another critic observed: "From the first nighters there was scarcely a ripple of reaction ... The audience wondered and wondered and the most sophisticated understood."[43] Another reviewer reported that "no blanched faces could be noticed, there were none who crawled under their chairs to hide their embarrassment."[44]

One of the first-night patrons, Broadway star Eva Le Gallienne, would four years later play a real-life role strikingly similar to that of Bourdet's Madame d'Aiguines. In a trial much publicized by the tabloids, a socialite sued his actress wife, Josephine Hutchinson, because, in his words, she preferred to be with Le Gallienne "morning, noon and night."[45] The *Daily News* referred to Hutchinson as Le Gallienne's "shadow,"[46] the euphemism for lesbian used in *The Captive*.

There were curtain calls after the first and second acts of *The Captive* amid an uproar of bravos and applause. After the second act ovation, co-star Helen Menken — never at a loss for words — made a short speech praising Gilbert Miller for having the courage to produce the daring, controversial play. Miller took his bow from a seat in the audience. The enthusiastic uproar, however, was not repeated at the end of the play. "A singularly silent and thoughtful audience walked out of the Empire Theater at 11:30 to think it over,"[47] the *Morning Telegraph* noted.

The next day producer-director Miller boasted, "The entire press resounded with the most lavish praise a play has received for at least a decade."[48] That appraisal was less than accurate. Miller's polished and professional direction and production were indeed highly praised, and Bourdet's dramatically effective and tastefully restrained play-script was also cited. Nevertheless, half a dozen critics protested that the subject matter was more appropriate to "the clinical laboratory,"[49] "the province of pathologists,"[50] or to "the field of medicine."[51] "Here is a play amazingly well done," one reviewer conceded, "that was not worth doing at all."[52] Another critic concurred: "Some tragedies cannot be viewed without disgust. There seems no legitimate excuse for staging *La Prisonniere.*"[53]

Although *Variety* called *The Captive* "the most daring show of the season,"[54] not even the most homophobic critics faulted the playwright for having sensationalized or vulgarized the lesbian attachment they found so loathsome. Alan Dale, a defender of Bourdet's drama, wrote: "Its author has dealt with its subject splendidly, reverently, and without the least ribaldry, or ridicule, or contempt, or any of the childish and quite ignorant moods of a small town community. There is not one risque line in the entire make-up of the drama."[55] Another critic pointed out: "The immoralist ever in search of the pornographic and obscene, as the Constockians ever snouting out 'vice and depravity,' are foredoomed to disappointment, for there is nothing mawkish or repellent in the drama."[56]

The show was the hottest ticket that season. At five dollars a seat, which was very high for the period, tickets to *The Captive* were the most expensive for a serious play: speculators were scalping tickets to the sold-out opening night for as much as twenty-five dollars.[57] One newspaper noted: "They stand in line to buy tickets."[58] *"The Captive,"* predicted Burns Mantle, "is now promising to be the season's sensation in practically every theatrical center of the world."[59]

Because of such publicity, as well as many positive reviews, *The Captive* was expected to settle down for a long, perhaps record-breaking engagement. The self-appointed watchdogs of public morality, it was felt, would have difficulty going after it. As Alexander Woollcott noted, "Bourdet had made the venture with infinite tact and reticence."[60] There were no erotic scenes of lesbian lovemaking such as those that had instigated the Grand Jury's investigation of *The God of Vengeance.*

George Jean Nathan initially reacted to the show with an open mind and jocund humor. Nathan was amused by much of what other New York drama critics wrote — or rather, failed to write. He chastised such reviewers as J. Brooks Atkinson and Burns Mantle for their timidity in writing about lesbians:

> The very critics who are perfectly willing to consider *Oedipus Rex,* for all its perversion, as a drama pure and simple seem to be indisposed to consider the present play in a like manner. Its Lesbian motif they don't seem to be able to get entirely out of their foreconsciousness. The old moral tone is to be detected in four out of every five reviews of the work. In this connection, it is the local reviewers in their attempt safely to get around a forthright statement of just what it is that Bourdet's play is about ... just what there is to offend any newspaper reader in the world is difficult to make out.
>
> Thus, we encounter in the *Times* such evasions as "twisted relationship with another woman," and "warped infatuation;" in the *World,* such euphemisms as "tormenting impulses" and "bondage;" in the *Evening World* such equivocation as "the poisonous serpent's spell of a decadent woman;" and in the *Daily News* such phrases as "a cancerous growth."[61]

That same day, in a similar column, Percy Hammond noted that reticent colleagues within the critics' circle were afraid to write with complete candor, because their critiques might be considered "as salacious as the play itself." Hammond described the way a critic was forced to deal with the subject:

> All he can do is to hint, and by the sly winking of his wicked eye convey the news that *The Captive* treats of a drama suitable only to the consideration of sex postgraduates...
>
> It may be whispered again, however, to those who are on the inside, that *The Captive* deals with a class of woman whose joys and sorrows are to be pitied and censored.[62]

At least two reviewers reacted to *The Captive* with such outrage that their readers could have no doubts about what was to be seen on the stage of the Empire Theater. Ironically, one such reviewer was

Arthur Hornblow, the father of *La Prisonnière's* English translator. In a review in *Theater Magazine,* Hornblow ranted:

> Sexual perversion as a subject for dramatic consideration is not new in the drama ... Until now, however, that form of sexual perversion known to physiologists as Lesbianism has not appealed to dramatists as a fit subject for the stage...
>
> ...It is a sad commentary on the decadent times in which we live that, amid the general chorus of praise which, with only few exceptions, greeted this play, no protesting voice was raised in the public press against its particularly offensive subject, or is it that, from now on, our wives, son, and daughters are free to discuss at the breakfast table the gangrenous horrors of sex perversion.[63]

In a darker vein, Frank Vreeland of the *Evening Telegram* alluded to a kind of evolutionary genocide that would dispose of lesbians and gay men:

> In considering such intolerance one must bear in mind Nietzsche's warning that the weak always destroy the strong who encourage them too much. In fact, it is quite possible that the subnormal, if allowed much sway, would deride — and persecute the normal as much as the latter outlaws them now ... The most charitable view one can take of such persons is that they have a defective nervous organization. One thing evolutionary theory makes plain — that species which survive always rid themselves of defectives, of abnormal beings who do not carry on the species ... Whatever you or I think of such arrested persons, history will dispose of them in the immemorial fashion."[64]

Such abhorrence and intolerance may not have been typical of audience reactions. The unrecognized minority had to be more clearly identifiable to elicit such a reaction. At least four reviewers in the play's first-night audience thought that in 1926 most Americans had no conception of lesbian relationships or lifestyles — even in cosmopolitan New York City. "I really think that a good percentage of the audience will fail to ascertain what it is all about,"[65] decided one reviewer from Brooklyn. Another from Manhattan reported that "among the first-nighters there was much speculation as to whether the extraordinary theme would be comprehensive to that coddled fellow, the man on the street."[66] After seeing *The Captive,* the critic from the *Sun* overheard two young girls in the lobby deciding that few persons would really know what it was all about: "'Well, my mother wouldn't,' said one of them."[67] Alexander Woollcott concurred:

I think the average playgoer straying within its doors (remembering, perhaps, that that is where he saw *Peter Pan* and dear Mr. Drew's comedies) would sit through the three engrossing acts without once suspecting the true nature of the Bondage which is the very sum and substance of *The Captive*.[68]

In the 1920s, the man on the street may not have comprehended the erotic infatuation of one woman for another; but that could hardly have been true of the more sophisticated social classes in either American or European society. Charles Brackett, the erudite drama critic for the *New Yorker,* resented "the hypothesis that the intimate circle of a worldly French diplomat would regard her idiosyncrasy as so unique or dumbfounding."[69] It is also difficult to believe that Irene's infatuation would have baffled those people aware of the gay lifestyles of an elite group of famous American and British superstars: those playwrights, songwriters, producers and directors working in the English-language theater between the two world wars.

Common gossip in the higher echelons of show business concerned the female attachments of Katherine Cornell, often referred to as "The First Lady of the American Theater," and the more blatantly gay activities of her husband, director-producer Guthrie McClintic.[70] Alfred Lunt and Lynn Fontanne, the illustrious husband and wife co-stars, were rumored to be discreetly gay.[71] So, too, were Broadway stars Jeanne Eagles, Libby Holman,[72] Alla Nazimova, and Clifton Webb.[73] Blyth Daly — daughter of stage star Arnold Daly, and herself a lesser-known Broadway actress during the 1920s — once said of Talullah Bankhead, Estelle Wynwood, Eva Le Gallienne, and herself: "We were dubbed 'the four horsemen of the Algonquin' by the Broadway wits and wise guys in those days when we all made the Algonquin Hotel our hang-out."[74]

Leonard Spigelgass, the Broadway playwright and Hollywood scenarist, gives us some idea of how open certain gays could be about their lifestyle, at least among an elitist clique of entertainers. Spigelgass recalls that:

> ...homosexuality in that period had two levels: One, it was held in major contempt, and the other was that among his [i.e., lyricist Lorenz Hart's] kind it was the most exclusive club in New York. That's terribly important to realize — that it was a club into which you couldn't get ...
> I mean, no ordinary certified public accountant could get in the Larry

Hart, Cole Porter, George Cukor world. That was *the* world. That was Somerset Maugham. That was Cole Porter. That was Noel Coward. That was *it* if you were in that, and I remember those houses on Fifty-Fifth Street, with the butlers and carryings-on ... You were king of the golden river! That was it! In spite of the attitude towards homosexuality in those days. On the one hand you said, 'They were homosexual — oh, my isn't that terrible!' On the other hand you said, 'My God, the other night I was at dinner with Cole Porter!' Immediate reaction: 'Jesus Christ, what did he have on? What was he wearing? What did he say? *Were* you at that party? Were you at one of those Sunday brunches?' So you had this awful ambivalence. Show folks; show biz people just couldn't make it.[75]

Edouard Bourdet also understood the homophobic public's intrigue with and horror of a minority whose very appearance could upset the intolerant. His most effective dramatic device in *The Captive* is, of course, never presenting on stage the pivotal Madame d'Aiguines. The character, consequently, becomes more threatening, mysterious, and fascinating. It would have been most difficult for any actress to portray a woman described as having "all the feminine allurements," and "being the most harmonious being that ever lived."[76] John Mason Brown noted the shrewdness of Bourdet's restraint in omitting Madame d'Aiguines. "Unseen and only talked about, she dominates three acts, a hundred times more vividly than if she had ever appeared."[77]

Perhaps the playwright thought it wisest to keep the aggressive lesbian offstage, rather than run the risk of horrifying bourgeois Parisians. Yet audiences were not really spared the trauma of seeing a lesbian character. *New Yorker* critic Charles Brackett protested: "I resent the implication that Irene is merely the captive of Madame d'Aiguines rather than being imprisoned by her own abnormality."[78] That is clearly the impression Bourdet wanted to convey. Inconsistently, he included a very telling scene in which Irene instinctively recoils from sexual contact with a man of whom she is very fond.

In creating Irene, Bourdet came closer than he might have expected to in approximating the real-life psyche of a congenital lesbian. Still, most critics did perceive Irene as such. Percy Hammond referred to the play's protagonist as "the hapless lady enslaved in the noxious chains of abnormality."[79] J. Brooks Atkinson called her "a young lady of good family who has fallen victim to the fatal fascination of a loathsome attraction for another woman."[80]

Actress Helen Menken admitted to an interviewer that she had been reluctant to do the role until her husband, Humphrey Bogart, persuaded her: "...I have seen girls like Irene. They are pathetic beyond all description. They are young women with great flights of poetic fancy, unless they become hardened to the point of viciousness."[81] After signing a contract to star in *The Captive,* Menken went to Paris to see how a French actress portrayed one of these young women. "I did not see Mme. Sylvie who created the sensation over there," the American star reported. "I am told she resembled a collection of all sins whereas, I concentrated on only one."[82] Menken did not specify the other sins of which Irene could have been guilty.

Helen Menken's conception of the title role, both on first reading *The Captive* and also after playing it for four and a half months, was that Irene was a normal being struggling against a powerful influence. The actress reasoned: "That she was a normal character is proven by the fact of her struggle; had she not been normal, there would have been no struggle."[83] Apparently even portraying a normal girl in a play dealing with a lesbian's powerful influence proved to be such an ordeal that Menken had a physical reaction to it. The actress explained:

> There had been a good deal of discussion of my make-up. The cause of the discussion was my state of intense nervousness on the first night. It showed in my pallor. I was dead white. I put on a great deal of rouge but the underlying whiteness showed through the coat of red.[84]

The pallor of the star's ghost-white make-up, in fact, was distracting to a number of reviewers. Those critics most distracted were also most unappreciative of her performance. The critic for the *Wall Street Journal* complained: "Miss Menken played the young woman with a ghastly white make-up and crouching movements which may have gained sympathy for the character as a neurotic defective but stirred no other emotion."[85] The *New Yorker* reported that, "New York is assembling to see *The Captive* with an idea that it is to witness a super special close-up of the Beast of Apocalypse — and I must admit that Helen Menken suggests something of the sort in the dead white make-up, writhing and twisting about the stage; either that or a recent and prolonged diet of green apples."[86]

Articulate, gregarious, and vivacious, Menken granted numerous interviews duuring the winter of 1926-27. She always had a great deal to say about her portrayal of a woman who was sexually, intellectually, and emotionally attracted to another woman. The actress warned that such a relationship should be avoided like "the black plague."[87] Years later, Menken was still being quizzed about *The Captive.* In a 1930 interview, the actress admitted something she had been careful to conceal while the show was still running and under attack. "While playing in *The Captive,*" Hollywood gossip columnist Sidney Skolsky learned from Menken, "she received on the average fifty letters a day from girls. She also received as presents many slave bracelets. The entire collection is now in the possession of Gilbert Miller."[88]

Ever since Anthony Comstock had headed the Society for the Suppression of Vice in 1873, numerous religious leaders had repeated their demands for some kind of censorship of the Broadway stage. In response, a voluntary "play jury" system of quasi-official citizens had been set up in Manhattan in 1922, even before the production of *The God of Vengeance.* After that show had been threatened with closure by a court order, playwright Zoe Akins noted that it had been a great mistake on the part of the producer "not to ask for the people's jury to pass upon the play and thus avoid your difficulty."[89]

Such a fate of arrests and court procedures did not seem to be in store for *The Captive,* which was presented before the play jury less than a month prior to its opening. The majority of jurors failed to find it objectionable. The District Attorney defended the jury system and agreed to abide by its decision. Although he admitted that the play jury had its weaknesses, he insisted that "it is the best thing we have so far."[90]

One of the Hearst newspapers ran a banner headline on its editorial page reading, "Don't Relax Mayor! Wipe Out Those Evil Plays Now Menacing Future Of The Theater."[91] Another paper, however, soberly reminded the District Attorney that he had bound himself to abide by the verdict of the play jury, "as a man of honor, whatever he or anyone else may think of the play."[92] The paper further editorialized that the District Attorney should not close the play despite reports that a citizens' committee had petitioned him to do so.

William Randolph Hearst, the best-known and most influential mass-media power boss in the United States in the 1920s, took particular exception to *The Captive* — even though his employee, critic Alan Dale of the *American,* was singularly tolerant of it. Hearst was a strong supporter of New York's motion picture censorship law which Governor Alfred E. Smith wanted repealed. In *The Captive*, Hearst had found an issue with which to challenge and embarrass the liberal governor, who, like himself, had presidential ambitions. Hearst wrote:

> The effect of censorship, or of this fear of censorship, can be easily estimated by the fact that the great firm which produces many of the best and cleanest and highest class of moving pictures in the United States is responsible for one of the most vicious and obscene plays that has disgraced the stage in this year nineteen hundred and twenty-six.
>
> Without the influence of censorship, this firm might have produced moving pictures as demoralizing as its stage play, and certainly under the influence of censorship it would have abstained, and would have been compelled to abstain, from inflicting the injury on American morals that it has inflicted with its degraded stage production.[93]

This editorial, which began the publisher's campaign for purification of the American stage, was an attempt to back the governor into a political cul-de-sac. The *Herald Tribune* informed its readers:

> A political movement is gathering throughout the state, under the leadership of William Randolph Hearst, to push a theater censorship bill through the state legislature and lay it before Governor Smith.
>
> It is politically recognized as an opportunity for Mr. Hearst to use this pure stage movement to produce a situation now which would embarrass Governor Smith in the 1928 campaign — in retribution for the public insults which the Governor in his last campaign hurled at Mr. Hearst...
>
> Hearst representatives for the last few weeks have been organizing committees throughout the state to stir up a general demand for state censorship of the theater.[94]

Variety was well aware of the press baron's campaign to produce "material against the governor"[95] by instigating public sentiment in support of stage censorship in New York State. Smith had won wide liberal support with his uncompromising stance for the abolition of the state's motion picture censorship board. If the governor did not veto any stage censorship bill placed before him, he would lose a sizable portion of that support. If, on the other hand, Smith vetoed such legislation he would enrage an even larger bloc of voters by seeming to condone the production of "dirty plays" on the American stage.

Of all the shows produced during the 1926–27 theatrical season, *The Captive* was understandably the one that Hearst should have singled out as an example of the decadent and sordid state of the Broadway theater. Hearst's attack on Bourdet's drama was, of course, supported by puritanical religious and political pressure groups. This attack reflected a widespead sentiment, popular during that prohibition-prone period in American history. At the same time, many opposed such prohibitions. They represented what drama critic Burton Rascoe called "the natural reaction of Americans against any threat of official censorship — against any form of regimentation."[96]

Certainly in 1927 one would have expected the prestigious drama critic George Jean Nathan to be in the front ranks of those civil libertarians and intellectuals ready to defend freedom of expression on the American stage. Since World War I, Nathan had led the fight for the drama of ideas. The perennial bachelor and man-about-town had mocked his more obviously homophobic colleagues for their moralistic prissiness when referring to the subject matter of *The Captive*. Nevertheless, Nathan had second thoughts about his initially tolerant reaction to lesbian characters in a Broadway play. Nathan's belated attack on Bourdet's drama came during the third month of its sensationally successful engagement.

In a magazine article, Nathan called *The Captive* "the most subjective, corruptive, and potentially evil-fraught play ever shown in the American theater."[97] Distressed that some of the audiences might have felt that the two women had gone on "to live happily ever after," Nathan fumed:

> Bourdet's play amounts in simple words to nothing more or less than a documentary in favor of sex degeneracy. It is the persuasive advancement of the assurance that a degenerate physical love between two women is superior to the normal physical love of the opposite sexes.[98]

Nathan told an interviewer, "It is certainly inviting to females with a leaning toward perversion; and certainly to such sisters on the borderline, this couple of hours of enchantment is not designed to bolster their wills."[99] Appalled by Nathan's statement that, "if he owned a daughter he shouldn't care to have her see *The Captive,"* fellow aisle-sitter Percy Hammond protested:

> That utterance from so wanton a pundit is the severest arraignment the current tendency toward fire and brimstone has suffered. When a scholar of Mr. Nathan's freedom of belief and expression admits that a masterpiece of the Drama might bring discomfort to a broadminded parent, it is a signal for us to worry about the state of the theater ... When the devil of Mr. Nathan's caliber turns in dread from the horrors of the theater it is time to be afraid."[100]

Nathan defended his position "for the simple reason that his fine play is a charming presentation of degeneracy and young girls are very susceptible to charm."[101] In his belated estimation, Bourdet's drama was "an exceptionally evil one so far as an impressionable portion of the public goes. Drama, like literature, can very easily throw morals off the track."[102]

Nathan was sure that girls were trying to sneak out of private schools up along the Hudson to run down for a matinee.[103] He wrote:

> To believe that such stuff does not at least pique curiosity on the part of susceptible young women — and the Empire Theater has been full of them since news of the play first got around the boarding schools — is to believe more than I, for one, am capable of.[104]

Of the make-up of *The Captive*'s audiences, the critic confided to an interviewer:

> I had been talking to a man who attended a matinee performance ... He told me that he, and apparently a mere handful of males in the house, felt embarrassingly conspicuous amidst such overwhelming feminine assemblance... If all the ladies present were not weakened they were at least made curious.[105]

Certainly the Empire Theater was being filled during the autumn and winter of 1926-27 by more than just young girls from boarding schools. The engagement was getting from $21,000 to $23,000 per week[106] — impressive box-office receipts for a serious play more than half a century ago. A police officer noted about the performance he saw four days before it was raided: "Seventy percent of the audience on Saturday night ... were under 25 years of age ... Women comprised 60 percent of the audience, and groups of unescorted girls in twos and threes sat together."[107]

In defense of *The Captive* the stage manager said that "girls came in school detachments to see the play. . . It added to the understanding of the audience by showing the devastating effect of such an attachment between women." He also confided that letters of praise were received by Helen Menken:

> They came from deans of women's colleges and heads of finishing schools; who said they were already concerned with the necessity of impressing the girls in their charge with the dangers of a reprehensible attachment.[108]

And from Menken herself:

> I believe *The Captive* is the greatest moral lesson Broadway has seen in many years. I think all girls should see it, that they may understand the horrible unhappiness a similar relationship may bring them. . .
> How could it be terrible when ministers write to me how glad they are to see such a problem set forth in its fearful unhappiness, when college heads ask me to come and lecture before their girls on such a problem[109]

During the winter Menken continued to receive mixed messages about her starring role in *The Captive*. Along with the invitations from ministers and college heads were those threats to the hit show's survival penned by George Jean Nathan and William Randolph Hearst. Even though both men eventually figured in the play's untimely end, neither contributed to that end as effectively as the out-of-town reviewers of another play, authored by Broadway star Mae West.

Notes

1. Burton Davies, "Much Talked Of 'Captive' Opens," *New York Morning Telegraph,* 30 September 1926.
2. "The Captive," *Variety,* 8 October 1926.
3. Frederick Lewis Allen, *Only Yesterday* (New York: Harper and Row, 1931), p. 113.
4. "'La Prisoniere' To Be Put On By Frohman Here September 29" *New York Morning Telegraph,* 28 August 1926.
5. "Gilbert Miller Preparing To Defy Mrs. Loomis By Producing 'The Prisoner,'" *New York World,* 20 August 1926.
6. John Anderson, "The Play," *New York Evening Post,* 30 September 1926.
7. Charles Parmer, "Bourdet Releases Himself From His 'Captive Myth,'" New York Telegraph, 28 November 1926.
8. "Parisian Plays Are Naughtier Than New York's," *New York Herald Tribune,* 20 February 1927.
9. Ray W. Harper, "Footlight Reflections," *Brooklyn Citizen,* 3 October 1926.

10. J. Brooks Atkinson, "The Play," *New York Times,* 30 September 1926.
11. *New York Telegraph,* 28 November 1926.
12. Edouard Bourdet, *The Captive,* Arthur Hornblow, Jr., trans. (New York: Bretano's, 1926), p. 145.
13. *Ibid.,* p. 148.
14. *Ibid.,* p. 149.
15. *Ibid.,* p. 150.
16. *Ibid.,* p. 151.
17. *Ibid.,* p. 157.
18. *Ibid.,* p. 169.
19. *Ibid.,* p. 170.
20. *Ibid.,* p. 178.
21. *Ibid.,* pp. 178-79.
22. *New York Telegraph,* 28 August 1926.
23. Frank Vreeland, "The Marble Bride," *New York Evening Telegram,* 30 September 1926.
24. E.W. Osborne, "The Plays," *New York Evening World,* 30 September 1926.
25. "'Captive' Breaks Berlin Records," *New York Morning Telegraph,* 16 January 1927.
26. Gilbert W. Gabriel, "'The Captive' From Paris," *New York Sun,* 30 September 1926.
27. Eleanor Barnes, "'The Captive' Good Play For Medical Student," unidentified Los Angeles newspaper, 1928, in *The Captive* file, Lincoln Center.
28. "The Premiere," *Brooklyn Citizen,* 30 September 1926.
29. Alexander Woollcott, "The Stage," *New York World,* 30 September 1926.
30. Sappho, *Sappho,* Mary Barnar, trans. (Berkeley, California: University of California Press, 1958), p. 42.
31. Abe Laufe, *The Wicked Stage: A History of Theatre Censorship and Harassment in the United States* (New York: Frederick Ungar Publishing Co., 1978), p. 61.
32. Percy Stone, "Bourdet Didn't Try To Shock When He Wrote 'The Captive,'" *New York Herald Tribune,* 12 December 1926.
33. *New York Telegraph,* 28 November 1926.
34. "New Plays," *Bronx Home News,* 1 October 1926.
35. J. Brooks Atkinson, *Introduction to The Captive* by Edouard Bourdet, Arthur Hornblow, Jr., trans. (New York: Bretano's, 1926), p. viii.
36. *Ibid.,* p. ix.
37. *New York Times,* 30 September 1926.
38. *Ibid.*
39. "Rumor Zukor-Lasky Split," *New York Herald Telegraph,* Weekly Motion Picture Section, 13 February 1926.
40. Percy Hammond, "The Theatres," *New York Herald Tribune,* 30 September 1926.
41. *New York Evening Post,* 30 September 1926.
42. Donald Freeman, "La Prisonniere," *Vanity Fair,* December 1926.
43. "'The Captive' At Empire," *Brooklyn Standard,* 30 September 1926.
44. *New York Herald Tribune,* 30 September 1926.
45. "Bell Divorces Actress Eva Le Gallienne's Shadow," *New York Daily News,* 8 July 1930.
46. *Ibid.*
47. *New York Morning Telegraph,* 30 September 1926.
48. "'The Captive' Is Withdrawn, Cast of Play To Escape Trial," *New York Sun,* 16 February 1927.
49. "The New Play," *Brooklyn Times,* 30 September 1926.
50. Robert Coleman, "'The Captive' Dazes," *New York Mirror,* 30 September 1926.
51. H.Z. Zorres, "'The Captive' Is Seen At Empire," *New York Commercial,* 30 September 1926.
52. *Brooklyn Times,* 30 September 1926.
53. *New York Commercial,* 30 September 1926.

54. "The Captive," *Variety*, 6 October 1926.

55. Alan Dale, "One Tragic Phase of Human Nature Frankly Staged," *New York American*, 30 September 1926.

56. Kelcey Allen, "Amusements," *New York Graphic*, 30 September 1926.

57. *New York Post*, 30 September 1926.

58. Percy Stone, "Helen Menken Defends English Translation of 'The Captive,'" *New York Herald Tribune*, 10 October 1926.

59. Burns Mantle, "'The Captive;' As Ugly and Devastating as Sin and as Common," *New York Daily News*, 30 September 1926.

60. *New York World*, 30 September 1926.

61. George Jean Nathan, "The Week in The Theatre," *New York Morning Telegraph*, 10 October 1926.

62. Percy Hammond, "The Theatres," *New York Herald Tribune*, 10 October 1926.

63. Arthur Hornblow, "Mr. Hornblow Goes To The Play," *Theatre Magazine*, December 1926, p. 16.

64. *New York Evening Telegraph*, 30 September 1926.

65. *Brooklyn Citizen*, 3 October 1926.

66. *New York Graphic*, 30 September 1926.

67. *New York Sun*, 30 September 1926.

68. *New York World*, 30 September 1926.

69. Charles Brackett, "The Theatre," *New Yorker*, 9 October 1926, p. 33.

70. Tad Mosel, *Leading Lady, The World and Theatre of Katherine Cornell* (Boston: Little, Brown and Company, 1978), p. 386.

71. Isobel Elsom, interviewed at the Motion Picture Country Hospital, Woodland Hills, California in April 1978.

72. Milt Machin, *Libby* (New York: Tower Books, 1980), p. 101.

73. Kathleen Mulqueen, interviewed in Newhall, California, 28 December 1983.

74. Blyth Daly, conversations with the author, Studio City, California, in 1948.

75. Samuel Marx and Jan Clayton, *Rogers and Hart, Bewitched, Bothered and Bedevilled* (New York: G.P. Putnam's Sons, 1976), p. 237.

76. Edouard Bourdet, *The Captive*, p. 150.

77. John Mason Brown, "Diadems Of Paste," *Theatre Arts*, December 1926.

78. *New Yorker*, 9 October 1926, p. 33.

79. *New York Herald Tribune*, 30 September 1926.

80. *New York Times*, 30 September 1926.

81. Wilma Soss, "Helen Menken Star of Exotic Play Talks In A Taxi," *Brooklyn Daily Times*, n.d., 1926.

82. *Ibid.*

83. Ada Paterson, "Miss Menken Defends 'The Captive,'" *Theatre Arts Magazine*, February 1927, p. 22.

84. Clare Ogden, "Captive Is Moral Lesson, Helen Menken, Star, Asserts," *New York Morning Telegraph*, 16 January 1927.

85. Metcalfe, "The Theatre," *Wall Street Journal*, 2 October 1926.

86. *New Yorker*, 9 October 1926, p. 33.

87. *New York Morning Telegraph*, 16 January 1927.

88. Sidney Skolsky, "Behind The News," *New York Daily News*, 7 July 1930.

89. Program for *The God of Vengeance*, p. 11

90. "Banton Defends Play Jury System," *New York Times*, 30 December 1926.

91. "Don't Relax Mayor! Wipe Out Those Evil Plays Now Menacing Future of Theatre," *New York American*, 26 January 1927.

92. "District Attorney and 'The Captive,'" *New York World*, 23 November 1927.

93. William Randolph Hearst, "The Best Treatment For Unclean Spoken Plays Is To Apply The Methods Which Protected Motion Pictures," *New York American*, 30 December 1926.

94. "Banton To Sift Stage Charges To Foil Hearst," *New York Herald Tribune*, 1 February 1927.

95. "Police Ready To Raid Theatres With 'Dirt' Plays," *Variety,* 9 February 1927.

96. Burton Rascoe, "'Trio' Is Good But Fails Buildup As Sensation," *New York World Telegram,* 30 December 1944.

97. George Jean Nathan, "Theatre," *American Mercury,* March 1927, p. 373.

98. *Ibid.,* pp. 373-74.

99. William Pendleton Gaines, fragment from an untitled, undated interview with George Jean Nathan on file in folder MWEZ, n.c. 6901, Lincoln Center.

100. Percy Hammond, "The Theatres," *New York Herald Tribune,* 16 January 1927.

101. William Pendleton Gaines interview.

102. *American Mercury,* March 1927, p. 375.

103. William Pendleton Gaines interview.

104. *American Mercury,* March 1927, p. 375.

105. William Pendleton Gaines interview.

106. "'The Captive' Quits But New Producer Will Defy Police," *New York Times,* 17 February 1927.

107. "Captive Immoral, Mahoney Decides," *New York Times,* 9 March 1927.

108. "Girls' Schools Upheld 'Captive' Says Shotac," *New York Herald Tribune,* 21 February 1927.

109. *New York Morning Telegraph,* 16 January 1926.

3

Introducing Gay Male Characters in a Broadway Play Secretly and by Night

The threat that lesbians, as characterized in *The Captive,* seemed to pose to the social order paled in the face of the news that Broadway would soon be playing host to gay male characters. During the winter of 1927 Burns Mantle informed readers of the *Daily News* that:

> The day after the mayor called the managers on the carpet and warned them that either they had to clean up their plays or he would do it for them, a comedy called "New York Exchange" was boldly advertised as "the story of a male 'Captive' and as ugly as a cage of snakes and as fascinating."[1]

Another journalist reported:

> Next we may have to look at "The Captive's" pale brethren, and then it will be over. There was, at least before the present hysteria over cleaning up the stage, two plays dealing with male perverts scheduled for New York production. One is by a Frenchman, Jacques Natanson, the title of which translates into something like The Butterfly Man! and the other by an American which is called The Drag. The last, as the title shouts, is quite frankly concerned with anything but he-men.[2]

During the first two weeks of February 1927, *The Captive* continued to play to packed houses without any indication that it was in imminent danger of being closed. During this time, a number of items appeared in the city's daily papers detailing what was considered a threat to the community: The *World* warned: "'The Drag,' Mae West's 'Homosexual comedy–drama,' the entry of which into New York would prove, it is feared, the last straw upon the back of the uncensored theater, opened a step nearer Broadway last night."³ The reference was to the opening in Paterson, New Jersey, for a three-day run prior to its planned Broadway premiere, of a show that had begun its tryout engagement in Bridgeport, Connecticut.

Almost every one of New York City's daily papers alerted its readers to the existence of *The Drag* with some mention of the show's out-of-town tryout, sometimes giving it front-page coverage. The *Herald-Tribune* ran such a report almost every day on the play's progress. On the other hand, after noting that *The Drag* had opened out-of-town, the *Daily News* never mentioned it again, not even when the play closed in New Jersey following a sensational raid.

To make matters worse, during the tryout of *The Drag,* C. William Morganstern, the play's nominal producer, announced that four other plays as daring as the censor-threatened piece would shortly appear in the city. "The four," said Mr. Morganstern, "are by Mae West."⁴ A week later the *Evening Post* revealed that "The district attorney and the Police Department have definitely decided to prevent the New York production of *The Drag* it was learned today from an official source in the district attorney's office."⁵ In a page-one warning the paper passed on the word that: "Police Won't Let 'Drag' Play Here. Will Arrest Everyone Connected With Show If Production Is Attempted."⁶ Other papers repeated the same threat.

Even theater people were up in arms. Seventy-six theatrical producers met at the Astor Hotel on Broadway presumably to discuss a censorship bill framed in Albany. The real purpose of the meeting, according to certain theatrical writers, was to oppose the appearance of *The Drag* on the New York stage for fear its presentation would result in censorship.⁷ Three committees, one composed of producers, another of actors and a third of playwrights, met at the Actors' Equity Association's offices to devise a plan to prevent *The Drag* from reaching Broadway.

Producer Al H. Woods had tried and failed to interest Chicago audiences in a lesbian love drama, entitled *Sin of Sins,* after *The Captive* proved a box-office blockbuster. While he had no qualms about producing a play with lesbian characters, Woods objected to the introduction of gay male characters into legitimate theater productions. Woods told the press, "If any New York theater owners or lessees permit such a show to go on the boards at their playhouse, they will not be deserving of anything else than the strictest kind of censorship."[8] John Golden, another very important Broadway producer, warned: "While I have not seen *The Drag* the things I have heard about the play have convinced me that its invasion of New York now would be the straw to break the camel's back."[9]

At the direction of the Police Commissioner, the secretary of the New York Police Department went to Bridgeport to see the "homosexual comedy-drama." A few curious New York drama critics also made the trip. One reviewer dismissed it as "a tawdry and badly written and insincere piece of catch-penny claptrap."[10] Another concluded that "The play was offensive, not for its bold invasion of an unexplored sociological area, but by reason of its bungling insincere treatment of that region of truth."[11]

Variety, which covers all out-of-town tryouts, reported from Bridgeport, Connecticut, the home base and final resting place of showman P.T. Barnum:

> If P.T. Barnum had ever been inspired to stage a grand and glittering spectacle entitled, for instance, "The Destruction of Sodom," this is about the way he would have gone about it. The whole play is a cheap and shabby appeal to sensationalism, done without intelligence or taste and in the spirit of a Winter Garden revue. If it ever gets to Broadway, it would be a calamity, ... *The Drag* is a dramatization of a wild party given by a rich pervert and bedizened men friends. This episode is staged with Hippodrome elaborations taking close to 20 minutes of the third act, and without dialogue or dramatic action of any kind.
>
>   ...The whole venture is without justification and merits the unqualified condemnation of the public, the theater and the authorities, not to speak of calling the prompt intervention of the police.[12]

An editorial in William Randolph Hearst's *New York American,* advocating the publisher's plan to censor the stage as motion pictures were being censored by the state of New York, informed readers:

> In a disgusting theatrical challenge to decency just revealed at Bridgeport, where the foulest use of sex perversion yet attempted by the theatrical baiters for dirty dollars is being polished for a metropolitan run, we see where the lack of censorship is bringing us.[13]

In the same issue of that paper, it was disclosed that John S. Sumner, secretary of the Society for the Suppression of Vice, had written a letter to Mayor Walker demanding immediate police action if the Morganstern production appeared on Broadway. William C. Morganstern had been hired by Mae West to put *The Drag* on the road, but it was an open secret that she was really the show's producer as well as its author. For reasons that she never clarified in subsequent interviews, West wanted no playbill credit for presenting *The Drag.* Apparently it had nothing to do with the daring subject matter: the previous spring, she had hired the same nominal producer and used the same pseudonym, Jane Mast, to stage another bold theatrical venture called *Sex,* in which she starred.

Making her dramatic Broadway debut in *Sex,* West's comic and coarse performance as a cliché whore-with-a-heart-of-gold was dismissed by the critics. The show became popular with less discriminating theatergoers attracted by its bold title. Even before West was being identified with *The Drag* by show business scuttlebutt, her name suggested theatrical poor taste and censorable salaciousness.

It was during the run of *Sex* that the thirty-four-year-old comedienne came up with the script for *The Drag.* West had been sued on at least two occasions for stealing the work of some playwright and passing it off as her own.[14] Since the production of *The Drag* provoked no lawsuits, it may be that the script was, at least in large part, her own invention. If so, West had obviously done some reading of contemporary sexual psychology and had made note of homophobic distortions of history. More certainly, her relationships with gay men were also incorporated in the comedy-drama. She had already worked for three decades in show business, starting as a child actress. As a vaudeville headliner, the tough, uneducated woman from Brooklyn came to know, and claimed to like, many effeminate chorus boys and professional female impersonators, referring to them with a mixture of amusement and contempt as "fags" and "fairies."

With the commercial success of *Sex,* West was also able to finance, for the most part by herself, a production of *The Drag.* She guessed correctly that its shocking subject matter would prove to have even more popular appeal than either her play about prostitution or *The Captive.* West's obviously mercenary motivation for introducing gay male characters in a Broadway-bound drama was readily identi-

fied by the press in the public uproar that greeted its tryout performances. However, her anti-gay bias completely eluded audiences in
1927.

Because of the sensational, amusing, and very theatrical drag
party scene in the play, it seemed to some of the critics — and possibly
even to gays in the audiences — that West was the first American playwright to "kind of glorify the boys."[15] That is what the film star had
boasted in her dotage. In her more lucid memoirs, *Goodness Had
Nothing to Do with It,* published in 1967, West confessed that with the
production of *The Drag,* she had hoped to begin a campaign to warn
the American public of the dangers posed by the unrecognized gay
minority. West was concerned, in her own words, about "its effects
upon the children recruited to it in their innocence."[16]

Mae West had some very strong and ambivalent feelings about
the gay men of her acquaintance. She was rather tolerant of effeminate men she considered "born inverts," at least until medical science
could help them. "Let them treat it like a disease," West demanded of
the government, "like cancer, for instance, discover the cause and if
its curable, cure it."[17] She had no such compassion for less easily discernible gay men whom she called "perverts." Almost obsessively
hostile, West decided that such masculine men had "become that way
because of weak characters or a desire for new thrills."[18] Her biographers noted that, "...although she related perfectly to the flamboyant homosexual's lifestyle, when she discovered that a relative
with a macho image was homosexual she became distraught and dis-
associated herself from him."[19]

West believed that with *The Drag* she was calling attention to "a
tragic waste of life that was spreading into modern society when any
mention of it was met by ordinary people with a state of shocked horror."[20] Her play was to "bring out in the sun" the threat to America's
survival, since those gay men whose sexual predilection was not readily identifiable constituted some sort of "a private pressure group"
that could "infect whole nations."[21].

West admitted in her autobiography that a perplexing personal
relationship had really been her prime inspiration for writing *The
Drag.* The frustrating experience — and perhaps many others like it —
obviously accounted for her homophobia. An insatiable, egocentric
nymphomaniac, West sensed that a certain "he-man" actor who had

intrigued her would probably have rejected her sexual advances. She had been suspicious of the gay company he kept. It is not too far-fetched to suppose that West realized something of a vicarious thrill when she wrote a scene in *The Drag* in which the "he-man" rejector of women is brought down with the blast of a gun.

The Drag opens in the library of the home of Doctor Richmond in New York City. The doctor and his spinster sister, Barbara, reveal in conversation that the old maid, a cynical, tough-minded woman, has kept house for her brother and raised his daughter after the death of his wife. Barbara is concerned that all is not well with the marriage of her niece and wealthy young industrialist Rolly Kingsbury, but the doctor pays her little attention since she is admittedly very suspicious of men.

A young man, David Caldwell, identified by the author as "an outcast" in the cast of characters because he is a drug addict, is brought to the doctor's home in an emergency by a friend, Clem Hathaway. David is very disturbed, but Clem is in a cheerful mood as he makes gay, campy jokes about the good-looking taxi driver who drove them to the doctor. "Ride around a while, dearie," Clem tells the driver, "and then come back for her if you're so inclined."[22] Referring to the driver as "rough trade"[23] — that is, a heterosexual male from a rough, working-class background who prostitutes himself for gays — Clem leaves the unsettled younger man saying, "Well, so long kid. I hope he's a gorgeous doctor and does you good."[24]

David breaks down before the doctor, pleading for help.

David. .... I'm one of those damned creatures, who are called degen-erates and moral lepers for a thing they cannot help — a thing that has made me suffer — Oh, God! — Doctor, I can't explain.

Doctor. Tell me everything — This perversion of yours — is it an ac-quired habit or has it always been so?

David. Always, from the earliest childhood. I was born a male, my mind has been that of a female. Whay *[sic]* as a child I played with dolls. I even cried when they cut my curls. As I grew older the natural desires of youth were unknown to me. I could not understand why women never interested me. I was attracted by my own sex. How was I to know it was wrong, when it seemed perfectly natural to me.

Doctor. Go on.

David. I soon realized I was not like other men. I sought those of my own kind as companions. I realize that we were outcasts. I suffered. I rebelled. I fought with myslf — but it was stronger than I. Then I gave

in. Why not? I was, what I was. There were others like me. Oh, we all fight in the beginning, but it was no use.
Doctor. What seems right to the normal men in the matter of sex, seems wrong to you?
David. As wrong as our desires seem to those others.
(Pauses)
In time I met another like me.
(Rises, paces floor)
How can I tell you? *(Pause)* We were attracted to each other. We loved each other. I worshipped him. We lived together. We were happy. The curse didn't seem to matter so much. We loved our own life — lived it in our own way. No normally married couple were happier than we were. Then — he married.[25]

David's lover had married, he tells the doctor, because his family insisted. To make matters worse, the young man has taken a new lover since his marriage, "a normal man."[26] David wants to kill himself; the doctor suggests he take up athletics. Becoming increasingly upset at this predicament, David is taken to another room where he can be given a sedative.

Judge Kingsbury comes to visit his old friend, Doctor Richmond. Barbara is still trying to figure out why the marriage of her niece and the conservative jurist's son does not seem to be happy. She repeats some gossip she has heard linking Claire's name to that of her husband's best friend, Allen Grayson, an engineer employed by the Kingsley company that Rolly manages.:

Judge. Bosh! Why Rolly's very fond of Grayson. If anyone's interested in Grayson, I'd say it's Rolly and not Claire.[27]

Claire Kingsbury, the doctor's daughter and the judge's daughter-in-law, enters the library interrupting a lengthy debate between the two men concerning society's treatment of gay males. The more tolerant doctor faults the law for imprisoning sexual inverts. The harsh, homophobic judge blames the medical profession for not finding a cure for this "disease." The men depart, leaving Claire with her suspicious, outspoken Aunt Barbara.

While the younger woman cannot bring herself to confide in her aunt, she assures her, at least, that neither she nor her husband are romantically involved with anyone else. Claire wants to escape and suggests that she and Barbara take a trip to Europe. Rolly Kingsbury arrives to join his wife. He is unable to understand why she would want to go abroad, but makes no objection to such plans. Dr. Richmond, on the other hand, hopes to dissuade his daughter from leaving her husband, as he feels this might threaten their marriage.

Rolly is just about to leave the library after Claire, Barbara, the doctor, and the judge have made their exits when:

> . . . David opens Door R. His coat and vest are off. He half staggers into room.
>
> *David.* Doctor — Doctor. . . It's no use I can't — Rolly!
>
> *Rolly.* You — What are you doing here?
>
> *David.* Rolly—
>
> *Rolly.* Why are you here?
>
> *David.* I couldn't stand it any longer — I came here to see the Doctor — thought—
>
> *Rolly.* You came here to tell him—
>
> *David.* It's not so. I didn't tell him I so much as knew you. I came because I thought he could help me.
>
> *Rolly.* You fool he can do nothing for you — For any of us.
>
> *(Takes out his wallet)*
>
> Here take this — and get out of here.
>
> *David.* I don't want your money — Rolly please—
>
> *Rolly.* Get out of here. I've had enough of you.
>
> *David.* I've heard all about you and Grayson, he doesn't give a damn about you.
>
> *Rolly.* Shut your mouth about Grayson — leave his name out of it.
>
> *David.* It's true and you know it. He doesn't give a damn for you.
>
> *Rolly.* Damn you — you — you
>
> *(Grabs David by the throat and swings him onto divan. Doctor enters)*
>
> *Doctor.* Rolly!
>
> *Rolly.* Who is this — this mad man — He tried to attack me.
>
> *Doctor.* My poor lad — What's got into you? It may be the drug I've given him — I don't know — poor devil — Thank God, Rolly, you're not what he is — Come, come, my boy — Come—
>
> *Doctor.* (Leads David R.L.E. David turns and looks at Rolly.)
>
> *Rolly.* Not what he is—
>
> *(Looks after doctor and David and then sinks in chair)*
>
> Good God!

CURTAIN[28]

Act Two takes place in the drawing room of Rolly Kingsbury's home. Claire is out for a drive which gives Rolly an opportunity to entertain some of his gay friends: Clem, Rosco, Winnie and the Duchess. Unlike their wealthy host, they are "campy," effeminate, and self-mocking young men jealous of one another. They play-act at being very "bitchy" as they deprecate their kind in petty, mindless raillery. Referring to themselves throughout their conversation as "queens," "molls," "Annie," "dearie," and "bitch," they use "she" instead of "he" and let out screams and call out "whoops!" Their mindless chatter concerns "drag" costumes they plan to wear when impersonating women and parties they have attended.

The Duchess, a big man of Swedish extraction, is the most flagrantly effeminate in his behavior, constantly powdering his face. Clem, who had brought David to Dr. Richmond, warns the Duchess of attracting the attention of the police with his powder puff.

> *Duchess.* Say — the cops, they like me. They all know me from Central Park.[29]

Clem tells of attending a "drag" "over at Peter Pan's"·

> *Clem.* ...It was a great party but the place was raided and when they backed up the wagon, they got all but one and she jumped out the window. That must have been you.[30]

The talk turns more serious as the men discuss young David's addiction, and they refer to him as "that sentimental Moll," a "poor queen" who takes "heroin and morphine by the barrels."[31]

> *Clem.* ...the trouble with her is he's sensitive of what she is. Now I don't give a Goddamn who knows it. If *[sic]* course, I don't go flouncing my hips up and down Broadway picking up trade or with a sign on my back advertising it. *(Aside — laughs)* But of course, I don't pass anything up either, dearie, I'm out to have a good time as well as the next.[32]

Clem has become involved with the taxi driver whom he described as "rough trade" in the first act. One of the other characters warns him, "Dish the dirt, because you won't be able to dump that bird so easily."[33]

Rolly Kingsbury has invited his employee and best friend, Allen Grayson, a handsome young bachelor, to visit him at home while Claire is out for a drive and he is entertaining his gay friends. The engineer has brought plans he has been working on for one of the Kingsbury companies to show to Rolly. "Yes, I'd love to stay and see your construction,"[34] Clem says to Grayson during his brief encounter with the engineer. "So glad to have you meet me," Winnie tells him as they are exiting, "come up some time and I'll bake you a pan of biscuits."[35]

When they are alone, Rolly wants an immediate reaction to Allen's impression of his friends.:

> *Rolly.* You've never met that particular type before?
> *Grayson.* I can't say that I have.
> *Rolly.* Perhaps you have and didn't know it.
> *Grayson. (Looks up)*
> *Rolly.* Why do you suppose I've had you come here so often. Haven't you noticed the friendship I've had for you since the day you stepped into the office? All I could do was eat, drink, sleep, think of Allen Grayson.[36]
> *Grayson.* Why, Rolly, I'd hate to have you think of me that way. *(Rises)* I've always looked at you as a he-man. God this is—...[37]

The young engineer is very distressed at his employer's confession. He begins questioning Rolly about his relationship with Claire. Rolly dismisses his marriage as a social convenience and his wife as a naive woman unable to understand his sexual proclivity.

> *Grayson.* Why I think that's that most contemptible thing you could do — marry a woman and use her as a cloak to cover what you are.[38]

In righteous and heated indignation, Grayson turns on his dissembling employer. "Go to hell," he tells Rolly, "I think you're a rotter! God!"[39]

Claire returns from her drive with her friend and confidante, Marion. When the two women are alone, the miserable younger woman confesses to the matron that her marriage to Rolly has never been consummated. Rolly announces that he is going to be out of town on business and has asked Allen to take his wife to the opera; after which she will spend the weekend at her father's home rather than be alone on her own. After Rolly's departure Claire and Allen are alone. She is miserable at Rolly's treatment of her and he is aware of her frustrating marital relationship. Weeping, Claire falls into Allen's comforting arms as the curtain descends.

While his wife is staying with her father over the weekend, Rolly is giving a drag party in the drawing room of his home. As the curtain rises on the last act, the guests in female attire are dancing. Parsons, the butler, introduces each new arrival as he enters, welcomed by screams of excitement and approval from the other transvestites. The

Duchess makes his entrance, followed by the Grand Duchess, Dolly, Kitchen Kate and the taxi driver. Clem becomes annoyed at the Duchess for flirting with the taxi driver.

> *Clem.* Listen, Bargain, if you don't want me to clean you out of this joint, lay off of Civic Virtue before I knock you loose from this flat breezer of yours. I've got what gentlemen want."[40]

One of the transvestites does a toe-dance number, followed by another number to the song "How Come You Do Me Like You Do?". Dolly then sings, "Goody-Goody-Good." The entertainment is followed by screams from the guests. Between numbers, the guests joke about their harassment by the New York City police and their appeal to heterosexual men. Discussing a recent raid at one of their drag parties, Kitchen Kate says:

> *H* — . . . we had a grand time — The police were perfectly lovely to us — weren't they girls?
> *Ensemble* — Yes!
> *O* — They were.
> *H* — Perfectly lovely, why the minute I walked into jail, the captain said — Well Kate what kind of a cell would you like to have? And I said — oh, any kind will do Captain, just so it has a couple of peep-holes in it. I crave fresh air.[41]

In another exchange, Kitchen Kate and another transvestite become involved in some self-mocking, salaciously suggestive badinage about their sex appeal to heterosexual men while, at the same time, mocking others in drag who compete for the same attention:

> *O* — . . . I'm the type that men prefer. I can at least go through the navy yard without having the flags drop to half mast.
> *H* — Listen, dearie — pull in your aerial, you're full of static. I'm the type men crave. The type that burns 'em up. Why, when I walk up 10th Avenue, you can smell the meat sizzling in Hell's Kitchen.[42]

Clem and Duchess have an offstage fight over the taxi driver. Duchess races back on stage minus his wig which Clem tosses at him. The doorbell rings.

> *(There is a sudden hush — then everybody in hushed tones says Oooh!)*
> *(Lights out)*
> *No. 1.* Oh, my God, it must be the cops!
> *No. 2.* My God, the place is pinched!

No. 3. Don't give your right name, dearie!
No. 4. The place is raided![43]

As the transvestites file out of the drawing room Rolly assures them that he will see to it that nothing comes of the raid on his party. The guests are resigned to such harassment:

No. 12. I don't care, I had a gay time.[44]
No. 13 I had a grand time.
No. 14. I had a gorgeous time.[45]

Rolly accompanies his guests off stage. Immediately after they depart, a gunshot is heard between the sounds of a door slamming. The butler rushes into the drawing room and phones Judge Kingsbury that something terrible has happened at his son's home as the drag party scene comes to a confusing close.

Judge Kingsbury, Claire, Allen Grayson and the butler are gathered in the drawing room for the last scene of the drama during which a police inspector is questioning them about the murder of Rolly earlier that same night. The gunman has escaped; the butler attempts to incriminate Allen by repeating some of that conversation between Rolly and Allen in which the deceased revealed his sexual preference to his employee. The butler makes no mention of the gay proposition made during the two men's last conversation. Allen, too noble to besmirch the dead man's reputation, does not divulge that information either, even though his interest in Claire makes him the prime suspect in the case.

With his drug-addicted patient David in tow, Dr. Richmond breaks into the police interrogation:

Doctor. This is the mad-man. The poor depraved, unfortunate, who shot our boy.
Judge. (Struggles with detective to get at David) You killed my boy — You killed my boy!
David. I killed him, because I loved him. *(He collapses)*
Judge. (Gazing at David) A mad-man, a mad-man.
Doctor. This is the poor abnormal creature we discussed the other day.
Judge. Take him out of my sight before I strangle him.
David. Strangle me, strangle me — You Judge Kingsbury — the great supporter of justice — You would crush me, destroy me — But your son was the same as I — yes, I killed him — when you condemn me, you condemn him.[46]

Unable to comply when David came to him begging for a cure for his sexual orientation, Dr. Richmond has since grown concerned about his patient and thus counsels his friend, the judge:

> *Doctor.* Bob, we don't know what we bring into this world. We are blind, deaf and dumb. We can see no faults, no sins, no wrongs in our own, [when] it's another man's son, you condemn him, it's true, it's true! You've sent many up the river, and you know it, Bob, but when it hits home it's a different story. In this civilized world, we are not civilized enough to know why or for what purpose these poor degenerates are brought into the world. Little did we know that a fine, strong boy, like Rolly, was one of them.[47]

The judge turns to the inspector:

> *Judge.* Report this — a case — of suicide...
> *Inspector.* Yes — your honor.
>   CURTAIN[48]

For more than half a century no scholars or critics were able to obtain a copy of *The Drag* to evaluate what William M. Hoffman posits may be "the first modern gay play."[49] After Hoffman located the Library of Congress's manuscript in 1978, he concluded:

> Although the play was billed as "a homosexual comedy in three acts," it is in fact an *extremely* serious melodrama that borders on a plea for tolerance of homosexuals. *The Drag* contains long, intense intellectual discussions based on the most advanced contemporary scientific opinion (Ulrichs, Krafft-Ebing, and a smattering of Freud).
> Sometimes the serious sections are unintentionally funny especially to a modern ear, but usually the characters ring true, especially when the gay people are talking among themselves. Gay slang seems to have changed little over the years.[50]

Hoffman noted that page fifteen in the Library of Congress's copy is missing, but such is not the case. Page fifteen of the carbon copy the author mailed to the copyright office is in the manuscript, numbered but left blank. On the bottom of page fourteen, Doctor Richmond tells Judge Kingsbury at the conclusion of their lengthy discussion, "There is a cure for this thing."[51] Perhaps West had hoped to find some information about a proposed cure and include it on the blank page fifteen before *The Drag* went into production. No reviewer, however, reported suggestions of such a miraculous remedy anywhere in the show.

None of New York's most prestigious drama critics went either to Connecticut or to New Jersey to catch the tryout performances of the controversial production. The reviewer for *Zit's* show business publication gave a plot resume of the play, but because he obviously left before it was over, he concluded that "In the end Alan chooses the woman to love and kills her homosexual husband."[52] *Zit's* critic had this reaction to the first scene of the last act, which may have driven him from the theater:

> The sensation of *The Drag*, however, is not the plot itself, but a party of homo-sexuals which takes place on the stage. This party is called, in the esoteric set, a "drag," and to go "in drag" means for a person to appear in woman's clothes.
>
> It is privileged for few to be present at one of these "drags," but to those who have attended them it is a never-to-be-forgotten sight, although it does leave a bad taste in the mouth. People who were, seemingly, males before they came to the party, suddenly are transformed to shrieking, screaming women. They hurl ribald epithets at one another, in jocular fashion, drink, and, if it happens to be a "drag" to which they bring their male sweethearts, then the function becomes the most disgusting orgy imaginable.[53]

After assuring readers of *Variety* that he went to Connecticut with no revulsion at the prospect of seeing "homosexuality as the subject matter of drama," the reviewer from that show business publication reported:

> But as treated in *The Drag* it illuminates nothing, serves no decent purpose and is altogether vicious. This is because its exploitation in this play is utterly insincere and everything urged in its favor is phoney, the object being an inexpressibly brutal and vulgar attempt to capitalize a dirty matter for profit and without a shred of decency in purpose or means.[54]

Another critic from Manhattan who went to Bridgeport to catch the out-of-town opening had an entirely different reaction. The reviewer from the *Graphic* entitled his appraisal, "Went To Be Shocked; Found *The Drag* Clean":

> It is a mighty daring theme, the first time that such a calcium light has been cast on those who will never get over to greet St. Peter — unless they fly over — that has ever been put on the speaking stage...
>
> The blood-red subject was laid bare with a scalpel of the surgeon, but done so nicely that it drove home a lesson. The scoffers remained to

praise. There were a dozen curtain calls after each of the three acts.

The play starts off with what Elmer Grandin, as Dr. Richmond, declares "Reveals 5,000,000 third sex people in this country alone and civilization has done nothing to cure them...

But it was life, if even not your life or mine. And it was put on (get this) to bring out the moral lesson of the play and the lesson there was to it all. A mighty lesson!...

The expected effluvium and stench were absent. It is true it featured the "culls and scraps" of a cross-section of humanity, but it did not debase, nor degrade...

There is not a ribald line in the whole play, unless you construe this: "You must come over some time, dearie, and I'll bake you a pan of biscuits."[55]

The same reviewer from the *Graphic* made mention of the "surprising fact" that women comprised the majority of the audience at the performance he attended. In that same audience sat the unhappy manager of the Lyceum Theater in Paterson, New Jersey. He had come to Bridgeport with his lawyer to serve notice of cancellation of a contract to house the show. But the man from Paterson left the theater telling his booking agent that he was only too glad to have such a production in his house. The manager of a theater in Stamford, Connecticut, who had cancelled *The Drag,* also expressed willingness to play it after he saw a performance in Bridgeport. It seems that before the show opened a police sergeant, acting as a censor for the department, had insisted on certain changes during rehearsals in the production with a cast that, according to *Variety,* included "about 40 young men from Greenwich Village."[56]

When a reporter from the *Evening Post* went to see the show in Paterson, he noted:

...visitors from New York — and fully a third of the audience was from the city, and few of them were women — The audience seemed to have been divided into two groups — those who fully understood the subject under discussion and those to whom the whole theme was a puzzle.[57]

Like the reviewer from the *Graphic,* who had seen the show in Connecticut, the *Evening Post* reporter found *The Drag* to be anything but shocking: "Strain their ears as they might, they heard no words which have not, in recent years, come into common usage at the bourgeois dinner table or were not at least pseudo-radical."[58]

There were as many reports that *The Drag* was "clean" as there were claims to the contrary; nevertheless, New York newspapers continued to keep the public keyed up with items concerning the show's out-of-town tryout that made it seem like a staged sex orgy. The *Herald-Tribune* reported on its Bridgeport opening on January 31, 1927:

> The show deals with a subject usually discussed only in medical works. One of the local critics describes one scene as being "in some ways as revolting a scene as Nero or one of the more decadent kings of France might have put on a few centuries or more ago."[59]

Obviously aware that they might be legally prevented from bringing the show into New York, those with vested interest in it attempted to give the impression that Mae West had done some sort of a dramatization of a medical argument. One backer protested: "This is a scientific play. Why, there's worse plays than this in New York right now. This is a medical play."[60] C. William Morganstern told the press that *The Drag* "has a moral just like 'Sex.' It deals with the discussion of a disease."[61] In another statement the producer proclaimed, "This play has to do with an abnormal sex condition which is widespread, and its purpose is to enlighten the public."[62]

Reports out of both Bridgeport and Paterson indicated that business for *The Drag* was nothing less than sensational and audiences, for the most part, were receptive. When the play opened in New Jersey, the *World* reported:"The house was a sellout and the ticket line a block long by eight P.M. The majority were men, with a fair turnout of women. Only two persons in the audience grew noisy, and they subsided when the rest of the audience hissed them."[63]

Certainly aware of such audience enthusiasm in New Jersey, Broadway theater owners were still afraid of having their playhouses raided under the state penal code prohibiting impure shows; they would not book the production. There were rumors that *The Drag* would either play on alternate nights with or replace *Sex* at Daly's Theatre. Because Mae West's starring vehicle was going so well there, that possibility never eventuated. At wit's end because he could not find a Broadway house, Morganstern seriously considered hiring Madison Square Garden for two performances of *The Drag,* asserting that it was "a moral play that could be given in a church."[64]

Mae West was accused by the *Variety* reviewer of exploiting gay transvestites in an insincere, phony and vulgar manner "for profit and without a shred of decency."[65] She defended herself in a magazine article published two years after *The Drag* folded::

> I admit that in my play "Drag" I was a little bit premature. The public is still too childlike to face like grownups the problem of homo-sexuality. How few are the people who even know what he word means?
>
> Because of the universal ignorance I wrote "Drag" with the intention of taking it to all the theaters in the country to teach the people. So much of a stir was made, however, that I voluntarily removed it and I must mark time until our country grows up to show them a vital truth.
>
> The time will soon come when homo-sexuality will be faced — open-mindedly... It is a great problem. Many of our famous lawyers, doctors, bankers and judges are homo-sexualists. Thousands of others suffer because they are starving for love both in body and soul, and they become mental prostitutes. Five thousand perverts applied for only fifty parts when we were casting for "Drag" because there only could he do what he was starving for — act like a woman and wear expensive, beautiful gowns. Some homo-sexualists are not to be blamed for their condition. They are the inverts or the ones born that way... Some, however, are perverts...
>
> The theater will be my medium to sex education. I pride myself on the fact that I have always been ahead of public teachers. I realized the importance of the problem and devoted my career in the theater to the education of the masses. I shall boldly continue to do so, in spite of criticism, insults, and narrow-minded bigots. I believe that when I have my own theater, as I hope to some time in the future, my purpose can go unhindered by silly and old fashioned taboos and busy bodies.[66]

In the same magazine article, West made clear what she meant by providing the masses with a sex education. She wanted to dramatize her theories about gay male sexual predilections, which she likened to a contagious social cancer. After West became a superstar of motion pictures, nothing more was heard from her about any plans for further dramatic exposés of the tragedy of "born inverts" and the threat of gay "perverts." When the subject came up again in interviews in the 1970s, West boasted that *The Drag* "glorified the homosexual" in order to give "gay boys" work on the legitimate stage.[67] Well aware that many of her most appreciative and faithful fans were involved in the gay liberation movement, West — already billed "the greatest female impersonator in the world" — began doing another sort of impersonation during the last decade of her long life. She began posing as a veteran in the battle for gay civil rights.

Mae West never made any mention, either in interviews or in her memoirs, of the part politics played in the closing of *The Drag*. "It's all politics,"[68] her producer, C. William Morganstern, cried out the day after one drama with a gay theme was closed on Broadway to prevent another from opening along the same streets. The *World* reported: "Morganstern said 'The Drag' had fallen victim to a 'hysterical condition,' which also forced action against 'Sex,' 'The Captive,' and 'The Virgin Man.'"[69]

"Walker Play Crusade Laid To Pre-Election Promise,"[70] the *Evening Post* informed its readers, echoing Morganstern's cry that "It's all politics.":

> Mayor Walker was called upon for point-blank statements by representatives of several religious faiths and he has acknowledged that he gave these representatives his word of honor that, if elected, there would be no occasion to regret any support the churches might give him in this campaign...
>
> The Catholic Church, through one of its two organizations, has been interested in the drive against unclean stage productions...
>
> Likewise, the Greater New York Federation of Churches, several times has taken official notice of the need of purifying productions.[71]

Baptist and Methodist clergymen took particular exception to much of what was playing on Broadway. The New York press publicized their pontifications throughout the 1920s and well into the next decade. One Protestant preacher, Dr. S. Parkes, raised his outraged voice on his popular radio program, calling for continued police action and stiffer state and city censorship. Similar sermons could be heard in many of the churches and synagogues throughout the five boroughs.

In Manhattan, Cardinal Hayes made the same demands from Saint Patrick's Cathedral. When the New York City police closed three Broadway shows in one night it was reported that Rabbi Wise, who was held responsible for the closing of *The God of Vengeance,* and Bishop Manning of the Anglican Church, "were about to wade into the situation when the raiders beat them to the front page."[72] Another rabbi, Nathan Kraus, while opposed to censorship, told a meeting of the Jewish Theatrical Guild:

> We don't want the stage converted into a dumping ground for the moral and spiritual garbage of the human race, and plays dealing with abnormality belong to the psychopathists and psychoanalysts.[73]

While all the major religious denominations made repeated calls for censorship of the American stage, only the Catholics had the political clout in the state of New York to force any action on the matter. Both New York City's mayor and the state's governor were Roman Catholics. On the last day of 1926, the *Evening Journal* reported:

> The other day the Mayor of New York called a number of commercial theatrical producers into conference and told them that there were only six current plays that were successful, that all six were dirty, and that unless they themselves undertook to clean up the stage they faced the prospects of censorship.[74]

Criticizing Jimmy Walker for being "New York's night-life mayor, the man who frequents night clubs and prize fights so much that his nocturnal excursions are a scandal among many sections of his people," the *Evening Journal* surmised:

> It may be that the impetus for his new drive has come from the Mayor's church organization. It is a fact that only recently Cardinal Hayes solemnly inveighed against what he called indecency on the stage, which address was promptly followed by Mr. Walker's action.[75]

At the same time that city religious leaders were pressing Mayor Walker to take action in the face of the imminent arrival of *The Drag,* Governor Smith, his fellow Democrat, was threatened by political embarrassment. Unless Mayor Walker had the Manhattan police close certain plays already on Broadway, *The Captive* in particular, Smith would be forced to sign legislation, proposed by state senator Greenberg, to censor the New York stage. But if the so-called "dirty plays" were wiped off the Broadway boards, the governor could dismiss Greenberg's bill as unnecessary.

The *Times* ran a piece with the headline "Smith Against Censor, Governor Is Said To Favor Activity By The Police."[76] The *World* elaborated: "Governor Smith expressed his opinion that no state censorship law was needed and the adequate statutes cover the situation if enforced."[77] The *Herald Tribune* explained the seemingly liberal governor's preference for strong-arm, night-stick censorship:

> As the Hearst state censorship campaign is understood politically the immediate purpose is to confront Governor Smith with a bill which his previous political utterances will compel him to veto. The governor has been uncompromising for the abolition of the state motion picture

censorship board. Now the Greenberg Bill proposes an enlargement of the duties of that board to include theatricals of all kinds...

After Governor Smith vetoed the Greenberg Bill he could be accused of protecting immoral shows and Tammany Hall accused of collecting Broadway graft.[78]

Hearst had singled out *The Captive* in his clean stage campaign in order to embarrass Smith, who had once insulted him publicly. Since another editorial in his paper deplored the possibility that *The Drag* would be seen on Broadway, both plays had to be prime targets in any police raid instigated by Smith to foil the press baron's plans. While waging his campaign for a state censor to check immorality on the New York stage, Hearst made sure the public was well aware of the sort of entertainment he endorsed. He ordered extensive press coverage of such movie musicals as *The Red Mill* starring Marion Davies; Hearst's dailies offered glowing reviews of his mistress's talents when *The Red Mill* opened on Broadway.

"We were gettin' up to $50 a seat; they came from all over the country to see it,"[79] Mae West recalled about the box office business that *The Drag* was doing by the time it reached Paterson, New Jersey. New Yorkers began to read reports about people fighting to see it. "Six patrolmen were sent to the theater to handle the crowd that stormed the door an hour before the curtain rose,"[80] reported the *Herald Tribune*.

Despite threats in the press emanating from the Office of the District Attorney and the Department of Police, West and her co-producers would not be intimidated. They were going ahead with plans to bring the moneymaker into New York. According to *Variety*, before they did so, the producers

...attempted to secure the endorsement of the medical fraternity and the city officials to the effect that "The Drag" is educational and a remedial gesture on behalf of the "Homos." According to the "author" of "Sex," the Homos number one male in 20 in the United States and a larger percentage in Europe.[81]

In the same article, under the headline, "Confidential Performance of 'Drag' For Endorsement," *Variety* divulged that:

A midnight performance of "The Drag" was scheduled for Daly's, New York, last night (Tuesday) after the regular performance of "Sex." ... Mae West staged the midnight show for city officials and 25 physicians, with newspapermen barred. No notice of the midnight show was sent out.[82]

For unknown reasons, perhaps even problems with Actors' Equity, this report was denied the following day by the producers. One police official, according to the *World*, "specifically denied he had attended the showing, but he would not say it had not been held."[83] It may very well be that the Broadway debut of gay males as characters in an American play took place in February 8, 1927, for a very limited, select audience, secretly and by night.

Notes

1. Burns Mantle, "Enter The Lord High Censor," *New York Sunday News,* 6 February 1927.
2. Fragment of an untitled, undated newspaper article in file folder MWEZ n.c. 6801, Lincoln Center.
3. "Paterson Sees 'The Drag' Billed as Medical Play," *New York World,* 4 February 1927.
4. " 'The Drag' and 'Sex' Not The Half Of It," *New York Evening Post,* 2 February 1927.
5. "Police Won't Let 'Drag' Play Here," *New York Evening Post,* 9 February 1927.
6. *Ibid.*
7. " 'Drag' Censored At Bridgeport; Battle On Here," *New York Herald Tribune,* 1 February 1927.
8. *Ibid.*
9. *Ibid.*
10. *New York World,* 4 February 1927.
11. "Boasting of Sex, 'The Drag' Goes On," *New York Sun,* 1 February 1927.
12. "Plays Out Of Town," *Variety,* 2 February 1927.
13. "Only A Major Operation Can Save The Stage," (editorial), *New York American,* 2 February 1927.
14. George Eells and Stanley Musgrove, *Mae West* (New York: William Morrow and Company, Inc., 1982), pp. 63-64, 82.
15. "Come Up and See Me," *Show Business Illustrated,* 3 October 1961, p. 36.
16. Mae West, *Goodness Had Nothing To Do With It* (Englewood Cliffs, N.J.: Prentice-Hall, Inc.) p. 94.
17. Mae West, "Sex In The Theatre," *Parade,* September 1929, p. 17.
18. *Ibid.*
19. *Mae West,* p. 94.
20. *Goodness Had Nothing To Do With It,* p.93.
21. *Ibid.,* p. 94.
22. Mae West, "The Drag," (Unpublished manuscript on file in the Library of Congress, Washington, D. C., dated February 1927), Act I, p. 6.
23. *Ibid.*
24. *Ibid.*
25. *Ibid.,* Act I, p.7.
26. *Ibid.,* Act I, p. 8.
27. *Ibid.,* Act I, p. 12.
28. *Ibid.,* Act I, pp. 23-24.
29. *Ibid.,* Act II, p. 2.
30. *Ibid.,* Act II, p. 5.

31. *Ibid.,* Act II, p.6.
33. *Ibid.*
34. *Ibid.,* Act II, p. 7.
35. *Ibid.,* Act II, p. 8.
36. *Ibid.,* Act II, p. 9.
37. *Ibid.,* Act II, p. 6.
38. *Ibid.*
39. *Ibid.* Act II, p. 10.
40. *Ibid.,* Act III, p. 2.
41. *Ibid.*
42. *Ibid.,* Act III, p. 3.
43. *Ibid.,* Act III, p. 4.
44. *Ibid.*
45. *Ibid.*
46. *Ibid.,* Act III, p. 6.
47. *Ibid.,* Act III, p. 7.
48. *Ibid.*
49. William Hoffman, introduction, *Gay Plays: The First Collection* (New York: Avon Books, 1979), p. xvi.
50. *Ibid.,* pp. xvi-xvii.
51. *The Drag,* Act I, p. 14.
52. "'The Drag' Mae West's New Play Has 'Poppa Loves Poppa' Theme, *Zit Theatrical Newspaper,* 5 February 1927.
53. *Ibid.*
54. "Plays Out Of Town," *Variety,* 2 February 1927.
55. "Went To Be Shocked, Found 'The Drag' Clean," *New York Graphic,* 1 February 1927.
56. "'The Drag's' Rehearsing With 60 Villagers," *Variety,* 14 January 1927.
57. "Banton Abandons Play Jury System," *New York Evening Post,* 1 February 1927.
58. *Ibid.*
59. "'Drag' Censored At Bridgeport; Battle On Here," *New York Herald Tribune,* 1 February 1927.
60. "Paterson Sees 'The Drag,' Billed As A Medical Play," *New York World,* 4 February 1927.
61. *New York Herald Tribune,* 1 February 1927.
62. "Stage Wants Police Power For Play Jury," *New York Herald Tribune,* 3 February 1927.
63. *New York World,* 4 February 1927.
64. "Actors Arrested With Producers in 3 'Sex' Plays," *New York World,* 16 February 1927.
65. *Variety,* 2 February 1927.
66. *Parade,* September 1929
67. Christopher Stone, "Mae West," *The Advocate,* 8 October 1975.
68. "3 Theatres Raided: 'Sex' and 'Captive' Players Arrested," *New York Herald Tribune,* 10 February 1927.
69. "'The Drag' Quits As 3 Sex Plays Reap Harvest," *New York World,* 13 February 1927.
70. "Walker Play Crusade Laid To Pre-Election Promise," *New York Evening Post,* 16 February 1927.
71. *Ibid.*
72. "The Talk Of The Town," *New Yorker,* 5 March 1927, p. 19.
73. Jonathan Katz, *Gay American History* (New York: Thomas Y. Cromwell Company, 1976), p. 89.
74. William M. Feigenbaum, "Does Stage Need A Censor?" *New York Evening Journal,* 31 December 1926.
75. *New York Evening Journal,* 31 December 1926.

76. "Smith Against Censor," *New York Times,* 4 February 1927.
77. *New York World,* 10 February 1927.
78. "Banton To Sift Stage Charges To Foil Hearst," *New York Tribune,* 1 February 1927.
79. "Playboy Interview With Mae West," *Playboy,* January 1971, p. 76.
80. "Crowds Fight To See 'The Drag,'" *New York Herald Tribune,* 4 February 1927.
81. "Confidential Performance of 'Drag' For Endorsement," *Variety,* 9 February 1927.
82. *Ibid.*
83. *New York World,* 10 February 1927.

4

Stopping the Captive's Pale Brethren in Their Tracks: the 1927 Broadway Show Raid

"To-day Broadway told itself the worst is true — the shows are going to be raided," New Yorkers read on the morning of February 9, 1927. "Pessimists think the night-sticks may descend tonight."[1] The same day *Variety* informed its readers, "Police Ready to Raid Theaters With 'Dirt' Plays." The weekly publication explained:

> Taking a tip from Governor Al Smith that the Penal Code covered the matter of salacious plays, District Attorney Banton and Police Commissioner McLaughlin came forth with statements late last week to the effect that presentation of dirt plays would bring arrests and prosecutions...
> The governor again made it plain that he did not believe in state censorship bills now pending in Albany. He even called attention to a Supreme Court decision wherein it was held that any play tending to incite or arouse impure imagination, constitutes the maintenance of a public nuisance, is punishable under the law, even though there be no indecent language or obscene exposure.[2]

The District Attorney agreed with Governor Smith that existing laws were more than adequate to handle the situation. Even so, the District Attorney was ready to renege on his promise that there would be no retroactive prosecution of plays approved by the play jury. "I am not in sympathy with these radical Bolshevist ideas that try to obliterate the distinction between decency and indecency,"[3] he announced.

Even Broadway ticket scalpers guessed correctly that the lesbian love drama was one of those earmarked for closing in the anticipated raid. Every seat was sold out before the curtain rose on the night of February 9. According to the *World*, "Hawkers in the street shouted, 'Here you are! Get your tickets for positively the last performance of 'The Captive!'"[4]

It came as a complete surprise that the District Attorney also decided to close a vapid comedy, *The Virgin Man*, which had run for a year in London after being approved by the office of the Lord Chamberlain. *The Virgin Man* was about to post closing notices because of disappointing reviews and business. The light comedy concerned a worldly wife who playfully arranges — without success it turns out — for the seduction of her young brother-in-law, an innocent college student.

It was even surprising to some people that *Sex* was also included in the raid. Percy Hammond, who had not bothered to see Mae West's starring vehicle when it first opened, decided, simply out of curiosity, to look in on the show the month before it was closed down for being a public nuisance. "'Sex' was in plight no worse than many of its reputable companions of the stage," Hammond reported in a very brief appraisal.[5]

If *Sex* was not worse than other stage productions seen at the same time on Broadway, why was it selected for closing? Heywood Broun was one of the few drama critics who wrote about the raid on the Broadway shows. Broun pointed out that "'Sex' has now been running for eleven months, and 'The Captive' has had more than 150 performances. If either or both of these plays constitute a scandalous condition, just what did they constitute three months ago?"[6]

Both Mae West and the lesbian love drama began to pose a threat to those who had been unsettled by *The Drag*'s out-of-town tryout engagements and possible future opening on Broadway. West, as the author and producer of *The Drag*, would certainly be intimidated after the police arrested her and closed her starring vehicle. At the same time, it had to be made clear that no play with "perverts" would be tolerated on Broadway, not even *The Captive*, even though it had escaped immediate criminal charges when it first opened. "*Sex* and

The Virgin Man appeal to morons," the District Attorney said. Singling out *The Captive,* he concluded, "The other two are indecent and vulgar, but this one is thoroughly bad."⁷

The Mayor of New York was out of town the night the actors and managers of three shows were arraigned on charges of being a "public nuisance," as well as "tending to corrupt the morals of youths and others."⁸ In Mayor Walker's absence it was up to the Acting Mayor to bring complaints to the attention of the District Attorney. He was also contacted by the New York Society for the Suppression of Vice which cited George Jean Nathan's "extremely caustic condemnation of the play *The Captive.*"⁹

During the second act of the February 9 performance of *The Captive*, the stage of the Empire Theater was suddenly filled with policemen. They stood blocking the set's entrances and staring at the performers. Basil Rathbone was so shocked and disconcerted that he forgot his lines. "The stage manager rang down the curtain," Helen Menken recalled, "and most of the actors became hysterical ... Basil was finally quieted when the policemen consented to retire to a corner of the stage. The curtain rose once more and the play resumed."¹⁰

The next day, neither headlines nor front-page accounts of the police raid made mention of any such hysteria. "Police Politely Serve The Warrants After Final Curtains; Victims Not Unwillingly Submit Cordially To Arrest, Which Will Be Repeated Till Plays Are Purged," the *Times* misinformed its readers.¹¹

Mayor Walker knew about the planned raids; in fact, he made special arrangements for Helen Menken's trip to court. Walker wanted to spare her the indignity faced by Mae West and other performers who were herded into waiting taxis. Menken recalled:

> I had visions of something terrible like a paddy wagon, but I had a pleasant surprise when I got my make-up off. A very nice chauffeur appeared at my door and announced that Mayor Walker, who was an old friend of mine, had sent his car for me. So I rode to court in the Mayor's private car enjoying the irony of the situation.¹²

On the whole, the experience of being arrested and brought to court was apparently less enjoyable for Menken than the ride in her friend's car. Menken finally took to her bed under the strain of the situation. On the very day she had a "nervous collapse," the *Herald Tribune* reported, "Walker at Palm Beach, Smiles Over Theater

Raids."[13] From a golf course in Miami, the playboy Mayor commented:

> I do not believe in censorship in any of its forms, and I think the producers will clean their own houses without interference from us. But, of course, the police have been ordered to interfere whenever a play offends public decency.[14]

The New York police were ordered to arrest without warrant anyone connected with a performance which, in the mind of any individual officer, seemed to violate common decency. Neither the order nor the night-stick raid drew any outraged editorial protests from the daily papers. Hearst's tabloid, *The Daily Mirror,* boasted of its support for the clean-stage crusade.[15] Both the *Morning World* and the *Evening World* blamed the producers rather than the police and politicians for the raid. "Something had to be done," the *Evening World* editorialized. "If it is not cleaned from the inside, it will certainly be from the outside."[16]

A couple of the newspapers objected to the raid primarily because it gave sensational free publicity to the offensive shows, thus increasing their patronage until the courts closed the productions. In an editorial about "Cleaning Up The Stage," the *Times* suggested some sort of play censorship committee empowered to prevent professional actors from appearing in any play found objectionable.[17] The *Evening Post*, like the *Times,* resented the fact that the shows were able to reopen for business after being raided. The *Post* noted, too:

> The players themselves were forced to go through an ordeal of public exploitation that was neither just nor necessary... Nevertheless, despite these evils, two plays, which in theme went further than any heretofore presented on the American stage are checked. However, haltingly, even stupidly, the subject of sex perversion has been prevented from establishing itself in the theater.[18]

The very week of the Broadway show raid, one New York newspaper announced, "We're Still the Wettest City Despite Those 39 Raids."[19] Federal agents of the Prohibition Administration repeatedly made strong-arm invasions of speakeasies and supposedly idle breweries. Perhaps because such activity was considered commonplace, there was no public outcry after the raid on the three "dirty" plays. Donald Stewart, a Princeton professor, was one of the few voices of protest, and mistakenly thought that he would be joined by many others. "The idea of Helen Menken going to jail for playing the part of *The Captive* is preposterous," he said. "The public will not tolerate such outrageous persecution."[20]

A few others eventually joined his protest. In *Theater Magazine,* one outraged writer attacked the Society for the Suppression of Vice and the Watch and Ward Society as being philistines. "What a pity that a great play like *The Captive* had to suffer," the writer concluded, "but again here was an example of spinelessness before the police."[21] Dr. Holmes of Manhattan's Community Church decried:

> The police, in attempting to clean the New York stage, have begun as usual by making fools of themselves. Yesterday they raided *"The God of Vengeance,"* the day before they raided Bernard Shaw's *"Widower's House,"* [sic] and now they run true to form by raiding *"The Captive,"* one of the really serious plays in town.[22]

Actors' Equity Association — which had been active in the campaign to keep *The Drag* out of New York — made no protest after its union members had been manhandled and publicly humiliated during the Broadway police raid. Counsel for the actors' union simply said it "washed its hands of the situation."[23]

Before the raid the *Morning Telegraph* reported, "One thousand Protestant clergymen of the Greater New York Federation of Churches yesterday passed a resolution backing up the District Attorney in his drive against objectionable plays."[24] Drama critic and columnist Heywood Broun took objection to at least one reason given by the Methodists for encouraging Banton's attack on Bourdet's play:

> Some of the Methodist Brethren who have paid their respects to *"The Captive"* have suggested that the particular aberrancy with which the play concerns itself is a matter in which cities alone are concerned. . . I must ask permission to meet his particular charge with an unholy snicker. The problem is neither local nor of our own age. Let the Methodist Gentlemen look to the Bible and they will find that long before there was a New York, curious pathological quirks did exist.[25]

In Washington, D.C., the representative from Mississippi, a state in which the legitimate theater was all but nonexistent, urged federal stage censorship. A bill to that effect was introduced in Congress; it cited sixty-seven lewd or obscene Broadway plays, but it never passed.[26] A New York City congressman, Sol Bloom, urged that the whole audience be arrested for patronizing immoral shows.[27]

An entirely different reaction to the raid came from across the Atlantic, Andre Gaillard, the first man to produce *La Prisonnière,* observed:

> After a play has run more than three months, . . . it seems strange that it should suddenly be banned. It is all the more surprising because it makes it appear that New York's morals are narrower than those of Berlin and Vienna and especially the French Provincial cities, noted for their straight-laced ideas, where *La Prisonniere* has been running lately.[28]

Also from Paris, Augustus Thomas, a major American dramatist, spoke out in annoyance at the heavy-handed police tactics. "There was no reason to close *The Captive* after a three-month run," said Thomas. "I consider *The Captive* handled delicately and artistically. The plot is legitimate and the theme of the twentieth century."[29]

All of New York's daily papers ran front-page headlines reporting the Broadway raid, and most of them published daily accounts of the ensuing court proceedings and of the imprisonment of Mae West. Even so, the drama sections of those papers made little mention of the sensation of the 1926–27 theatrical season. Percy Hammond, one of the few critics who made any comment at all wrote: "We should all have faith in the mayor, the police and the district attorney, and trust no matter in which direction they squirt their hoses, purification will be the result."[30]

The other most important newspaper critics — J. Brooks Atkinson, George Jean Nathan, Burns Mantle, and Alexander Woollcott — were all curiously silent after the raid. After having attacked Nathan for his narrow-mindedness, though, Hammond himself expressed some sober second thoughts about the advisability of allowing females to see *The Captive.* He declared that if the new producer who takes over the show "will debar weak women and children from attendance and confine its audience to men only, *The Captive* should be allowed to continue its career as a fine play, illustrating a sinister topic."[31]

Mae West and her titular producer finally realized the futilty of attempting to bring *The Drag* into New York. The day after she was arrested for appearing in *Sex,* an assistant prosecutor in Bayonne, New Jersey, directed that *The Drag* be closed. "'The Drag' Dragged Off The Board in Bayonne,"[32] the *Daily Mirror,* announced. It was accompanied by a full front-page photo of a crowd of would-be patrons in front of the Bayonne Opera House: eight hundred theater-goers had seen the matinee and final performance of *The Drag* at the Opera House, while five hundred[33] more had waited in vain to buy tickets for the evening performance that was cancelled by the city's assistant prosecutor and police chief.

Except for the *Daily News,* which ignored *The Drag* after first reporting on its Connecticut opening, all of the major daily newspapers connected the out-of-town threat of *The Drag* and the closing of the three Broadway plays. Details of court proceedings in the aftermath of the raid shared front-page space with announcements of *The Drag*'s demise. Headlines read: "Bayonne Bars 'The Drag,'"[34] "'The Drag' Ends Hectic Career; Morganstern out,"[35] "'The Drag' Quits,"[36] and "'The Drag' Stopped."[37]

Morganstern protested: "Five million people in the United States are interested in conditions similar to those pictured in *The Drag.* There is no reason why the stage should not deal with their problem."[38] There was a reason, of course, for the uproar. The contempt in which gay men were held in the 1920s is evident in one newspaper's characterization of *The Drag*'s cast. The piece also reflects the once widespread impression that this still unrecognized minority was limited to just the sort of outrageous transvestites created by Mae West for her tragicomedy:

> Now that *The Drag* has been dumped into the garbage heap, and at least a score of its former players must go back to trimming hats and selling ribbons, it may not be amiss to describe some of the "queer" characters who are said to have appeared in *The Drag* during the brief time it dragged itself about.
>
> It is certain that Mae West, who sponsored the play, didn't have to work hard to complete the homosexual cast. The nature of these creatures is such that they will snap at a chance of appearing in public. And, when they are offered a chance to appear on the stage in gowns, dearie, real gowns; well — woops!
>
> Chief among those reported to have appeared in the last act of *The Drag,* which was the big "camp" scene of homosexuals, was a person known as "The Duchess." ... [S]he is the arbiter of homo-land. There is no greater authority of manners and etiquette ... and whenever one of "her" tribe is found guilty of a lapse in the most correct social usage "the Duchess" deals harshly with "her.". . .
>
> Another celebrated homo said to have played in *The Drag* is called

"Mother Superior." This character is an indefatigable correspondent. He is said to have studied for the priesthood at one time, but abandoned taking holy orders for the more exciting life of a homosexual in the great city. "Mother Superior" is the confessor and spiritual advisor of a large group of homos and both he and "The Duchess" hold court in a certain eating place on Fifth Avenue in the forties. Whenever a publication takes the queer clan to task, it is always "Mother Superior" or "The Duchess" who wrote a defense...

Incidentally the entire "queer" crew think it is terrible that the play should have closed. Most of them have been convinced, for the last several years, that they can act much better than regular Broadway actors or actresses, and they think it's "too dreadful, dearie," that the rude police should have stopped the play."[39]

Had Mae West agreed to close *Sex* as quickly as she called it quits with *The Drag,* she never would have gone to jail — nor would she have emerged as a nationally recognized celebrity. Released on bail after the raid, the feisty comedienne obtained a court injunction against further police interference as she continued starring in *Sex* for another six weeks. During that time, the grand jury indicted all those involved with the production for "maintaining a public nuisance." West, Morganstern, and West's business manager, James Timony, were convicted and sentenced to ten days in jail. West was also fined $500. The sensational press coverage of the trial and the imprisonment of the stage star was worth a million dollars in personal publicity.

The cast and managing director of *The Captive* never went to trial. The State Supreme Court also granted an injunction restraining the politicians from raiding that show again, and it played five more days. Gilbert Miller, admitted to the Legion of Honor in Paris for producing the English translation of *La Prisonnière,* was arrested in New York the day after he was decorated by France. Proud of having both produced and directed the show, Miller was determined to keep it running. However, as Broadway producer Horace Liveright confided to an inteviewer: "Mr. Lasky and Mr. Zukor brought pressure to bear on Mr. Miller and forced him to close the play because they were afraid of what their small town public might think of their producing a play like 'The Captive' in New York. I don't like to think the legitimate stage is dominated by motion picture interests."[40]

Liveright, a well-known publisher as well as a producer, announced that he would take over production of the play from the

Famous Players Lasky in Hollywood. The company had suffered a considerable financial loss by abandoning the production; more than $80,000 had to be given back at the box office to ticket-holders who would never get to see *The Captive*.[41]

A week after the Broadway raid the newspapers ran more articles concerning *The Captive*. The *Times* announced with front-page headlines: " 'The Captive' Quits, But New Producer Will Defy Police."[42] Liveright obtained an affidavit declaring that Bourdet's drama "has been approved by responsible psychiatrists and doctors." With that, he began a court battle to reopen *The Captive* on Broadway. To this end, he hired Arthur Garfield Hays, former counsel in the famous Scopes Monkey Trial. Determined to defend *The Captive* by making a "Scopes case in New York," Garfield declared:

> We laugh at those people down in Tennessee, ... but we do the same thing in New York. In Tennessee, it was held you should keep people ignorant to save their souls. Here the police attempt to say you should keep them ignorant to save their morals.[43]

Supporting Liveright, Menken, Rathbone and other members of the cast of *The Captive* retracted the promise they had made to the judge that they would not reappear in the play. "Far from seeing that we have been engaged in the commission of a crime,..." read the statement signed by the show's cast, "we feel that we have been privileged in using our talents in a play of the highest merit and social value."[44] But an editorial in the *Evening Post* declared:

> The cast of 'The Captive' appeals to so very lofty principles in behalf of a very weak case. "We owe it to ourselves, our profession and to the public to refuse to be intimidated." This sounds brave and fine. But in behalf of whom is it made? Why, in behalf of the right to introduce the theme of sex perversion on the American stage. We hope the city will continue to fight to prevent "The Captive" from reopening.[45]

Exactly one month to the day after the cast and producer of *The Captive* were arrested, Supreme Court Justice Jeremiah A. Mahoney ruled that "the stage is not a place for the portrayal of grossly immoral human emotions."[46] Holding that the police had acted correctly in stopping the show and preventing its revival, Mahoney declared, "The law recognizes the fact that many people must be protected from their very selves."[47]

Mahoney's ruling was headlined in some of New York papers. The case itself, when it was appealed, failed to excite the press, the general public, or even the civil libertarians enough to make it in any way comparable to the Scopes Monkey Trial, as Liveright's counsel had hoped. "The subject matter of 'The Captive' has been dealt with in some of the most famous classics of history," Attorney Hays argued, appealing Mahoney's ruling. "The matter is handled in a delicate, artistic, subtle and inoffensive manner. There is not an offensive, or vulgar line in the play, nor is there any obscene or unrefined situation or action."[48]

Roger Liveright had no choice but to abandon his plans for putting *The Captive* back on Broadway. Less than two months after the police raid, the Republicans in Albany slipped through the State Assembly, during the closing hours of the session, legislation amending the Penal Code of 1909. Not only was a specific reference to prohibiting plays "depicting or dealing with, the subject of sex degeneracy, or sex perversion,"[49] added to the public obscenity restrictions of the revised code, but also a much-publicized amendment. Section 1140A directed that theater-owners could have their playhouses padlocked for a year if they rented to a producer of a show which a jury decided "would tend to the corruption of youth or others."[50] The Wales Law, named after the legislator who introduced it, became popularly known as the Wales Padlock Law. Padlocking would be possible only if the district attorney's office received a guilty verdict from a jury after trying a producer for presenting an immoral show. Even after such a conviction, the theater could not be padlocked unless the owner still refused to evict the production from his property.

"I fear it does not go far enough," complained a state senator from Brooklyn the day the measure was voted on. "It is a slap on the wrist when a good, man-sized punch in the jaw is what is needed. When sex degeneracy and sex perversion have been shown on the stage, it is time to call a halt."[51]

The Broadway show raid failed to save the man who instigated it from having either to veto or to sign a bill increasing state censorship of the New York stage. Tammany Hall's strong-arm tactics had not placated those religious leaders and pressure groups who wanted a law to curtail freedom of expression of the legitimate theater in America. On the contrary, the headlines engendered by the sensational raid called national attention to their condemnations. It also won widespread popular support for Hearst's campaign to prohibit impure and perverted plays on Broadway. Instead of the proposed Greenberg amendment that had so provoked Governor Smith, the even more restrictive Wales Padlock Bill was placed before him.[52]

" 'The Drag' brought on the crisis," prestigious producer Winthrop Ames declared. Homophobic passions were inflamed much more by the existence and success of a play with gay male characters than they had been by the seemingly less threatening appearance of a lesbian love drama. Since the press reported no opposition to legal prohibition of further dramatizations of "sex degeneracy, or sex perversion," Governor Smith had no expedient political alternative but to sign the bill with no more fanfare than the Republicans had passed it in Albany. Had he not done so, his archenemy William Hearst could have accused the liberal Democrat of fostering "crimes against nature."

In 1927, at least one attorney declared that the Wales Law was unconstitutional.[53] Forty-eight years later, the US Supreme Court finally extended to the legitimate theater the same kind of constitutional protection against advance censorship and prohibition that newspapers and books enjoy. A theater-owner or operator in America cannot legally bar a production, sight unseen, from his stage, although the Wales Law was on the books in New York State for more than four decades.

While Alfred E. Smith signed the law that drove lesbian and gay male roles back into the closets of certain playwrights' imaginations, it was William Randolph Hearst who had personally initiated the prohibitive legislation. Mae West's play provided Hearst an example of what theatergoers might expect to see in such shows. The comedienne reinforced the libel that gay men are a sexual threat to children by including in *The Drag* a neighborhood boy who has been made so welcome in the home of a sexually promiscuous man that he wanders in and out of the house at will. The doctor's arguments for compassion in the comedy-drama are negated by the unsympathetic and bizarre gay roles West created. By dramatizing the madcap antics of the transvestite minority, the author's script left the general impression that "drag queens" represented the majority of the invisible gay community in the 1920s, rather than its exceptions.

For almost half a century after *The Drag* and *The Captive* were forced to close, a penal code prohibition inhibited the emergence of lesbians and gay men in Broadway dramas. Consequently, their real-life counterparts bore the stigma of being the only citizens of the United States adjudged too loathsome and morally infectious to be seen even in fictitious characterizations in legitimate theater productions.

Except for Mae West's mention of her landmark play during interviews and in her autobiography, one would have been hard-pressed to find any mention over the past half century of *The Drag, The Captive* or even the Broadway show raid that put them out of business. Theater historians have chosen to ignore the socio-theatrical phenomenon of the abortive emergence of lesbians and gay men as characters in English-language drama in the 1920s. During the last half of the 1970s, Alan Churchill devoted three pages to the sensation of the 1926–27 Broadway season in *The Theatrical Twenties*. Abe Laufe covered it in four pages in *The Wicked Stage*. Jonathan Katz, in his massive documentary *Gay American History,* included a note on *The Drag* in eight pages of newspaper excerpts concerning the closing of *The Captive.*

In 1970, Brooks Atkinson filled a paragraph about *The Captive,* but made no mention of *The Drag,* in *Broadway,* his cursory study of New York's theatrical activity since the turn of the century. Blaming the district attorney for closing *The Captive* because he was unable to "tell the difference between literature and hokum,"[54] the retired dean of Broadway critics made no reference to his initial revulsion at the plight of lesbian lovers in Bourdet's play.

Atkinson's homophobia was, however, no match for that of his colleague, Burns Mantle, who obviously wished he could expunge any evidence of a lesbian love drama having been performed on the Broadway stage. Even though his fellow critics voted that Mantle include a plot resumé of *The Captive* as one of the best plays of the 1926–27 New York theatrical season, he refused to do so in his annual yearbook of the drama in America. "So far as this book and this editor are concerned," wrote the drama critic for the *Daily News,* in defense of the egregious omission, "the show remains where fate and circumstances have placed it."[55]

Notes

1. "Will Raid 'The Drag' If It Opens," *New York Sun,* 9 February 1927.
2. "Police Ready To Raid Theatres With 'Dirt' Plays," *Variety,* 9 February 1927.
3. "Mr. Banton Goes To The Play," *New York Evening Post,* 12 February 1927.
4. "Actors Arrested With Producers In 3 'Sex' Plays," *New York World,* 10 February 1927.
5. Percy Hammond, "The Theatres," *New York Herald Tribune,* 4 February 1927.
6. Heywood Broun, "It Seems To Me," *New York World,* 4 February 1927.
7. W. J. Blalock Jr., "The Night They Raided Three Broadway Shows," *New York Sunday News,* 22 April 1956.
8. "Sex Plays Are Raided," *New York Daily Mirror,* 10 February 1927.
9. John S. Sumner, "For The Ultimate Good Of Society There Must Be A Cessation Of Dirty Plays — Hence The Theatre Closings," *Theatre Magazine,* August 1928, pp. 11-12.
10. "Helen Menken Recalls 'Captive' And Her Arrest," *New York Herald Tribune,* 9 June 1935.
11. "Police Raid Three Shows, Sex, Captive and Virgin Man: Hold Actors and Managers," *New York Times,* 10 February 1927.
12. *New York Herald Tribune,* 9 June 1935.
13. "Walker At Palm Beach, Smiles Over Theatre Raids," *New York Herald Tribune,* 18 February 1927.
14. "Walker Backs McKee," *New York Times,* 15 February 1927.
15. "Sex Plays Are Raided," *New York Daily Mirror,* 10 February 1927.
16. "The Warning To The Stage," *New York Evening News,* 10 February 1927, and "Mr. Banton's Raids," *New York Morning World,* 11 February 1927.
17. "Cleaning Up The Stage," *New York Times,* 11 February 1927.
18. "The War On Unclean Plays," *New York Evening Post,* 18 February 1927.
19. "We're Still The Wettest City Despite Those 39 Raids," n.p., New York Newspaper Clipping, 12 February 1927, in file MWEz, b.c. 4415, Lincoln Center.
20. "Clean Stage Drive Halts For Courts," *New York Evening Post,* 12 February 1927.
21. Benjamine De Cassers, "Smash The Panders and Smuthounds!" *Theatre Magazine,* July 1928, p. 12.
22. "Clergyman Flays Police For Raid on Captive," *New York Morning Telegraph,* 11 February 1927.
23. "Press Old Charges Against Liveright, Backer of 'Captive,'" *New York Times,* 18 February 1927.
24. "Banton Will Make Cops Play Critics," *New York Morning Telegraph,* 8 February 1927.
25. Heywood Broun, "It Seems To Me," *New York World,* 4 February 1927.
26. "Arrest Sex Play Audiences, Urges Bloom," *New York Morning Telegraph,* 14 February 1927.
27. *Ibid.*
28. "New York Modesty Tardy Says 'Captive' Originator," New York Morning Tribune, 11 February 1927.
29. "Augustus Thomas in Paris Assails Banton Play Raid," *New York Morning Telegraph,* 12 February 1927.
30. Percy Hammond, "The Theaters," *New York Herald Tribune,* 13 February 1927.
31. Percy Hammond, "The Theaters," *New York Herald Tribune,* 20 February 1927.
32. "'The Drag' Dragged Off The Boards in Bayonne," *New York Daily Mirror,* 10 February 1927.
33. "Bayonne Bars 'The Drag,'" *New York Times,* 10 February 1927.
34. *Ibid.*
35. "'The Drag' Ends Hectic Career; Morganstern Out," *New York Morning Telegraph,* 13 February 1927.

36. "'The Drag' Quits as 3 Sex Plays Reap Harvest," *New York World,* 13 February 1927.

37. "'The Drag' Stopped," *New York American,* 11 February 1927.

38. *New York Morning Telegraph,* 13 February 1927.

39. Untitled New York newspaper article dated 11 February 1927, no publication in the clipping file for *The Drag,* Lincoln Center.

40. "Horace Liveright Clatters Down B'Way On Rosintante," *New York Post,* 17 February 1927.

41. "'The Captive' Quits, But New Producer Will Defy Police," *New York Times,* 17 February 1927.

42. *Ibid.*

43. "Fight To Save 'Captive' Like Scopes Case," *New York Herald Tribune,* 19 February 1927.

44. "Raided Shows Are More Defiant," *New York Sun,* 11 February 1927

45. "Editorial," *New York Evening Post,* 17 February 1927.

46. "'Captive' Immoral, Mahoney Decides," *New York Times,* 19 March 1927.

47. *Ibid.*

48. "Legislature Gets Play 'Padlock Bill,'" *New York Times,* 19 March 1927.

49. Jonathan Katz, *Gay American History* (New York: Thomas Y. Crowell Company, 1976), p. 90.

50. *New York Times,* 19 March 1927.

51. "Padlock For Stage Voted By Senate," *New York Times,* 24 March 1927.

52. "Liveright Appeal To Reopen 'Captive,'" *New York Times,* 20 February 1927.

53. "Smith Approves Theatre Padlocks; Vetoes Gas Cut-Off," *New York Times,* 8 April 1927.

54. Brooks Atkinson, *Broadway* (New York: The MacMillian Company, 1970), p. 248.

55. Burns Mantle, ed., *The Best Plays of 1926-27* (New York: Dodd, Mead, & Company, 1927), p. vii.

5

A Horrible Thing of Soul
Leprosy Stalks a Chicago Stage

During the run of *The Captive,* an interviewer wrote of Helen Menken:

> There is only one regret she has about the whole thing. Now that
> "The Captive" is a success, she is afraid that the school of playwrights
> that copies successes in the hope of catching some of the overflow will
> begin toying with the theme of "The Captive," and she knows only an
> artist can handle the subject in such a way. That is, not unpleasant in
> presentation.[1]

Another lesbian love drama, the very first by an American playwright, had already opened and closed by the time Menken's qualms
were being read in *Theater Arts Magazine.* This play was either
already written when *The Captive* premiered, or had been dashed off
in a great hurry by William Hurlbut, author of more than a dozen
other plays produced on the New York stage. Just one month after
The Captive proved such a box office sensation, A.H. Woods had
opened Hurlbut's *Hymn to Venus* for its out-of-town tryout in Atlantic City.

Woods was the producer who had successfully fought to keep *The
Demi-Virgin* running when the license commissioner attempted to
close that slightly risque hit in 1921. One would have thought, however, that he would have been the last producer in the business to
mount a gay play. One drama critic in Atlantic City chided:

> Oh, Mr. Woods! And you were the sage who predicted Mr. Gilbert Miller would be immediately carted off to jail if he lifted the Empire curtains on "The Captive."
>
> Nothing encourages like success. So Mr. Woods has followed Mr. Miller's lead and forthwith we have the William Hurlbut play "Hymn to Venus," which emerged from the enshrouding mystery of its advance notices at the Apollo Theatre last evening.[2]

William Hurlbut, who had been writing prolifically for the stage since 1908, had his biggest hit with *Bride of the Lamb*. It appeared in New York the same season (1926–27) that *Hymn to Venus* failed critically and financially in its Chicago debut. Woods selected that city to premiere *Hymn to Venus* because, despite its success in New York, Gilbert Miller had yet to announce plans for a Chicago company of *The Captive*. Apparently the Shubert brothers who rented him the Empire Theatre had already booked all their Chicago playhouses for that season.

Abraham Erlanger, who ran the other national theatrical syndicate, had not rented Miller a Broadway theater and refused to lease him one in Chicago, objecting to the dramatization of such subject matter. The breach between Erlanger's syndicate and its long-time lessee, the Charles Frohman Production Company, afforded Woods an opportunity to cash in on *The Captive*'s success and nationwide publicity. The *Chicago Daily News* noted:

> In a rather spectacular race between the two producers as to which of them shall first reach Chicago, A.H. Woods has evidently won out. For he announced the production here, at the Adelphi Theatre, of William Hurlbut's sensational play, *Hymn to Venus*. The fact that he has his own theater here while his rivals, producers of *The Captive,* like it in theme, had to accept the bookings of a syndicate; these bookings being largely contingent on the plays current in the theaters at their command.[3]

The title *Hymn to Venus* — the title of one of Sappho's poems — was changed to the more provocative *Sin of Sins* after the play's Atlantic City tryout. Starring English-born Isobel Elsom and Robert Warwick, the drama disappointed one Atlantic City drama critic who compared it to *The Captive*:

> Mr. Hurlbut has not displayed the sentiment, the tact, and the reticence of the wary Bourdet. He has preceded the action with lengthy

preambles, particularly the first 15 minutes which are intolerably exasperating...

As long as "The Captive" is playing to capacity houses on Broadway, "Hymn to Venus" may thrive on the overflow.[4]

The critic for *Zit's,* the show business publication, was no more enthusiastic about Hurlbut's dramaturgy:

Lesbianism on the stage is a touchy topic, one generally spoken in nervous whispers. Mr. Hurlbut treats the subject relentlessly but rather clumsily.

He arouses a sympathy for the unfortunate woman, but it is a feeling tinged with horror. Her life has been one of complete inner turmoil, bringing havoc to all those living in intimate contact with her.

The play gains speed and interest as it progresses and its absorbing moments, many of them intensely melodramatic, and all leading up to the only possible solution for the poor victim of her own nature — suicide.

The brunt of the performance falls upon Miss Isobel Elsom who carries off the hapless lady with thrilling effectiveness. She has a deep sensitiveness to the character and a realization of its impending doom.[5]

Sin of Sins was advertised with a quote from Spinoza's *Ethics,* which the playwright and the producer used to justify the drama's daring subject matter:

I have labored not to mock, lament or excoriate but to understand human actions; and to this end I have looked upon passions not as vices of human nature but as properties just as pertinent to it as heat, cold, storm, thunder and the like to the nature of the atmosphere.[6]

While there were fifteen daily drama critics covering the New York stage in the 1920s[7], Chicago had only three important daily newspapers: the *Daily News,* the *Daily Tribune,* and the *Herald Examiner.* When *Sin of Sins* opened on November 8, 1926 at the Adelphi Theater with no advance sale, it was doomed after two of the three daily critics panned the play. John Joseph of the *Herald Examiner* was most appreciative of Wood's production, and his review contains a brief plot resumé. Hurlbut's play was never published; thus, the critique is valuable because it gives some idea of this first drama containing a lesbian character written by an American.

In his review entitled, "*Sin of Sins* Brings Strange Fish into Adelphi Aquarium," and subtitled, "Play Sort of Clinical Study But

English star Isobel Elsom played a seducer of females in the first play with a lesbian character written in the English language. Sin of Sins, *authored by an American, failed in its Chicago premiere in 1926 after an Atlantic City tryout in which Gladys Lloyd, better known as Mrs. Edward G. Robinson, played the object of an aggressive, murderous lesbian's affection.*

It Is a Drama Whose Power Is Enhanced by Fine Cast,'' Joseph wrote:

> The topic of ''Sin of Sins'' is one generally discussed in text books, though I believe it might have been mentioned in the Loeb-Leopold drama. In other words, perversion, and what it may lead to was the message that Mr. Hurlbut felt a crying need to express. So the heroine is not quite right, as we say ... Indeed, so far from right is the lady (who has had two husbands and is tormenting a third) that all of her mental and physical affection darts towards members of her own sex. She has, poor soul, apparently kept her strangeness to herself. And she has selected a nice girl on whom to shower what everybody considers motherly affection.
>
> When the nice girl falls in love — with a man, I might add, naturally, or rather unnaturally, the lesbian lady is moved to jealousy. And before the *Sin of Sins* has gone an act the girl's sweetheart is dead. Suicide, they think. But it's murder, and murder will out. Which it does in a breathless third act when the strange, female fish confesses her crime and the reason for it. She atones, too, but not, let it be said, by entering a convent.
>
> Weird as all this may sound, ''Sin of Sins'' is delicately written, acted and staged. There will be, doubtless, many who will see it and not know what it's all about, even in this very public age. There will be others, too, who will see it and dislike it intensely. But I don't feel they'll be offended ... In spite of the clinical subject, Mr. Hurlbut manages to create sufficient sympathy for his central character to make her real. In this he is superbly aided by Isobel Elsom, who acts the pathological lady for all the role's pathological power and none of its sensationalism. In fact, throughout a filthy affair, anybody desiring to wallow had better go elsewhere.
>
> *Sin of Sins* will not run as long as *Abie's Irish Rose,* but it has power and it brings into the theater a new (at least to my big, young eyes) topic for dramatization and it is finely done.[8]

Mathilde Len, reviewing *Sin of Sins* for the *Chicago Daily News,* had a mixed reaction. While she detested the subject matter, she appreciated the author's tactful handling of it and applauded Elsom's portrayal of the murderous lesbian. Len wrote in a review entitled, ''*Sin of Sins* Fails to Impress Critic; Marvels Only at Daring of Producer in Presenting So Unclean a Thing'':

> Cloaked by a quotation from Spinoza, a horrible thing of soul leprosy stalked its way into the consciousness of a first-night audience at the Adelphi Theater during the unfolding of *The Sin of Sins* at its world premiere yesterday.

William Hurlbut, its author, and A.H. Woods, the sponsor, are already well enough known for their daring. Having astutely labeled their play "a study" and cannily cast its character delinations into the hands of a seasoned and personable group of actors, they get away with the most unclean thing yet produced in the theater ... Paraphrasing the lines of Robert Warwick, spoken as Byron Carlin, "There are no words to express my disgust" — with an author, and a producer and an actor who, for the sake of the almighty dollar, drag into the glare of the footlights a loathsome diesase from out of the psychomedical clinics.

Isobel Elsom, new to Chicago, is an actress of such unquestionable ability that admiration for her art overcomes revulsion for her part. With a sensitive, spiritual beauty and a low voiced, perfect diction of the cultured Englishwoman, she won immediate sympathy by giving the audience the feeling of having to do with one walking on the brink of insanity...

There is nothing salacious about the play, so it has no appeal to the sensationally inclined; so it affords nothing by way of beguilement, so it will fail to please the amusement seeker, and surely there are happier and saner avenues of psychological research to furnish plots and an emotional outlet for good acting.[9]

Frederick Donaghey, the critic for the *Chicago Daily* and *Sunday Tribune,* liked nothing about *Sin of Sins,* neither the play itself nor the performances. Accusing all involved with the production of being unscrupulous mercenaries, Donaghey wrote:

Mr. Woods, in a line carried beneath the title in the playbill, indicates that he regards *Sin of Sins* as "a study"; meaning, perhaps, a study of the boxoffice takings of *The Captive,* retailing in New York at five dollars a seat. Three of four persons of proved judgment and controlled enthusiasms who have seen *The Captive* tell me that it is, regardless of its theme, a good play. *Sin of Sins* isn't. It isn't regardless of the theme and of the authorship, which Mr. Woods seems to think should be credited to the late Baruch Spinoza, leaving one to wonder what Mr. Hurlbut had to do with it, but the important aspect of "Sin of Sins" is the proof it conveys that actors may be hired to do anything: the limit, if they knew one, has been kicked across the well-known and highly-lauded horizon. Their employment here is consciously in willful, deliberate vileness...

The big odor of the piece is supposed to be exuded in a scene of eccentric lovemaking by a female urning[10] with an ingenue whose fiance the former has murdered. It is, in the writing, and the indicated "business," more nearly explicit than even the episode in *God of Vengeance* which landed the management and actors in jail; but it is such weak, tawdry drama that it doesn't evoke even the reaction of

nausea... [S]pecial matinees for the children will, maybe, be a matter
of late announcement.[11]

Except for the daily ads for *Sin of Sins* in all the Chicago newspapers, there was no follow-up news or publicity, not even in the Sunday drama sections which ran photos and interviews of stars of current shows. Nor were the city's pressure groups, the politicians or the
religious leaders quoted in the papers after the show had opened. It
would seem that the press had decided that a news blackout was the
best way to cope with a show that the critic for *Variety* called "not fit
for public presentation." Predicting its demise, the same reviewer
wrote:

> It is safe to say that one-third of the first night house never under-
> stood what it was all about ... This one's chances are few. Firstly, the
> type of audience which will be drawn by the title will be disappointed
> and bored — and the word spreads fast among that class. Secondly, the
> theme is revolting and the average playgoer will stay away.[12]

Wood's attempt to profit from the publicity fallout from *The Captive*
failed: after a three-week run, *Sin of Sins* closed for lack of business
on December 4, 1926.

There was some positive response to Hurlbut's drama; that is evident in Frederick Donaghey's defense of his dismissal of the play and
of his disdain of the performances which he characterized as "pure
ham."[13] In his Sunday column, he wrote the last words Chicagoans
were going to read on the subject:

> The use of the theme — that of female urning — in the drama or in
> any other form of art would have to be the ultimate justification. It has
> such justification in the Yiddish piece named *God of Vengenace:* not
> that the piece, itself, is of importance as art, but that the episode which
> caused the New York police to put the actors in an English version in jail
> is integral, and serves the purpose of the drama in the author's clear
> design, however unlovely and repellant the play and the characters may
> be. I have not seen *The Captive,* and have been unable to obtain real in-
> formation as to its form and contents from either the twaddle written
> about it by the New York reviewers or the twitter printed about it in the
> Continental journals.
> But it is not necessary to know anything about any other play deal-
> ing with the homo-sexual, as a type or as an individual manifestation of
> psychopathic affliction, for the purpose of authentic reporting on *Sin of
> Sins.* Its sole importance resides in Mr. Woods' justified, if leering

audacity in putting it before the public. Not even its author can conceivably believe it to be worth three cents a dozen as a play; and all the brains, the wisdom, and the learning of that Spinoza, from whom Mr. Woods quotes so liberally without knowing who he is, could not make the thing appear even to the consciousness of mattoids as other than planned, willful, eager vileness.[14]

Isobel Elsom, the star of *Sin of Sins,* remembered very little about the production. This is understandable, since it was only one of the many shows in which she had appeared since going on the London stage. Elsom did say about this failure:

> I was simply unaware of gay people who may or may not have been in the English or American theater working at the same time that I was. So the subject neither interested nor threatened nor had anything to do with me. And I didn't get to know any big name stars, playwrights or producers who might have been gay. One heard very little on the subject — which was simply taboo among show business gossips — except it was said that Katherine Cornell and her husband, director Guthrie McClintic, and Lynn Fontanne and her co-starring husband, Alfred Lunt, were all supposed to be gay, but I don't know if this was so.
>
> I was not at all afraid of playing a lesbian. I thought it was a good role and right for me, what I could do with it on the stage. I wasn't shocked or made uncomfortable playing the love scenes in *Sin of Sins.* I don't remember receiving either mash notes or any insulting mail. Only the critics' reaction was distressing because it puzzled me.
>
> No, I never did see *The Captive* in New York before or after doing the show for Al Woods in Chicago. I never met Hurlbut, the playwright, who, I understood, was not gay.[15]

Perhaps because *Sin of Sins* met with such an unappreciative critical reception in Chicago — "the most offensive offering in the annals of the theater in Chicago,"[16] as one critic called it — *The Captive* did not play the city when a national company took it on the road after the nightstick raid on Broadway. *The Captive* was seen in Baltimore, Cleveland, Detroit, San Francisco, and Los Angeles. Baltimore saw it in two different fortnightly engagements and Cleveland, where it had its longest engagement on the road, saw it in a five-week stand. The performances in Baltimore and Cleveland went without interruptions. Police officers in San Francisco, however, stepped onstage to halt *The Captive* when it opened there in the summer of 1927. The police also raided the show in Los Angeles and Detroit, piling the cast into paddy wagons.

Eleanor Barnes, a Los Angeles reviewer, called *The Captive* "cancerous" and dismissed it as "A Good Play For Medical Students."[17] But another Los Angeles critic, Harrison Carroll, was very impressed. "A masterly written, superbly acted, and intelligently directed drama," he wrote, but added, "I will not attempt to pass judgment on the advisablity of discussing such a subject in the theater."[18] Don Wiley of the *San Francisco News* wrote a rave review for "the relentless and absorbing tragedy," which he found enthralling despite a police raid in the middle of the opening night performance. He reported:

> But even the ridiculous spectacle of a squad of decidedly unaesthetic looking policemen trampling about the stage, trying to prevent people from saying things couldn't lessen the tremendous dramatic effect of Edouard Bourdet's fascinating drama.[19]

Only nine years after she had been arrested as the star of *The Captive,* Helen Menken had these thoughts about the reaction to the play:

> I'm absolutely certain that *The Captive* wouldn't create even a ripple of excitement here and now. The subject has been written about since with amazing frankness, and nobody seems the worse for the freedom of discussion. "Other days — other morals."[20]

Veteran drama critic Richard Watts, Jr., mused about his initial reaction to *The Captive,* forty years later:

> I'm afraid that its moderation, reticence and carefulness would cause the present day spectators either to laugh at it for its timidity or to be terribly bored by its tentative manner of beating around the amorous bush. You had to figure it out between the lines.[21]

When Bourdet's drama was revived in San Francisco in 1951, the reviewer from *Variety* had this disinterested reaction:

> But it's doubtful if it will stir the police to action as it did when it first showed its distorted face 25 years ago. Compared to the atomic problem facing mankind, it is now mild fare, milk and water stuff. The boys and girls of Nethersex Village and farm will just have to work out their problems for themselves, it seems. These are days of bigger revulsions.[22]

In 1959, Arthur Hornblow, Jr. announced plans to make a film version of *The Captive.* Columbia Studios was reportedly considering its super-star sex goddess, Kim Novak, for the title role. Hornblow and his wife had also written a new version which director Leland Hayward hoped to stage. Neither the Hollywood film nor the Broadway revival ever materialized. In 1959, the industry's Motion Picture Production Code still banned lesbian and gay male characters from the screen, and the New York stage censorship law remained on the books.

Notes

1. Ada Paterson, "Miss Menken Defends 'The Captive,'" *Theatre Arts Magazine,* February 1927, p. 22.
2. George R. Weintraub, "The Play," *Atlantic City Union,* 2 November 1926.
3. "Amusement Notes," *Chicago Daily News,* 1 November 1926.
4. *Atlantic City Union,* 2 November 1926.
5. "'Hymn To Venus' Has Some Hymn; Second Lesbian Play Opened by A. H. Woods at Atlantic City," *Zit's Weekly,* 6 November 1926.
6. *Chicago Daily News, Chicago Daily Tribune, Chicago Herald Examiner,* 8 November 1926.
7. Brooks Atkinson, *Broadway* (New York: The MacMillan Company, 1970), p. 251.
8. John Joseph, "'Sin of Sins' Brings Strange Fish Into Adelphia Aquarium, Joseph Reports," *Chicago Herald Examiner,* 9 November 1926.
9. Mathilde Len, "'Sin of Sins' Fails To Impress Critic," *Chicago Daily News,* 9 November 1926.
10. Karl Heinrich Ulrichs, the German historian and sex researcher, coined the word "urning" since Plato in *Symposium* wrote that the goddess Urania watched over the "heavenly love" of two males. Through the 19th century, "uranian" was in general use until, in 1869, Hungarian Doctor Daroly Maria Benkert coined the word "homosexual."
11. "Theatre," *Chicago Daily Tribune,* 9 November 1926.
12. "Plays Out Of Town," *Variety,* 24 November 1926.
13. *Chicago Daily Tribune,* 9 November 1926.
14. Frederick Donaghey, "This Thing And That Thing Of The Theatre," *Chicago Sunday Tribune,* 14 November 1926.
15. Isobel Elsom, interviewed in the Motion Picture Country Hospital, Woodland Hills, California, April 1926.
16. Frederick Donaghey, "The Season In Chicago," in *The Best Plays of 1926-27,* Burns Mantle, ed. (New York: Dodd, Mead & Company, 1947), p. 19.
17. Eleanor Barnes, "'The Captive' Good Play For Medical Students," n.d., n.p., fragment in *The Captive* file, Lincoln Center.
18. Harrison Carroll, fragment of review entitled "'The Captive' In Mayan Bow," n.d., n.p., in *The Captive* file, Lincoln Center.
19. Don Wiley, "Rentless And Absorbing Tragedy in 'The Captive,'" *San Francisco News,* 15 July 1927.
20. "Helen Menken Recalls 'Captive' and Her Arrest," *New York Herald Tribune,* 9 June 1935.
21. Richard Watts, Jr., "Two On The Aisle," *New York Post,* 17 January 1970.
22. "The Captive," *Variety,* 18 July 1951.

6

Closeted Gays Onstage in the 1920s

Less than a year after *The Captive* was raided, another gay male character appeared on the Broadway stage. Despite the newly enacted stage censorship code in New York, Eugene O'Neill included a gay male role in his play *Strange Interlude*. O'Neill created Charles Marsden, a celibate character who was as carefully closeted as his real-life counterparts of the period. Marsden consequently went unrecognized — or at least unidentified in print — as being gay.

"I've known many Marsdens on many different levels," O'Neill said, "and it had always seemed to me that they've never been done in literature with any sympathy or real insight."[1] In one of his biographies of O'Neill, Louis Shaeffer has been able to identify Charles Marsden's real-life counterparts. Shaeffer divulged:

> The character was based on Charles Demuth, the painter whom O'Neill had known in Provincetown and Greenwich Village; and the playwright also had in mind another noted artist, Marsden Hartley (hence the name "Charles Marsden"), who was a good friend of Demuth's. The two artists were homosexual — as is the play's Marsden, though he flees from himself — and Demuth, like his fictional counterpart, had a strong, protective and jealous mother.[2]

Strange Interlude, was a great Theater Guild hit both in New York and on the road. The play ran six hours, with a dinner-break in-

Eugene O'Neill, America's most renowned playwright in the 1920s, believed that he had written the first gay character in English dramatic literature with "any sympathy or real insight." Tom Powers played that role in O'Neill's 1929 Broadway success Strange Interlude, *which starred Lynn Fontanne. None of the critics identified Powers' role as being gay in the reviews of the drama.*

termission, during which it slowly detailed the lifelong suffering of a woman's relationships with her father, romantic lover, gay male confidant, husband, adulterous lover, and son. In the tradition of French classical drama, Charles Marsden functions as confidant to the distressed protagonist, Nina Leeds, throughout the play's nine acts. While she relates to him as she might to an older brother, she refers to him as a protective father-figure after losing her own father. Over the years, Nina loses her first love and her husband to death, her son to marriage; she also loses sexual interest in her longtime lover. At the play's end, she retires emotionally and physically in a marriage of convenience with Marsden.

Describing Charles Marsden as having an "indefinable feminine quality about him, but ... nothing apparent in either appearance or act," O'Neill has other characters in the play react to the character as if his manner were flagrantly feminine. Behind his back, Marsden is referred to disparagingly as: "this ladylike soul," "fussy old woman," "slacker bachelor," "an old maid who seduces himself in his novels," "queer fellow," "mother's boy," "like a woman," "the damned old woman," "old sissy," "queer creature," and "one of those poor devils who spends his life trying not to discover which sex they belong to." O'Neill describes the character being as "scandalized as an old maid" when he comes upon young lovers petting.[3]

To explain his gay character's celibacy, the playwright used a slightly fictionalized account of his own first traumatic encounter with a prostitute.[4] After a heterosexual fiasco, Marsden confesses that he "sobbed ... thinking of my mother ... feeling I had defiled her ... and myself ... forever." O'Neill's own sexual experience apparently did not cripple him, according to biographers; he enjoyed many satisfying heterosexual relationships.

In *Strange Interlude* O'Neill used a theatrical device that permitted his characters to speak their inner thoughts in lengthy soliloquy-asides while engaging in conversation with other characters. Marsden never has anything to say to the audience about being physically attracted to his own sex. There does not seem to be a single gay thought in his supposedly gay head. No matter how socially closeted O'Neill intended his creation to be, his device might have served to reveal Marsden's most intimate thoughts.

The critics had much to say about *Strange Interlude* in 1927, but there was only passing mention of Marsden's characterization. None of the critics identified it as gay. Atkinson of the *Times* dismissed the bachelor as a "timid and petty novelist."[5] John Mason Brown referred to him as "Mollycoddle Charlie,"[6] and *Theater* magazine noted that "good Old Charlie suffers from an acute mother complex."[7] Other critics made no mention of Marsden at all.

Thirty-six years later, many reviewers reacted to Marsden almost as unsympathetically as do the other characters in the play. In the 1963 Broadway revival at the Actors' Studio, Charles Marsden is described in reviews as: "spinsterish,"[8] "all but neuter ... the weak one ... in his fussy, brittle shallowness,"[9] "a victim of momism,"[10] "undersexed,"[11] "sexless,"[12] and "Oedipal Charles Marsden, the intellectually sterile author who makes a fetish of devotion and descends like a carrion hawk to profit at the presence of death by marrying at the play s end."[13] But even in the Sixties, critics did not identify the character as gay.

Nor did other reviewers, twenty-two years later, do so. In a third Broadway revival of *Strange Interlude* in 1985, Marsden was played by English actor Edward Petherbridge. The critics were unanimously delighted with his performance. Still, there was no mention of the character's obvious gay identity. According to the reviewer for *The Advocate,* Marsden's sexuality goes unmentioned because of entrenched homophobia:

> My guess: Given what O'Neill wrote, a critic, to confront this sexuality, would have to admit that gays might have a sensitivity, emotional awareness, and depth of caring that most American men don't. . .
>
> Marsden, who is variously referred to as "the old woman," the "sissy," the "sexless" man, is the only one who sees all, knows all and, ultimately, heals all. O'Neill makes the man who abhors sex with women the only sane, whole, rational one in the bunch.[14]

Three theatrical seasons before Charles Marsden appeared in *Strange Interlude,* two other closeted characters were portrayed in British dramas that opened in the U.S. The first, Michael Arlen's dramatization of his best-selling novel *The Green Hat,* was staged by Guthrie McClintic. Co-starring his wife — Katherine Cornell — and Leslie Howard, it proved to be a popular hit even though the critics were more impressed with the actors' work than with the playwright's.

The Green Hat concerns a young bachelor enraged at his sexually promiscuous twin sister, Iris March, after her bridegroom's mysterious suicide on the first night of their honeymoon. At the play's climax it is revealed that the groom, Boy Fenwick, killed himself because he was syphilitic. To protect Fenwick's good name, his noble bride says that he died "for purity,"[15] thus adding further dishonor to her own tarnished reputation. Her brother, Gerald, had passionately idolized Fenwick and was led to believe that the playboy killed himself upon learning that Iris had been promiscuous before their wedding. Iris felt that Gerald would commit suicide too if he learned that his tin god was "dirty." Gerald refuses to talk to her for ten years, and, unable to function after Boy's death, he dies an alcoholic.

The brother's supposedly platonic adoration of Fenwick must have seemed suspicious, perhaps even amusing, to gays in those mid-twenties audiences . Broadway critics made no mention of the unusual relationship. Arlen's novel gives no clear indication that he intended the sexually repressed brother to be gay, yet in his dramatization

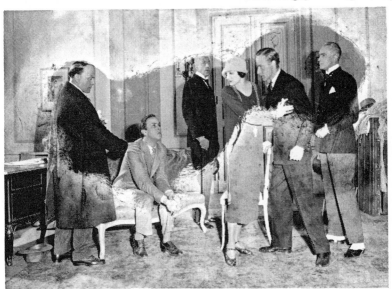

Katherine Cornell has to hold back Leslie Howard, her leading man, from assaulting her gay twin brother, played by Paul Guilfoyle, in a scene from the 1925 hit, The Green Hat. *The brother becomes hysterical upon learning that his sister's bridegroom, a man he idolized, had committed suicide on the couple's honeymoon. None of the critics recognized the closeted gay brother, nor did Britain's stage censor, who approved the original London production.*

Gerald's obsessional idolizing is certainly as impassioned as Antonio's self-destructive devotion to Bassiano in Shakespeare's *The Merchant of Venice.*

In the first scene of *The Green Hat,* Gerald March, played by Paul Guilfoyle, attempts to defend his hysterical, verbal attack on Iris to astonished onlookers:

March. "Look here." I want you to understand something — Boy and I were friends. Got that? Friends, friends, friends! ... I never wanted Iris to marry Boy, I knew it wouldn't do. Boy Fenwick was the cleanest man in the world.

Continuing to scream desperately in the same scene, Gerald feels the need to explain his strong feelings about his late brother-in-law:

March. ...The only person I ever met in my life for whom I had an admiration was Boy Fenwick. That's why I'm so excited now, but you mustn't think I'm mad. Look here, I admired Boy because he was the only person I've ever met who had really clean ideals and wasn't a bit of a prig or anything like that. And another thing: Boy was like a God in his contempt for shoddiness! ... Mental and physical shoddiness.[16]

None of the critics from the daily papers made any mention about the possible implication of a grown man's hysterical infatuation for his best friend. Most filled their reviews comparing and contrasting Katherine Cornell with the heroine of Arlen's widely read and much-admired novel. *The Green Hat* has never been revived. If it had been, especially in the last twenty-five years, American audiences might have cringed or smirked at the equation of puritanical sexual self-denial with "cleanliness" and "contempt for physical shoddiness" in the brother's hysterical outburst. Someone in a modern audience might even laugh aloud at the sister's explanation that her bridegroom "died for purity"[17] by plunging from his hotel window upon discovering that she was not "chaste" — followed by her brother's reaction to this lie with a wild cheer, crying "Bravo Boy! Hurrah, Hurrah!"[18]

The play has never been published, nor included in any anthology other than in a brief synopsis in Burns Mantle's *Yearbook of the Drama*.[19] Because *The Green Hat* has never been revived, there has been no occasion for contemporary drama critics to identify — as some surely would — a covert but rather transparent gay characterization.

Had it not been for Michael Arlen, New York audiences that season might never have seen the second of those two British dramas with covert gay characterizations. Arlen had become great friends with Noel Coward, who had completed a run in his first stage hit, *The Vortex*. Coward had written it as a starring vehicle for himself, and it had made him the overnight sensation of the English theatrical scene. Nevertheless, he was having trouble with backers after making plans to take *The Vortex* to New York. When Coward told Arlen of his financial problem, Arlen wrote out a check for £250, and handed it to his friend with no stipulations attached.[20]

Both *The Green Hat* and *The Vortex* became Broadway hits. Arlen — still a bachelor at thirty — and twenty-seven-year-old Coward intrigued gossips with their friendship. Coward's longtime companion and confidant, Cole Lesley, recalled:

> The smell of success was in the air for Michael Arlen and for Noel, relished by both, though the smarties made up their minds that they were rivals, and must be bitterly jealous of each other. To scotch this

they could be seen dining, just the two of them, at least once a week in the most prominently fashionable restaurants in New York until rumors swung the other way and had it that they were having an affair, which of course added to their enjoyment more than ever.[21]

Once again, the newspaper critics of half a century ago were unable to recognize a closeted gay character. Percy Hamond was the only reviewer among the first-nighters who suggested that Coward's role was "a little effeminate and neurotic."[22] Only in a single slur by his mother's virile young lover does Coward identify the protagonist of *The Vortex* as "effeminate."[23] The *Times* observed only that *The Vortex* concerns "ridiculous, effeminate manners," and "effeminate wrangles."[24]

"I play the part of a neurotic misfit," Coward wrote in his memoirs, "who took drugs, made sharp, witty remarks and was desolately unhappy."[25] In none of his memoirs did Coward ever identify his own gay lifestyle, nor did he identify the role he wrote for himself in *The Vortex* as being in the same closet as the playwright was — at least in the eyes of the public. In 1975, after Coward's death, Cole Lesley was the first to write, "He was a homosexual."[26] Dr. W. David Sievers seemed to be the first to recognize "the element of latent male inversion . . . suggested in . . . Noel Coward's *The Vortex*"[27] in *Freud on Broadway*, published in 1970. Seven years later scholar Martin Green noted that *The Vortex* was "about drugtaking and homosexuals."[28] Green made the observation in a passing reference to *The Vortex* in *Children of the Sun,* his study of the cult of beauty and brilliance among young Englishmen — many of them gay.

Had Green noted that *The Vortex* was a play about drug-taking and *a* homosexual, it would be clear that he was referring to one character: Paucefort Quentin, called "Pawnie," described by the author as "an elderly maiden gentleman."[29] A venomously sarcastic snob, in no way involved with the play's main plot, Pawnie was obviously meant to add humor to the decadent society Coward was portraying. Pawnie is the "bitchy fag" stereotype, probably the kind of character that Eugene O'Neill contended had been drawn without "sympathy or real insight."[30]

Since Pawnie elicited no cries of horror from either the Lord Chamberlain's office in London or the New York drama critics, they probably considered him another amusing asexual descendant of the

In 1925 twenty-seven-year-old Noel Coward established himself as a star of the Broadway stage with his London hit, The Vortex, *which he wrote for himself. Coward played an unrecognized closeted gay who blamed his sexually promiscuous mother, played by Lillian Braithwaithe, for his addiction to drugs.*

Restoration fop or a close relative of one of Oscar Wilde's drawing
room wits. Although he makes no sexual references or innuendos, certain of Pawnie's lines should make clear today — even if they did not
in 1925 — his sexual disposition.

Feuding for no good reason with one woman in his circle of
rather silly acquaintances, Pawnie proves himself a devastating wit, if
not a very charitable human being. He remarks: "Poor Clara — she
eternally labours under the delusion that she really matters."[31]
Distaste for such a character probably provoked the comments from
the *Times*' reviewer about "ridiculous, effeminate manners," and
"effeminate wrangles."[32]

Although his overtly gay Pawnie was surprisingly bold for the
mid-twenties, Coward was commensurately cautious in defining
Nicky, the protagonist of *The Vortex*. Nevertheless, Martin Green
probably meant to include Nicky in his plural reference to "homosexuals"[33] in the drama since no other character qualifies.

The Vortex concerns a young English pianist who returns home
after studying on the Continent, to introduce his English fiancée to his
parents. The engaged couple joins other houseguests at the family's
country retreat. Nicky's glamorous mother, Florence, has included
her young gigolo lover among her guests.

Soon after arriving, Nicky and his fiancée break off their engagement because there seems to be no real attraction between them. The
young lady had once been romantically involved with the virile gigolo,
and the two decide to resume their relationship. There is an embarrassing scene between the rejected, furious hostess and her young
lover, witnessed by her hurt and horrified son. Confused at his passive
father's obtuseness and tolerance and enraged at his aggressive
mother's blatant infidelity, Nicky turns on her viciously in a melodramatic climactic scene — reminiscent both of the Hamlet-Gertrude
closet scene and Mrs. Alving's final scene with her son in Ibsen's
Ghosts:

> *Nicky.* You've wanted love always — passionate love, because you were
> made like that — it's not your fault — it's the fault of circumstances
> and civilization — civilization makes rottenness so much easier — we're
> utterly rotten — both of us—
> *Florence.* Nicky — don't — don't—
> *Nicky.* How can we help ourselves? — We swirl about in a vortex of
> beastliness—[34]

Blaming his mother not only for making a mess of her life ("you're an awfully rotten woman, really"[35]), Nicky finally shatters her by showing her a small box. Florence throws it out the window upon realizing that he uses it for drugs. They confess their love for one another, despite their new awareness of one another's failings. The curtain falls as the son takes his mother in his arms:

> Nicky. ... —Promise me you'll be different—
> Florence. Yes, yes — I'll try—[36]

Perhaps audiences concluded that Nicky suffered from a weltschmerz not unfamiliar to many of "the lost generation" during that unsettled decade following World War I. Nicky blames his mother for the troubles that drove him to drugs, but Coward does not say just what these are. Passionate lovemaking encouraged by a permissive society is what he deplores in Florence. Since he concludes "we're utterly rotten — both of us"[37] one can only wonder whether Nicky's own sexual passion has unsettled him, too. No passion is apparent in Nicky's platonic scenes with his fiancée, and there is no mention of any other woman in his life except, of course, his mother.

Coward does drop some subtle hints about Nicky's rather curious preference in women. His girlfriend is described as "more attractive than pretty in a boyish way."[38] His mother, with whom he is still very much emotionally involved (Nicky is in his mid-twenties), is described in one scene as looking like "an heroic little boy."[39]

Whatever Noel Coward's private sexual activity may have been when he was writing *The Vortex,* his public stance — at least on the stage — was a puritanical denunciation of any but the hard-working middle-class, heterosexual and monogamous lifestyle. This was apparent to only one of the reviewers at its premiere in 1924, when *The Vortex* took London by storm. While others damned it or praised it as a reflection of the liberalizing moral attitudes in British society, playwright-critic John Ervine suggested that *"The Vortex* is a very moral play, dedicated to the old fashioned virtues of hard work and clean living, by which most of the characters are judged and found wanting."[40] Within this frame of reference, Coward paints a damning portrait not only of a sexually liberated matron, but of his covertly gay protagonist as well.

In both London and New York, *The Vortex* was particularly

popular with younger theatergoers. "Noel Coward was the Beatles of our day," one Englishwoman recalled, discussing the impact of *The Vortex* on the second half of the 1920s.[41] Despite its initial success, *The Vortex* has not been seen in a revival.

Some consider *The Vortex* one of the most significant British dramas of this century. In his biography of Coward, Charles Castle wrote of this drama about the sophisticated, witty, decadent upper-middle-leisure class: "It is probably fair to say that this play changed the face of the British theater in the twenties in the way that Osborne changed it in the fifties with *Look Back in Anger.*"[42]

Notes

1. Louis Shaeffer, *O'Neill, Son and Artist* (Boston: Little, Brown and Company, 1973), p. 242.
2. *Ibid.*
3. Eugene O'Neill, *Nine Plays by Eugene O'Neill* (New York: The Modern Library, 1959).
4. Sheaffer, pp. 241-242.
5. J. Brooks Atkinson, "The Play," *New York Times,* 18 December 1928.
6. John Mason Brown, "Intermission, Broadway in Review," *Theatre Arts Monthly,* April 1929, p. 238.
7. "The Editor Goes To The Play," *Theatre Magazine,* April 1929, p. 40.
8. Howard Taubman, "Actors Studio Presents O'Neill Revival," *New York Times,* 13 March 1963.
9. Whitney Bolton, "'Strange Interlude' Wears Well, Acting Honors to Page, Prince," *New York Morning Telegraph,* 13 March 1963.
10. George Oppenheimer, "One Stage," *Newsday,* 20 March 1963.
11. Richard Watts, Jr., "O'Neill's 'Strange Interlude' Still Retains Its Dramatic Power," *New York Post,* 12 March 1963.
12. Edward Southern Hipp, "King-Size In Spades," *Newark Evening News,* 12 March 1963.
13. Larry Van Gelder, "Interlude Still Tops," *New York Mirror,* 12 March 1963.
14. Robert Silver, "Theater," *The Advocate,* 30 April 1985.
15. Michael Arlen, *The Green Hat,* (Typewritten copy on file), Lincoln Center, p. 20.
16. *Ibid.,* pp. 12-13.
17. *Ibid.,* p. 20.
18. *Ibid.*
19. Burns Mantle, ed. *The Best Plays of 1925-26,* (New York: Mean and Company, 1937), pp. 121-159.
20. Charles Castle, *Noel,* (Garden City, New Jersey: Doubleday & Company, Inc., 1973), p. 62.
21. Cole Lesley, *Remembered Laughter* (New York: Alfred A. Knopf, 1976), p. 89.
22. Percy Hammond, "The Theaters," *New York Herald Tribune,* 17 September 1926.
23. Noel Coward, *Play Parade I* (London: William Heinemann Ltd., 1950), p. 198.
24. "The Play," *New York Times,* 17 September 1926.
25. Noel Coward, *Future Indefinite* (London: William Heinemann, Ltd., 1976), p. 168.
26. *Remembered Laughter,* p. 93.

27. W. David Sievers, *Freud On Broadway,* (New York: Cooper Square Publishers, Inc., 1970), p. 93.
28. Martin Green, *Chidren Of The Sun* (New York: Basic Books, Inc., Publishers, 1976), p. 171.
29. *Play Parade I,* p. 176.
30. Louis Shaeffer, *O'Neill, Son and Artist* (Boston: Little, Brown and Company, 1973), p. 242.
31. *Play Parade I,* p. 202.
32. "The Play," *New York Times,* 17 September 1926.
33. *Children of the Sun,* p. 171.
34. *Play Parade I,* pp. 238-239.
35. *Ibid.,* p. 244.
36. *Ibid.,* pp. 244-45.
37. *Ibid.,* p. 239.
38. *Ibid.,* p. 189.
39. *Ibid.,* p. 192.
40. Sheridan Morley, *A Talent to Amuse* (Garden City, New York: Doubleday and Company, Inc., 1969, p. 172.)
41. *Noel,* p. 65.
42. Ibid.

7

Seventeen Live Fairies Onstage During a Presidential Year When New York Had to Be Good

In the autumn of 1928, Mae West was ready to try a second time to put a play on Broadway that included flamboyant, gay transvestites. It had been less than two years since West had to close *The Drag,* under duress, during its financially rewarding engagement in New Jersey. "I had gotten back all my money and made about thirty thousand dollars,"[1] she recalled concerning the play's out-of-town tryout. Her new production, West boasted to Noel Coward, would have "seventeen live fairies on stage."[2]

It is ironic that Mae West was the first to defy the censorship statute which appeared on the New York lawbooks in the homophobic wake of *The Drag.* West decided that she was not going to let the district attorney halt her at the city's gates again. Her new play, *Pleasure Man*, began its tryout engagement at a theater in the Bronx. If it survived the surveillance of the law in that borough of the city, the move downtown to Broadway would be only a subway ride away.

West's flaunting of the law for a second time, though obviously motivated by greed, was not a thoughtless gamble. *Pleasure Man,* West and her attorneys were ready to argue, concerned a protagonist of a more conventionally acceptable sexual promiscuity than that of the gay cad in *The Drag.* Those "seventeen live fairies" were necessarily included in a drama of heterosexual concerns to authenticate the play's settings.

Pleasure Man is a backstage melodrama about a vaudeville troupe in some American city. The main plot concerns one of the performers, Rodney Terrill. An insatiable, brutal womanizer, he is found dead and castrated during a climactic costume party. The play becomes a murder mystery in its brief, final scene; the irate, alcoholic husband of a woman who had been in love with Terrill comes under suspicion. As it turns out, Terrill died at the hands of a young stage electrician avenging the honor of his sister, whom Terrill had battered while she was begging him not to end their affair.

In structure, *The Drag* and *Pleasure Man* are strikingly similar. The main character of each play is a sexually promiscuous male, ruthless and unfeeling, who batters a cast-off lover. Both are murdered after attending a costume party. Both melodramas end with a last-minute revelation of the killer's identity, clearing an innocent man.

Among the performers in the backstage hustle-and-bustle of the first two scenes, and at the party in the third, are five (not seventeen) female impersonators. Four are silly, effeminate young men: two of these indistinguishable minor characters flitting about backstage are identified as Bunny and Peaches. These performing transvestites are part of an act headed by one of the play's major characters, Paradise. This tough, vulgar female impersonator — a sort of gay old whore with the cliché heart of gold — provides most of the humor throughout the play's three acts with his self-deprecating, obsessive, sexually suggestive retorts. He is mocked repeatedly by the stagehands, stage manager and house manager. Nevertheless, Paradise proves himself braver and more compassionate than the men who bait him, gallantly rescuing Terrill's mistress during the battering scene.

During the first scene when the performers are arriving to prepare for the next attraction, one of the men backstage asks Paradise what he does in the show:

Paradise. O— Oh! I'm Bird of Paradise and my four Many-kins.
Stan. . . .He chases butterflies on the dewy grass.
(Illustrates)
And makes delicious fudge on Sundays and holidays.
(Up to table)
Steve. What kind of an act do you do?

Paradise. Oh, I get down on my knees — and sing a couple of Mammy songs ... You see I'm a character imperson-eater.
Steve. A what?
(Enter two boys of Paradise Co.)
Paradise. A female impersonator...
Steve. I guessed as much.
Stan. Have you had your cream puff this morning?
(Down S.R.)
Paradise. Oh, I always eat early.
(To Steve)
You know it's the early bird that catches the worm, dearie.[3]

The female impersonators get a dressing room next to the acrobats and have to be told, "And don't push the chewing gum out of the knot-hole."[4] Stan also tells Paradise:

Stan. And don't you annoy the boys, Violet.
Paradise. Lavender, maybe but violet never.[5]

"They are so queer," one of the vaudevillians says to another performer on the same bill. He replies, "Yes, my dear ... extraordinarily queer."[6]

In the second act, while a performance is going on, there is other evidence of the vaudevillians' discomfort with working with gays. Chuck, a dancer, is disturbed because he suspects his new dancing partner, who makes lampshades in his spare time. It is in this act that Paradise stands up to Terrill and comforts the battered mistress because he is sympathetic to a "sister" being abused by a man.

A backstage visitor invites the whole company to a costume party given in their honor by an retired vaudevillian. The party will afford "the pleasure man," as the other performers contemptuously call Terrill, the opportunity to seduce the married woman who is flirting with him behind her suspicious husband's back.

The professional transvestites appear in drag at the costume party, but they are only five among the large company of performers. Among themselves, they chatter about their costumes and their sexual activity:

1st Boy. I hear you're working in a millinery shop.
2nd Boy. Yes, I trim rough sailors.
3rd Boy. My, what a low-cut gown you've got.
4th Boy. Why, Beulah, a woman with a back like mine can be as low as she wants to be.[7]

"It is interesting that some of the dialogue duplicates that of *The Drag,*" William M. Hoffman observed after reading the playscript in 1978, "as if West was determined to make sure that New York audiences were going to hear what had been banned earlier."[8] Hoffman also noted: "In the backstage world that West portrays, gay is usually accepted."[9] That conclusion is hardly supported by other characters' remarks. The transvestite performers are tolerated, but mocked with an unmistakable contempt shared, it would seem, by the playwright herself: West refers to them as "fags" in her stage directions.

West was so intrigued with the plot that she reworked it as a novel, also entitled *Pleasure Man,* published in 1975. West could have included the female impersonators in that version of *Pleasure Man*, but there is not a single mention of such characters in the novel. Nor was the party during which Rodney Terrill is castrated identified in the book as a costume party. For reasons best known to herself, West had expurgated from the novelization much of the sensation of her original playscript.

Pleasure Man premiered at the Biltmore Theatre on October 1, 1928 — a night most first-string critics elected rather to attend one of the performances opening at two respectable repertory companies. Seats for *Pleasure Man*'s opening had been selling for between $70 and $100,[10]: apparently West would have a financial bonanza on the order of *The Drag.* "That West girl knows her box-office," *Variety* reported, "and this one is it right now."[11]

"The excitement that the play had created in its break-in weeks had saturated Broadway and theatergoers with great expectations of seeing a sensational piece of entertainment," West recalled forty-five years later. "My name was up in lights as the author, and only two blocks away I was still appearing in *Diamond Lil.*"[12]

Pleasure Man was such a sellout that the police, out in great numbers on orders to raid the show, had to keep the crowd orderly as hundreds of disappointed theatergoers were turned away from the box office. Before reaching Manhattan, *Pleasure Man* had had a two-week tryout in the Bronx and Queens. The district attorneys of those boroughs allowed the play to run after certain lines and situations to which they had taken exception were eliminated. Preparing for *Pleasure Man*'s move downtown, the Manhattan authorities sent stenographers disguised as suburbanites to the theater in Queens to jot down objectionable dialogue.

"Police around the Biltmore Theatre did nothing to break up the first Broadway performance of Mae West's new smutch, *Pleasure Man,*" reported Gilbert Gabriel of the *Sun,* the only first-string critic to review the show's opening night. Gabriel continued:

> But, afterwards, fortified by fresh air, a good third of the audience regathered in the stage door alley, passed out cigarettes and latest rumors, and waited to see the actual collision of the actors and the law. This extra act was by far the best of the evening.[13]

A throng estimated at two thousand gathered around the Biltmore Theatre to watch as paddy wagons pulled up to hustle the fifty-five performers,[14] some still in make-up and costumes, off to the police station. The playwright, the producer, and the theater-owner were also booked for presenting impure entertainment. A critic wrote:

> "At first it was planned to prosecute under the Wales Law, which requires arrest and conviction before it can be invoked. Later the district attorney, with his characteristic good sense, decided that the police had ample powers under the penal code without resorting to that new emblem of American liberty, the padlock...
>
> The Wales Law can only be invocated where the theater manager or owner refuses to alter or eject a play which the police adjudged obscene. In an undefendable case like that of *Pleasure Man* no producer or owner is going to defy a clear police order. But in a case like that of *The Captive* it may be the right and the duty of the producer to protest the irresponsible decision of a police official and insist on a fair trial in the courts,...
>
> This is the ultimate absurdity of the Wales Law, that it is not, and probably never will be, invoked against downright obscenity; but it is almost certain to be invoked against any sincere producer who, believing his play to have artistic merit, insists on his constitutional right to a fair trial.[15]

Describing the final scene in *Pleasure Man,* and the police raid immediately afterwards, the *Daily News* reported:

> All the gentle-voiced boys are holding their merry party when suddenly some sober big rough policemen burst onto the stage and start asking questions.
>
> There is much hysterical giggling and soprano shrieking, and the skirted youths fainted upon each other's powdered shoulders.

The scene was repeated almost in duplicate behind the scenes after the last curtain went down, when the real police came galloping through the stage doors.[16]

According to the *Sun:*

The throng in the street included practically the entire audience that had witnessed the show. These evidently had a bad taste in their mouths. They spat (some of them) upon the pavement and booed and hissed as the "female impersonators" in the cast were brought out of the stage entrance, where here and there was heard a frail falsetto cheer.[17]

About the scene at the police station, the *World* reported:

Some of them tried to laugh it off. Some of them expressed anger at the police. But most of them were silent and nervous.

The women seemed to take it the hardest. Two or three of them sobbed convulsively on the shoulders of other women and looked with frightened glances at the crowd outside which could be seen whenever a door was opened.

The whole affair, from start to finish, was handled without disorder; in this the police were helped by the bravado which most of the prisoners affected.[18]

The night-stick raid on *Pleasure Man* made front-page headlines — most often accompanied by a photo of Mae West — in all the New York newspapers. The play itself, according to a police observer quoted by the *Daily News,* had "to do with the pastimes and preoccupations of female impersonators," and was "the most sinister show ever produced on Broadway."[19] A detective was quoted by the same tabloid as saying, "I couldn't describe the show ... without using words that I don't like to see used in print."[20] According to *Variety, Pleasure Man* was "the queerest show you've ever seen. All the queens are in it."[21]

The plot concerning the castration and murder of the heterosexual was included, rather sketchily, in all the press accounts of the police raid on *The Pleasure Man*. Neither the police nor the press passed judgment on this, the major concern of the drama. They concentrated instead on the climactic costume party scene, in which female impersonators appear "in drag."

According to some press reports, nearly half of the cast were female impersonators. West claimed only five of the fifty-five performers were.[22] However many there may have been, the public's discomfort was fanned to a frenzy by West's second attempt to put gay transvestites on the stage. "*The Pleasure Man* threatened us last season," a Hearst editorial said, "but under the name of *The Drag*... Rewritten in parts, Monday it again reared its ugly head and was so obnoxious that it disgusted confirmed first nighters and hard-boiled cops."[23]

West reacted angrily:

> They are proceeding against *Pleasure Man* simply because word has got around and they believe that it is *The Drag*. It is not. There is no part of *The Drag* in *Pleasure Man*. *The Drag* was about a homosexualist. Who was married to a doctor's daughter. This play is about a normal man and women...
>
> I have some lady impersonators in the play. In fact, I have five of them. But what of it? If they are going to close up the play and prevent these people from making a living because they take the part of female impersonators, then they should stop other female impersonators from appearing on the Keith Circuit ... How many thousand female impersonators do you think there are in the country? Are they going to put them all out of business?[24]

Not every newspaper reviewed *Pleasure Man* in its entertainment section, but almost all of them included a brief synopsis of the plot in detailed front-page accounts of the raid. A second-string critic for the *Times* dismissed West's drama in a very brief, negative review: "By and large, *Pleasure Man* is a coarse, vulgar and objectionable specimen of its author's theatrical writings. As a play it is ... a hodgepodge, scrambled in theme and poorly written."[25] In its news coverage of the play's opening, the *Times* commented that "it must be said that some of the players seemed to glory in the opportunity for exhibitionism."[26]

In his report subtitled "*Pleasure Man* — Something of a Description of the Somewhat Indescribable," Gilbert Gabriel wrote:

> No play of our times has had less excuse for such a sickening excess of filth. No play, I warrant, has set out more deliberately to sell muck to the jeerful...
>
> ...I saw a "drag" and its inhabitants ... But seeing was only half of the sickening. The — shall we call them female impersonators? — were many, and were made to go through all sorts of Harlem bacchanales in various stages of robe and disrobe. What they had to speak was worse.

Perhaps they enjoyed it. The fouler phases of exhibitionism may be interesting to pathologists — but they make for pathetic playgoing.[27]

The critic from the *Evening Post,* just as outraged as Gabriel, subtitled his review "They Don't Come Any Dirtier." He wrote:

> To the three tiresome and unspeakably slimy acts of *Pleasure Man* the police, by arresting the entire cast, contributed a fourth, and even the most rabid opponent of official interference would find it hard to protest on this occasion...
>
> The bulk of Mae West's latest is feeble back-stage melodrama, relieved by some midly amusing characters and local color. If this were all, *Pleasure Man* would die unnoticed in a few weeks. But it is smeared from the beginning to end with such filth as cannot possibly be described in print, such filth as turns one's stomach even to remember...
>
> Nearly half of the performers are cast in the roles of what, for lack of a more printable term, may be called "female impersonators." One scene shows them in women's clothes, dressing and undressing. The final act shows us a "drag," or party given by one of this kind for the other of his kind, and when I add that the dialogue, throughout is full of revolting innuendo of perversion I have said enough.[28]

Two years after his office acted quickly to close *Pleasure Man,* the Assistant District Attorney gave this assessment of its artistic and entertainment merit:

> This play ... was a deliberate attempt to capitalize on the effect of a large number of men on the stage who were portraying perverts. That was relied on to fill the box office. The story of Mary Ann, who was ruined by the Pleasure Man, wouldn't have gotten them $10 a week.[29]

The reviewer for the *Brooklyn Eagle,* far less revolted than some other aisle-sitters, wrote in his critique, "Mae West Again; *Pleasure Man* Jewel from Her Pen Proves Tame":

> A little more than a year ago, Mae West and her associates were given a broad hint that it would not be advisable to bring to New York a play called *The Drag.* The objection to the piece, which Miss West-proudly acknowledged as one of her brain children, was based upon the fact that its theme was sexual perversion, and that such a theme was without the law ... Being evidently enamored with the subject, Miss West wrote another play and called it *Pleasure Man* ... Although the story is not the same, there are a number of characters in *Pleasure Man* that would have fitted ideally into the cast of *The Drag.* Also, it is an open secret that there are lines and scenes in both plays that are very similar ... to bring these characters on stage, Miss West hit upon the

idea of writing a "back-stage" play. Female impersonators are common enough in vaudeville houses.

... They are seen on the stage at an early morning rehearsal, and later snapshots are given of the dressing rooms of the theater. The humor of the piece — if humor it can be called — is of the same type that one sometimes finds in cheap burlesque houses. It is about the only type of humor that is found in the Mae West stamp. At first, it seemed to meet with some favorable response on the part of the audience. Later it began to pall terribly. In the end, it was a rather tired audience that waited for something to happen ... Nothing really happened. In the main they were disappointed. Evidently a blue pencil has been freely used. Little is heard that is objectionable as was heard in *Sex,* the play that sent Miss West to jail. Still the whole piece is so common and vulgar that it is not worth considering.[30]

Critics' reactions to *Pleasure Man's* premiere were as widely divided as audience reactions. One critic observed that, "Perversion was never before used to give diversion like it was last evening. People winked both eyes and looked straight ahead. Modesty forbade them to look left or right."[31] According to the *World,* the audience, "at first inclined to shout hilariously at the more suggestive lines, did not seem pleased with the exhibitions of female impersonation which were part of the festivities of the third act."[32] The incensed man from the *Evening Post,* on the other hand, had this to report on one group of first-nighters:

Pretty nearly the most nauseating feature of the evening was the laughter of the audience, or at least that part of it which howled and snickered and let out degenerate shrieks from the balcony. If a first-night audience doesn't whistle or throw vegetables or leave the theater or call for the steward when such muck is put under its nose but laughs and laps it up, there is no sense in taking the performers to the police station. The real culprits are on the other side of the footlights.[33]

Despite a restraining order from the state supreme court directing Manhattan police not to interfere with the production of *Pleasure Man* until the case was tried, the nightsticks came down on Mae West once again. This was an election year, when Alfred E. Smith would run for governor and Franklin D. Roosevelt for the presidency: Mayor Walker was not going to allow a play with characters prohibited by law to reflect adversely on the city, the state or any Democratic politician from New York. "Persons close to the Mayor," reported the *Evening Post,* "said that he had told Police Commissioner Warren that any dastardly drama even slightly odorous were not to be tolerated on Broadway this season. New York must be good in Presidential years.''[34]

A detective, followed by a squad of police officers, entered the stage of the Biltmore Theatre during the third act of *Pleasure Man*'s second and final performance. At the sight of the police, one actor stepped out on the stage's apron and addressed the audience:

> "This play is going to be stopped before it has been brought to trial," he said. "Do you folks think it's fair?"
> "NO!" thundered the audience.
> "The newspapers have tried to make it out a play of degeneracy. They have tried to cover the cast with filth and mire. Is that fair?"
> "NO!" cried the audience.[35]

The actor was seized by the police and pushed under the curtain as the audience cried out, "Let him finish!''[36] The actor did not get that opportunity; the second performance of *Pleasure Man* was never completed.

The leadership of Actors' Equity did nothing to protest the treatment of members of its union. "In general the stand of the Actors' Equity Association on alleged salacious plays is well known," a union spokesman announced to the press. "Equity has preached against them and the columns of its magazine teem with articles condemning them.''[37]

Back in court a second time in as many days, West and her company again pleaded not guilty to taking part in an indecent performance, and the show was closed indefinitely. The trial, which became very long and highly publicized, did not take place until a year and a half later. It included one spectacle in which the District Attorney asked a police officer to show the jury how female impersonators walked on stage. The man rose, put a hand on his hip, and while swaying mincingly back and forth, explained that they "walked like this.''[38]

"Your honor, . . ." West's lawyer declared at one point, "there is nothing indecent in female impersonations on the stage." "No," said the prosecutor, "but it is possible to have an obscene, lascivious performance under cover of a female impersonation.''[39]

The judge told the jury:

A performance based on innuendo and double meaning, as the police say *Pleasure Man* was, is more dangerous to public morals than a "crude strip poker show."

The latter may arouse impure thoughts, ... but it is more apt to excite disgust. The greater danger lies in an appeal to the imagination, and, when the suggestion is immoral, the more that is left to the imagination, the more subtle and seductive the influence.[40]

After ten hours of deliberation, the jury could come to no decision. The charges against West and the players of *Pleasure Man* were dropped when the District Attorney's office decided against a retrial.

After the exhausting ordeal of her second trial, Mae West finally gave up on her designs to cash in at the box office with a public spectacle of gay transvestites. "There was an advance ticket sale of two hundred thousand dollars, which was enormous in those days when the American dollar was worth a lot more," West recollected, writing about *Pleasure Man* in 1975.[41] Even though her two flamboyant plays never got to profit by a Broadway engagement, they still earned West a profit during their tryout engagements.

Mae West's role in bringing gay male characters onto the American stage had never been carefully and clearly examined during her long lifetime. In numerous interviews from Hollywood she has spoken affectionately of her many fans among gay men, and boasted of her role in presenting them for the first time as characters in a legitimate play in America. Actually, her persistent, mercenary attempts to exploit gay transvestites in the 1920s stirred neither public tolerance nor compassion. It reinforced the stereotyping of gay men as vulgar, sex-obsessed effeminates who wear women's clothing at drag parties.[42]

The following excerpt from an editorial in the *Morning Telegraph* testifies to the damage that Mae West had wrought:

> Everybody knows the kind of boys who inhabit the Broadway Fairyland. They are unfortunate victims of nature...
>
> Abnormality in any form is repulsive. It's repulsive in the physical blemish that Providence sometimes places on human beings. It is repellent even in gorging appetites or gaudy showiness. But when it reaches the stage of abnormal passions, it become hideously repugnant.
>
> Scientists, psychiatrists and biologists admit that such abnormalities exist. The cause nobody has been able to definitely determine in spite of the fact that many reasons have been provided. A play of this character built from a psychological or philosophical standpoint, with its theme handled by a delicate or refined innuendo, might pass muster,

but when done only with the eye on the box office, it becomes a menace to the theater, its performers and the theater-going public.[43]

Notes

1. Mae West, *Goodness Had Nothing To Do With It* (Englewood Cliffs, New Jersey: Prentice-Hall, Inc.), p. 95.
2. George Eells and Stanley Musgrove, *Mae West* (New York: William Morrow and Company, Inc., 1982), p. 80.
3. Mae West, *Pleasure Man* (Typewritten copy on file in the Manuscript Division, Thomas Jefferson Building, Library of Congress, Washington, D. C., dated 1928), Act I, p. 10.
4. *Ibid.,* Act I, p. 25.
5. *Ibid.,* Act I, p. 13.
6. *Ibid.,* Act I, p. 23.
7. *Ibid.,* Act III, p. 1.
8. William M. Hoffman, *Gay Plays: The First Collection* (New York: Avon Books, 1979), p. xvii.
9. *Ibid.*
10. Jon Tuska, *The Films of Mae West* (Secaucus, New Jersey: The Citadel Press, 1973), p. 46.
11. Jack Conway, "Pleasure Man," *Variety,* 19 September 1928.
12. Mae West, *Pleasure Man* (New York: Dell Publishing Co., 1975), p. 7.
13. Gilbert Gabriel, "Last Night's First Night," *New York Sun,* 2 October 1928.
14. "Mae West and Cast of 55 Players Plead in Court," *New York Sun,* 2 October 1928.
15. Hiram Mothersill, "Sense and Censorship," *Theatre Guild Magazine,* November 1928, p. 11.
16. Charles Moran, "Police Seize Cast As New Play Opens," *New York Daily News,* 2 October 1928.
17. *New York Sun,* 2 October 1928.
18. "Mae West and 61 of 'Pleasure Man' Cast Are Arrested," *New York World,* 2 October 1928.
19. *New York Daily News,* 2 October 1928.
20. "Police Planning More Raids to Halt Production," *New York Daily News,* 3 October 1928.
21. Jack Conway, "Pleasure Man," *Variety,* 19 September 1928.
22. *New York Daily News,* 3 October 1928.
23. "There's No Place On Stage For Money-Mad Exploiters of Filth," (editorial), *New York American,* 3 October 1928.
24. "Mae West Defies Police, Continues To Present Play," *New York World,* 3 October 1928.
25. "West Play A Hodge-Podge," *New York Times,* 2 October 1928.
26. "Raid Mae West Play, Seize 56 At Opening," *New York Times,* 2 October 1928.
27. Gilbert Gabriel, "Last Night's First Night," *New York Sun,* 2 October 1928.
28. Robert Littell, "The New Play," *New York Evening Post,* 2 October 1928.
29. Fragment of an untitled New York newspaper article in "Censorship: U.S. Stage, 1920–26," file, Lincoln Center.
30. "Mae West Again, 'Pleasure Man,' Jewel From Her Pen Proves Tame," *Brooklyn Eagle,* 2 October 1928.
31. "'Pleasure Man,' Mae West Play, Given Premiere," *New York American,* 2 October 1928.
32. *New York World,* 3 October 1928.
33. Robert Littell, "The Play," *New York Evening Post,* 2 October 1928.

34. Milton MacKaye, "Mae West Asks Writ To Block Raid Tonight," *New York Evening Post,* 2 October 1928.

35. "Mayor's Filth War Raids West Play," *New York Daily Mirror,* 4 October 1928.

36. *Ibid.*

37. *New York World,* 3 October 1928.

38. "Blushing Raider Re-enacts Scene of 'Pleasure Man,'"*New York Herald Tribune,* 22 March 1930.

39. "Judge Breaks Gavel Over 'Pleasure Man,'" *New York Daily News,* 27 March 1930.

40. "Mae West Case Given to Jury," *New York Daily News,* 27 March 1930.

41. *Pleasure Man*, p. 7

42. The wearing of apparel of the opposite sex is far more widespread among heterosexuals than it is among gays according to W. B. Pomeroy. "The diagnosis and treatment of transvestites and transexuals," *Journal of Sex and Marital Therapy,* 1975 (Vol. I, No. 3.) as cited by C. A. Tripp, *The Homosexual Matrix* (New York: The New American Library, 1976), p. 26.

43. "Now Our Idea Is This," (editorial), *New York Morning Telegraph,* 3 October 1928.

8

Getting Even With Sappho in Overalls in 1929

During the last month of the last year of the Roaring Twenties, Broadway audiences got their first look at a female character who might have been crudely called a "bull dyke." Only the playwright seems to have been horrified that so many critics reacted to his creation as such, though none ever used that epithet — at least not in print. The author's widely publicized protests, as well as the fuzziness of his protagonist's characterization, kept the play on the stage for a month, unchallenged by the custodians of public virtue or those responsible for enforcing the penal code.

The play, Thomas H. Dickinson's *Winter Bound,* ran for thirty-nine performances at the Garrick Theater just off Broadway.[1] Produced by the Provincetown Players of Greenwich Village, it lost no money but drew only fair-sized audiences: for the most part, critics were confused by the playwright's intentions and by the contradictory characterization of his interesting, enigmatic heroine in male attire. Burns Mantle, who admired the play, claimed that it failed because "most of its reviewers and the less charitable and intelligent of its patrons read the taint of Lesbianism into it [and] the piece was foredoomed."[2] According to another critic it was "[a] curious, glum, muddled play, occasionally interesting, but more maddeningly misleading."[3] Perhaps *Winter Bound,* rather than being doomed by its subject matter, never came into clear focus because the playwright was "inhibited by our censors,"[4] as Gilbert Seldes contended.

Dickinson had been a professor of English literature and drama at the University of Wisconsin before retiring with his wife to a farm in Connecticut. He was well known in his time, at least to theater students and historians, as the prolific editor of several authoritative anthologies of contemporary drama and the author of critical works on the theater. *Winter Bound* was his first and last effort to reach the Broadway stage.

A year before *Winter Bound* was produced, Radclyffe Hall's *The Well of Loneliness* was published in the United States. This widely read lesbian novel became a bestseller in this country after a temporary but highly publicized censorship bout and a long period of suppression in England. *The Well of Loneliness,* authored by a lesbian[5], concerns a tomboyish woman who falls in love with another woman. At the novel's climax, the latter settles down with the man who has come between the two women. The plot of *Winter Bound* bears a striking resemblance to the novel's, as some reviewers pointed out. Dr. Dickinson insisted that his play had been written a dozen years before Radclyffe Hall's novel appeared in the United States, and four years before *La Prisonnière* was produced in Paris.[6]

Set in a farmhouse in Connecticut, *Winter Bound* concerns two women from urban backgrounds who set out to live compatibly alone in the country, free from the oppression of male-dominated American society. The idea for this experiment comes from one of the women, Tony, described as "a virile looking creature in blouse and short trousers; ... bobbed hair under a battered felt hat; ... no breasts, lanky limbs."[7] Her companion is Emily, "a healthy girl. Thoroughly feminine," whose "emotions tend to be influenced by the latest strong spirit that comes into her orbit."[8]

Tony, swearing and dressing like a man and preferring outdoor activities and male companionship, is rather unpleasant, gruff and bumptious. She is even physically threatening, especially in one early scene; wearing a sheep-lined great coat over trousers, with a whip in her hand, she attempts to bully a visiting female friend. "Don't try any of your strong arm stuff on me," the spunky young woman tells Tony, "I'm not married to you, you know."[9]

It almost seems, at least in the first scene, that thoroughly fem-

In 1929 Aline MacMahon played tough Tony, a disgruntled, pugnacious cross-dresser in Winter Bound. *Tony was the first "bull-dyke" character ever seen on an English-language stage. However, MacMahon became infuriated upon hearing it characterized as such forty-eight years after originating the role, preferring to remember having played an early-day feminist who was "normal."*

inine Emily is "married" to tough Tony. After their company departs and the two women embark upon their experiment of liberating themselves from male oppression, Tony comments:

> *Tony.* Alone at last. Gosh, that's what honeymooners say, isn't it?[10]

By the second scene it is apparent, however, that Emily and Tony are no honeymooners. Bored and peevish, Emily complains about being left alone all day while Tony is out riding with her stable boy. She resents having to sleep alone, after having had a male lover less than a year before. Tony cannot understand Emily's dissatisfaction and her bad humor:

> *Tony.* ...It's the time of month, eh?
> *Emily.* Worse luck.
> *Tony.* I might have known it. I forgot. It's too bad. I'm sorry, kid. It's what you women are up against.
> *Emily.* Don't say "you women" to me. I can't stand it.

Tony. Why not? You are a woman, aren't you?
Emily. If I am, so are you.
Tony. I'll be damned if I am. Not your kind anyway.[11]

Afraid that Emily is ready to leave her and the country, Tony argues:

Tony. . . . You and I have to make a go of this. We've got to show that two women can get along. I'm tired of the idea that you've got to have a man around. I've got nothing against men. They're better than most women, I'd say. But this little old world has had just about enough of some things I could mention. Just about enough. Women have got to learn to get along with each other, the way men get along.[12]

Annoyed at their constant bickering, and at Tony's preaching feminism to her, Emily will not be placated with words:

Emily. We might as well be man and wife the way you jaw at me.
Tony. There's one difference anyway, we don't eat each other up with sex passion.[13]

Tony is not only a militant feminist and a misogynist, but also a misogamist and a female Hippolytus. She explains to Emily why her young husband killed himself:

Tony. . . . I told him there were higher and better things than going to bed together, and I didn't go to bed with him, do you hear? . . . I haven't found any man yet who is willing to be friends in any way. So until I do I'll stick to women.[14]

At the end of the second scene, Emily goes off to Tony's bed to wait for her there. Tony is going to make supper and bring it to her bedroom so they can eat together. Since Emily is so desperate for physical affection, once again the playwright ends a scene on a note that would indicate a sexual relationship is in the offing.

Nothing has changed in the women's sexually empty lifestyle, so they are back to bickering in the next scene. Emily cannot figure Tony out:

Emily. I know you don't think much of women. What are you but a woman?
Tony. I dunno. I'd hate to think I was a woman.
Emily. I sometimes think maybe you're not. You're something like a boy — a boy that never grows up, and hasn't got any heart in him.[15]

Indeed, Tony does behave like a young boy at times. For instance, once she squares off Emily as if boxing, calling out "hold up your hands."[16] Like a boy she cannot understand what she cannot feel, saying that she'd like to abolish sex. "Love is rotten. It always wants to own someone,"[17] Tony has decided. In some of her tirades she sounds not only like a boy, but a very puritanical one at that:

> *Tony.* ...Everything is based on woman. Sex. Sex. Sex. And the women are the worst ... And everywhere women with their naked bodies showing. As if she didn't have anything but body.[18]

When a stranger comes to the door, it is Emily who objects to his intrusion:

> *Emily.* ...Don't let him in. We've been so happy here. And quiet. Don't spoil it now. Please, Tony![19]

Since the women have been seen doing little more than bickering, Emily's reference to quiet and happiness is puzzling. The stranger, of course, turns out to be a virile, aggressive young man, with a farm down the road. At first sight, he likes Emily and dislikes Tony whom he mocks by calling her "fella."

The bickering intensifies as Emily meets her suitor on the sly because Tony objects to her involvement with a man. Emily finally turns on Tony viciously before racing off for another tryst with her farmer:

> *Emily.* Are you jealous of him? Do ... you want him for yourself?
> *Tony.* That's not worthy of you.
> *Emily.* Or do you want me? Tell me that? Do you want me? No thank you, Tony Ambler. No, thank you ... Don't touch me.[20]

A scene later, Tony and Emily are engaged in another of their tedious discussions concerning their disintegrating relationship since a man has come into the picture. Always on the defensive, Tony attempts to explain herself:

> *Tony.* ...I'm not going to touch you. But I'm going to tell you something you won't understand. I have loved you cleanly and purely. More than I ever loved anyone in this world. I guess with new kinds of love we get new kinds of pain.[21]

Frustrated by Emily's determination to set up housekeeping with the farmer, in the last act Tony destroys the statue she had been working on. Once she realizes that her feminist experiment has failed, Tony turns soft and so incredibly generous that she insists on giving her farmhouse to Emily and her prospective bridegroom. Emily believes that she finally understands Tony:

> *Emily.* The trouble with you is you're neither a man or a woman. You're a he-woman.[22]

Tony sees herself in a different light:

> *Tony.* Perhaps I'm a woman who doesn't want to be considered a walking baby basket. Not to have every man who looks at me think of me as a piece of amusement.[23]

Tony is very attractive to the young stable boy; he follows her around, spying on her, until she finally fires him. In the last minutes of the drama, it is revealed that the young man was accidentally killed when he tried to leave the farm community by hopping a freight train. The play closes after Tony appraises her relationship to others:

> *Tony.* ...Every life I touch I spoil. But, maybe in a million years they will find out, I was right.[24]

The drama ends after Tony departs for the big city. Emily and her farmer fiance watch her go. He stops calling her "fella" in the last scene to show his appreciation for the gift of her farm.

Six years before Dickinson's drama was produced, D.H. Lawrence's novella *The Fox* was published. Apparently the work was unknown to the New York drama critics or they would have mentioned the similarity between *Winter Bound* and *The Fox,* which was far more striking than its resemblance to *The Well of Loneliness.* In *The Fox,* a young man succeeds in breaking up the relationship between two women who have been living together on a farm in England during the First World War. He marries one of them. The farm setting, the male intruder's hostility, the women's domestic bickering, and the fact that a youth falls in love with a woman in masculine attire ten years his senior are all to be found in both works.

The critical reaction to *Winter Bound* was divided. Either reviewers compared and contrasted it to *The Captive,* or, as often as not, to *The Well of Loneliness*, or they saw no such connection and resented that others did so. One reviewer predicted that the Garrick Theatre was "going to be packed by the same type of morbid[25] audiences that made *The Captive* so much talked about..."[26] Another critic noted that "[a] few curious ones were there to revel in *The Captive* theme."[27] Apparently negative word of mouth, plus many bad reviews, kept the theater from being filled enough to justify more than a five-week run.

Richard Watts, Jr., of the *Herald Tribune,* reported:

> There was considerable confusion at the Garrick Theater last night concerning the intentions of Mr. Thomas H. Dickinson, the author of *Winter Bound*... At the end, it remained something of a mystery play, as far as the author's purpose went, with one man's guess as good as another's. What can be stated pretty dogmatically, though, is that *Winter Bound* is a bad play, confused, tedious, hysterical and uncertain.
>
> The safest assumption last night was that Mr. Dickinson's work was a new version of *The Captive* theme without the courage of its ill-fated predecessor. All the evidence was that the author intended to treat the pathological subject of what must be loosely, vaguely and inaccurately described as decadent love.
>
> Certainly when *Winter Bound* is set against such a memorable statement of the same problem as Edouard Bourdet made ... Mr. Dickinson's attempt cannot but seem colorless and clumsy, not to say tedious.[28]

The critic from the *Evening Journal* was sure that Dickinson had "penned a play treating homosexualism, withal handling as delicately as possible this more or less 'verboten' topic."[29] John Mason Brown described Dickinson's drama as "lumbering down that Brimstone Path which leads to *The Well of Loneliness.*"[30] The man from the *Times* also saw the drama moving "along Devious Paths, " with "A theme of twisted impulses that wander along the path of *The Captive.*"[31] The reporter from the *Morning World* described *Winter Bound*'s theme as "usually confined to medical discussions and surreptitious readings in the freer haunts of Greenwich Village."[32]

In an assessment entitled "No-Man's Land, Sappho in Overalls," the reviewer from the *Morning World* wrote:

> It is this reporter's guess that the reason *Winter Bound* had so confusing an effect on its first night audience was because Mr. Dickinson was so unsure where he was driving.
>
> The shadow of Sappho hovers across the scene, yet in certain dialogue sequences the author seems to be disclaiming such a purpose.[33]

Critic Gilbert Seldes, who also felt that the audience was confused at the unfocused, contradictory characterization of Tony Ambler, reported:

> Essentially you have to puzzle out the mystery of a woman who at one time is a crusader for the freedom of her sex, at another is a vicious creature bent on wrecking the lives of other people, at another is the ordinary invert, and finally is a blight, a sterile woman corrupting and spoiling whatever she touches.[34]

Professor Dickinson's defenders attempted to dismiss charges or suspicions concerning the nature of his subject matter. One outraged reporter fumed, "Some of the drama writers with their usual hate and seeking labels, compared the play to *The Captive.*"[35] Another insisted Dickinson wrote "with no trace whatsoever of Lesbianism even though the author composed some dangerous sounding lines."[36] Burns Mantle, Dickinson's staunchest supporter in the press, insisted:

> There is neither sign, nor word, nor scene in *Winter Bound* that could by the wildest margin be considered offensive to the most sensitive or even the reasonably clean minded.
>
> It probably is the most highly moral sex experiment the stage has ever entertained.
>
> In *Winter Bound* he had dared assume that certain misunderstood females are none the less clean of mind and purpose.[37]

The *Bronx Home News,* which reported to its readers that "there is nothing vulgar about the play," commented upon its morality:

> *Winter Bound* is the latest play to deal with the affection of a woman for one of her own sex, but it is far from another *Captive,* either in its story or in its telling ... In the latter play we have the tale of a woman unable to break away from her unfortunate associations, while the newest offering portrays a woman who experiments with such associations, but ultimately revolts against them and finally seeks the seclusion of a normal married life.[38]

Some reviewers believed the failure of *Winter Bound,* particularly the characterization of its protagonist, could be attributed to the playwright's timidity in the face of the New York state penal code and the Wales Padlock amendment. Professor Dickinson was certainly aware of the raids on *The Captive* less than two years earlier. There had also been a highly publicized closing, in 1927, of a Shubert production entitled *Maya,* starring Aline MacMahon — who played Tony in *Winter Bound.* In the Shuberts' show MacMahon had played a prostitute. *Maya's* run was brief because the Shuberts agreed to close it rather than run the risk of a police raid and a session in court for presenting a play with a prostitute protagonist.

Helen Deutsch and Stella Hanau, in their history of the Provincetown Players' productions, comment that "However fair the criticism of obscurity, Dickinson was not, with a timid eye to the censors, as some implied, trying to write a watered *Captive!*"[39]

However, according to *Billboard:*

> The problem posed in *The Captive* is studiously avoided by the author. He wavers and teeters on the point of reaching some clarification, but frightened, possibly through fear of the censors, he limns his female protagonist in the ambiguous way which vitiates the portrait.
>
> *Winter Bound* is a wholly decent study, which will offend no one. But it seems that the author in his unwillingness to give offense spoiled what might have been a fine play.[40]

The *Brooklyn Daily Eagle* noted that *Winter Bound* was "sailing very close to an absurd law,"[41] and Alison Smith, the only woman drama critic to cover the play for the New York papers, observed:

> It is at once less honest and less reticent than *The Captive.* From time to time the author seems to pull himself together (remembering that some motifs are not graciously received by Mrs. Grundy) and introduces some line indicating that the two women have fled to their retreat solely in the desire for mild and innocuous serenity.
>
> In the next line, the well of loneliness gushes forth through the frenzied jealousy of the more masterful member of the union whenever a man ventures to court the timid companion. There is nothing actually offensive in the play, but it brings the dreary distaste of prolonged inepitude.[42]

Repeatedly, play reviews not only identified the subject matter of *Winter Bound* as lesbian love, but also faulted the author for handling it with timidity, if not cowardice. The critic for *The Stage* wrote:

> This play is curiously open to misinterpretation; for while Dr. Dickinson has not introduced into *Winter Bound* the subject of perversion, the recent vogue of the novel called *The Well of Loneliness* and the less recent performance of the *The Captive,* and the streaks of masculinity in Tony Ambler, have already led many commentators to jump to the conclusion that *Winter Bound* was a timorous handling of a similar theme.[43]

Dr. Dickinson wrote a letter defending himself, and his protagonist, to many of the drama critics. The letter read, in part:

> In view of the fact that my play, *Winter Bound,* has been subject to
> false and, I feel, unjust interpretations, I wish to make the following
> statement in its behalf:
> Neither in substance nor intention does my play deal with the sub-
> ject of lesbianism ... Tony Ambler, in *Winter Bound* is simply trying to
> free herself and womanhood in general from the slavery of sex, ... it is
> ridiculous to suppose that a woman of her idealism would be the victim
> of a far worse slavery. As Tony's creator, and as one who knows her
> well, I deny this outlandish charge that has been made against her.[44]

The reviewer from the *Evening Sun* supported the playwright's
defense:

> Unless the much-used word "abnormal" is to be taken at precisely its
> meaning, and not as a synonym for one or other of the aberrations with
> which every one seems so concerned nowadays, Thomas H. Dickinson is
> entirely justified in the protest he has raised against the use of it as
> descriptive of his play.[45]

The critic for the *Journal,* on the other hand, took the time to pen
a thorough reply to the playwright blaming him for the controversy:

> Tony Ambler is being mistreated every night at the Garrick by her
> paternal ancestor, Professor Thomas H. Dickinson ... who ... has
> written an elaborate defense of his child, declaring that she is good,
> pure, honest and altogether normal. If she seems otherwise on the stage
> at the Garrick he cannot blame it entirely on those of us who have met
> her in the theater. She behaves in a certain way; the critics called her
> names for it, and instead of correcting her behavior so as to remove all
> suspicion, Professor Dickinson is content merely to say that they are
> mistaken.
> In their reviews Miss Alison Smith of the *World* and Mr. Brown of
> the *Evening Post* reported that the play deals with the same theme of
> sexual abnormality that lives in *The Captive.* Prof. Dickinson hotly
> denies this and declares it is false and unjust interpretation. "Tony," he
> writes me in a letter, "is an absolutely honest woman trying to work
> through the sex miasma to rational thinking. She is the synthesis and
> representation and mouthpiece of many of the finest women who are
> weary of the age-old role to which woman has been limited, the role of
> biological activity."
> ...if Prof. Dickinson doesn't mean the plain implications in the
> play he has done Tony a great injustice himself, a far greater one than
> his critics did. In word and action he arouses repeatedly the suspicion of
> abnormal relations. The suspicion is aroused not only in the audience

but among the other characters. Tony dresses in men's clothing, is even mistaken for a man by a visitor and three times leaves unchallenged the intimation of aberration ... Instead of defending Tony in letters he ought to defend her in his manuscripts, and if the charge is so awful to him, it seems, surer, and more sensibly honest to refute it utterly in the only way it can be refuted, and that is by removing the basis of it. Otherwise, his defense has about as much weight as a letter from Eddie Cantor protesting against the critics because they think he's funny.[46]

Dickinson added further confusion by contradicting himself in the press during the run of the play. After having defended his protagonist for "simply trying to free herself and womanhood in general from the slavery of sex,"[47] he altered his earlier, seemingly fairminded feminist stance:

We are moving inevitably from a man-made world into womanmade world. The feminine struggle for freedom has turned into a struggle for dominance. There is offered to men a dilemma which can be avoided only by men building up a self-protection against women. Either men must grow increasingly subordinate, or they must create a technique by which the masculine principle may again assert its integrity.[48]

Aline MacMahon somehow managed to have "endowed the role of Tony Ambler with the suffering of a personality divided against itself,"[49] according to the authors of The Provincetown. The Times cited MacMahon for bringing "a well-molded and decisive assurance that illuminates, at least in part, a character that is as ill-defined as the play itself."[50] In an interview during the run of the play in which she discussed the role, MacMahon made no mention of lesbianism[51]. Almost half a century later, MacMahon was enraged at the suggestion that Tony might in any way be related to the emergence of lesbians in American drama. "Of course, I knew what a lesbian was in 1929, but I never thought of the character as being one!" the veteran actress fumed. "The friendship between the two women was very clearly the usual, normal and platonic female relationship." Apparently the director had other thoughts on the matter since MacMahon did remember that, "James Light said he always thought that Dickinson had fallen in love with a lesbian and this was his way of getting even."[52]

When audiences for Winter Bound decreased to half houses, the Provincetown Players were unable to meet the rent asked for by the

Shuberts for the Garrick Theater. Attendance further decreased during the first week after the 1929 stock market crash. When *Winter Bound* closed, the Provincetown Playhouse closed with it. Had *Winter Bound* been done at their famous little experimental playhouse off Washington Square, it might have run longer than it did on Broadway where production costs were so much higher. Those sponsors who encouraged the Provincetowners to move uptown were financially unable to support the group after the shattering break in the stock market. "The death of the Provincetown Playhouse after fourteen years devoted to pioneer experiment in the theater," one reporter commented at the time, "is the first major fatality in the arts traceable directly to the Wall Street Crash."[53]

Lesbians, as first seen on the American stage in *The God of Vengeance* and *The Captive*, were in fairer hands than were the mannish women of *Winter Bound* and *The Well of Loneliness*. In both Asch's drama and Bourdet's, the lesbian characters were attracted by their own kind and able to consummate their affectional preferences despite social abhorrence. The publication of *The Well of Loneliness,* labeled "anti-homosexual propaganda" by Henry Gerber,[54] America's pioneer gay activist, was permitted in the United States two years after *The Captive* — in which lesbian love wins out — was closed. Gerber wrote of Hall's heroine:

> She tried to win the sympathy of ostracizing so-called "normal" society and falls in love with a heterosexual girl, who is snatched away from her arms by a male competitor in love. Had she joined her own circle, which is large in every metropolitan city ... and had she chosen a homosexual girl as her partner, there would have been no morbid story; it would not have been such ideal anti-homosexual propaganda, and the publisher would have rejected the manuscript, well aware of the fact that he could be sent to jail for saying anything in favor of homosexuals.[55]

Since their characterizations and their plots are so similar, charges leveled at *The Well of Loneliness* might well have been directed at *Winter Bound*. Of course, had Tony tried her feminist experiment with a lesbian, the Provincetown Players might have rejected Dickinson's playscript, the production of which would have been a criminal misdemeanor.

Notes

1. Burns Mantle, ed., *The Best Plays of 1929-30* (New York: Dodd, Mead and Company, 1940), p. 440.
2. Burns Mantle, "It is a Tough Year for Failures," *New York Daily News,* 17 December 1929.
3. Philo Higley, "No-Man's Land, Sappho In Overalls," *New York Morning World,* 14 December 1929.
4. Gilbert Seldes, "Second Sights," *New York Graphic,* 16 November 1929.
5. Una Vincenzo, Lady Troubridge, *The Life Of Radclyffe Hall* (New York: Scribners, 1963).
6. Helen Deutsch and Stella Hanau, *The Provincetown* (New York: Russell & Russell, 1931), p. 183.
7. Thomas H. Dickinson, *Winter Bound* (typewritten copy), Lincoln Center, p. 1-1-6.
8. *Ibid.,* p. 1-1-1.
9. *Ibid.,* p. 1-1-10.
10. *Ibid.,* p. 1-1-19.
11. *Ibid.,* p. 1-2-6.
12. *Ibid.,* p. 1-2-7.
13. *Ibid.,* p. 1-2-8-.
14. *Ibid.,* pp. 1-2-11, 1-2-12.
15. *Ibid.,* p. 1-3-5.
16. *Ibid.*
17. *Ibid.,* p. 1-3-7.
18. *Ibid.,* p. 1-3-11.
19. *Ibid.,* p. 1-3-9.
20. *Ibid.,* p. 3-2-6.
21. *Ibid.,* p. 3-3-5.
22. *Ibid.,* p. 3-2-6.
23. *Ibid.,* p. 3-3-7.
24. *Ibid.,* p. 3-3-10.
25. The word "morbid" was a euphemism for gay.
26. "'Winter Bound' is an Unusual Study of a Peculiar Woman," *Brooklyn Daily Eagle,* 13 November 1929.
27. "'Winter Bound' is Presented by Provincetown Players," *New York Evening Journal,* 13 November 1929.
28. Richard Watts, Jr., "'Winter Bound' Is Provincetown Players' Offering," *New York Herald Tribune,* 13 November 1929.
29. *New York Evening Journal,* 13 November 1929.
30. John Mason Brown, "The Play," *New York Evening Post,* 13 November 1929.
31. "'Winter Bound' Moves Along Devious Paths," *New York Times,* 13 November 1929.
32. "Other New Plays," *New York Morning World,* 13 November 1929.
33. *New York Morning World,* 14 November 1929.
34. *The Provincetown,* p. 182.
35. Jack Charash, "Circling Times Square," *New York Today,* 21 November 1929.
36. "Perplexing Drama," *New York Campus,* 4 December 1929.
37. Burns Mantle, "'Winter Bound' Agitates Suspicious," *New York Daily News,* 23 November 1929.
38. "New Plays," *Bronx Home News,* 14 November 1929.
39. *The Provincetown,* p. 183.
40. "Winter Bound," *Billboard,* 23 November 1929.
41. *Brooklyn Daily Eagle,* 13 November 1929.
42. Alison Smith,"Other New Plays," *New York Morning World,* 13 November 1929.

43. Untitled fragment from *The Stage,* dated 15 December 1929 in Aline MacMahon Scrapbook, Lincoln Center.

44. Bide Dudley, "The Stage," *New York World,* 18 November 1929.

45. "'Winter Bound' and the Mind Bound," *New York Evening Sun,* 25 November 1929.

46. John Anderson, "Author's Responsibility to His Brain Child, Tony in 'Winter Bound' Play Suffers From Neglect," *New York Journal,* 18 November 1929.

47. *New York World,* 18 November 1929.

48. Untitled newspaper article from *Light,* 9 December 1929, in Aline MacMahon Scrapbook, Lincoln Center.

49. *The Provincetown,* p. 183.

50. "'Winter Bound' Moves Along Devious Paths," *New York Times,* 13 November 1929.

51. "'Winter Bound' Actress Had to Pick Part," *New York American,* 13 November 1929.

52. Telephone interview with Aline MacMahon, New York City, November 1977.

53. "Footlights — The Stage," *Light,* 16 December 1929.

54. Jonathan Katz, *Gay American History* (New York: Thomas Y. Cromwell Company, 1976), p. 401.

55. *Ibid.,* p. 405.

9

The 1930s: A Moral Constabulary
with Seats on the Aisle

"By the 1930s, people were simply sick of the whole business of stage censorship, theater people and theater audiences, too. We were fed up with the threat of it,"[1] producer-director Herman Shumlin recalled while discussing his 1934 production of *The Children's Hour*. The Protestant contingent of those self-appointed watchdogs of public morality had also grown tired of following in the tracks of their late mentor, Anthony Comstock. The once formidable Society for the Prevention of Vice, still headed by John S. Sumner, had lost its impact during his lengthy tenure in office. When Sumner formed a group to fight against a proposed appeal of the Wales Law, seven people joined him at a meeting in 1930. Fifty invitations had been sent out to thirty organizations.[2]

Even with the decline of their arch-enemies in the Society for the Prevention of Vice, theater people in the thirties had reason to still feel threatened by the possibility of more stringent stage censorship. The Irish Catholic clergy wanted city and state officials to curtail, more drastically, the freedom of expression on the American stage. The press had never tired of reporting attacks on the theater, nor of giving puritanical pressure groups their editorial support; thus, the issue remained as highly publicized in the thirties as it had been in the twenties. In a headline reminiscent of many others that helped incite the

Broadway Theater Raid of 1927, one of William Randolph Hearst's tabloids printed a threat, in the winter of 1930, that read, "Clean Up or Be Cleaned Up, Mayor Walker Warns Stage."[3] Throughout the entire decade there were similar threats repeated by both political and religious officials.

In 1930, many of the nation's newspapers ran daily, detailed accounts of Mae West's lengthy trial for having written and produced *Pleasure Man.* That same year, the author of *Frankie and Johnny* and nine members of the cast were arrested for having given an indecent performance after plainclothes policemen raided the show. "The principal objection to it," the police said, "was the language used."[4] Throughout the decade the climate of opinion in the United States continued to be puritanical and prohibitive. Despite the press, the politically powerful Catholic Church and the homophobic statutes still in effect, thirteen plays with covert and even overt gay characters were seen on the Broadway stage.

For a number of reasons, productions with illegal gay roles were able to appear and even remain on the Broadway boards without being harassed by the police or closed by the courts. More than half of the plays were flops. Most of these eight unsuccessful shows folded so quickly that investigators from the non-theatergoing pressure groups never had a chance to see them. Nothing came of their very brief engagements except the homophobic reviews of newspaper critics. An inept playscript or a poorly mounted production caused critics to become more obviously intolerant of a show that seemed to be concerned with lesbians and gay men. However, the sort of obsessed, homophobic tirades on editorial pages and in critics' columns, occasioned by *The Captive* and *The Drag,* were no longer found in New York newspapers during the thirties. It was as if the Great Depression had knocked the wind out of those members of the press who had once reacted as if America's theatrical fare was a major threat to the nation's very survival.

In spite of their bias, it was the New York drama critics who decided which of the plays prohibited by the penal code should run unmolested on Broadway during the thirties. The rave reviews they wrote provided protective armor for two shows with unquestionably gay protagonists. Director Herman Shumlin was well aware of the reviewers' power when he decided to run the risk of producing *The*

Children's Hour in 1934. "I knew that we'd be safe if the reviews turned out to be as good as I had hoped for, " Shumlin recalled. "With raves, nobody would dare to touch us. The critics in defending themselves, would have to come to our defense."[5]

The influential, prestigious and celebrated New York drama critics of the thirties were the only repesentatives of the establishment constantly alert to everything appearing upon what many puritans still thought of as the wicked stage. As such, these newspapermen became, as one of their colleagues put it, "a sort of moral constabulary in their reports on the theater."[6] Their rules of conduct upon the Broadway stage were limited to theatrical effectiveness so long as prohibited subject matter was handled with subtlety and sensitivity. This sense of morality did not satisfy the Catholic clergy, who would have preferred a stricter commissioner of licenses with as much power over Broadway as the Lord Chamberlain exercised over the London stage.

Not even the British censors could cope with those circumspect English playwrights who closeted their gay creations so discreetly that it would have been difficult to justify banning public performances of their plays. Be that as it may, it is astonishing that the Lord Chamberlain's office still failed to recognize a perfectly apparent gay role in *Dangerous Corner.* J.B. Priestley's play was not only the first of the thirteen shows with illegal characterizations seen on the New York stage in the thirties; it was also the first new drama staged in London with an unmistakably gay character since Restoration audiences saw the comic Matchmaker in Sir John Vanbrugh's farce, *The Relapse,* in 1697.

There were very few references to the gay role in *Dangerous Corner* in the London, Philadelphia and New York reviews of the play's premieres. Such an omission may be attributed to the very nature of the drama. It is a murder mystery, and any revelation detailing the play's characterizations would have spoiled the impact of the show's shocking personality exposés for theatergoers who read the reviews. Even so, *Variety* did mention that one character was "a pervert."[7] The *Herald Tribune* listed "homosexualtity"[8] among the many vices exposed in the mystery drama. Brooks Atkinson noted that the play concerned "a pack of degenerates and dissemblers."[9] The word "perversion"[10] was used in a follow-up review in the *London Times,* some months after its premiere in 1932.

Only three of the New York reviews of *Dangerous Corner* mentioned actor Cecil Holm's performance. Without identifying the character he played as gay, one critic saluted Holm for being "brave beyond Broadway words, thoroughly good and tactful and decent in a most embarrassing role."[11] On the other hand, John Mason Brown complained that "though Cecil Holm acts sincerely as the abnormal husband, he fails to bring to the part the warped intensity which was so disturbing — and so right — a feature of the London performance."[12] The reviewer for the *Times* preferred the performance of Holm's successor: Warren Ashe as "the abnormal Gordon Whitehouse." Ashe, the critic concluded, "gives one of the best performances I have seen in months. He is exactly right."[13]

Except for those few vague references to an abnormal character, the drama critics gave law enforcement officers no other clues that might have alerted them to a production in violation of New York's Penal Code. So, with the inexplicable approval of the Lord Chamberlain, *Dangerous Corner* was seen in numerous English-language productions, despite puritanical prohibitions on both sides of the Atlantic. The show was such a hit on Broadway that it ran for three hundred performances in 1931 and 1932.[14]

Mixed reviews both in London and New York hardly reflected theatergoers' unflagging enthusiasm; an enthusiasm sustained for decades for *Dangerous Corner,* a short three-act mystery that Priestley wrote in a week. The novelist and playwright recalled:

> It was received in Shaftesbury Avenue so tepidly that only my own insistence carried it past the initial five performances. It then became the most popular play I have ever written. I doubt that there is any country in the world possessing a playhouse that has not seen *Dangerous Corner,* or if any other play written during the last thirty years has had more performances.[15]

Dangerous Corner, which at least one theater historian has praised as "perhaps the most ingenious play ever put together,"[16] takes place one evening in the drawing room of an English publishing magnate's home. A chance turn in a casual after-dinner conversation forces the characters to reveal sordid secrets about themselves; each one had been involved with the magnate's late brother, Martin, supposedly a suicide. The results are devastating. In an ingenious dramaturgical device, the first minutes of the play are repeated at its climax.

In 1932 Cecil Holm was the first actor to play a role, unmistakenly gay, in a successful production on Broadway. Dangerous Corner *had also been the first drama with a gay character seen in a public theatre production in London since Restoration audiences saw the gay matchmaker in* The Relapse. *The New York critics identified the gay husband with an embittered wife, played by Barbara Robbins, as being "abnormal," but, inexplicably, neither the police nor pressure groups attempted to close the show for a legally prohibited characterization.*

When the critical turn in the conversation comes up again, it is by-passed simply by chance. The characters, safe behind their masks, go on living in genial, comfortable humor with one another, their illusions and deceptions all intact. The scene is played the second time, as critic Burns Mantle pointed out, "to show that had those sleeping dogs of suspicion been permitted to lie, there would have been no unpleasantness — and no play."[17]

Gordon Whitehouse's unmasking reveals his amorous obsession with Martin (a charismatic drug addict), but Martin's sexual bent is never clarified by the playwright. He seems to have been a bisexual who seduced women while encouraging the attentions of an idolizing young man who had been his traveling companion. It turns out that Martin did not commit suicide; in a drug-induced rage, brandishing a revolver, he was accidentally killed by a woman as he attempted to rape her.

Gordon not only grows sentimental during the after-dinner discussion of Martin's mysterious demise, but hysterical and hostile when the deceased playboy is maligned:

> *Gordon.* ... You couldn't dislike him, nobody could. I don't mean he hadn't any faults or anything, but with him they just didn't matter. He was one of those people. You *had* to like him. He was Martin.
> *Betty.* In other words — your God! (Gordon *turns sharply*) You know Gordon literally adored him. Didn't you, darling?[18]

Gordon's wife, Betty, is not the only woman who is aware of his infatuation with another man. His sister, Freda, exchanges insults with him after Gordon says that Martin did not really care for her even after seducing her. In retaliation, Freda claims that Martin had done everything he could to get rid of Gordon because he was a nuisance who was always becoming hysterical:

> *Freda.* ...I see what he means now. Every time he's been mentioned tonight, you've been hysterical. What are you trying to make me believe you are?
> *Robert.* Freda, you're mad.
> *Gordon.* It's all jealousy, jealousy! If he'd thought I was a nuisance, he wouldn't have kept asking me down to the cottage. *(Turning to* Freda) But he was tired of you, pestering him and worrying him all the time. He didn't care for women. He was sick of them. He wanted me to tell you so you'd leave him alone.[19]

Robert, Freda's husband and Martin's brother, thinks Gordon must be drunk:

Gordon. I'm not. I'm as sober as you are.
Robert. Well, behave as if you were. You're not a child. I know Martin was a friend of yours—
Gordon. (Turning on Robert, *hotly and scornfully)* Of course he was! Martin was the only person on earth I *really* cared about. I couldn't help it. There it was. I'd have done *anything* for him. Money, my God, I'd have stolen ten times the amount from the firm if Martin had asked me to. He was the most marvelous person I'd ever known. Sometimes I tried to hate him. Sometimes he gave me a hell of a time. But it didn't really matter. He was Martin, and I'd rather be with him even if he was jeering at me all the time, than be with anybody else I've ever known. I'm like Freda — since he died, I haven't really cared a damn. He didn't really care for women. He tried to amuse himself with them, but he distrusted them, disliked them. He told me so, many times, Martin told me everything. And that was the finest thing that ever happened to me. *(Sits on sofa)* And now you can call me any name you like, I don't care.[20]

While the characters in the play do not call Gordon either a homosexual or a pervert after his candid declaration of love for Martin, a couple of the critics did so in their reviews.[21] The playwright did not include any admission of a sexual attraction in Gordon's confession. Priestley makes it perfectly clear that there was no sexual activity in the young husband's relationship with his pretty wife. Betty is very embittered about their marriage, which she calls "the biggest sham that has ever been."[22] She cites Gordon's sexual indifference to her in an attempt to justify her affair with another man:

Betty. ...It's *your* fault really, Gordon. Because you're responsible for everything that happened to me. You never should have married me.
Gordon. I didn't know. It was a mistake...
Betty. I ought to have left you long before this. That was *my* mistake — staying on — trying to make the best of it — pretending to be married to one who wasn't there — simply dead!...
Gordon. ...What would have happened if we'd gone on pretending like hell to be happy?
Betty. Nothing.
Gordon. No. If we'd gone on pretending long enough, I believe we might have been happy together, sometime. It often works out like that.
Betty. Never.[23]

"If this play does not take the town," reported London's *Sunday Times* in the spring of 1932, "it will be the town's fault."[24] Gilbert Miller — who had produced *The Captive* — opened Priestley's mystery drama in London at the Lyric Theatre in a production by Tyrone Guthrie. It was a sensation. "And in the West End, mind you," the *New York Telegram* noted in its negative review, "for an entire season cash customers flocked to see it..."[25] After a tryout in Philadelphia, *Dangerous Corner*'s Broadway premiere at the Empire Theatre on October 22, 1932 drew mixed notices. Nevertheless, its popular appeal was such that after completing a successful twenty-six-week engagement in April, it was revived in July at the Waldorf Theater for another three months.[26]

With the exception of the transvestite entertainers in Mae West's *Pleasure Man,* Gordon Whitehouse in *Dangerous Corner* was the first self-identified gay male character ever seen by the public in a Broadway play. It is not surprising that the critics reported no outrage over Whitehouse's appearance in 1932, even though *The Drag* had incited homophobic rage only six years before. Priestley's gay creation was a refined upper-middle-class gentleman; West's coarse working-class characters were flagrant, promiscuous transvestites. While it is unlikely that Priestley was familiar with the plight of *The Drag*, he was undoubtedly familiar with the success of Michael Arlen's *The Green Hat*. Gordon Whitehouse bears a striking resemblance to Arlen's covert gay character, Gerald March. Like Gordon Whitehouse, March also worships a womanizer. Each character is in competition with his sister for the affection of the same man. Each becomes so distraught that he makes a rather indiscreet declaration of his affectional preference in a drawing-room gathering. After the demise of their idols, life loses its meaningfulness for both Gerald and Gordon.

It is interesting to note that the three female characters in *Dangerous Corner* never became hysterical, although two are forced to admit to an adulterous affair and the third confesses to having killed Martin. Gordon, on the other hand, is repeatedly referred to as hysterical. Both Priestley and Arlen must have thought that hysteria was an earmark of gay males. A female playwright from Germany created a teenage lesbian for *Gestern und Heute* who, while not actually hysterical, was still emotionally out of control. Three months after *Dangerous Corner* settled down for its long successful engagement,

Christa Winsloe's drama reached Broadway with the title *Girls in Uniform.* Like Arlen's and Priestley's hysterical gay creations, Winsloe's distraught lesbian makes an indiscreet public declaration of her infatuation.

The office of the Lord Chamberlain had approved Barbara Burn- ham's English-language adaptation of Christa Winsloe's Berlin stage hit. Entitled *Children in Uniform* for a London production, it opened in October of 1932 at the Duchess Theatre with Jessica Tandy portray- ing the schoolgirl and Cathleen Nesbitt playing her Prussian persecu- tor. The play had "stormed the principle cities of Europe," according to the *Morning Telegraph,* before it "had been turned into one of the great motion pictures of our times."[27]

Fifteen weeks before Broadway audiences saw *Girls in Uniform,* the German-language motion picture version of the drama opened at the Forty-fourth Street Theatre, just a block away from the Booth Theatre. After being temporarily obstructed by the U.S. censors, the film *Mädchen in Uniform* was released in New York City to unanimous critical acclaim. The play was seen in only a dozen performances,[28] but not because it met with hostile or indifferent critical reception, or because it was threatened by the district attorney's office. The play version of Winsloe's drama was doomed even before it appeared on Broadway because of the success of the film version.

Sidney Phillips' production, titled *Girls in Uniform* for American audiences, opened on December 30, 1932, the day before the New York film critics named *Mädchen in Uniform* the best motion picture of the year.[29] Most of the play's reviews were raves for the film ver- sion, to which the Broadway production was compared. The majority of reviewers preferred the motion picture even though they praised the stage production. "As a play *Girls in Uniform* is still deeply moving," the *New York Times* reported, adding at the same time, "*Mädchen in Uniform* is a masterpiece of audible screen photography."[30] *Theater Arts Monthly,* on the other hand, saluted the Broadway production as "infinitely superior to the more popular film version with its deliber- ate evasions and forced happy ending."[31]

The *World Telegram* noted that "You came away from the mo- tion picture with the joyous assurance that life in the Prussian girls' school was about to become more humane and more compassionate.

The theater, with the courage of its convictions, is less obliging."[32] Recommendations made by critics appreciative of the play's tragic, depressing, but more realistic climax could hardly help bring the public into the Booth Theatre. It was the winter of one of the worst years of the Great Depression when hordes of hungry Americans were lined up at soup kitchens and bread lines even along Broadway's Great White Way.

The reviewer for the *Daily Mirror,* in a report favoring the stage production, wrote, "*Girls in Uniform* is a meaningful and tense experiment in the theater which no intelligent playgoer can afford to miss."[33] All too aware that many intelligent theatergoers could no longer afford the legitimate theater, the management of the Forty-fourth Street motion picture theater cleverly placed a large advertisement for *Mädchen in Uniform* in the *New York Times* on the same page that the play's review appeared. "As Good as the Day They Were Written Fifteen Weeks Ago," the ad read, above such excerpts as "A work of art! Something to revive one's faith in the cinema," quoted from the many rave reviews for the film. "At Prices Everyone Can Afford," the ad concluded with a list of admission costs which ran as low as twenty-five cents for a matinée and forty cents for an evening performance.[34] Orchestra seats for Broadway plays in 1933 cost three dollars, although seats at the back of the balcony of some shows did cost only fifty cents.[35]

Girls in Uniform, which can be read under the title *Children in Uniform* in *Famous Plays of 1932-33,*[36] concerns a sensitive, highly emotional, motherless fourteen-year-old who is brought to a Prussian boarding school for aristocratic young ladies by the unaffectionate aunt who has raised her. Starved for attention and searching for a surrogate mother, tomboyish Manuela develops a schoolgirl crush on Fräulein von Bernberg, a popular, sympathetic, young teacher among a faculty that is rigid, puritanical and impersonal. After drinking some heavily-spiked punch, the guileless, theatrical and often embarrassingly expansive adolescent declares her affection for von Bernberg at a school party at which the Headmistress is in attendance:

Manuela. I am so happy, so ... so blissfully happy ... because now, I know for certain — she loves me *(laughs).* She ... opened her wardrobe ... and took out a chemise ... one of her own! ... And gave it to me! I was to wear it and think of her. *(softly)* She didn't say that ... *(aloud)*

But she doesn't need to tell me anything. Her hand on my head tells me everything — sweet, good, dear white hand, that can hold so tenderly ... Nothing can happen to me now — nothing in the whole world ... She loves me! I know it — I feel it — it gives me strength ... it makes me feel holy... *(softly)* From now on I will be quite different. I will have only good pure thoughts ... and I will serve her ... life has no other meaning...[37]

Horrified at the implications she reads into the slightly tipsy teenager's overwrought tirade, the Headmistress sputters:

Head. Revolting! A scandal! A scandal![38]

For her punishment, Manuela is isolated from the other students and removed from the dormitory to a room of her own. Fräulein von Bernberg visits the girl to tell her that for her own good they must have nothing more to do with one another:

Fr. von B. (Painfully). You must not love me so much — it is wrong, it is harmful — it is a sin—[39]

After rejecting the devastated teenager, the young teacher confronts the Headmistress to defend herself for having cared about the motherless, affection-starved adolescent and for having given her an undergarment to replace one which was full of holes. In a blistering attack on the suspicious, evil-minded older woman, the young teacher berates her for the way she runs the regimented boarding school:

Fr. von B. This house is a rat-trap. This is a house of death. You kill the soul, the spirit! This galvanized suppression is spiritual death. Only women can do such terrible things to women![40]

Defending her contempt for any deviation from the norm among the student body, and her dedication to the rigid and impersonal Germanic educational system, the Headmistress declares:

Head. ...here, Fräulein von Bernberg, we remain true to the ideals that made Prussia great and will make her great again. Here it is our sacred duty to rear Spartan women, not weaklings.
Fr. von B. In Sparta the boys and girls competed together naked!
Head. This is a Christian community!...[41]

The women's heated confrontation is interrupted when a student bursts in to the room. The student announces that Manuela has killed herself. Concerned only about the effect news of the suicide might have on the school's royal patroness, the Headmistress devises a cover-up as the drama closes:

> *Head.* ...Tell the Grand Duchess there has been an accident.[42]

At least two drama critics warned potential playgoers against entertaining the same suspicions about Manuela as the Headmistress, whom the reviewer for the *Morning Telegraph* called "that grim old warhorse, who places an ugly construction on the child's affection." He also advised:

> I think you should see *Girls in Uniform* but — please with a mind closed to depraved curiosity or vulgar jesting. You will be disappointed if you expect a course in lesbian suggestiveness. It isn't there. The play is real and fine, and touching.[43]

Richard Lockridge of *The Sun* had this warning, lest theatergoers turn as evil and mean-minded as the Headmistress:

> As was probably inevitable, the play has been interpreted by some who have seen it, on the stages of London and Berlin and on the screen here, as a study of those tendencies described by one of the mistresses as "unhealthy." And, of course, if a schoolgirl "crush" is unhealthy, then Manuela's feeling for her teacher was something to be hushed. But if we are not too regimented by prevailing misinterpretations of "modern psychology" — if we are not unperceptive as Manuela's persecutors — we can see it only as a story of an innocent child cruelly and needlessly murdered.[44]

Lockridge was not the only critic to note that some viewed *Girls in Uniform* as a lesbian love drama. The *Morning Telegraph*'s reviewer wrote:

> There was complaint the First Night, by those who go about seeking unhealthy implications in affections between persons of the same sex, that Mr. Phillips had borne down too bluntly in the first two acts on the possiblity of Sapphic love between the girl and teacher. These surmises, as is customary, were blasted away in the last act when the innocence of the girl's love is made not only plain but heartbreaking.[45]

Those who blamed producer Sidney Phillips for the sexual implications in *Girls in Uniform* had possibly not read the playscript; otherwise, the finger would have been pointed at the dramatist. Manuela is by no means an ordinary teenage girl, nor is her obsessive crush on her teacher the familiar, almost universal one. Furthermore,

Fräulein von Bernberg's reaction may very well be interpreted as somewhat provocative. In one scene von Bernberg says to Manuela:

> *Fr. von Bernberg.* ...You know I mustn't make any distinction between one girl and another, because that might lead to jealousy, don't you? That I mustn't single anyone out?
> *(Manuela nods.)*
> *(Very earnestly)* But I want you to know this, Manuela, that I think about you very, very much. I see more than you imagine, and sometimes I am grieved about you, while at other times I am glad. But I mustn't show all this, you know that, don't you, my dear?[46]

Some of the students and instructors sense that Manuela is unusual. One of the girls comments:

> *Johanna.* ...Fräulein Manuela is different... I always said she was different...[47]

One of the instructors uses a euphemism to describe Manuela that implies sexual abnormality:

> Fr. von Kesten. ...Manuela is — well — to put it mildly ... morbid.[48]

Just as others sense something unusual about Manuela, she has similar feelings about Fräulein von Bernmberg:

> *Manuela.* ...I believe she is unhappy ... I feel she has suffered in some way ... that ... there is another side to her quite different from the one she shows us.[49]

Even before the Headmistress learns of Manuela's attraction, she has eyed the girl disapprovingly. One of the students quotes her in a conversation with Manuela:

> *Ilse.* ..."Dear me, the little Meinhabis looks just like a boy—"...
> *Manuela.* ...I'd like to look like boy. But I don't want her to say it. I hate her.[50]

Manuela becomes the sensation of the boarding school when she appears in a play portraying a knight, a role she sought and feels comfortable in. Talking to one of her friends, she confides:

> *Manuela.* ...I'm so terribly happy, for now I shall be able to show her myself — as I really am! When I'm dressed in my silver armor, with my hair quite free, then, then, she will see me properly for the first time...[51]

When Manuela gets a chance to declare her love for Fräulein von Bernberg, she does so with intensity.

Manuela. (first stammeringly, afterwards more freely): I don't know how to say it ... but ... every time you say goodnight to me, and then go away, and shut the door of your room, I feel so terribly lost ... I stare at your door through the darkness... I keep on staring and staring ... and I long to get up ... open your door, creep up to your bed, and kneel beside it. I want to take your hand, and ... and tell you ... but I know I mustn't, so I have to clutch hard to my bed — I grip it so tight that it hurts ... Oh, I love you! I love you like my mother. But you are always so far away, so distant. I can never talk to you, never come into your room, never be near you...[52]

The critics in 1932 viewed *Girls in Uniform* as an examination of the brutal, prudish reaction of an individual personifiying the Prussian educational system to a harmless, passing schoolgirl's crush. In that case, the Headmistress must seem solely responsible for the teenager's tragic end. However, to any who might have interpreted the student-teacher relationship differently, Fräulein von Bernberg's rejection of the adolescent brings about the tragedy. In order to spare them both in a hostile environment, the teacher becomes a more significant factor in the girl's decision to kill herself. In the latter interpretation, the young lesbian is destroyed not so much by the Headmistress's intolerance — since she holds the Headmistress in contempt — but by her idol, who is forced to behave expediently rather than compassionately.

However fine Leontine Sagan's motion picture adaptation of the Winsloe drama, the happy ending of *Mädchen in Uniform* reduces the schoolgirl's crush on a teacher to a passing trauma which she will survive. In her stage version, Christa Winsloe was the first playwright to dramatize the self-destruction not uncommon among lesbians and gay men who have been unable to deal with personal rejection and social ostracism. Half a century after the brief Broadway engagement of *Girls in Uniform,* suicides such as Manuela's are unfortunately still familiar enough that the title of Eric Rofes' 1983 study, *I Thought People Like That Killed Themselves,*[53] really needs no further clarification.

168   WE CAN ALWAYS CALL THEM BULGARIANS

Notes

1. Interview with Herman Shumlin, New York City, 3 March 1979.
2. "Sumner Forms Group For a Stage Clean-Up," *New York Times,* 6 December 1930.
3. "Clean Up Or Be Cleaned Up, Mayor Walker Warns Stage," *New York American,* 26 December 1930.
4. "Play Frankie and Johnnie Raided By Police As Indecent; Fifteen Arrests Are Made," *New York Times,* 11 September 1930.
5. Interview with Herman Shumlin, New York City, 3 March 1979.
6. Frederick Donaghey, "This Thing and That Thing Of the Theatre," *Chicago Sunday Tribune,* 14 November 1926.
7. "Plays On Broadway," *Variety,* 1 November 1932.
8. "Dangerous Corner," *New York Herald Tribune,* 20 October 1932.
9. Brooks Atkinson, "The Play," *New York Times,* 28 October 1932.
10. "Dangerous Corner," *London Times,* 13 August 1932.
11. "Gabriel Sees New Play," *New York American,* 28 October 1932.
12. John Mason Brown, "The Play," *New York Post,* 28 October 1932.
13. "Dangerous Corner," *New York Times,* 18 July 1933.
14. Burns Mantle, ed., *The Best Plays of 1932-33* (New York: Dodd, Mead & Company, 1933), p. 423.
15. Stanley Richard, ed., *Best Mystery and Suspense Plays of the Modern Theatre* (London: Oxford University Press, 1967), p. 762.
16. A. V. Cookman, "Priestley, John Boynton," *The Oxford Companion To The Theatre* (London: Oxford University Press, 1967), p. 762.
17. *The Best Plays of 1932-33*, p. 6.
18. *Best Mystery and Suspense Plays of the Modern Theatre* (New York: Dodd, Mead & Company, 1971), p. 692.
19. *Ibid.,* p. 710.
20 *Ibid.*
21. "Dangerous Corner," *New York Herald Tribune,* 20 November 1932; "Plays On Broadway," *Variety,* 1 November 1932.
22. *Best Mystery and Suspense Plays*, p. 724.
23. *Ibid.,* p. 725.
24. James Agale, *London Sunday Times* review as quoted in program for the Lyric Theatre premiere, *Dangerous Corner* clipping file, Lincoln Center.
25. Robert Garland, "'Dangerous Corner' London Sensation Opens At Empire," *New York Telegram,* 28 October 1932.
26. Burns Mantle, ed., *The Best Plays of 1933-34* (New York: Dodd, Mead & Company, 1934), p. 423.
27. "'Girls In Uniform' As A Play Is A Moving And Distinguished Production," *New York Morning Telegraph,* 1 January 1933.
28. *The Best Plays of 1932-33*, p. 445.
29. William Boehnel, "Three Foreign Films First In Ten Best Exhibited in 1932," *New York World Telegram,* 31 December 1932.
30. "The Play," *New York Times,* 31 December 1932.
31. "Broadway In Review," *Theatre Arts Monthly,* January 1933, p. 186.
32. "'Girls In Uniform' Stages Well," *New York World Telegram,* 31 December 1932.
33. Bernard Sobel, "School Play Proves Impressive," *New York Daily Mirror,* 1 January 1933.
34. "As Good As The Day They Were Written Fifteen Weeks Ago," *New York Times,* 31 December 1932.
35. "Amusements," *New York Morning Telegraph,* 12 March 1933.
36. *Famous Plays of 1932-33* (London: Victor Gollancz, Ltd., 1934).
37. *Ibid.,* p. 69.
38. *Ibid.*

39. *Ibid.*, p. 91.
40. *Ibid.*, p. 94.
41. *Ibid.*
42. *Ibid.*, p.95.
43. *New York Morning Telegraph,* 1 January 1933.
44. Richard Lockridge, "The New Play," *New York Sun,* 31 December 1932.
45. *New York Morning Telegraph,* 1 January 1933.
46. *Famous Plays of 1932-33,* p. 56.
47. *Ibid.*, p. 59.
48. *Ibid.*, p. 86.
49. *Ibid.*, p. 47.
50. *Ibid.*, p. 49.
51. *Ibid.*, p. 47.
52. *Ibid.*, p. 56.
53. Eric Rofes, *I Thought People Like That Killed Themselves* (Grey Fox Press, 1983).

10

Two Closeted Smash Hits
Courtesy of Noel Coward

During the economically depressed winter of 1932–33, *Girls in Uniform* was hardly escapist entertainment with its suicide of a guileless schoolgirl who was, in the words of the *World Telegram,* "charged with the unspeakable sin."[1] Theatergoers who instead went to the movie version saw a happier climax. It was the right winter for a refreshingly shocking, seemingly heterosexual comedy of outrageous, amoral manners. *Design for Living* concerned a very gay bohemian trio, untouched by and unaware of the Great Depression, which still wracked the whole of the Western world.

The adjective "gay," ironically enough, was used in almost every review to describe Noel Coward's *Design for Living.* In 1933 the word still meant, to most people, an open lightness of heart and mood. In that sense, the play was unmistakenly gay; yet it seemed to a number of theatergoers to be "gay" in the sense the word was being used that decade by some American lesbians and gay men, especially in theatrical circles.

A week after Coward's comedy opened in Manhattan to unanimous rave reviews, Percy Hammond confided to his readers:

> *Design for Living* arrived in New York preceded by a scandalous reputation, acquired through its performances in other towns. Mortified playgoers in Pittsburgh, Cleveland, Washington and elsewhere

had sent word along that the conduct of its heroes was effeminate, and that the heroine was cursed with irregular ideas about love life.[2]

"All of the stories that got about beforehand to the effect that there was going to be a touch of lavender in the thing," scoffed Arthur Pollock of the *Brooklyn Daily Eagle,* "turned out to be silly."[3] Among the New York critics, only Brooks Atkinson of the *Times* made any allusion to the possible gay relationship of the two bachelors in the play, but he quickly passed over it because of the nature of Coward's comedy of bohemian bed manners. "Although there is a constant odor of abnormality about this one," Atkinson observed, "it is no more sensuous or erotic than a highly polished blade of steel."[4]

Percy Hammond, who had criticized other reviewers for searching *Design for Living* for "hints of degeneracy,"[5] also noted that other New Yorkers had voiced suspicions about the relationship of the two young men in the play and the credibility of their sexual attraction to the character played by Lynn Fontanne:

> The sophisticated acclaim it is as flagrantly falsetto, sounding none of the masculine chest-notes appropriate to healthy romance...
> At the risk of being considerd an ingenue, I confess that I see nothing in the performance of Mr. Alfred Lunt and Mr. Noel Coward that suggests anything more than a fervent friendship, tinged a little with the bizarre.[6]

Another reviewer, Whitney Bolton, was also annoyed at objections he had heard raised about the play. In an article for the *Morning Telegraph* entitled, "Moralists Make Jackasses of Themselves with *Design for Living,*" Bolton did not specifically identify the nature of the criticism he was replying to when he raged:

> I take it that we will stand for crude suggestiveness, blatant obscenity and coarse characterizations and hail it as realistic drama, but we must not have gaiety and wit and intelligence as ingredients of plays about men and women who are not married.[7]

Dedicated to Alexander Woollcott, a critic renowned for his gaiety and wit, *Design for Living* concerns a trio of British bohemians: Gilda, an interior decorator, and her two bachelor intimates, Otto, a painter, and Leo, a playwright. Described by Coward as the legend of "three people who love each other very much,"[8] Leo explains to Gilda that "the actual facts are so very simple. I love you. You love me. You love Otto. I love Otto. Otto loves you. Otto loves me...'"⁹ Coward had, as the *New York Times* noted, "taken to fooling around with the eternal triangle."¹⁰

Gilda is living with Otto in a rather shabby studio in Paris at the play's start. While he is out of town, his former roommate, Leo, has arrived from London where productions of his plays have earned him a great deal of money. Before Leo drops by to visit the couple, a mutual friend of the trio, Ernest, reminds Gilda:

> *Ernest.* Otto and Leo knew each other first.
> *Gilda.* ...I know about all that! I came along and spoilt everything!
> *Ernest.* I didn't say that.
> *Gilda (sharply).* It's what you meant.¹¹

Leo arrives at his ex-roommate's studio flat and spends the night with Gilda. Upon his return home, Otto becomes so enraged when the couple tell him what transpired that he storms out, leaving the man and the woman he loves to their own devices.

In the second act Gilda is living with Leo, author of yet another hit play, in a London flat. While he is out of town, Otto arrives to make peace with his ex-mistress and his ex-roommate. He remains to spend the night with Gilda. Because she feels useless and unfulfilled now that both men are successful in the arts, Gilda leaves in the company of Ernest, a wealthy art dealer headed for New York. When Leo returns and he and Otto learn that Gilda is gone, the ex-roommates get drunk. "They both sob hopelessly on each other's shoulders as the curtain slowly falls."¹²

Gilda, married to Ernest, is living in a New York penthouse at the beginning of the third act. Otto and Leo, who are back living together and have been traveling about the globe for the past two years, arrive in Manhattan to rescue her from the dull and shallow respectability of middle-class married life. Although by now Gilda is a successful interior decorator and has made many friends in New York, she is as restless and discontent with her marriage as she was when she tired of living with Otto. After a brief attempt to escape their influence, Gilda agrees to leave her husband and take up with the two bachelors once again. Ernest is shocked and furious, calling the trio "a disgusting three-sided erotic hotch-potch," and "unscrupulous, worthless degenerates."¹³ Ernest rushes out of the apartment in a rage, falling over something in the hallway. *"This is too much for Gilda, and Otto and Leo; they break down utterly and roar with laughter. They groan and weep with laughter; their laughter is still echoing from the walls as the curtain falls."*[14]

Robert Benchley, who was reviewing plays for the *New Yorker,* concluded that the trio, "all very clever," planned to live happily ever after "getting along under one roof without sex — if they can."[15] "You say, 'Such people don't exist,' and enjoy their pretended unreality,"[16] observed the critic for the *World-Telegram.* "A jolly *ménage à trois,"*[17] commented the reviewer for the *American.* One of Coward's biographers, Sheridan Morley, contended that "American reaction to the play was somewhat guarded,"[18] yet it received unanimous rave reviews and became one of the biggest hits of the 1932–33 theatrical season. "The sleekest and most persuasive play in town,"[19] raved the *Morning Telegraph;* "the gayest comedy of Mr. Coward's repertory,"[20] concluded the *Herald Tribune.*

According to the *New York Times,* during the comedy's tryout run in Washington, D.C., "They were putting chairs in the orchestra pit to accommodate extra patrons."[21] By the time *Design for Living* arrived on Broadway for its New York premiere "excited peasants gathered in such throngs about the Barrymore Theater that mounted policemen were forced to ride upon sidewalks and chase them away."[22]

Noel Coward was the talk of the town in January 1933. The film version of his London success, *Cavalcade,* had just opened to rave reviews. "The best motion picture in the English language,"[23] Richard Watts, Jr. of the *Herald Tribune* wrote. A second popular film based on another of Coward's dramas was also playing on Broadway: *Tonight Is Ours,* starring Claudette Colbert and Fredric March. "They adore Noel Coward in England," Ursula Jeans, one of the stars of *Cavalcade* confided to the *Herald Tribune,* "He's such a likeable human person, you couldn't help adoring him."[24] Americans were singing, along with the British, songs by Coward such as "I'll See You Again," "A Room with a View," and "Mad About the Boy." Rumors were flying that, despite his gay predilection, Coward would soon be knighted because of the sensational success of both the stage and film versions of *Cavalcade,* his salute to the British Empire.[25]

Noel Coward wrote Design for Living *so that he could costar with his intimate friends Alfred Lunt and Lynn Fontanne. Coward dedicated the comedy to celebrated New York drama critic and radio personality Alexander Woollcott, who was as witty and closeted as the two gay gentlemen in the 1933 Broadway hit.*

Despite the Depression, *Design for Living* played to sold-out houses for the first three months of its run: "When a break did come," Burns Mantle noted, "it was comparatively insignificant and other weeks were added."[26] The comedy was seen in 135 performances,[27] and there was no mention, at least in the press, of it being overtly threatened with censorship. Percy Hammond hoped that "Mr. Sumner [head of the Society for the Suppression of Vice], if he is still abroad, will deal more or less gently with it."[28]

Had Sumner decided to go after *Design for Living,* he would have had to focus his attack on Gilda's sexual promiscuity. Leo and Otto's relationship as traveling companions, which can be viewed as purely platonic, pales beside the lady's seduction of them and the shockingly off-handed termination of her marriage. That Sumner did not complain may be attributed to the prestige and popularity of the comedy's co-stars. The *Times* hailed the trio as "three gay and thoroughly distinctive actors."[29] Alfred Lunt and Lynn Fontanne, the most successful husband and wife co-stars on the English-language stage in the 1930s, were every bit as renowned as Coward. Perhaps no other theatrical personalities could have gotten away with *Design for Living* as a co-starring vehicle during a period so fraught with censorship threats.

If Sumner had picked over the playscript he might have noted certain lines in Coward's comedy that may have been self-mocking pet names shared by the playwright and his co-stars in their intimate personal relationship. Gilda, for instance, may be alluding to the stars themselves and their vehicle rather than to the characters in the play in this rather baffling snatch of dialogue:

> *Gilda.* ...Look at the whole thing as a side show. People pay to see freaks. Walk up! Walk up and see the Fat Lady and the Monkey Man and the Living Skeleton and the Three Famous Hermaphrodites!...[30]

Even if Sumner had been able to point to such cryptic lines in *Design for Living,* they would hardly have served to support a police raid because one of the characters facetiously makes allusions about them all being hermaphrodites. There is one speech, ostensibly a defense of heterosexual free love, that might be taken as a closeted defense of Coward's own lifestyle; but it would have been impossible to use as evidence that the comedy depicted, even esoterically, prohibited subject matter:

> *Otto.* ...There's no sense in stamping about and saying how degrading it all is. Of course, it's degrading; according to a certain code, the whole situation's degrading and always has been. The Methodists wouldn't approve of us, and the Catholics wouldn't either; and the Evangelists and the Episcopalians and the Anglicans and the Christian Scientists — I don't suppose even the Polynesian Islanders would think very highly of us, but they wouldn't mind so much, being so far away. They could all club together — the whole lot of them — and say with perfect truth, according to their lights, that we were loose-living, irreligious, unmoral degenerates, couldn't they?
> *Gilda (meekly).* Yes, Otto, I expect so.
> *Otto.* But the whole point is, it's none of their business. We're not doing any harm to anyone else. We're not peppering the world with illegitimate children. The only people we could possibly mess up are ourselves and that's our lookout...[31]

In 1944, eleven years after *Design for Living* ran on Broadway, A.A. Brill, a psychoanalyst, was certain after examining Coward's text that Otto and Leo were lovers:

I don't know whether the author of the play knew our psychological concept of homosexuality, but all the essential factors of it were clearly depicted. The narcissism was expressed by making the two men look and dress almost exactly alike; they even kiss each other. The overevaluation of the penis ... is reflected in the line: "But don't forget, it's in the *London Times* — it's the organ of the nation."[32]

After his examination of *Design for Living,* Robert Wood, a noted English sexologist, concluded:

Ostensibly the men are in love with the girl, Gilda, but it is clear that they are even more deeply in love with each other. They approach each other symbolically through her.[33]

Percy Hammond might have been very distressed had he lived to read these appraisals of Otto and Leo's relationship, since he dismissed just such speculations as "viciously erroneous" after *Design for Living* opened in 1933.[34] Half a century later the New York drama critics were so familiar with such suppositions about this "antiseptic sex comedy," that many quoted them in their reviews of the Broadway revival. Some reviewers even contended that *Design For Living* is actually an esoteric defense of Coward's own gay lifestyle, and that of his costars, the Lunts.[35] The *Village Voice* assumed that the whole point of the script was a defense for homosexuality.[36]

The *New York Times* protested that critic John Lahr went too far with his postulation that *Design For Living* involves "the homosexual daydream of sexual abundance." The paper's critic, Benedict Nightingale, referring to the final moment of the comedy, asked:

Is what Mr. Lahr calls "the victory of the disguised gay world over the straight one" the reason for their rather callous and vindictive glee? ... whether or not its roots are in the homosexual experience, the morality jauntily espoused by Coward's sophisticates is one that heterosexuals can share. Cant, moral pretension, and emotional staleness are the great vices, honesty and affection the great virtues...[37]

John Simon, the arch homophobe among drama critics, also protested Lahr's conjecture:

I doubt the play is covertly about an all-male triangle. Rather it seems to be a genuine tribute to polymorphous perversity.[38]

Noel Coward was largely responsible for bringing New York theatergoers yet another sensational and successful stage production

Laurence Olivier made his Broadway debut playing the pampered, perverted ward of a gay foster-father, portrayed by James Dale, in the 1933 hit, The Green Bay Tree. *Olivier won the role because of the suspiciously gay part he played so effectively in his London stage debut in* The Rats of Norway.

in the 1930s. And it included a gay character more discernible than the bachelor buddies in *Design for Living.* Although he did not write *The Green Bay Tree, Variety* erroneously reported before its opening that "some observers figure Noel Coward did the playwriting because many lines are typical of his style."[39] Coward did encourage Jed Harris, the director-producer wonderboy, to bring *The Green Bay Tree* to Broadway after both men saw it performed at King's Theatre, Hammersmith. "No play in recent years in London," the *New York Times* reported, "has been more widely and vivaciously discussed," yet Harris had serious reservations about mounting the production for American theatergoers.[40] The producer told critic Douglas Gilbert:

> I like the theme — the vicious influence of an older man on a younger, but if it hadn't been for Noel Coward I doubt if I should have produced it. The play as it was done in London was atrocious. But Noel liked the script and I went ahead with it...[41]

The Green Bay Tree was written by Mordaunt Shairp, author of three successful plays and an assistant master at University College and extension lecturer to the universities at Oxford and London. It was such a hit in London that, according to the *New York Times,* "The author was duly entitled to assume a position as one of England's literary lions."[42]

In an interview, Shairp revealed his inspiration for the drama about an affluent, cultured bachelor's adoption of a motherless, working-class boy:

> The idea which grew into *The Green Bay Tree* came to Mr. Shairp one day when he was walking on Hampstead Heath, near his home, he saw a man and a boy driving together and something in the boy's wistful expression suggested to him the theme which is the basis for the play. When he returned home he told his wife he had found a new subject and then went directly to work.[43]

The Green Bay Tree, set in London, opens in the elegant flat of Mr. Dulcimer, a very wealthy gentleman of leisure. "The atmosphere of the room is one of luxury, fastidiousness and just a touch of the abnormal," according to the author.[44] Dulcimer is described as:

> A man of about forty-five, immaculately turned-out, ... speaks exquisitely ... with now and then a slight drawl... Though a complete dilettante,... an alert, vibrating personality. A man who could fascinate, repel and alarm.[45]

The fussy, rather irritable, anti-proletarian bachelor lives with his butler and a young man whom he adopted fifteen years before. The motherless boy's father had turned him over to Dulcimer for a considerable financial settlement. Julian, Dulcimer's ward, is "a handsome boy in his early twentites, charming, well made, but self-assured and self-indulged."[46] The playwright adds that "there is ... a rather grotesque likeness between him and Mr. Dulcimer."[47]

Dulcimer is so precious that, in the first few minutes of the drama, he wears gloves to arrange flowers in a vase while peevishly complaining that the gardener has cut the stalks not exactly to his liking. Julian arrives announcing to his foster-father that he has fallen in love and plans to marry. Though somewhat skeptical, Dulcimer has a reasonable reaction to this news. Julian, however, thinks him most unreasonable when Dulcimer refuses to continue supporting him:

Julian. I did rather hope you'd increase my allowance.
Dulcimer. I see.
Julian. You will, Dulcie, won't you?

Dulcimer. I've always loved your ingenuousness, Julian. It's one of your greatest charms,. I shouldn't dream of increasing it. In fact, if you leave me, I don't propose to make you any allowance whatever.[48]
Julian (laughing). Then you're turning me adrift?
Dulcimer. That's hardly the way I should describe a young man who proposes to support a wife.[48]

Julian has a second surprise for Dulcimer when his love, Leonora, arrives at the flat. Dulcimer is gracious and hospitable, and Leonora is at first fascinated by him. In an easy conversation Dulcimer confesses:

Dulcimer. He's more than a son to me, and it will mean more to give him up...[49]

At the end of the first scene Dulcimer is left alone when the young couple go off to see the ballet.

Later that night, Julian returns to tell Dulcimer that instead of going to the theater, they had gone to see his natural father in his working-class neighborhood. The man, now a part-time preacher, has been sober since turning Julian over to Dulcimer. Julian tells his benefactor that he now wants to return to live with his natural father. While living with him, the young man plans to study, coached by Leonora, for the entrance examination to a veterinary school so he can someday go into practice with his wife. Dulcimer is hurt and angry at being deserted by his foster-son and blames Leonora for coming between them. Julian wants to retire for the night with a handshake and no ill will, but Dulcimer ungraciously refuses to take his hand as the first act ends.

The second act begins in Julian's father's small, commonplace living room three months later. Julian has been studying very hard for his examination so he is overjoyed when Dulcimer's butler arrives to invite him and Leonora to dinner. The young woman does not want to go, and Owen, Julian's father, does not want him to have anything more to do with Dulcimer, whom he blames for spoiling his son in the lap of luxury. Owen quotes a passage from the Bible warning Julian of Dulcimer's decadent influence: "I have seen the wicked in great power and spreading himself like a green bay tree..."[50]

Julian will not listen to his fiancée nor to his father. He is convinced that Dulcimer has grown so lonesome for him and anxious for a reconciliation that he may now reconsider giving Julian an allowance. Leonora agrees to accompany Julian only after he reveals his true feelings for the man who raised him:

> *Julian.* . . . I don't like him, really, anymore than you do. . .⁵¹

The next scene takes place in Dulcimer's flat. After dinner, Leonora departs to look after a sick dog. This affords Julian an opportunity to talk to Dulcimer, but his pleas for money are wasted on the man who once indulged him: Dulcimer will not support Julian as a married man. Unable to bring himself to return to the grind of studying for the veterinary medical exam while living on the meager subsistence he has borrowed from his father, Julian breaks down weeping in frustration, falling upon the couch. Dulcimer smiles and instructs the butler to get Julian's room ready. The phone has been ringing. Knowing it is Leonora attempting to reach him, Julian refuses to answer it, as the second act curtain comes down.

At the opening of the last act, Julian comes down for breakfast after spending the night in his old room and announces that he needs a holiday. He has decided that he cannot live on his wife's salary while he goes to school. Julian wants to vacation in Dulcimer's villa in Italy. As they prepare for a departure that night, Leonora arrives wanting to know why Julian did not join her the night before as planned, and why he would not answer the phone. Owen, very distraught because his son has remained with Dulcimer, stands outside looking up at the apartment window, waiting for Julian to come out with Leonora.

Julian is fed up with work and poor surroundings and will not consider going back to studying with Leonora and living with his father:

> *Julian.* I hate everything that's cheap and ugly and second-rate.⁵²

Julian insists that he must have a holiday and leaves Leonora with Dulcimer while he dresses. She admittedly despises Dulcimer, who now becomes just as openly hostile to her. He explains his interest in Julian:

> *Dulcimer.* I didn't adopt him to please my conscience, if I have one, or
> to give him what was best for him. My aim was to make him like, and
> unable to do without, what was best for me. . .⁵³

Leonora, angry and hurt at being rejected by the man she loves, turns on the millionaire who had perverted Julian's values by raising him to be a parasitic drone in society:

> *Leonora.* You get what you want simply because you can pay for it. It wouldn't take much to wipe you out. Another convulsion in the world and you'd vanish tomorrow.[54]

Owen, crazed with anxiety, bursts into the flat demanding that Dulcimer give him back his son:

> *Owen.* There was nothing in the contract, Mr. Dulcimer, that gave you the right to corrupt my boy![55]

Julian's father has a revolver:

> *Owen.* ...once I take him off your hands, he'll forget all about the soft and corrupt way, and curse you as I have cursed you![56]

Owen shoots Dulcimer, then turns to his son, calling him by the name he had been baptized:

> *Owen.* Now you're free, Davy, at last![57]

The curtain falls.

When it rises again for the final scene, three weeks have passed. Leonora is visiting Julian in Dulcimer's flat. Once again she begs him to leave and come away with her. Julian has inherited the apartment and all of Dulcimer's wealth and property. We learn that Owen has been adjudged insane and is now committed to a prison asylum. Leonora will not marry Julian unless he refuses his inheritance; this he cannot bring himself to do, although he insists that he still loves her and wants her.

Leonora leaves Julian; but the butler, who had warned that he would not stay on if a woman became part of the household, agrees to remain to serve the young man as he did Dulcimer.

There are two endings for *The Green Bay Tree*. In the original New York production, the butler goes out to fetch some flowers so Julian can arrange them as was Dulcimer's habit. The young man is alone smoking as the lights are lowered. A death-mask of Dulcimer with a smile on his lips hangs on the wall behind him: *"The death-mask continues to smile. Gradually all the lights fade, leaving only a pin-spot on the death-mask and the end of Julian's cigarette."*[58]

We can be certain that ending was used in Harris's production, at least on opening night, since one critic took marked exception to it. Describing the audience's last sight of Julian, the *Brooklyn Daily Eagle* noted:

> His head sways daintily and his manner is mincing, like the manner of the dead man. From the back wall a mask of the corrupter smiles over at him and on the the mask shines a stupid green light such as used to shine on ghosts in the old dramas. Rather clumsy trick, this mask business.[59]

In the abridged version of Shairp's drama published in *The Best Plays of 1933–34,* the play ends this same way.[60] For the 1952 Broadway revival of the drama, starring Joseph Schildkraut, director Shepherd Traube used the ending that can be read in *Sixteen Famous British Plays,* published in 1942,[61]. In the Traube production the butler brings flowers into the living room, and Julian arranges them as preciously as his late guardian in the first scene. The death mask is on the wall behind Julian as he puts on a pair of gloves, selects a vase to his taste, and complains about the way the gardener has cut the flower stalks. The curtain falls.

"I'd almost swear that, as the curtain came down in the original Broadway production," Herman Shumlin reminisced, "the boy was fussing over flowers the way the old prissy had done earlier in the play."[62] Jed Harris explained:

> In the last scene the butler never takes his eyes off him. There is not the slightest hint of anything queer, nothing spoken, nothing said. Just the butler quietly watching him. "The flowers have come," he says, and goes out. No reaction from Julian, just sitting there with a cigarette and brandy. Curtain. It knocked the audience flat. He never arranges the flowers as the final curtain comes down. Yet there were many people who were convinced they saw it.[63]

"The theater has unleashed one of its thunderbolts,"[64] Brooks Atkinson reported when Jed Harris's production of *The Green Bay Tree,* financed by Lee Shubert, opened on October 20, 1933. Another critic elaborated:

> Impatiently awaited, promising one of the most interesting evenings of the theatrical season, Jed Harris' production of *The Green Bay Tree* came into the Cort last night. I think that in it Mr. Harris has given us by far the most exciting, arresting and provocative play of the new season — a brilliantly directed, absorbing and adult drama.[65]

Greeted by unanimous critical praise, *The Green Bay Tree* became one of the biggest hits of the season, running twenty-two weeks for 166 performances.[66] Harris, a wonder boy in the twenties with such hits as *Broadway, The Royal Family,* and *The Front Page,* had taken an extended leave from show business; resuming work in the theater, he seemed unable to pull his career out of an eclipse. Harris had produced five costly flops in a row, but the sensational success of *The Green Bay Tree* was such that the *Times* hailed him as "one of the most clairvoyant minds in the theater."[67]

Robert Edmund Jones, one of America's most eminent set designers, did the sets and famed interior decorator Elsie De Wolfe supplied the rare antiques in Dulcimer's stunning salon. The pale green and gold setting was so exquisitely done that one newspaper columnist was concerned about its deleterious effects on impressionable young theatergoers. He warned:

> No matter how seductive a vice may become, even though it is surrounded by the excessive beauty of *The Green Bay Tree* atmosphere, it nearly always, according to the nature of things, ends in disaster and decay. That scene in the second act when the boy gives way to the anguish is proof enough of the grief, frustration and misery which comes to the man who swerves from the normal pattern.[68]

Harris hired the English actor James Dale, known to New York audiences as the Jew in John Galsworthy's *Loyalties,* to portray Dulcimer. Leo G. Carroll played the butler, and Laurence Olivier and the first of his actress wives, Jill Esmond, were cast as the young couple. Harris "thought that it would be very clever to have such masculine types as Olivier and Dale cavorting on the stage as a couple of classy queens."[69]

"There was nothing homosexual or swish in the performances or in the dialogue," Jed Harris said, "yet the suspicion had to be there. That's the only way you can explain what was going on."[70] When the play had been done in London nine months earlier that same year, at least one critic attacked actor Frank Vosper for his "exaggeratedly mincing deportment and his ugly caressing of chairs," in an "excessively hysterical" portrayal of Dulcimer.[71] The *London Observer* had an different reaction to Vosper's performance:

> We are most of us, I suppose, wearied beyond words with the easy laughter raised by parading effeminate men with all the mincing move-

ment of their kind. Neither Mr. Shairp nor his players stoop to conquer by these methods. The effeminate is either a victim of physiological misfortune or a revolting poseur. Mr. Shairp's Mr. Dulcimer is something, one gathers, of both. But he is not put up to shock us vulgarly or to amuse us basely; he is there as the objectively studied specimen of a rare and unhappy species.[72]

The New York critics' reaction to James Dale's playacting was uniformly appreciative. Wolcott Gibbs of the *New Yorker* gives us some inkling of what the actor and his director made of a role that could have been either campy or offensively effeminate:

> James Dale plays it splendidly. Mr. Dulcimer is funny at first in his matronly preoccupation with the arrangement of his tulips and the year of his wine, and then gradually becomes a tragic and even a shocking figure in his murderous urbanity toward his ward's fiancée, and in his subtle and venomous campaign to get rid of her.[73]

Dale had reservations about the effectiveness of Olivier's work in *The Green Bay Tree,* even if the critics did not. Dale felt that his co-star:

> . . .wasn't nearly as successful . . . as the man who played the part in London — Hugh Williams.
> Of course, Larry is a man of action . . . The character in *The Green Bay Tree* was a limp, wet, lackadaisical, rather effeminate lad — the very last thing that Larry Olivier was, is, or ever will be. I understand he didn't like himself in the part.[74]

"It's a terrible thing for an actor to say isn't it?" Olivier confessed about his performance as Julian, "but honestly I've never hated playing any part so much before."[75] The actor also loathed working with ruthless, exacting, and sarcastic Jed Harris, so much so that some years later "he thought about him and about Adolph Hitler in preparing his characterization of *Richard III.*"[76] Olivier's unhappiness with Harris and uneasiness in the role of Julian did not diminish his performance. One critic raved:

> In the horrifying scene where he is beaten in slavish submission by his benefactor's abnormal attraction for him, his acting becomes not *acting,* but an exhibition of emotional collapse so painful to witness that the eyes of the audience are torn away; the spectacle of his ignominy actually becomes too terrible to bear.[77]

"He is the best actor in England," Jed Harris said of Olivier, but "he has no mind at all." The director remembered:

> In the scene in which he tells his girl he is going back to see the older man who had kept him, I told him to play it like a whore telling her pimp, "Don't worry. I'm not going to get involved. I'm just going over to get the money out of him." Olivier was shocked, offended.[78]

There is not a single line of dialogue, that can be cited as giving sexual implications to Dulcimer's relationship with Julian. *The Green Bay Tree* was approved for production in Great Britain by the office of the Lord Chamberlain. In New York, there were no charges of breaking the state law prohibiting dramas depicting sex degeneracy or perversion.

Burns Mantle informed his readers:

> *The Green Bay Tree* has come from London tagged with the report that it is sort of *Male Captive*. Recalling that the police closed the local performances of *The Captive* after it had flourished abundantly for a matter of months, some seasons back, there was an eager and receptive audience at the Cort Theater last night prepared to absorb what *The Green Bay Tree* had to offer before other censors descended upon it.
>   Well, there is little danger that this play will be attached.[79]

According to Burns Mantle, Shairp dramatized the emasculating and demoralizing effects of luxurious aestheticism:

> It is in effect a revealing study of a certain social decadence, a habit of luxurious living, the tendency of which is to weaken the moral fiber and corrupt the souls of its practitioners.[80]

The reviewer for *Stage* concurred:

> No doubt psychology has much to say on the subject, but as it is acted on the New York stage the play can be taken at its face value: a highly special type of man, who receives his emotional stimuli from color, form, design, and luxury in the outer world, and seeks to bring up a young man in his image.[81]

Brooks Atkinson also took the text literally, concluding:

> It may as well be noted that one may read anything one chooses, or very little if one chooses, into Dulcimer's feeling for his ward. The author more of less lets the point go by default, devoting himself in the main to an attack on luxury.[82]

Only the *London Times* made no reference whatever to a possible gay motif in *The Green Bay Tree*. Reviewers for other British newspapers doubted that the drama was as asexual as the Lord Chamberlain thought and the American critics concurred.

Robert Garland of the *World-Telegram* described *The Green Bay Tree* as a study of the sexual perversion of a basically normal but weak-willed boy:

> My brothers of the First Night garden, remembering the bad luck of *The Captive,* are prone to pretend that Mr. Shairp's play deals with a couple of things.
>
> Mr. Dulcimer's admiration for Julian's wavy hair, for instance. Or the manner in which that personable young fellow occupies a couch, purring like a cat in the lap of luxury. Reading the reviews printed while I was out of town, I gather that *The Green Bay Tree* has nothing to do with the way of a man with a man. Well, if it has nothing to do with that it has nothing to do with anything.
>
> If it has nothing to do with that (and "that" is an incident not unknown to the public in general and to patrons of revues in particular) Mr. Shairp's play is the most meaningless play ever written by anybody.
>
> But Mr. Shairp's play isn't the most meaningless play ever written by anybody. It is, as London has known week after week, month after month, a poignant study of a not-infrequent peculiarity in the relationship of one human being to another. Centuries back the Greeks had a word for it, a nicer word than we have today.[83]

Percy Hammond of the *Herald Tribune* wanted to believe that Dulcimer's relationship with his ward was platonic, and blamed both the director and the playwright if theatergoers thought otherwise.

> I am not one of those who believe in everything they hear about the exquisite Mr. Dulcimer in *The Green Bay Tree*. As you know, "foul whisperings are abroad" concerning his character, and he is accused of impurities too serious to be charged against him without evidence less fallible than that offered in the play...
>
> I cry that Mr. Dulcimer's addiction to embroidering, double-breasted evening jackets and the companionship of an attractive young man is no excuse for putting him on the spot for depravity. Acquaintance with him will prove to any just drama-lover that at his worst he is merely an asexual voluptuary, ... he may make you suspicious when, for instance he dons an apron and white gauntlets while arranging a bowl of tulips. But I can remember that not so long ago George M. Cohan, and other super he-men, regarded the wrist watch as an emblem of pansiness...

If there is aught that is "queer" in his attitude toward Julian, Julian obviously does not know it, and neither does keen Leonora. It is beyond belief that either of these normal and experienced persons would not have detected and have fled from any such vile shenanigan...

Of course he is being corrupted, but not the way that Mr. Shairp, the British author, and Jed Harris, the American producer, shrewdly and slyly intimate for purposes of argument.[84]

Mordaunt Shairp was both commended and faulted for ambiguity, yet none of the reviewers remarked on the necessity of such a treatment given the American and British laws forbidding the portrayal of gay characters. John Mason Brown was uncomfortable with Shairp's expedient reticence:

In *The Green Bay Tree* it is somewhat difficult at times to discover what *is* at the bottom of Mr. Mordaunt Shairp's garden...

Mr. Shairp's drama, which has been the center of much discussion in London, is certain to provoke the same discussion here. It is an inspiring study of the disintegration of character, and one which is capable of several interpretations.

...one may wish that Mr. Shairp had been more forthright in clarifying his issue and had not hesitated to call a spade a spade.[85]

Wolcott Gibbs, writing for the *New Yorker,* felt that the dramatist had drawn his characterizations very clearly. In sharp disagreement with John Mason Brown, he wrote:

The subject of abnormality is usually discussed on the stage with such a misty delicacy that is hard to tell just exactly what the author had on his mind, or else with a humor hearty and explicit enough to engage the indignant attention of the Police Department. It is a relief to see it treated for once, in *The Green Bay Tree,* at the Cort, without either coyness or the nasty joviality of a Minsky blackout.[86]

Understandably, the English-import was repeatedly compared and contrasted by many of the critics to the French-import closed down by the law just six years before. "If *The Greenbay Tree* were only, as has frequently been said, a variant of *The Captive*," the reviewer for *The Stage* wrote, "it would have limited dramatic interest. But as the play is presented, it acutely analyzes the epicene influences in society."[87]

Since *The Green Bay Tree* was never known to be under surveillance by the Manhattan District Attorney, no reports from police spies are available to give us an idea of the audience make-up at the Cort Theatre in the winter of 1933–34. In the 1920s, some drama critics had mentioned a gay presence in audiences of *The Captive, The Drag,* and *Pleasure Man,* but no such references were made about *The Green Bay Tree.* That the gay underground was out in force for at least one performance seemed evident to veteran and inveterate theatergoer, Reginald Cockburn. He recalled, "...looking back and up at the balcony audience when a companion called my attention to it. 'My God, would you look at them!' he whispered laughing. 'The gay bars must all be empty tonight.' "[88]

Notes

1. "'Girls In Uniform Stages Well," *New York World Telegram,* 31 December 1932.
2. Percy Hammond, "The Theaters," *New York Herald Tribune,* 5 February 1933.
3. Arthur Pollock, "The Theater," *Brooklyn Daily Eagle,* 25 February 1933.
4. Brooks Atkinson, "Boiled-Shirt Comedy," *New York Times,* 29 January 1933.
5. *New York Herald Tribune,* 5 February 1933.
6. *Ibid.*
7. Whitney Bolton, "Moralists Make Jackasses Of Themselves With 'Design For Living,'" *New York Morning Telegraph,* 26 January 1933.
8. "This Week's Openings," *New York Times,* 22 January 1933.
9. Noel Coward, *Play Parade* (New York: Garden City Publishing Company, Inc., 1924), p. 19.
10. *New York Times,* 22 January 1933.
11. *Play Parade,* p. 11.
12. *Ibid.,* p. 83.
13. *Ibid.,* p. 111.
14. *Ibid.*
15. Robert Benchley, "Goings On About Town," *New Yorker,* February 1933, p. 4.
16. "Comedy By Coward Daring and Witty, Too," *New York World-Telegram,* 25 January 1933.
17. Gilbert W. Gabriel, "Design For Living," *New York American,* 25 January 1933.
18. Sheridan Morley, *A Talent To Amuse* (Garden City, New Jersey: Doubleday & Company, Inc. 1969), p. 225.
19. Whitney Bolton, "'Design For Living' Sleekest and Most Persuasive Play In Town," *New York Morning Telegraph,* 26 January 1933.
20. Percy Hammond, "The Theaters," *New York Herald Tribune,* 25 January 1933.
21. "Gossip Of The Rialto," *New York Times,* 22 January 1933.
22. *New York Herald Tribune,* 5 February 1933.
23. Richard Watts, Jr., "Cavalcade," *New York Herald Tribune,* 22 January 1933.
24. "Film Personalities," *New York Herald Tribune,* 22 January 1933.
25. Sheridan Morley, *A Talent To Amuse* (Garden City, New York: Doubleday & Company, Inc., 1969), p. 213.
26. Burns Mantle, ed., *The Best Plays of 1932-33* (New York: Dodd, Mead & Company, 1933), p. 134.
27. *Ibid.,* p. 454.
28. *New York Herald Tribune,* 25 January 1933.

29. *New York Times,* 29 January 1933.
30. *Play Parade,* p. 14.
31. *Ibid.,* p. 58.
32. A. A. Brill, *Freud's Contribution to Psychiatry* (New York: W. W. Norton, 1944), p. 131.
33. Robert Wood, "Homosexuality On The Modern Stage," in *The Third Sex,* I. Rubin, ed. (New York: New Books, 1961), p. 88.
34. *New York Herald Tribune,* 5 February 1933.
35. Douglas Watt, "'Design For Living' Still Fun," *Daily News,* 21 June 1984.
36. Michael Feingold, "The Earnestness of Being Unimportant," *Village Voice,* 3 July 1984.
37. Benedict Nightingale, "Coward's Wit Carries Thru 'Design For Living,'" *New York Times,* 8 July 1984.
38. John Simon, "...There Is Little Of Coward's Style In This Flat 'Design For Living'..." *New York Times,* 16 July 1984.
39. "Inside Suff-Legit," *Variety,* 24 October 1933.
40. A. V. Cookman, "Note On Mordaunt Shairp," *New York Times,* 12 November 1933.
41. Douglas Gilbert, "Jed Harris Flourishes Anew," *New York Times,* 31 October 1933.
42. *New York Times,* 12 November 1933.
43. *Ibid.*
44. Mordaunt Shairp, *The Green Bay Tree,* (typewritten copy), Lincoln Center, Act I, Sc. 1, p. 3.
45. *Ibid.*
46. *Ibid.,* I-1, p.4.
47. *Ibid.,* I-1, p. 11.
48. *Ibid.,* I-1, p. 20.
49. *Ibid.,* II-1, p. 29.
50. *Ibid.,* II-1, p. 13.
51. *Ibid.,* II-1, p. 23.
52. *Ibid.,* III-1, p. 9.
53. *Ibid.,* III-1, p. 10.
54. *Ibid.,* III-1, p. 11.
55. *Ibid.,* III-1, p. 12.
56. *Ibid.,* III-7, p. 16.
57. *Ibid.*
58. *Ibid.,* III-2, p. 22.
59. Arthur Pollock, "The Theater," *Brooklyn Daily Eagle,* 21 October 1933.
60. Burns Mantle, ed., *The Best Plays of 1933–34* (New York: Dodd, Mead & Company, 1949), p. 414.
61. *Sixteen Famous British Plays,* compiled by Bennett A. Cerf and Van H. Cartmell (Garden City, New York: Garden City Publishing Co., Inc., 1942); *The Green Bay Tree* was also published by Baker International Play Bureau, but copies of it are not to be found in the New York Public Libraries.
62. Interview with Herman Shumlin, New York City, 3 March 1979.
63. Television interview, Jed Harris, "The Dick Cavett Show," WNET-TV, Channel 13, New York City, 25 March 1980.
64. Brooks Atkinson, "The Play," *New York Times,* 21 October 1933.
65. William Boehnel, "'The Green Bay Tree' Exciting Adult Drama," *New York World Telegram,* 21 October 1933.
66. *The Best Plays of 1933–34,* p. 445.
67. Brooks Atkinson, "The Seal of Good Producing," *New York Times,* 29 October 1933.
68. Untitled, New York newspaper fragment, dated 18 November 1933, on file in *The Green Bay Tree* file, Lincoln Center.
69. John Cottrell, *Laurence Olivier,* (Englewood Cliffs, New Jersey: Prentice-Hall, Inc., 1975), p. 86.

70. Television interview with Jed Harris, 25 March 1980.
71. Paul Banks, "The Green Bay Tree," *London New English Weekly,* 16 March 1933.
72. Ivor Brown of the *London Observer,* as quoted in "The Green Bay Tree for America," *New York Evening Post,* 2 March 1933.
73. Wolcott Gibbs, "The Green Bay Tree," *New Yorker,* 28 October 1933, p. 26.
74 *Laurence Olivier,* pp. 86-7.
75. Felix Barker, *The Oliviers* (New York: J. B. Lipincott Company, 1953), p. 82.
76. *Laurence Olivier,* p. 209.
77. *Ibid.,* p. 87.
78. Television interview with Jed Harris, 25 March 1980.
79. Burns Mantle, "'Green Bay Tree' Highly Emotional," *New York Daily News,* 21 October 1933.
80. *Ibid.*
81. K. McK, "Shapes Of The Soul," *The Stage,* December 1933, p. 21.
82. *New York Times,* 21 October 1933.
83. Robert Garland, "Fine Fusion Of Arts Is The Play At The Cort," *New York World Telegram,* 29 October, 1933.
84. Percy Hammond, "The Theaters," *New York Herald Tribune,* 5 November 1933.
85. "The Play; By John Mason Brown," *New York Evening Post,* 21 October 1933.
86. Wolcott Gibbs, "The Green Bay Tree," *New Yorker,* 28 October 1933, p. 26.
87. *The Stage,* December 1933, p. 21.
88. Telephone interview with Reginald Cockburn, New York City, 10 October 1978.

11

A Most Revolutionary Play
And a Commissioner of Licenses
on the Prowl

"If I hadn't seen how subtly and elegantly Jed Harris had done *The Green Bay Tree,*" Herman Shumlin said forty-five years after he directed *The Children's Hour,* "I wouldn't have dared to touch Lillian Hellman's script. It was a risky venture since that Moss person, the Commissioner of Licenses, was on the prowl back in 1934."[1]

The Green Bay Tree had appeared in its out-of-town tryout, on Broadway, and in a road show without once inciting a police raid. Mr. Dulcimer was too discreetly closeted to have justified legal action, nor was any such action taken the next autumn, when an overt lesbian character appeared in *The Children's Hour.* "They wouldn't have dared come near us, after we got such rave notices!" Herman Shumlin recalled, bristling even at the thought of that possibility. "My real problem was how to keep that Moss from going after us before the show opened. I had to devise a way to handle that very real threat."[2]

Shumlin was determined that *The Children's Hour* was not going to be harassed or closed during rehearsals or during an out-of-town tryout just because it contained a scene in which a character confesses her love for another woman. "After all," Shumlin said, "that was just one element, however shocking it may have seemed to some, of a larger, more universal consideration the playwright was concerned with: the devastating effects of vicious slander."[3]

Shumlin's initial reaction to a play concerned with lesbian love was negative. A writer for the *New Yorker* reported that:

> At a party given by Ira Gershwin in the fall of 1933, Hellman asked Shumlin, "What would you think of a play about a couple of school teachers accused of being lesbians by a brat student?" "I wouldn't waste time on it," Shumlin answered kindly.[4]

Lillian Hellman, a New York University graduate who had been working as a press agent and a playreader for MGM Studios, had already spent several months on such a project. Hellman had finished only one other play, an unproduced farce entitled *Dear Queen* written with critic Louis Kronenberger. While living with mystery writer Dashiell Hammett, Hellman had read the true account of a couple of slandered Scottish schoolmarms.

Robert Benchley, reviewing plays for the *New Yorker,* researched Hellman's source material for *The Children's Hour:*

> It may be pointed out that Miss Hellman has court records to substantiate her story, records on which she must have based it, so identical are the main circumstances.
>
> In Edinburgh, in 1810, two school mistresses, the Misses Woods and Pirie, were similarly accused by a girl pupil, who had even less to recommend her than the young villainess of Miss Hellman's play. A suit for slander was instituted (and, by the way, shouldn't this one have been for slander instead of libel? It was all done by word of mouth.) against the girl's grandmother, and after ten years of losing, appealing, winning, appealing, and endless legal haggling, with no evidence other than that of the already discredited viper, the case finally came before the august House of Lords. Here a technical verdict was awarded the schoolmistresses, but further legal haggling set in and there is no record of their ever having received a shilling for their ruined lives.
>
> So, to doubters, Miss Hellman may offer as evidence (as she already must know) pages 111–146 of a reputable volume called *Bad Companions,* by William Roughead, published in 1931 by Duffield and Green.[5]

To some, Hellman's failure to publicize the source of *The Children's Hour* seemed less than professionally ethical. Richard Moody reported in his biography of the playwright:

> Neither the program, the advance notices, nor the published text, which appeared the day after the opening, indicated that the story was not original. John Mason Brown, in his *New York Post* review

(November 21, 1934), was the first to refer to the source. A letter to the *Saturday Review* (March 16, 1935) reported that after the opening Miss Helllman said that the satanic "imp came out of my own head." She should have said that the imp came out of my own Roughead. But perhaps Miss Hellman doesn't like wisecracks.[6]

Unaware of her source material, Arthur Pollock of the *Brooklyn Daily Eagle* speculated:

Lillian Hellman has apparently wondered what would be the effect on the lives of two nice girls who found pleasure in each other's company if gossips took it into their heads to spread about precise whispers concerning the nature of their morals. In New York it would not matter too much. In a small town it might matter enormously.[7]

Despite Shumlin's initial reaction to the idea, Hellman worked for another six months on the script. According to the *New York Times,* while employed in his office in 1934:

She had written five drafts ... Then she handed her boss the sixth, ... and he read it while she waited...

"Swell," Mr. Shumlin said after the first act. "I hope it keeps up," he said after the second. After the third, he said simply, "I'll produce it."

In the months that followed, Mr. Shumlin and Miss Hellman worked painstakingly over the production, with occasionally brooding silences, they recalled, with some arguing about the title.[8]

"Miss Hellman loved its irony," Gary Blake noted in his study of Shumlin's directing techniques, "while Shumlin feared audiences would mistakenly misjudge the title and buy tickets thinking they would be witnessing a children's play."[9] The playwright borrowed her title from Henry Wadsworth Longfellow's 1860 poem, "The Children's Hour," in which children are described as being innocent and angelic.

Casting *The Children's Hour* posed quite a problem for the producer-director. Anne Revere, who played the schoolmarm who confesses her love for another woman, remembers that "The stars that rejected these roles could fill a book."[10] Revere recalls:

I wasn't shocked when I read the script. Nothing in the theater shocks me. My agent Jane Broder showed me the play and I wanted to do it, but I had trouble with Lillian Hellman. She wanted to go for the stars. They turned it down because of the kid's part. It wasn't because of the lesbian thing. They simply didn't want to do a play with a little girl taking over, which they knew would happen. At any rate, Herman liked my reading from the start, but Lillian, who is a real monster, fussed about my hair being too fuzzy and too short. It wasn't really but I think I'd just been to the hairdresser. "What would you do with your hair?" she asked me. "Wear a wig, if I have to!" I shot back at her. I ended up adding a switch, I think, to settle the matter.[11]

In the summer of 1934, Shumlin saw a young actress, Florence McGee, performing in a straw-hat theater production. Revere and Katherine Emery were in the same cast and impressed Shumlin. McGee, who had played one of the Prussian schoolgirls in *Girls in Uniform,* was set to portray Mary, the schoolgirl brat in *The Children's Hour.* Katherine Emery won the role of Karen, and Revere that of Martha.

Act One of *The Children's Hour* is set in the living room of a farm house, converted by two young teachers into a boarding school for girls. *"Karen* is an attractive woman of twenty-eight, casually pleasant in manner, without sacrifice of warmth or dignity,"[12] according to the author, and Martha, the other schoolteacher, "about the same age as *Karen.* She is a nervous, high-strung woman."[13] The school is such a success that the women expect to be out of debt by the end of the term, so Karen begins talking about marrying Joe, a doctor. Martha becomes very nervous and insecure when the subject comes up. Karen insists that marriage will not interfere with her work.

Martha becomes more edgy when her Aunt Lilly Mortar, the school's elocution teacher, reacts badly to the suggestion that Mrs. Mortar return to live in London where she had worked as an actress in the theater. A shallow, selfish woman, Mrs. Mortar cannot get along with Karen and is an inadequate teacher. Martha generously offers to support her in London. Resentful at being turned out, Mrs. Mortar makes a personal attack on her niece while Joe is visiting the school. He has come to check on one of the students, his troublesome cousin Mary, another nuisance Karen and Martha would like to be rid of:

Mrs. Mortar. I know what I know. Every time that man comes into this house, you have a fit. It seems like you just can't stand the idea of them being together. God knows what you'll do when they get married. You're jealous of him that's what it is.
Martha (her voice is tense and the previous attitude of good-natured irritation is gone). I'm very fond of Joe, and you know it.

Mrs. Mortar. You're fonder of Karen, and I know that. And it's unnatural, just as unnatural as it can be. You don't like their being
together. You were always like that even as a child. If you had a little girl
friend, you always got mad when she liked anybody else. Well, you'd
better get a beau of your own now — a woman of your age.[14]

Unfortunately, a couple of students eavesdrop on this conversation and they repeat what they have overheard to Mary. Because she
has been caught lying again, Mary won't be able to see the boat races
on Saturday. She hates the school and, as the first Act comes to a
close, tells her chums that she is going to go home to her grandmother,
Mrs. Tilford. The other schoolgirls are shocked:

Peggy (shocked). You're just going to walk out like that?
Evelyn. What are you going to tell your grandmother?
Mary. Oh, who cares? I'll think of something to tell her. I can always do
it better on the spur of the moment.[15]

In the first scene of Act Two, set in Mrs. Tilford's elegant living
room, Mary tries unsuccessfully to coax her grandmother not to send
her back to school. She claims that her teachers pick on her because
they are afraid she will tell her grandmother a terrible personal secret.
Mary repeats what the other schoolgirls overheard Mrs. Mortar say to
Martha. Mrs. Tilford dismisses it as trivia. Mary becomes desperate
because her grandmother does not react as she had hoped. She decides
to tell a more egregious lie suggested, perhaps, by a novel she has just
finished (Théophile Gautier's *Mademoiselle de Maupin,* in which a
woman falls in love with another woman who wears male attire):

Mary. And we've seen things, too. Funny things. *(Sees the impatience
of her grandmother)* I'd tell you, but I got to whisper it.
Mrs. Tilford. Why must you whisper it?
Mary. I don't know. I just got to...[16]

Mrs. Tilford is so appalled at what she hears that she assures
Mary that she does not have to go back. As soon as Mary leaves the
room, the distraught Mrs. Tilford goes to the phone. After asking her
nephew, Dr. Joseph Cardin, to come to see her right away, she dials
another number:

Mrs. Tilford. ...Mrs. Munn, please. This is Mrs. Tilford. Miriam?
This is Amelia Tilford. I have something to tell you — something about
school and Evelyn and Mary—[17]

The curtain comes down on her conversation.

In the next scene, Rosalie arrives to spend the night with Mary. Rosalie says that all the girls are being taken out of school. She is confused, wondering if someone has scarlet fever. When Mary says that she may have quoted Rosalie when telling her grandmother the secret responsible for the students' removal, Rosalie announces that she is going to tell Mrs. Tilford that it is not so and starts for the door. She is stopped in her tracks when Mary threatens to inform her grandmother that Rosalie stole another student's bracelet. Terrified that she will go to prison, the girl promises to do and say whatever Mary tells her.

Joe arrives to see Mrs. Tilford just as she is sending the girls off to bed. After asking him why Karen and he have decided to marry now after such a long engagement and wondering why Martha is sending her aunt away, she tells him:

> *Mrs. Tilford.* You must not marry Karen.
> *Cardin (shocked, he grins).* You're a very impertinent lady. Why must I — *(imitates her)* not marry Karen?
> *Mrs. Tilford.* Because there's something wrong with Karen — something horrible.[18]

Before Mrs. Tilford can say any more, Karen and Martha break into the room, very upset. The two women tell of the chaos at their school as chauffeurs and parents came to take girls home. One woman finally told them what it was all about:

> *Karen.* That — that Martha and I are — in love with each other. In love with each other, Mrs. Tilford told them.[19]

Mary's grandmother admits it was she who spread the story, and then insists that both young women leave her house at once; but they remain to rage at her, threatening to sue her for libel.

Mrs. Tilford objects, but Joe insists upon bringing Mary into the room to repeat some of what she has said. Mary is immediately caught in a lie when she claims to have seen the two teachers kissing by looking through the keyhole of their door; there is no keyhole. She changes her story, claiming it was Rosalie who saw the women kissing once when they left their door open. When Rosalie is brought into the room, Mary makes a reference to the missing bracelet. Rosalie becomes hysterical and supports Mary's lie as the curtain falls.

Act Three takes place in the living room of the school. Martha and Karen have become recluses since losing the libel suit. They are even afraid to shop in the town. A grocery boy, who stares and giggles at them, drops by to bring some things they ordered. Mrs. Mortar arrives, much to Karen and Martha's astonishment:

Martha. Where the hell have you been.[20]

It seems that her Aunt Lily has been on the road traveling with a theatrical company. Mrs. Mortar had refused to answer her niece's telegrams, that begged her to come back and testify on Karen and Martha's behalf:

Martha. . . . Listen, Karen Wright and Martha Dobie brought a libel suit against a woman called Tilford because her grandchild had accused them of having what the judge called "sinful sexual knowledge of one another." *(Mrs. Mortar holds up her hand in protest, and Martha laughs)* Don't like that, do you? Well, a great part of the defense's case rested on the telling fact that Mrs. Mortar would not appear in court to deny or explain those remarks.[21]

Martha orders her aunt to leave town on the next train as Joe comes to visit them. The young physician announces that he has sold his practice and intends to return to Vienna, where he had studied, taking both Karen and Martha with him. He even plans to take Martha with Karen and himself when they go on their honeymoon. When the young couple is alone, Karen realizes their relationship has been spoiled by the scandal. "Say it now, Joe," Karen insists, "Ask it now.":

Cardin. I have nothing to ask. Nothing — *(quickly)* All right. Is it — was it ever—
Karen (puts her hand over his mouth). No. Martha and I have never touched each other. . .[22]

Karen knows that she can never really be sure Joe believes her:

Cardin. . . . We love each other. *(His voice breaks)* I'd give anything not to have asked questions, Karen.[23]

She asks Joe to leave, to go away for a couple of hours and think things over by himself. "I'll be back, Karen." "No, you won't. Never, darling," she says to herself.

When Martha asks where Joe has gone, Karen tells her:

Karen (in a dull tone). He won't be back anymore.

Martha is confused and wants to know what happened:

Karen. He thought that we had been lovers.[24]

Both young women are deeply distressed at Joe's departure and want to flee. But their libel suit has gained national publicity and they don't know where they can go without being recognized:

Karen (as a child would say it). Is there anywhere to go?
Martha. No. There'll never be any place for us to go. We're bad people...
Karen (shivers, listlessly gets up, starts making a fire in the fireplace). But this isn't a new sin they tell us we've done. Other people aren't destroyed by it.
Martha. They are people who believe in it, who want it, who've chosen it. We aren't like that. We don't love each other. *(Suddenly stops, crosses to fireplace, stands looking abstractly at Karen. Speaks casually)* I don't love you. We've been very close to each other, of course. I've loved you like a friend, the way thousands of women feel about other women.
Karen (only half listening). Yes.
Martha. Certainly that doesn't mean anything. There's nothing wrong about that. It's perfectly natural that I should be fond of you, that I should—
Karen (listlessly). Why are you saying all this to me?
Martha. Because I love you.
Karen (vaguely). Yes, of course.
Martha. I love you that way — maybe the way they said I love you. I don't know. *(Waits, gets no answer, kneels down next to Karen)* Listen to me!
Karen. What?
Martha. I have loved you the way they said.[25]

Stunned by Martha's confession, Karen sits alone for a few minutes without moving after Martha leaves her. When a shot is heard, Karen springs to her feet and rushes into the room Martha had entered. Mrs. Mortar, highly excited, also runs in to see what has happened. There is nothing they can do for Martha.

Mrs. Tilford arrives to speak to Karen. Aunt Lilly leaves them to converse alone during the denouement of the drama. The rich old lady wants to make financial amends for the damage she has done: she has learned that Mary and Rosalie lied. After announcing that Martha is dead, Karen rages at the culprit for a few minutes. She becomes compassionate, however, and agrees to allow Mrs. Tilford to help her, perhaps even to attempt to reconcile her with Joe. The curtain falls as Karen smiles and waves goodbye.

Lillian Hellman had found a wealth of detail for *The Children's Hour* in the story of Marianne Woods and Jane Pirie, the libeled Scottish schoolteachers. Professor Moody, in his biography of Hellman, pointed out that:

> Miss Wood's aunt, a former actress, lived with them and earned her keep looking after the girls' wardrobes...
>
> Among the pupils, all from Edinburgh's first families, was the black granddaughter of Lady Cumming Gordon. Lady Gordon's son had died in India, "bequeathing to his aristocratic parent a bastard, borne to him by a black woman..."
>
> One bit of evidence that weighed strongly against the teachers was supplied by Charlotte Wiffin, a maid at the school. She swore that "looking through the keyhole of the drawing room door, [she] beheld her mistresses in a compromising situation on the sofa." The Judges, disturbed by this charge, went to Drumsheigh to investigate and found that there was no keyhole in the drawing room door.[26]

Even the blackmailing of Rosalie by Mary follows the actual case history, since Jane Cummings had coached a fellow student to support her in her slander against their innocent teachers.[27] Perhaps fearing that she might be suspected of some racial inference, Lillian Hellman chose not to use the details of Jane Cummings' background as possible motivation for the disturbed behavior of Mary Tilford.

It took six months for Herman Shumlin and Lillian Hellman to cast *The Children's Hour*.[28] The task was made especially difficult since they not only had to sign two little-known actresses capable of handling roles that ordinarily would have been played by stars, but they had also to find experienced actresses who looked young enough to pass as schoolgirls onstage. During their summer search, a threat appeared on their horizon in the person of License Commissioner Paul Moss. Earlier that year he had announced, "I don't want to be a censor, but certain indecent performances should not be permitted."[29] The *New York Times* reported, "In the fall Mr. Moss expects to have representatives of his department inspect plays during the rehearsal period. Realism on the stage has reached an unnecessary and often offensive point, Mr. Moss said."[30]

Herman Shumlin recalled:

Just as soon as I read *The Children's Hour,* I not only decided I wanted to produce it, but that no one was going to ruin it on me with a lot of nasty, controversial pre-production publicity that would stir things up. I wasn't going to have it labeled a homosexual play and start a fuss because it was more than just that. I decided not to allow anyone in the theater during the rehearsals except those working on the production. Nobody got near it to label it before we opened. We did not go out of town either for the usual tryouts. All rehearsals were done in the Maxine Elliott Theater, a little jewel of a playhouse perfect for intimate dramas.

I got a phone call from Lee Shubert, who never read a play himself and gave me $20,000 or whatever it was, sight unseen, because a friend of Lillian's, a publicist, had recommended it to him.

"Herman," he said, "what's this I hear about your show? There's not going to be a problem, is there, that will cost me the license on the theater?"

"There will be no problem," I said emphatically. "You have nothing to worry about and you'll be proud to be financing such a show." That seemed to be the end of that until I got another phone call from that Commissioner of Licenses.

"Shumlin," he said, "I think I ought to see a rehearsal of that show you're doing. I hear I ought to."

"No, you won't. You won't come near it," I replied, "until opening night. I'll send you tickets." I never heard from Moss again.[31]

Despite Shumlin's assurance that he had nothing to be concerned about, Lee Shubert — who produced the first drama to be affected by the Wales Padlock Law — came to see a rehearsal. Lillian Hellman remembered:

Mr. Shubert, who had been standing back watching the play for which he had put up the money, came down and sat behind me.

"This play," he said to the back of my head, "could land us in jail." He had been watching the confession scene, the recognition of the love of one woman for another.[32]

"I was always deeply moved by that scene," Shumlin said, "no matter how many times I watched it. Tears actually came to my eyes every time."[33]

Shumlin had decided how he wanted to see Martha portrayed in *The Children's Hour* based on an experience he had while one of his earlier hits, *Grand Hotel,* was running on Broadway:

One day Eugenie Leontovich, who was the star of *Grand Hotel,* asked me if I would like to meet Katherine Cornell whom I had much admired. There were some very sordid stories about her husband, Guthrie McClintic, carrying on — even something about having boys in the back of the balcony while she was performing — but I had never heard anything about Cornell. We went to her house on the East Side and watching Leontovich and Cornell together — there was a certain subtle intimacy in their rapport from which I was excluded — I understood why she would be married to a man like McClintic.

Of course, a woman can be as flagrant as he was as I found out while rehearsing Tallulah Bankhead in *The Little Foxes;* she was so coarse and campy about it. I wanted none of that obvious element in Martha's character any more than it was obvious in Leontovich or Cornell, on stage or in private, or in others I directed like Margaret Webster and her good friend, Eva LeGallienne, all of them refined, very feminine gentlewomen."[34]

Anne Revere, who played Martha in Hellman's drama, had some very different and definite ideas of her own about the character. Yet these did not conflict with Shumlin's concept of the role of a congenital lesbian, as he understood it. Revere recalled:

I did not play the role as a lesbian, that is like gals I had seen who were slightly "butch." Of course, I never thought that Martha was a lesbian. She and the other girl were just good friends, in my mind, nothing more. Under stress she cracks and thinks she is. She felt guilty and would have thought or said anything under the circumstances, done anything to take the blame on herself for what happened to them.

When Hellman directed the revival in 1952 she had Patricia Neal play Martha very "butch," going around lighting other women's cigarettes. What a mistake! It didn't work and the revival was a flop. Hellman had talent and intelligence, but she never really knew what she had come up with in a play. Monster that she was, she'd botch things up if she got her hand in a production. Herman stood up to her. It was her first show and she wasn't so sure of herself. Later on, she cruelly dropped Herman and turned her scripts over to someone with whom she could have her way.

I made a prediction, when I was starring for her in *Toys in the Attic,* that if her boyfriend, Dashiell Hammett ever died, she'd never write another play. She never did and never could after her editor and her advisor weren't around anymore. She needed Hammett and Herman to come up with her biggest hits.[35]

For the second time in little more than a year, a drama with a gay motif "struck Broadway like a thunderbolt."[36] *The Children's Hour* had its world premiere on November 20, 1934 at the Maxine Elliott Theatre. Shumlin's production proved an even greater hit than his boyhood chum Jed Harris had had the season before with *The Green Bay Tree*. Hellman's drama played 691 performances in New York, and over 100 performances on tour. "We did the show over 800 times," recalled Anne Revere.[39]

There wasn't a single negative review of the play, and most of the notices were outright raves. Robert Benchley wrote in the *New Yorker:*

> *The Children's Hour* came in, without one initial fanfare, and quietly set itself up as the season's high-water mark....
>
> It tells a story which would have been impossible of telling in public in the days when *Rain* was considered daring, and *The Captive* was being banned by the police.
>
> The language is frank, franker than we have yet had on the subject, but it is immaculate. I doubt if there will be any giggling, even at nervous matinées. Certainly there can be no offense to the adult mind. On the contrary, the effect should be highly salutary in the horror aroused at the enormity of irresponsible slander in such matters...
>
> In producing *The Children's Hour,* Mr. Herman Shumlin has shown not only courage but a fine sense of casting and direction (it is a marvelous job he has done.)
>
> *The Children's Hour* is possibly not for the children, but for any grown up with half a mind, it is almost obligatory.[39]

Walter Winchell declared in the *Daily Mirror,* "A theme that once excited the law to action is handled with such good taste and restraint ... [it] probably will attract playgoers for a long, long run."[40]

"The earnestness with which it was produced and the honesty with which it was written, cannot fail to impress," reported *Variety.*[41]

Lesbian love was referred to by one critic as a "monstrous sexual perversion,"[42] and Percy Hammond could not bring himself to spell it out, writing "l-----n" in his review and calling it a "naughty word."[43] However, a number of the critics were struck by a noticeable lessening of public and critical reaction to certain aspects of the play.

Robert Garland wrote in the *World-Telegram:*

> Eight years have passed since M. Edouard Bourdet's *La Prisonnière* was produced as *The Captive* at the Empire. An almost equal number of years have passed since Miss Radclyffe Hall's *The Well of Loneliness* was the literary sensation of the day.
>
> At Maxine Elliott's Theatre *The Children's Hour* dwells even more

determinedly on the affection that passes normal understanding and the wreckage it is able to create in otherwise well-ordered lives.

...Even when the onlooker's tears are falling, he has a suspicion that the not-like-other-girls up on the stage are taking their alleged aberration somewhat too seriously.

After all, certain things have been true about certain people, and they manage to keep their heads, to hold their horses.

...When all is said and sobbed, you wonder if people are as blindly intolerant as that nowadays.[44]

From Brooklyn, Arthur Pollock observed:

Many things have happened to increase the national breadth of mind since Bourdet's *The Captive* having enjoyed several fat months of success, was suddenly discovered to be improper and hurried from the stage, and *The Children's Hour,* a more sincere and less mysterious treatment of the same topic, should now be safe.[45]

Percy Hammond wrote:

Its subject has been forbidden in the theater as unfit for public illustration and a previous attempt to discuss it in *The Captive* was discouraged by the forces of law and order. That drama and the novel *The Well of Loneliness* were, in comparison to *The Children's Hour,* mere timid hints. Miss Hellman, with a gallant indifference to what has been termed the proprieties, speaks out, although with artistic discretion, and she leaves not even the most innocent drama lover in the dark. No tot, attending a matinée with its mother, will need to inquire. "Mama, what is it all about?"[46]

Richard Lockridge of the *Sun* questioned the young teachers' dilemma after they lost their court case. He wrote, "'There is not anywhere we can go,' one of the characters laments. You immediately think of half a dozen, including the city of New York."[47] Arthur Pollock also thought Hellman exaggerated the women's plight in implying there was nowhere they could make their living. "They never think of the stage!"[48] the critic exclaimed.

George Jean Nathan questioned Hellman's honesty in dealing with the subject of lesbian love. Nineteen years after the drama's premiere, Nathan complained:

There has always been one element in the otherwise cunningly written play that has bothered me. It is the business of having the child whisper her accusations of perversion against the two school mistresses

Anne Revere originated the role of a closeted lesbian who kills herself after confessing her love for her best friend played by Katherine Emery, at right, in The Children's Hour. *Herman Shumlin, who produced and directed the 1934 Broadway dramatic sensation, remembered that tears came to his eyes no matter how many times he watched the confessional scene.*

into her grandmother's ear because, she insists, she cannot bring herself to speak them aloud. Why can't she? Everything in her character would not only allow her to speak them openly but would indeed gratify her in the proclaiming of them. It isn't the child that is hesitant about articulating them; it is the playwright, who evidently has qualms about putting them into words and who shrinks from possible censorship (vide *The Captive*). Miss Hellman has cheated.[49]

Some of the critics, Brooks Atkinson chief among them, faulted Hellman for adding an anti-climactic denouement to an otherwise skillfully constructed drama. The critic for the New York *Times,* who praised the work as "a venomously tragic play of life in a girl's school,"[50] added:

Please, Miss Hellman, conclude the play before the pistol shot and before the long arm of coincidence starts wobbling in its socket. When two people are defeated by the malignance of an aroused public opinion, leave them the dignity of their hatred and despair.

...Instruct the guardian of the curtain to ring down when the two young women are facing a bleak future. That will turn *The Children's Hour* into vivid drama.[51]

In 1942 Hellman commented on *The Children's Hour* for the first time since its completion:

> There are, of course, many things wrong with *The Children's Hour*. (Even with my new clarity I have not seen them all, which is just as well, and better for my health.) The play probably should have ended with Martha's suicide: the last scene is tense and overburdened. I knew this at the time, but I could not help myself. I am a moral writer, often too moral a writer, and I cannot avoid, it seems, that last summing-up. I think that is only a mistake when it fails to achieve its purpose, and I would rather make the attempt, and fail, than fail to make the attempt.[52]

"I remember that I used to get a lot of mail while I was doing the show, none of it hostile or critical, but one letter in particular distressed me," Anne Revere recalled. "A woman wrote and asked me if that was the only answer for lesbians — suicide? I answered her immediately to assure her it wasn't. That reaction to the play really upset me."[53]

If she had it to do over, Hellman would still keep Martha's suicide in the script. But Herman Shumlin, like Atkinson, would have attempted to dissuade the author from retaining it if he had his way with a rewrite. In 1979, he said:

> Today I find that suicide unconvincing and unrealistic, but even in the 1930s, it seemed like something a woman might very well do even if she thought she was a lesbian. Why I remember how stunned everyone was in the 1920s when Le Gallienne's affair with Josephine Hutchinson hit the headlines. People thought it was simply frightful and I wondered how they would have the courage to go on with their careers or simply to go on. But they did and Martha probably would have and should have — gone on living as best she could.[54]

"That Hellman had great difficulties winding up *The Children's Hour*," observed Richard Moody, "are obvious from a study of the collection of her manuscripts at the University of Texas."[55] Moody also reports that critic Joseph Wood Krutch found the third act so improbable and boring that "[He] was amazed that 'anything so inept was ever allowed to reach production.'"[56] Dr. Annette Borgman Johnson concluded in "A Study of Recurrent Character Types in the

Plays of Lillian Hellman," that the author drove Martha to suicide to punish her for being a lesbian. Johnson wrote:

> ...if Martha's action during Act Two was motivated by a fear that there might be some truth to Mary's charges, Karen's actions may well stem from the same fear. When Martha tells Karen that there can be no tomorrow for herself, Karen cries and tells her to "Go and lie down." (p. 80) This is the first time Karen has commanded Martha or attempted to direct her life. Surely Karen knows that she is sending Martha to her death. After Martha has left the room, Karen sits motionless, certainly she is waiting for the shot. She does not move and she does not cry, it is easier for her also to believe that Martha was guilty.[57]

Only once during its long run were the police involved in *The Children's Hour.* Brooks Atkinson reported:

> For all the talk about the sinister charges against the teachers in the play, *The Children's Hour* has been honored by but a single visit from the gendarmerie. Because the Police Department must take official recognition of any complaint, no matter how ill advised, two interpreters of the law visited Maxine Elliott's Theatre of a Saturday afternoon and sat through the tense proceedings. They both emerged, better men, they said, for what they heard.[58]

After an eighty-six week Broadway engagement,[59] Herman Shumlin toured *The Children's Hour* for a year. It played many of the country's more cosmopolitian cities, but the Mayor of Boston banned it when he "insisted it violated the regulation against the portrayal of perverts." Moody reported in Hellman's biography:

> Shumlin volunteered to bring the entire production to Boston at his expense for a private showing for the Mayor and his board of censors. When that was refused, he filed a suit in Federal Court for $250,000 in damages. He lost.[60]

The Children's Hour, acclaimed "the season's high-water mark"[61] by Robert Benchley in the *New Yorker,* did not receive the Pulitzer Prize. In *The Wicked Stage,* a history of theatre censorship and harassment in the United States, author Abe Laufe explains that :

> *The Children's Hour* by Lillian Hellman was rumored to be a leading contender for the Pulitzer Prize for 1934–35, but it was bypassed, presumably because it dealt with charges of lesbianism ... its supporters denounced the Pulitzer Committee for cowardice and censorship.[62]

Hellman's drama did not stand a chance, according to her biographer, because "William Lyon Phelps, who dominated the committee, was revolted by advanced reports and refused to see it."[63]

The Lord Chamberlain banned *The Children's Hour* from the British public stage since it depicted a lesbian character, but it was eventually produced at London's Gate Theatre, a private playhouse, in November 1936. Like *The Captive,* it proved to be "more than a success, it was a sensation, particularly for audiences and censors who were shocked by the subject matter."[64] "The critics complained vigorously," Moody reported, "why should a play dealing with Sapphism — their word — be forbidden when the London stage was filled with bedroom farces, crude and vulgar jokes, and half-nude girls?"[65]

When Hollywood producer Samuel Goldwyn purchased the screen rights to Hellman's drama, he hired her to do the screenplay while the show was still running in New York. Entitled *These Three,* the 1936 release co-starred Merle Oberon and Miriam Hopkins, caught up in a heterosexual slander suit with Joel McCrea. It was not until 1962 that Hollywood dared film the original stage version, directed by William Wyler — who had also directed *These Three.* It starred Shirley MacLaine as Martha and Audrey Hepburn as Karen.

In 1934, the book reviewer for the *Saturday Review of Literature* commented:

> Twenty or thirty years ago, Miss Hellman's play, enthusiastically received in New York, would have been stopped by the police. As it is both engrossing drama and a sincere study of abnormal psychology, this change may imply a certain progress in the public's discernment.[66]

Doris Falk pointed out in her 1978 biography of Lillian Hellman:

> In Hellman's source, *Bad Companions,* the author-editor, William Roughead, had declared *emphatically* (his italics), "My interest in the case resides in the fact that the *charges were false.*" Roughead was apologizing for handling such a distasteful subject at all, but his is just the kind of statement that would inspire Hellman to react with the opposite view. What if the charges were *not* false? What if, after all, one — or even both — women had such feelings, consciously or unconsciously? Would the "guilty" deserve destruction at the hands of society? Changing mores between 1934 and 1978, the open treatment of homosexuality on the stage and elsewhere today, make the answer of most audiences, clearly, no; in fact, it is ironic that this most outspoken and revolutionary play in its time should now seem so old-fashioned.[67]

Notes

1. Interview with Herman Shumlin, New York City, 3 March 1979.
2. *Ibid.*
3. *Ibid.*
4. Margaret Case Harriman, "Profiles. Miss Lilly of New Orleans," *New Yorker,* 8 November 1941, p. 25.
5. Robert Benchley, "The Theatre," *New Yorker,* 1 December 1934, p. 34.
6. Richard Moody, *Lillian Hellman, Playwright* (New York: Pegasus, 1972), pp. 56–57.
7. Arthur Pollock, "The Theatre," *Brooklyn Daily Eagle,* 21 November 1934.
8. Eric Pace, "Herman Shumlin, 80, Dies; Leading Producer-Director," *New York Times,* 15 June 1979.
9. Gary Blake, "Herman Shumlin: The Development of a Director," (Unpublished doctoral dissertation, The City University of New York, 1973), p. 38.
10. *Ibid.*
11. Telephone interview with Anne Revere, Locust Valley, New York, 28 May 1979.
12. Lillian Hellman, *Four Plays by Lillian Hellman* (New York: Random House, 1942), p. 10.
13. *Ibid.,* p. 14.
14. *Ibid.,* p. 21–22.
15. *Ibid.,* p. 31.
16. *Ibid.,* p. 42.
17. *Ibid.,* p. 44.
18. *Ibid.,* p. 51.
19. *Ibid.,* p. 52.
20. *Ibid.,* p. 68.
21. *Ibid.,* p. 69.
22. *Ibid.,* p. 74.
23. *Ibid.*
24. *Ibid.,* p. 76.
25. *Ibid.,* pp. 77–78.
26. *Lillian Hellman, Playwright,* pp. 39–40.
27. *Ibid.,* p. 39.
28. John Chapman, "The Right People," *New York Daily News,* 23 December 1934.
29. "Clean-Up Of Stage, Dance Hall and Poolrooms Ordered By Moss," *New York Times,* 21 January 1934.
30. "Film Heads Make A New Concession," *New York Times,* 12 July 1934.
31. Interview with Herman Shumlin, New York City, 3 March 1979.
32. Lillian Hellman, *Pentimento* (Boston: Little, Brown and Company, 1973), p. 153.
33. Interview with Herman Shumlin, 3 March 1979.
34. *Ibid.*
35. Telephone interview with Anne Revere, 28 May 1979.
36. Burns Mantle, ed., *The Best Plays of 1934–35* (New York: Dodd, Mead & Company, 1935), p. 33.
37. Burns Mantle, ed., *The Best Plays of 1936–37* (New York: Dodd, Mead & Company, 1937), p. 501.
38. Telephone interview with Anne Revere, 28 May 1979.
39. Robert Benchley, "The Theatre," *New Yorker,* 1 December 1934, pp. 34 and 36.
40. Walter Winchell, "Tense Drama At Elliot, A New Hit," *New York Daily Mirror,* 21 November 1934.
41. "The Children's Hour," *Variety,* 22 November 1934.
42. John Anderson, "How Children's Lie Brought Ruin to 2 Teachers' Lives, Told in Play," *New York Evening Journal,* 21 November 1934.
43. Percy Hammond, "The Theaters," *New York Herald Tribune,* 21 November 1934.

44. Robert Garland, "Children's Hour A Moving Tragedy," *New York World-Telegram,* 21 November 1934.
45. *Brooklyn Daily Eagle,* 21 November 1934.
46. *New York Herald Tribune,* 21 November 1934.
47. Richard Lockridge, "The New Play," *New York Sun,* 21 November 1934.
48. *Brooklyn Daily Eagle,* 21 November 1934.
49. George Jean Nathan, "George Jean Nathan's Theatre," *New York Herald Tribune,* 11 January 1953.
50. Brooks Atkinson, "The Play," *New York Times,* 21 November 1934.
51. *Ibid.*
52. *Four Plays By Lillian Hellman,* pp. XII-XIII.
53. Telephone interview with Anne Revere, 28 March 1979.
54. Interview with Herman Shumlin, 3 March 1979.
55. *Lillian Hellman, Playwright,* p. 56.
56. *Ibid.*
57. Annette Bergman Johnson, "A Study of Recurrent Character Types in the Plays of Lillian Hellman," (Unpublished doctoral dissertation, Graduate School of Univeristy of Massachusetts, 1970), p. 24-25.
58. Brooks Atkinson, "8,752 Children's Hours," *New York Times,* 22 November 1935.
59. *Lillian Hellman, Playwright,* p. 38.
60. *Ibid.*
61. Robert Benchley, "The Theatre," *New Yorker,* 1 December 1934, p. 34.
62. Abe Laufe, *The Wicked Stage* (New York: Frederick Ungar Publishing Co., 1978), p. 87.
63. *Lillian Hellman, Playwright,* p. 56.
64. *Ibid.,* p. 38.
65. *Ibid.*
66. H. S. C., "The New Books," *Saturday Review of Literature,* 2 March 1934, p. 523.
67. Doris V. Falk, *Lillian Hellman* (New York: Frederick Ungar Publishing Co., 1978), p. 41.

12

Saving the American Theater — Except for Those They Could Always Call Bulgarians

In the spring of 1937, one man rallied many thousands of theater workers *and* theatergoers in a campaign to defeat the most serious threat to freedom of expression that the American stage had ever faced. The *New York Times* reported: "Herman Shumlin ... drew the theater together to fight the Dunnigan Bill."[1] State Senator John J. Dunnigan, called "A Terrible Man"[2] in a *Daily News* editorial, had authored the bill making the commissioner of licenses a political appointee, as powerful on Broadway as the Lord Chamberlain was in Great Britain.

Earlier in the decade, Cardinal Hayes of Manhattan had declared that the Broadway "stage was reeling with filth, and there seems no power in New York to stop it."[3] In a bulletin of the Catholic Theater Movement, the rector of Saint Patrick's Cathedral asserted that the theater in New York had sunk so low as "to become an outrage to public decency."[4] When the Catholic clergy finally found a champion of their cause in Dunnigan, Cardinal Hayes announced to the press that he was backing the censorship bill.

Theater people, in a campaign spearheaded by Shumlin, collected some 63,000 or more signatures[5] from Broadway audiences petitioning Governor Herbert Lehman to veto the bill. Some of the biggest stars in show business aided Shumlin's campaign. Chief among them

was Helen Hayes, who proved to be one of the most articulate oppo-
nents of the proposed legislation. *Life* magazine reported in May
1937:

> This spring, for the first time, the freedom of the New York stage
> was seriously threatened. Largely at the instigation of the Catholic
> Church, which had cleaned up the movies with its Legion of Decency, a
> bill was hastily passed by the legislature, empowering New York City's
> Commissioner of Licenses to close any play he deemed "immoral."
> Since most U.S. drama flows from the fountainhead of the New York
> stage, this measure would have made a political job-holder the supreme
> censor of the American theater.
>
> Actors, playwrights, producers and audiences promptly attacked
> the bill. Petitions were sent to Albany with audience approval. At a
> climactic meeting of 2,000 theater workers and theatergoers in New
> York's New Amsterdam theater, Helen Hayes ... was cheered when she
> spoke the lines of the historic Queen she acts in *Victoria Regina:* "We
> are not amused." Three days later Governor Herbert Lehman vetoed
> the bill and the U.S. theater was saved again.[6]

"An Admirable Veto," reported the *New York Times* in an
editorial on May 20, 1937:

> Governor Lehman has earned the gratitude of all liberals, of all
> who value freedom of speech and of the arts, by his veto of the Dun-
> nigan One Man Censorship Bill... There are fully adequate laws for
> dealing with indecency on the stage.[7]

One such law was, of course, the penal code's prohibition of any
play "depicting or dealing with, the subject of sex degeneracy or sex
perversion." Shumlin's campaign and Lehman's veto had saved the
American theater from a dictatorial censorship by a political appointee, but the prohibtion of gay roles remained in effect until the
penal code was recodified in 1967.

The defeat of the Dunnigan Bill came in the midst of a foursome
of Broadway productions with covert gay male and lesbian roles, all
of which failed to entertain the critics. The death notices written by
unimpressed reviewers closed these four plays just as quickly as any
commissioner of licenses could have. Such poor productions as these
so provoked the reviewers that they not only attacked the playwrights,
but also gay men and lesbians as well. There was often snide mockery
in the reviews attesting to the homophobia still prevalent among the
critics.

The sensational success of both *The Green Bay Tree* in 1933, and *The Children's Hour* the following season, made possible the Broadway premiere of J.R. Ackerley's *Prisoners of War*. The New York critics had proven themselves to be tolerant, even protective, of plays with gay characters when the productions were intelligent and tasteful. Ackerley's drama was first seen in 1935 by the general public in Manhattan, although it was written for the London stage in 1925. The first English-language drama with a gay protagonist written for the London stage since Christopher Marlowe's *Edward II* in 1593, *The Prisoners of War* was rejected by the Lord Chamberlain for public performances.

Ackerley's drama opened in London in 1925 at the private Three Hundred Club. The club had been founded the year before to present "drama of distinguished merit . . . likely to appeal in the first instance to a small public."[8]

The London *Times*'s reaction to Ackerley's openly gay character was awed and appreciative. It was hailed as "an arresting and dreadful story."[9] Its critic concluded his lengthy review by contending that:

> . . . it is impossible to imagine that the play could have been better produced, or better acted. Let me add my voice to the many which are asking that the performance shall be repeated.[10]

Two months later, *The Prisoners of War* was revived at the Playhouse, another private theater, in an engagement limited by British law to a few weeks. With somber second thoughts, the London *Times* reviewer was less enthusiastic with the Playhouse production. He wrote, "moving though it was, it had all the air of being a record."[11] A reference to the protagonist being "afflicted by a romantic attachment"[12] was the only hint that the main plot was a fictionalized dramatization of the playwright's actual infatuation with another young soldier while they had been interned in Switzerland during World War I.

At its Broadway premiere in 1935, *Prisoners of War* "gave its first night audience a number of laughs," one reviewer reported, "none of them intended."[13] The New York *Times* observed that;

> A decade ago, before the Depression turned values upside down again, the bare mention of those neuroses and the suggestion of homosexual attachments were sufficient for an evening of speculation in the

theater. *Prisoners of War* falls in that category ... such themes need deeper clarification today. They are no longer fascinating in themselves.[14]

Rejected by reviewers from nine other New York dailies, *Prisoners of War* had only eight performances at the Ritz, where it opened in January 1935.[15] Predicting an early demise, Percy Hammond wrote, "*Prisoners of War* is not so deep as *The Children's Hour,* nor so wide as *The Green Bay Tree,* and in my guess it will not quite serve."[16]

Ackerley, who some say became the greatest London literary editor of his day,[17] had written the first draft of *The Prisoners of War* in the early months of 1918 while he was a British prisoner of war. Ackerley was gay, identifying himself as such in his memoirs, *My Father and Myself.*[18] While Ackerley's autobiography was highly acclaimed by the critics, his sexual autobiographical drama was mocked and rejected by the American drama critics.

Captain Conrad, the protagonist of *The Prisoners of War,* is a twenty-four-year-old virgin whose sexual orientation is apparently obvious to the other four officers who have been quartered with him in the same hotel in Mürren, Switzerland, for half a year. "I have heard you do not like the fair sex," a flirtatious Swiss widow visiting the officers says to Conrad. "The fair sex?" the young officer retorts, "Which one is that?"[19] Foul-humored, antisocial, and hostile ever since handsome Lieutenant Grayle has rejected him, Conrad confesses to an older soldier that being imprisoned has psychologically unsettled him. The frustrated young officer confides that he finds himself "attracted to others in a way that terrifies me."[20]

In a futile attempt to affect a reconciliation with the teenage officer with whom he had once been on friendly terms, Conrad speaks to Grayle about his unhappiness while he "strokes the curly head affectionately"[21]:

Grayle. (who has been educated at a Good Public School). Look out! Someone might come in![22]

Conrad's plea for Grayle's affection and companionship serves only to alienate him further. Opportunistic Grayle, described by one of the officers as "terribly heartless,"[23] wants nothing more to do with Conrad personally, yet continues to help himself to the Captain's cigarettes and to use his large room to entertain friends when he is not around. The London *Times* described Grayle as "a thorough-going little cad, impervious alike to kindness and snubbing."[24]

In Act Two we learn that another officer, Captain Rickman, "seems to have taken a great fancy to young Grayle lately."[25] This distresses not only Conrad, but also young Lieutenant Tetford who is jealous that Rickman, his best friend and constant companion, is interested in the handsome teenager. Rickman placates Tetford, assuring his buddy that he is interested in young Grayle only so that he can fleece him at cards. Tetford's jealousy flares again when Rickman cancels their standing engagement to have tea together, joining Grayle for tea instead. The squabble is settled when Grayle announces his preference to have tea that afternoon with the lively Swiss widow. In the climax of Act Two, Conrad can no longer deal rationally with Grayle's treatment and picks a quarrel. He hits Grayle so hard on the mouth that he goes sprawling on the floor.

Tetford and Rickman are reconciled in a scene in the last act. They vow to stick together for the duration of their internment and then to go into partnership after the war, operating a farm in Rickman's native Canada. During this scene, Tetford slips his hand on Rickman's shoulder. Responding to this gesture, the older officer links a finger in Tetford's dangling hand. They shake, and while holding hands, according to the stage directions, they contemplate life together in Canada, caring no more how much longer they will be interned. In striking contrast to the happy resolution of this relationship, Conrad goes mad and begins carrying around a wilted azalea. The rejected lover reaches out and touches Grayle's sleeve before going out on the veranda to sit with the plant in his lap as the final curtain falls.

In his memoirs, *My Father and Myself,* Ackerley confessed, "The hero Captain Conrad is myself of course."[26] He also identified the inspiration for Grayle's characterization, "a consumptive boy who died of his complaint soon after the Armistice."[27] Half a century after writing *The Prisoners of War* Ackerley regretted that he had shown the play's first draft to the object of his affections before the youth died, which:

> ...the poor fellow, having identified himself in it, thought it awfully unkind, as well he might, since I accuse him, in the character of Grayle, of a heartless unresponsiveness to love without, in reality, ever having

made my own feelings toward him plain — if indeed I knew what my own feelings were.[28]

Ackerley became irritated when some London reviewers identified *The Prisoners of War* "as a homosexual play"[29] after it was revised in the autumn of 1955 at the London's Irving Theatre. "The rest of the characters," he insisted, "are entirely normal."[30] Ackerley wrote to a friend:

> As for homosexuality, I'm sorry you thought that there were "one or two" homosexual characters. If that were so I would certainly be at fault, but it was not intended, and production is always at pains ... to emphasize the normality of the Rickman-Tetford set-up. There is only one homosexual character, Conrad himself. The rest are entirely normal. And although Tetford regards Rickman as *his* pal, the notion of them going to bed together ought to be as unthinkable to the audience as I mean it to be to them ... If I had more of a hand in the production the relationship would, I think have been less ambiguous.[31]

The American critics who rejected *Prisoners of War* after its Broadway premiere in 1935 also found the relationship of Rickman and Tetford as sexually suspect as Conrad's unrequited passion for Grayle. Only Brooks Atkinson used the word "homosexual" to identify these troubled relationships.[32] The other reviewers were more euphemistic: one used the word "epicene,"[33] another referred to "the middle sex,"[34] and a third wrote of men who were "a little on the distaff side."[35]

Some reviewers mocked the characters with pejorative allusions to colors, flowers, and slang synonyms commonly used to identify gay males. The reviewer for Hearst's *Journal American* observed that the officers in the play "are all supposed to be wearing the usual olive-drab clothes of their army, but Mr. Ackerley, the author, prefers to paint them in such a light that these uniforms look utterly, utterly lavender."[36] The same critic added, "Most of them wear silver wings on their tunics, to symbolize aviation ... but this may indicate the elfin strain in them, too."[37] Burns Mantle suggested that when Conrad transfers his affection from the unresponsive Grayle to a potted plant, the flower ought not to have been an azalea, but a pansy.[38]

Just ten years before these mocking reviews, the *London Times* had been deeply moved by *Prisoners of War*: "Not for a long time have I seen anything more wholly beautiful than that last scene in which the wretched man, now beyond human companionship, sought communion with his plant."[39]

American audiences were much ruder than their English counterparts. The scene in which the Captain strikes Grayle caused "a ribald first-night audience to hoot up its sleeves at it,"[40] according to Percy Hammond. When Grayle runs out of the Captain's room crying, "Leave me alone, you beast! It was a foul blow!"[41] there were reports of "loud laughter at the Ritz."[42]

Six months after the failure of *Prisoners of War,* there was more "snickering in the audience,"[43] when New York theatergoers saw another drama with a gay motif. *Reprise,* by W.D. Bristol, was so "sophomoric"[44] and "one great big yawn"[45] that it was no wonder that it closed after a single performance at the Vanderbilt Theater on May 1, 1935.[46]

"A tragic drama of a brother and a sister who compete for the affection of the same man,"[47] *Reprise* concerned the Carters, an affluent Southern family living in a penthouse in Manhattan: Roy, a bachelor, Julie, his recently divorced sister, and their brandy-drinking, tough-minded old grandmother. A despondent young man named Peter attempts to commit suicide by jumping from the building in which the Carters reside, but is saved by Roy when he falls onto the terrace of the penthouse. John Anderson noted:

> Roy's interest was somewhat less than, shall we say, philanthropic. He wished, I gathered, to save Peter from worse than death, but poor Peter, alas! fell in love with Roy's sister, Julie. Roy was jealous, and his jealousy flourished as the green bay trees, as Roy struggled to make Peter, to make him, I mean, captive.[48]

Apparently the bachelor brother's designs on Peter were not obvious to most of the audience during the first act, but Arthur Pollock reported that:

> ...[a] handholding episode, however, which came in the second act, saved the show. At least it persuaded the audience to come back for a third, hoping to discover just what the meaning of it. The play, however, did not turn out to be anything like *The Captive* or *The Green Bay Tree.*[49]

In order to marry Julie, Peter betrays Roy in a dishonest business transaction. When this comes to light, both brother and sister turn their backs on the man they had been fighting over "like two fishwives over a herring."[50] The family gets even when the grandmother talks Peter into making a second suicide attempt. At the final curtain she joins Roy and Julie; neither are aware that Peter has plunged to the pavement while they listened to a recording.

During the late 1930s, two British dramatists turned out plays about lesbians which fared no better in their American productions than did *Prisoners of War* or *Reprise.* Lillian Hellman was not the only woman intrigued with the dramatic possibilities of the lesbian's dilemma in society. Neither Mrs. Guy Bolton, wife of the successful playwright, nor Aimee McHardy Stuart, who collaborated on her play with her far less successful playwriting spouse, Philip Stuart, were in Hellman's class — according to American critics. The Broadway productions of both Bolton's and the Stuarts' London hits were rejected by New York's critics and theatergoers.

Like *The Children's Hour,* these two plays concerned a possessive female's emotional or sexual attachment to another woman who is engaged or married to a man. Because *Wise Tomorrow* and *Love of Women* needed the approval of the Lord Chamberlain before they could be produced on a public stage in Britain, both plays were, of necessity, sexually ambiguous. And perhaps because of the touchiness of the subject matter both plays were billed and performed as comedies.

Wise Tomorrow, which Bolton wrote under the pseudonym Stephen Powys,[51] had met with success in its original London production, starring Marita Hunt, at the Lyric Theatre in the winter of 1937. "Roars of applause greeted the final curtain,"[52] according to the *London Daily Telegraph. Variety* reported, "Piece was received with considerable warmth at the premiere and ticket agencies have made a buy."[53]

The title *Wise Tomorrow* — inspired by Alexander Pope's observation, "Tomorrow's wiser than today," from his *Essay on Criticism* — confused at least one critic who could not relate it to anything in the play.[54] Although the play has never been published, reviewers have given us some idea of the plot. John Anderson provided this résumé for *Wise Tomorrow,* which:

...tells of a young woman, Joan Campion, with a modest talent for the stage, who is happily engaged to a young man named Peter Marsch, but who falls under the influence of an elderly actress whose sex desires . . . are fanned by winds from Lesbos Isle, "Where burning Sappho loved and sang." Mme. Dracula sets out to destroy the simple, normal happiness of the girl, and just when Joan's sweetheart seemed to be saving her from worse than death he ups and falls in love with her sister Tony . . . Anyway Mme. Dracula dies conveniently . . . and at the end Joan is going off with the lady friend of Mrs. Hideous to what seems to be a life of shame, leaving Tony and Peter to live happily ever after.[55]

Diana, the aging star who falls in love with Joan, "left a good husband for the companionship of her poisonous secretary,"[56] who, according to *Variety,* "dresses and walks and conducts herself in a masculine fashion."[57] The same reporter noted that at the conclusion of *Wise Tomorrow:*

> [Joan] is at last freed by the pursuer dying and willing her house and fortune to her. Equipped with wealth, the young woman seems to have inherited the characteristics of the deceased, and proceeds to conduct herself in a similar manner, even to engaging of the mannish secretary.[58]

The *London Times* did eventually run a follow-up evaluation of *Wise Tomorrow,* reporting that "Mr. Powys's plot is one which Sappho would have enjoyed."[59] But there was no hint in its first-night review that the show had to do with a lesbian attachment.[60] "The play from the English reviews," Burns Mantle noted, "carried no such taint."[61] A Hollywood studio was as oblivious as the Lord Chamberlain's office and the London drama critics to what seemed obvious to most New York critics. Warner Brothers bought the film rights to Bolton's work and made plans to produce it on Broadway. This prompted columnist Wilella Waldorf to comment:

> It has been whispered the theme has a touch of Lesbianism about it, which sounds a little odd when you consider that the Warners, presumably, have in mind a picture version eventually. However, as Samuel Goldwyn or somebody once said, "We can always call them Bulgarians."[62]

During its Baltimore tryout "audiences found it interesting and provocative,"[63] reported the *New York Times,* and *Variety* predicted that "New York audiences would be likely to receive the piece with as much fervor as the first-night West-Enders."[64] *Wise Tomorrow*

Wise Tomorrow *was the distaff version of the sensational London and New York hit,* The Green Bay Tree. *The original London production starring Marita Hunt, at center, as an aging lesbian stage star, was a success in 1937. The Broadway version, with a less accomplished cast, flopped. Diana Churchill, left, played the lesbian's protege who inherits her fortune and the services of her mannish secretary played by Olga Lindo.*

opened at the Biltmore Theater on October 15, 1937. It played three performances after an indifferent-to-hostile critical reception. The play was called "poor ... and dull,"[65] "dismal,"[66] and "terrible."[67] Brooks Atkinson wrote, "The topic is sufficiently malodorous. The author does nothing to redeem it in the frowziness of his playwriting."[68]

Only a few of the New York drama critics did not detect anything sexual in Diana's interest in her protégée;[69] most found it obvious despite the author's device of keeping the lesbian character closeted in a so-called comedy. Burns Mantle, who was unable to recognize the "bull dyke" character eight years earlier in *Winter Bound,*[70] was somewhat piqued at those who voiced suspicions of lesbianism in *Wise Tomorrow:*

> There has been a more or less determined effort to read a sugges-
> tion of Lesbianism into *Wise Tomorrow*...
>
> There really isn't much excuse for that.... It is pretty easy to read
> abnormality into almost any provocative drama dealing with any un-
> conventional relationship of the sexes. If that is the way your mind
> runs.[71]

"It is the subject of homosexuality," John Anderson bluntly concluded.[72] *Variety* tagged Bolton's work "an unvarnished tale of a woman's yen for another,"[73] and Robert Coleman wrote, "*The Captive* theme reared its ugly head last night in *Wise Tomorrow.*"[74]

Variety reported:

> Program announces this play as a comedy, which it is in treatment,
> although it has an underlying story constantly touching on homosexual-
> ity, but never quite saying so. Hints and situations continually recur, but
> a meticulously exacting censor could not legitimately raise any
> objection.[75]

The *World Telegram* also noted the care the author had taken to avoid a prohibition of the work by the British government censors:

> There's nothing forthright about *Wise Tomorrow*. The unfor-
> tunate situation is hinted at rather than explained. There are innuendos
> and hints and implications, plus certain pauses in the conversation that
> are intended to convey to the audience what the actors don't care or
> don't dare to say.[76]

Two of the first-night reviewers made mention of the striking resemblance of *Wise Tomorrow* to *The Green Bay Tree*. *Variety* noted that "there was a similar strain in the story, a sort of *Green Bay Tree* with its sexes in reverse."[77] Richard Watts, Jr., elaborated:

Someone was foolish enough to believe that since *The Green Bay Tree* was an admirable play, a distaff version of the same theme would be even better. It isn't ... The chief difference between the two plays, outside of the change in the sexes, is that *The Green Bay Tree* was a powerful and beautifully written drama, which had dignity as well as force, and that *Wise Tomorrow* is a weak and fumbling work that has no possible virtue to recommend it. There is a wide-eyed attempt to express the Lesbian theme in the new play, but it doesn't even give the drama the box office quality of being shocking.[78]

The second play with a covert lesbian theme, *Love of Women,* failed less than two months after *Wise Tomorrow* closed. A collaborative effort by Aimee and Philip Stuart, *Variety* said that *Love of Women* "flies over, under and around the Lesbian theme, but never alights directly on it."[79] To escape detection by the Lord Chamberlain, the authors included so many contradictory clues to the character of Vere, the older, stronger woman, that the role made little sense. Many of the critics were as confused and annoyed by Vere in *Love of Women* as they had been by Tony in *Winter Bound.*

Brooks Atkinson gave readers this brief plot summary:

Love of Women is the story of two young women who have lived together for five years and have made their mark in the world by writing a successful drama. A brilliant surgeon has fallen in love with one of them. For her it is a choice between love and a successful career at dramatic collaboration. For her comrade of five industrious years it looks like calamity. It turns out that way, for the brilliant surgeon captures his bride and her comrade is left frightened and alone.[80]

Robert Coleman reported that *Love of Women* was "one of London's biggest recent hits."[81] The Shuberts brought the comedy to Broadway, which had already seen at least three of Aimee McHardy Stuart's plays: *Lady Clara, Sixteen* and *Birthday.* The British cast in the Broadway production was headed by Valerie Taylor and her husband, Hugh Sinclair. *Love of Women* marked the Broadway debut of pretty English film star Heather Angel. Leo G. Carroll, who appeared as the butler in *The Green Bay Tree,* directed and played a supporting role. Their performances received higher acclaim than their play: "Clumsily written ... plot rickety ... characters implausible," complained John Anderson.[82] *Variety* identified it as "a dull drama,"[83] while the *Brooklyn Daily Eagle* called it "a very pale and anemic comedy."[84]

Love of Women opened on December 13, 1937 at the Shuberts' John Golden Theater and lasted five days.[85] John Mason Brown called it "the story of a cure"[86] since the two women "are shown the psychological dangers they run"[87] by the virile young doctor who breaks them up, thus preventing their relationship from evolving into a sexual one. Yet this would have been unlikely since, as Brown notes, "the authors would have us know that the girls are healthy and normal."[88] To prove just how heterosexual the older, more aggressive woman actually is:

> There is an odd moment at the end of the second act when the man and the possessive woman suddenly interrupt their argument to fall into an embrace, thus proving there is nothing out of the way about her, and completely reversing the apparent direction of the drama.

The reviewer for the *Sun* added, "It is always possible, incidentally, that someone has been doing house cleaning on the play, and left behind the confusion and muddle characteristic of house cleaning."[89] Citing the same confusion and contradictions especially in the characterization of one of the two women, Richard Watts, Jr., concluded that *Love of Women* is:

> a hollow and aimless work that has been so carefully cleansed of its dangerous sex matters that it has lost whatever dramatic point it may once have possessed. In the current version it is a very mild little comedy.[90]

Watts also reported:

> In an early scene of the drama, one of the characters suggests that children born in England during wartime, having been raised while their fathers were in the trenches and their mothers were doing men's work, tend to become effeminate if they were boys, and masculine if they were girls. However, the idea is immediately cast aside and we should do the same, pausing to remark that the play toys gingerly with its lesbian theme and pushes it, too, aside carefully.[91]

Just as there was considerable confusion about the drama's genre, there was divided reaction to the nature of its resolution. Atkinson mentioned the older woman being left "frightened and alone"[92] at the final curtain, yet the reviewer for the *Brooklyn Daily Eagle* — who mentioned nothing about lesbian innuendos in his critique — remembered:

Despite strict government censorship, British playwrights turned out no less than eight dramas with both overt and covert gay characters during the 1920s and 30s. Half became hits, but not For Love of Women, *which failed in 1937. Hugh Sinclair played a man who came between two women, Valerie Taylor and Heather Angel, in a drama that* Variety *reported "flies over, under and around the Lesbian theme, but never alights directly on it."*

The final tableau leaves her broken and weeping on the stage alone, as the happy couple take their departure. Still, things are not as bad as they sound, for we are led to suppose that a very pleasant neighbor is ready and willing to make everything up to her.[93]

John Anderson's report of the play's conclusion, on the other hand, would seem to support Atkinson's version. The abandoned woman tells her neighbor, who has a schoolgirl crush on her, to go away: "Go away and love a man, and have children and build a home, and leave me alone."[94] Anderson thought this "a handsome moral lesson,"[95] but to John Mason Brown it was a surprising incongruity in characterization when the woman, "suddenly mounts the rostrum to preach a three — or four — line anti-Lesbian sermon to another girl who has a crush on her."[96]

Robert Coleman of the *Daily Mirror* wished that neither *Wise Tomorrow* nor *Love of Women* had been seen by the public — because of the subject matter *and* because they were poorly written.

224 WE CAN ALWAYS CALL THEM BULGARIANS

Of *Wise Tomorrow,* Coleman wrote, "...such matters as those with which it concerns itself are best left to the consulting rooms of psychiatrists. They do not add to the health and well-being of the theater."[97] He decided that the subject matter of gay emotional or physical involvements was more than dramatists could handle: "Somehow it baffles playwrights and usually fails to stimulate box office patronage in New York. The exceptions to the rule can be numbered on half the fingers of one hand."[98]

Coleman's count was not quite accurate. Since the 1920s, there have been half a dozen hits out of the fourteen plays with overt and covert gay motifs: *God of Vengeance, The Captive, The Green Bay Tree, The Children's Hour, The Vortex* and *Design for Living.* Upon examination of the reviews of the eight flops, it seems that their authors not only lacked dramaturgical skills but were also handicapped by censorship prohibitions. The controversial subject matter of those well-written plays that won rave notices certainly contributed to the strong patronage they attracted.

With the possible exception of Irene in *The Captive,* all the other emerging lesbian characters in the '20s and '30s met with misfortune at the hands of their creators. One was forced into prostitution; three were driven to suicide; two were abandoned by the heterosexual object of their affection; one succumbed to a heart attack. Gay male characters fared somewhat better. While two were murdered, one driven mad, two driven to drugs, and another to alcohol, the gay confidant ended up with the leading lady in *Strange Interlude*; a pair of traveling companions went their merry bisexual way in *Design for Living,* and a gay good samaritan continued to enjoy Debussy in *Reprise*, although he never did get to seduce the would-be suicide he had saved.

Notes

1. "News of the Stage," *New York Times,* 22 May 1937.
2. "A Terrible Man, This Dunnigan," (editorial), *New York Daily News,* 17 November 1933.
3. "New York Stage Indecent, Says Cardinal Hayes," *New York Herald Tribune,* 10 October 1930.
4. *Ibid.*

5. "Cardinal Backing The Dunnigan Bill," *New York Times,* 18 May 1937.
6. "Helen Hayes Helps Save The American Theatre From Censorship," *Life,* 31 May 1937, p. 17.
7. "An Admirable Veto," (editorial), *New York Times,* 20 May 1937.
8. J. R. Ackerley, *The Ackerley Letters,* Neville Braybrook, ed. (New York: Harcourt Brace Jovanovich, 1975), p. 13.
9. "Three Hundred Club," *London Sunday Times,* 12 July 1935.
10. *Ibid.*
11. "The Playhouse," *London Times,* 1 September 1935.
12. *London Sunday Times,* 12 July 1935.
13. Arthur Pollock, "The Theater," *Brooklyn Daily Eagle,* 29 January 1935.
14. Brooks Atkinson, "The Play," *New York Times,* 29 January 1935.
15. Burns Mantle, ed., *The Best Plays of 1934–35* (New York: Dodd, Mead & Company, 1925), p. 445.
16. Percy Hammond, "The Theaters," *New York Herald Tribune,* 29 January 1935.
17. *The Ackerley Letters,* p. xxvii.
18. J. R. Ackerley, *My Father and Myself* (London: The Bodley Head, 1968).
19. J. R. Ackerley, *The Prisoners of War* (London: Chatto and Windus, 1935), p. 68.
20. *Ibid.,* p. 86.
21. *Ibid.,* p. 24.
22. *Ibid.*
23. *Ibid.,* p. 27.
24. *London Sunday Times,* 12 July 1935.
25. *The Prisoners of War,* p. 42.
26. *My Father and Myself,* p. 116.
27. *Ibid.*
28. *The Ackerley Letters,* p. 132.
29. *Ibid.*
30. *Ibid.*
31. *Ibid.,* pp. 112–113.
32. *New York Times,* 29 January 1935.
33. *Brooklyn Daily Eagle,* 29 January 1935.
34. "Prisoners of War," *Variety,* 5 February 1935.
35. *New York Herald Tribune,* 29 January 1935.
36. "Prisoners of War," *New York Journal American,* 29 January 1935.
37. *Ibid.*
38. Burns Mantle, "'Prisoners of War,' Aimless Drama," *New York Daily News,* 29 January 1935.
39. *London Sunday Times,* 12 July 1935.
40. *New York Herald Tribune,* 29 January 1935.
41. *The Prisoners of War,* p. 72.
42. John Mason Brown, "The Play," *New York Post,* 29 January 1935.
43. Percy Hammond, "The Theaters," *New York Herald Tribune,* 2 May 1935.
44. Robert Garland, "'Reprise' New Play At The Vanderbilt," *New York World Telegram,* 2 May 1935.
45. John Mason Brown, "The Play," *New York Post,* 2 May 1935.
46. Burns Mantle, ed., *The Best Plays of 1934–35* (New York: Dodd, Mead & Company, 1935), p. 476.
47. Brooks Atkinson, "The Play," *New York Times,* 2 May 1935.
48. John Anderson, "Reprise," *New York Evening Journal,* 2 May 1935.
49. Arthur Pollock, "The Theater," *Brooklyn Daily Eagle,* 2 May 1935.
50. *New York Post,* 2 May 1935.
51. "Rehearsals Today For 'Gibson Girls,'" *New York Times,* 26 October 1935.
52. W.A. Darlington, "A Well Acted Play," *London Daily Telegraph,* 18 February 1937.
53. "Wise Tomorrow," *Variety,* 10 March 1937.

54. Richard Lockridge, "The New Play," *New York Sun,* 15 October 1937.
55. John Anderson, "New Drama Strikes Old Sour Note," *New York Journal American,* 16 October 1937.
56. Robert Coleman, "Powys Play At Biltmore," *New York Daily Mirror,* 16 October 1937.
57. "Wise Tomorrow," *Variety,* 10 March 1937.
58. *Ibid.*
59. "Wise Tomorrow," *London Times,* 21 February 1937.
60. "Entertainments," *London Times,* 18 February 1937.
61. Burns Mantle, "'Wise Tomorrow' Is a Drama About a Couple of Harpies," *New York Daily News,* 16 October 1937.
62. Wilella Waldorf, "Edith Barett To Play A Role In 'Wise Tomorrow,'" *New York Post,* 17 September 1937.
63. "Powys Play In Baltimore," *New York Times,* 5 October 1937.
64. *Variety,* 10 March 1937.
65. John Mason Brown, "Two On The Aisle," *New York Post,* 16 October 1937.
66. Sidney B. Whipple, "Powys Brings A Play," *New York Tribune,* 16 October 1937.
67. Richard Watts, Jr., "The Theaters," *New York Herald Tribune,* 16 October 1937.
68. Brooks Atkinson, "The Play," *New York Times,* 16 October 1937.
69. Robert Francis, "The Theater," *Brooklyn Daily Eagle,* 16 October 1937; *New York Daily News,* 16 October 1937.
70. Burns Mantle, "'Winter Bound' Agitates Suspicions," *New York Daily News,* 23 November 1937.
71. *New York Daily News,* 16 October 1937.
72. *New York Journal American,* 16 October 1937.
73. "Wise Tomorrow," *Variety,* 16 October 1937.
74. Robert Coleman, "Powys Play At Biltmore," *New York Daily Mirror,* 16 October 1937.
75. *Variety,* 10 March 1937.
76. *New York World-Telegram,* 16 October 1937.
77. "Wise Tomorrow," *Variety,* 18 October 1937.
78. *New York Herald Tribune,* 16 October 1937.
79. "Love of Women," *Variety,* 15 December 1937.
80. Brooks Atkinson, "The Play," *New York Times,* 14 December 1937.
81. Robert Coleman, "Love of Women," *New York Daily Mirror,* 14 December 1937.
82. John Anderson, "'Love of Women' Debuts at John Golden Theatre," *New York Sun,* 14 December 1937.
83. *Variety,* 15 December 1937.
84. Robert Francis, "The Theater," *Brooklyn Daily Eagle,* 14 December 1937.
85. Burns Mantle, ed., *The Best Plays of 1937–38* (New York: Dodd, Mead & Company, 1938), p. 402.
86. John Mason Brown, "Two On The Aisle," *New York Post,* 14 December 1937.
87. *Ibid.*
88. *Ibid.*
89. Richard Lockridge, "The New Play," *New York Sun,* 14 December 1937.
90. Richard Watts, Jr., "The Theaters," *New York Herald Tribune,* 14 December 1937.
91. *Ibid.*
92. *New York Times,* 14 December 1937.
93. *Brooklyn Daily Eagle,* 14 December 1937.
94. *New York Journal-American,* 14 December 1937.
95. *Ibid.*
96. *New York Post,* 14 December 1937.
97. *New York Daily Mirror,* 14 December 1937.
98. *Ibid.*

13

Oscar Wilde's Ghost
Conjured Up Upon the Broadway Stage

It was as if the New York penal code forbidding the appearance of sexual deviants in plays had been rescinded when Governor Lehman vetoed the Dunnigan Bill in the spring of 1937: in the last third of the decade, six shows with gay characters appeared on Broadway. Lehman's veto had apparently dampened the ardor of the Catholic clergy, who had instigated the Dunnigan Bill.

Nor did any of the "Comstockians" decry the theatrical violations of the New York law. William Randolph Hearst remained understandably silent on the liberties taken by certain playwrights. Near bankruptcy, Hearst had relinquished control of his publishing empire to the banks in 1937. He stopped his moralizing editorials protesting the inactivity of the District Attorney, the Commissioner of Licenses and the Chief of Police. Vacillating George Jean Nathan, whose critique was cited to justify the police raid on *The Captive* in 1927, was, a decade later, ridiculing moralists still protesting the inclusion of lesbian and gay male roles in Broadway plays.[1]

Four of the six plays in the 1930s with gay motifs or characters did not last long enough to test the tolerance of the establishment. *Oscar Wilde,* the last of these shows, was a sensational critical and commercial success in 1938. Before it had conjured up the ghost of that most famous, and most tragic, of gay poet-playwrights, Manhattan theatergoers saw three other unexpected gay characterizations. One was a degenerate Nazi created by an American playwright who was passing on to the American public the homophobic propaganda of Paul Joseph Goebbels. In one of the other two plays, a teenager escapes his troubled, unsympathetic parents by running away with his lover. In the second play, starring Ethel Barrymore, another teenager inherits a considerable fortune, allowing him to escape his hateful family and study abroad.

"Ethel Barrymore Triumphs in Matriarch Role at Hudson,"[2] reported the *World-Telegram* on March 24, 1938, the morning after Barrymore appeared as the 101-year-old woman in *Whiteoaks* by Mazo de La Roache. The playwright adapted her play from her novel *Whiteoaks of Jalna.* According to *Variety,* "tryout showings in Canada, the drama's setting, were well supported. Play clicked on the London stage, too."[3] A modest success at the Hudson Theatre on Broadway with 104 performances,[4] Barrymore's performance was far more appreciated than de La Roache's playscript. Burns Mantle gave this brief synopsis of *Whiteoaks:*

> Gran Whiteoak, still alive and active at 101, is completely aware of the subtle scheming many of her relatives are doing in the hope of being named in her will. Her interest in the career of the least stable of her grandchildren, young Finch, who would devote his life to a study of music, is stimulated by visits with that young man. The old lady makes Finch her heir, causing considerable consternation when she dies.[5]

Complaining that "so much of the boy's character and problem is left out," critic Arthur Pollock still detected "a hint ... that Finch has fallen among evil companions, such young men as write love letters to each other. That is not gone into."[6] Richard Watts, Jr., thought the closeted character "might have been psychoanalyzed."[7] *Variety* called him "an almost pathological case."[8]

The three children and five grandchildren of old Ma Whiteoaks are a dull, mercenary lot. They typify Toronto's "horsey upper-middle class," except for Finch. Sidney B. Whipple observed:

> Finch is a musician and, externally, at least, a weakling. How far the mass persecution of the others may have beaten him into a sort of pulp of effeminacy and how much of it is congenital is a question, but it is there, as is demonstrated when the brothers (smelling strongly of dogs

and horses, no doubt) discover a letter, couched in terms of endearment, that has been sent to him by a friend named Arthur.[9]

Finch drops the letter, which is picked up by his brother Piers, Finch's habitual tormentor. Renny, an older brother whom Finch adores, has been asking him where he spent the night:

> *Piers.* A letter of yours, eh? Listen to this Renny! "Darling Finch." My God! That this sort of muck should be written to a brother of mine! Here, Renny, read it yourself. Who the hell is Arthur?
> *Finch.* He's a friend of mine; he helps me with my music.
> *Renny. (after reading the letter).* I'm disgusted with you!
> *(Finch feels annihilated. His face is drawn.)*
> *Finch.* I don't understand!
> *Piers.* He doesn't understand.
> *Renny.* Do you know what this leads to?
> *Finch.* To the orchestra?
> *Renny.* No, not the orchestra! *(Striking the letter.)* I'd rather find you spent last night in a brothel than to find you carrying that sloppy letter about! *(He tosses the letter into the fireplace.).* .[10]

Renny warns his younger brother to stay away from Arthur, and the subject never comes up again. At the play's end, Finch announces that he is going off to Europe to pursue his musical ambitions as soon as he comes into his grandmother's great fortune. Finch is the very first gay character on the English-speaking stage who is rewarded, rather than punished or condemned, for being different: "I know you're a queer boy," Ma Whiteoaks tells her grandson, "but I like you — yes, I like you very much."[11]

During the same year, 1938, another unhappy teenager escaped his oppressive surroundings in Chester Erskin's *The Good*. This drama, with as much suffering as is generally found in a popular soap opera, left the critics uniformly unenthusiastic. *The Good* appeared at the Windsor Theatre for only nine performances.[12] Erskin handled the subject of gay emotional and possible sexual involvement explicitly and sympathetically. More significantly, the attachment involved two gay males. The couple in *The Good* feel neither shame nor guilt; on the contrary, one character defends his orientation in the face of physical violence.

John Anderson said *The Good* concerned "the evil that a good and pious woman may do."[13] Burns Mantle observed that "Harriet, like her minister father before her, is a hard, unyielding, and thoroughly 'good' person who would hold all her neighbors to a strict accounting of the moral laws."[14] During the course of the play, the audience learns that the frigid woman drove her bitter, frustrated husband to find comfort in a mistress's arms. She also pushed a young Jewish boy to suicide because of her lack of compassion for the failings of others. She is held responsible — in part by the author and in whole by some of the critics — for overprotecting and emasculating her own child. "Her coldness," Burns Mantle concluded, "drives her sensitive son into an abnormal friendship with a choir master."[15] Brooks Atkinson blamed her for "the homosexual practices of her son."[16]

In the first act, the author describes Howard as "a slender, sensitive looking lad, about sixteen or so. An emotional boy. Earnest. Sincere. Gentle."[17] The choir master, Francis Duncan, is "a trim, well-built man somewhere in his thirties. He is a man of culture and education. A quick and alert mind. A complete absence of the flamboyance usually found in men of his type."[18] The man and boy have only one scene together in the play during which, *Variety* reported, "Conversation between them clearly indicates an unnatural affection."[19] The choir master's "attitude toward Howard is wholly sincere and honest,"[20] according to the stage directions. The teenager is emotional and rash, anxious to escape his loveless home and his artistically stifling hometown:

> *Howard (sudddenly in a burst of emotion).* Francis, let's not wait any longer! Let's run away from here. You and I, tonight! Let's start to do all the things we've planned to do.[21]

The choir master is a cautious, calm and steady man. He wants Howard to finish his senior year of high school and go on to college:

> *Mr. Duncan.* Howard! Please, you're making things so difficult, we must be patient. That's part of our understanding. Isn't it? We've so much ahead of us, we can afford to wait a while, can't we? Think of our whole lives full of adventure and excitement and all the things we've planned. You don't want to throw them up just for a silly mood, do you? We've so much to gain, what do a few months, or even a few years matter?[22]

Duncan is aware that Howard has been unusually unsettled since he went to the family doctor for a physical earlier that day. Howard admits that at Dr. Ten Broek's "something happened." Duncan immediately suspects the worst:

> *Mr. Duncan (tensely).* You didn't tell him?
> *Howard.* I didn't have to. He told me.
> *Mr. Duncan.* Oh, God! Howard! Oh, God! That was a terrible thing! Why didn't you tell me?
> *Howard.* I am telling you.
> *Mr. Duncan (a little frantic).* A terrible thing. You should have told me right away. You denied it, of course.[25]

> *Howard (looking at him strangely).* No, I didn't. I thought it was a senseless thing to do. I told him the truth, I'm not ashamed of us, so I told him the truth.
> *Mr. Duncan;.* You told him about me, too?
> *Howard.* He guessed.[23]

Duncan is deeply distressed at Howard's guilelessness, but Howard is convinced as the first act ends that professional ethics will keep the confession safe.

In Act Two, Howard has confrontational scenes with both his mother and father exploring their strained relationships. Duncan has sent a dozen roses to Howard's mother with a note apologizing for having taken so much of her son's time. In a scene very reminiscent of the flower-arranging scene in *The Green Bay Tree,* Howard insists on arranging the roses, fussing over the length of the stems and being very particular about the color of vase he selects.

When the boy's father comes home, he notices the roses and is openly contemptuous that the arrangement is so exotic. He complains that his son never played baseball as a boy. Howard blames his mother's overprotectiveness as well as his own lack of physical coordination. Attempting to establish some sort of rapport with his scholarly, artistic son with whom he has never been comfortable, the father admits to writing poetry, but only once: when he was infatuated with a girl. He warns his son not to take poetry too much to heart.

Walter Winchell reported in the *Daily Mirror:*

> Mr. Erskin, in a sentence, offers a pale, male version of *The Captive* . . . [T]he outstanding scene, perhaps, arrives just before the second act curtain descends when the family doctor tells Malcom and Harriet Eldred . . . that their 17 year old son is abnormal and that there is no hope for him. . .[24]

Dr. Ten Broek. A type, both of them. A baffling type.[25]

Enraged to hear their son's friendship with a man twice his age described by the doctor as "unnatural," the couple turn in frustration on one another. Malcom blames Harriet for overprotecting the boy, while she blames him for rejecting Howard. In a screaming rage, the father announces that he is going to find and kill the man who ruined his son. Howard overhears the raucous scene in the living room and comes downstairs to defend his lover. Beside himself with revulsion, Mr. Eldred strikes his son, throwing the teenager to the floor.

In a later scene, Howard turns to his mother for help:

Howard. Will you defend me against them? Will you? Will you tell them you were wrong and that I'm right. Will you do that? No, you can't. You believe what they do too.
Mrs. Eldred. No matter what I believe, I want to help you.
Howard. You couldn't. There's no changing me. I told you that. I'm not so sure I'd want to if I could. From one ugliness to another. It's all vulgar. The whole of life. Vulgar and stupid...[26]

In the last scene, Mrs. Eldred learns about an abortion her husband's mistress had, and is blamed for driving the Jewish boy to suicide. She finds solace only in having a son whom she hopes will someday become a Protestant minister, like her late father. Her embittered husband informs her, however, that Howard has run away with Duncan.

No longer as revolted by gay roles as most had been just eleven years before when Mae West's *The Drag* was kept out of town, some of the reviewers credited the performances by actors playing gay men for making *The Good* tolerable. "Jarvis Rice and Eric Kalkhurst, as the homosexuals," reported the *Daily Worker,* "were able to spare the audience as much embarrassment as possible."[27] Brooks Atkinson, too, praised Rice for managing "to make something palatable of the unsavory character of the abnormal son."[28] Sidney Whipple added his appreciation of Rice in his column for playing "the part of the confused young man without making it offensive."[29]

Despite his plaudit for the performer, Whipple was the only reviewer who still objected to the inclusion of a gay character in a play. He protested:

It has always been my belief, or prejudice if you will, that explorations into the field of abnormal sexual psychology were better left to the scientific world and not forced upon the public ... This is not prudery,

In the 1938 flop Waltz in Goose Step, *Henry Oscar played a role based on the characters of two of Hitler's earliest gay supporters, Nazi Captain Ernst Roehm and clownish Munich millionaire Putzi Hanfstaengel. Leo Chalzel portrayed a Hitler-like leader who offered the drama's despicable gay protagonist a chance to commit suicide after he failed to organize a* putsch.

human abnormalities are subjects for serious and sincere study. Public demonstration of them becomes dangerous in two phases — when they are burlesqued and when they are exposed for the satisfactions of morbid and unthinking curiosity.

...I think it is a futile, disappointing, inconclusive attempt to drag certain case histories from Krafft-Ebing or Havelock Ellis before the footlights...[30]

Despite Whipple's warning that it was dangerous to display case histories of "human abnormalities," two plays, based on the case histories of internationally known gay personalities, were produced before the end of the decade. One failed, but the other was a great critical and popular success. Ernst Röhm, one of Adolph Hitler's earliest supporters and the founder of the National Socialist Militia, provided the inspiration for the failure: Oliver H.P. Garrett's portrait of a diabolical gay Nazi in *Waltz in Goose Step*. Garrett had been a New York newspaperman turned Hollywood scenarist. Despite the fact that the drama was staged by Arthur Hopkins, considered one of America's most accomplished directors, *Waltz in Goose Step* was a flop.

Four years before Garrett's drama was staged, Nazi captain Ernst Röhm was arrested with several of his officers in a small vacation resort near Munich. Richard Plant, a historian of one of the lesser-known atrocities of the Nazi regime, the extermination of countless gays throughout Europe, describes the arrest of Röhm, a man Plant describes as "a 'butch lover' of handsome boys"[31]:

...A few SS bullies stormed into the hotel in the early morning hours, broke down the doors, arresting everyone. SA General Edmund Heines, Röhm's ally, was allegedly found in bed with a young SA man. Neither Röhm nor any of the SA men knew why they were arrested and put into prison. Heines and a few others were machine-gunned right away; Röhm, invited to shoot himself, refused and was killed a few days later by a special extermination squad.[32]

Röhm was so powerful at the time of his murder that he posed a threat to Göring, Goebbels and Himmler with whom he has political differences. According to Plant, in order to explain Röhm's death,

...Goebbels had concocted a cover story: not only had Röhm schemed up a putsch to overthrow the Führer, but his moral conduct had become unacceptable to true Swastika standards. Therefore, Hitler himself had stormed into the rooms of Röhm and Heines, disarmed and arrested them single-handedly. Hitler was so shocked by the depraved scene he uncovered, he ordered "the ruthless extermination of this pestilent tumor." Since the putsch story didn't go over well — how could the SA have planned it when most of them were on vacation — Goebbels stressed "the homosexual horror."[33]

Newspaperman Garrett had obviously been familiar with Goebbels' propaganda releases when he sat down to write this anti-Nazi and anti-gay *Waltz in Goose Step*.

"For the the first half of its First Act, I would have sworn that Mr. Garrett had written the inevitable play about the Nazis," critic John Anderson wrote, "but after that it veered off into a fragile and rather foolish little melodrama, concerning not Der Führer so much as the effeminate leader of what I suppose you could call the Lavender Shirts."[34]

Waltz in Goose Step begins in the interior cabin of a private plane used by August, a character called The Leader, as his flying office. The hysterical, clownish madman is "returning without shame," as John Mason Brown recognized, "from such a bloody expedition as the Röhm Purge represented."[35] The pilot of the plane becomes very upset upon learning how the Leader slaughtered a faction of his followers called the Blue Shirts. He holds his passengers at gunpoint and threatens to crash the plane:

Straub. ...you shot them down like dogs. Unarmed men. Your own friends.[36]

The angry, almost hysterical pilot is finally placated by the drama's anti-heroic protagonist, Count Gottfried von Laidi, one of The Leader's top two accomplices. The Count asks the mutinous young man:

Von Laidi. What would you say if I told you they were a perverted little clique—[37]

Von Laidi enrages The Leader, already suspicious of him, when he attempts to hide a locket on his person that he had taken from the corpse of a young man named Tony, slaughtered in the purge. Von Laidi, who ghoulishly licks Tony's dried blood from his fingers, admits that he had given it to the youth, and simply wanted it back.

The second and third acts take place in Von Laidi's sumptuous apartment suite. Although the playwright never identified Von Laidi's depraved existence as a gay lifestyle, most of the critics called the Count "effeminate." Some, like Richard Watts, Jr., were even more specific, categorizing him as a "sardonic, cultured, piano-playing homosexual."[38] Watts continued, "He might be a proper character in a Noel Coward social drama, but is an ineffective focal point for the burning indignation of Mr. Garrett's editorial thesis."[39] Even though Von Laidi is a treacherous, despicable Machiavellian, John Anderson also saw him as "a Noel Coward character playing with perfumed firecrackers."[40]

The evening after the mass slaughter of the Blue Shirts, Heit, their former commander, visits Von Laidi in his apartment. An intimate of the Count's, and of the same sexual persuasion, Heit is on the run. Saved from being cut down with the others in his command by an anonymous tip, which he learns came from Von Laidi, Heit rages at the Count for not also saving Tony, the youth they had both known intimately. The fugitive loved the youth, whom Von Laidi speaks contemptuously of as a waterfront hustler. The Count blames Tony for tipping off the Leader to their planned *putsch*.

Von Laidi refuses to help save Heit from August and his henchmen who are combing the city for him. The Count explains:

Von Laidi (Flinging the homosexual's worst insult). You bore me![41]

Before The Leader and his lieutenants come bursting into the room, the Count tells Heit where he can find a gun in his bedroom as he flees. The Blue Shirt Commander is gunned down as he is going down the rear staircase of the residence. Von Laidi denies ownership of the weapon found on the dead man, realizing that once that is established, he will be doomed. August realizes that the effeminate Count was one of the conspirators in the Blue Shirts' plot to assassinate him. To cover up his involvement in the plot, Von Laidi informed on his co-conspirators, and then, as head of the Secret Police, planned their execution in a surprise attack.

Von Laidi is unsuccessful at enlisting August's disgruntled mistress, and a dissident group of religious and political activists in a new plot. When finally arrested, the Count is given an opportunity to kill himself; the same opportunity that was given to Ernst Röhm. He is too cowardly to commit suicide, but is gladly shot by his former valet, whom he has betrayed along with everybody else. "The Von Laidi,"

Burns Mantle observed, "should you miss the suggestion in the name, is a rather precious person who is fierce enough to bite his hangnails but not his enemies."[42]

According to *Variety*, Von Laidi was "a thinly disguised prototype of Putzi Hanfstängel," and August's mistress, "a thinly disguised Leni Riefenstahl, ex-actress, and now head of Germany's film industry."[43] Hanfstängel was one of Hitler's earliest financial backers, and one of the first members of the upper class to support him politically. Like Von Laidi, the clownish Munich millionaire played the piano and was shallow, eccentric and sardonic,[44] so Garrett's creation was a composite of both Röhm and of Hanfstängel, whose piano playing often placated Hitler.

Variety gave a plot outline of *Waltz in Goose Step* which more closely follows Goebbels' version of the Röhm affair than was reported by the first-night critics. According to a typewritten script used for the Broadway production,[45] Von Laidi is executed by his ex-butler. *Variety* reported another ending that may have been seen in rehearsals before cuts and changes were made eliminating material that would have provoked the police or politicians. According to the trade paper, The Leader warns Von Laidi at the end of the first act, after they talk the pilot out of killing them, "to keep his hands off the good-looking kid."[46] The play ended, when *Variety*'s reviewer saw it, when "the kid is killed along with Von Laidi when the dictator breaks in and catches them together,"[47] just as Hitler was supposed to have caught Röhm according to Goebbels' fabricated report.[48]

"*Waltz in Goose Step* is stale stuff destined for immediate failure,"[49] Walter Winchell accurately predicted in the *Daily Mirror*. Arthur Hopkins' production of *Waltz in Goose Step* lasted only seven performances[50] at the Hudson Theatre during the first week of November 1938. Never before nor since have Broadway audiences seen a more despicable, depraved gay male characterization than that of Count Von Laidi.

That very same season, other audiences saw a most sympathetic portrait of a tragic gay figure. The playwrights, Leslie and Sewell Stokes, used their research for *Oscar Wilde* far more credibly than Garrett used the anti-gay propaganda of the Nazis in *Waltz in Goose Step*.

Edmond Rostand's son, Maurice, had written a play about Oscar Wilde that managing director Norman Marshall planned to produce in

Robert Morley was voted the season's best actor by the drama critics for his performance in the title role of the 1938 Broadway hit Oscar Wilde. *In one scene of the British import, foolhardy Wilde, who dared to be uninhibitedly gay in Victorian London, went out on the town with a stable-boy hustler played by John Carol.*

1936 at the Gate Theatre, a 200-seat private playhouse in London whose programs did not come under the jurisdiction of the Lord Chamberlain. It was at the Gate — whose audiences were made up "mostly of barristers and doctors,"[51] — that American plays such as *The Children's Hour* were first produced in London, for runs limited by law to only six weeks.

Oscar Wilde's most intimate friend, Lord Alfred Douglas, whose father brought about the playwright's downfall, was still alive in the 1930s. After reading Rostand's playscript, Douglas was so distressed, he considered suing for libel:

> I intervened and objected to the production. My objection, as I explained it to Mr. Marshall, ... was simply because Monsieur Rostand's play was a travesty of the truth and a deliberate misrepresentation of well-known and often recorded facts.
> ...The whole idea of Rostand's play was based on the false assumption that I had never seen or spoken to Oscar Wilde again after he came out of prison.[52]

The wealthy English nobleman had, in fact, housed Wilde at his villa in Naples for several months and had seen him constantly for three years in Paris, but Wilde's estranged wife and Douglas's mother threatened to cut off their allowances if they ever lived together. Wilde's friend supplied him with money and paid for his funeral at which he was the chief mourner.

The Rostand production was cancelled, but the manager-director of the subscription playhouse still felt the time was right for a dramatization of Wilde's tragedy. According to Sewell Stokes:

> Norman Marshall suggested to my brother Leslie and myself that we write a play about Oscar Wilde for his Gate Theatre...
> After we read together everything written on the subject of Wilde, and came to the inevitable conclusion that the dramatist, apart altogether from the scandal of which he became the center, was a very great wit, and a very great gentleman ... We went to see Lord Alfred Douglas ... and the play was based largely upon evidence which he very kindly placed before us. Rather inaccurately, several persons have declared the play to be based on Frank Harris's celebrated "Life" of Wilde.[53]

Douglas was pleased with the work the Sewell brothers had done for the Gate Theatre. "I agreed at once to its performance, with a few minor alterations in the text," the poet wrote. "As it now stands it represents an historically true story, allowing, of course, for dramatic license."[54]

Actor Robert Morley, newly successful as a playwright, was not particularly keen about playing the title role that was to make him a star on both sides of the Atlantic. According to an American interviewer for *Colliers* magazine:

> When *Oscar Wilde* was being cast, producer and playwrights sent for Morley, thinking that at least he'd be delighted at a chance to try for the part. He wasn't but he agreed just out of a genial desire to help them out in a tight spot, but he felt rather doubtful about the whole thing.[55]

Morley's stunning performance became the talk of London, despite the cool reception accorded the play by the *London Times*. "Upon Wilde the artist the play has no comment of importance to make, and of Wilde the man it merely relates what were best forgotten."[56] The *London Daily Telegraph* also attempted to dismiss the play, reporting that *"Oscar Wilde* which the Gate Theatre studio presented last night, left a slight unpleasant taste in one's mouth."[57] Playwright Sewell Stokes remembered similar reactions from the British public. "In England," he said, "when we did *Oscar Wilde* in 1936 at the Gate Theatre, anyone you mentioned the play to would simply lift an eyebrow and murmur 'Do you really think it's wise to write a play about Wilde?'"[58]

The Stokes brothers begin their drama, which has been published by Random House,[59] on the terrace of an elegant hotel in Algiers in 1895 where the thirty-nine-year-old Wilde and his twenty-year-old protégé, Lord Alfred Douglas, are vacationing. There are no explicit references to their lifestyle other than that Wilde delights in roaming the streets throwing money to the Algerian boys. The dialogue sparkles with Wilde's witty epigrams, which were taken from his writings. There is an ominous threat which Wilde takes lightly at the end of the first scene of Act One, when a letter arrives for young Douglas. His father, whom he claims is mad, has written forbidding him to stay with the famous poet and playwright.

The second scene takes place in a private room of London restaurant. Wilde arrives after the triumphant premiere of *The Importance of Being Earnest*. In the same evening that he has become the toast of London, he has been insulted by the eccentric Marquis of

Queensbury, Douglas's father, who brought a bouquet of vegetables to the premiere to present to the playwright. Wilde is unperturbed by a warning, given to him by his friend, the London editor, Frank Harris, that rumors about his scandalous, unconventional lifestyle might be used by his enemies to hurt him. The scene ends with the blithe and foolhardy celebrity dancing out of the room with a teenage Cockney stable boy named Charlie Parker, whom he had invited to join him for an after-the-theater supper.

Wilde's study is the setting for the third scene of the first act. Again Frank Harris advises Wilde to be more circumspect. The editor is appalled that the playwright is mixed up in a family feud, suing Queensbury, with young Douglas's encouragement, for having written that Wilde "poses as a sodomite."[59] After Harris's departure, Wilde cleverly gets back a compromising letter he wrote to Douglas by outwitting rather than paying a blackmailer.

Both scenes of the second act take place in the Old Bailey Courthouse in London with Wilde in the witness box. Carson, Queensbury's defense attorney, cross-examines Wilde about his numerous relationships with working-class young men to whom he has given presents and money. He had taken one on a trip to Paris. In the exchange, taken verbatim from excerpts of the actual trial in 1895, Wilde replies as frivolously and flippantly as the characters usually do in his comedies. One such flip reply compromises him. Quizzing him about one young man, Queensbury's barrister asks:

Carson. Did you ever kiss him?
Wilde. Oh, dear no, he was a peculiarly plain boy, he was. Unfortunately, extremely ugly. I pitied him for it.
Carson. Was that the reason you did not kiss him?[60]

Aware of the implications of his reply, Wilde suddenly becomes flustered, apologizing for his flippant manner. He loses his composure and become tongue-tied as the lawyer hammers relentlessly at his witness for having mentioned that the boy was ugly. There is a blackout.

When the lights come up:

The Judge. I shall have to tell the jury that justification was proved, and that it was true in substance and fact that the prosecutor had "posed as a sodomite." *(The Judge raps with his gavel.)* I must add that in view of the evidence which has come to light it will be my duty to send the papers in the case to the Public Prosecutor. Gentlemen of the jury — your verdict will be — not guilty.

CURTAIN[61]

In the second scene of the second act, Wilde is being tried for sodomy. After one of his friends, nineteen-year-old Charlie Parker, appears as a witness for the prosecution, Wilde is back in the witness box, this time to be interrogated by the Solicitor-General. He is doomed before he defends himself because of the teenager's testimony.

In the last act of *Oscar Wilde,* the playwright is a broken man after spending two years at hard labor. In the first scene, at his house in Chelsea, Wilde comes home to find some loyal friends waiting to greet him. He has decided that he must have a new name for his new life. He hopes to call himself Sebastian Melmoth. Within minutes after he is back home, whatever optimism he has been able to muster in facing the world again is shattered when he learns that his request to spend time at a Catholic retreat has been rejected:

> *Wilde. (Takes the letter and crumbles it in his hand.)* They won't receive me. Even they won't receive me. *(He sinks into the packing box.)* I thought my punishment was ended. It has just begun.[62]

Wilde is last seen in a small café in Paris. He has turned to heavy drinking and is in need of money since he survives on a very meager allowance from his estranged wife. Frank Harris pays the waiter what Wilde owes the café and Lord Alfred Douglas drops by to leave some money for him. All alone and half drunk Wilde calls to the waiter just before the curtain comes down:

> *Wilde.* Waiter! Ask the orchestra to play something gay.
> *Waiter.* Something gay? Oui, M'sieur.[63]

Not surprisingly, Lord Alfred Douglas was pleased with the production at the Gate Theatre. He said:

> I could have wished that poor Wilde had not been shown in the last act drunk on the stage. On the other hand, it is idle to deny that he was drunk, on occasions, at that period of his life ... I did not see the play myself, because I thought that it would be too painful for me ... I am glad to know from the evidence of numerous people who witnessed it that it aroused great sympathy for a man whom I consider to have been

cruelly and unjustly treated ... Let England bear the responsibility for what she did to him.[64]

Frustrated by the Lord Chamberlain's power over the British stage, the proprietor of the Gate Theatre, Norman Marshall, turned to the New York stage where *The Children's Hour* had not stirred up any censorship threats. Calling the American theater "the 'white hope' of the English stage," Marshall told an interviewer:

> The latitude permitted on the American legitimate stage ... is a tremendous tonic to the English theater. By latitude, I don't mean promiscuous indulgence in bad taste, but rather the tolerance of political and social themes which are impossible under the regulations and traditions as they are in the English theater...
>
> In the United States you are singularly fortunate in your type of theater audience whose general sophistication and knowledge of the world make any form of censorship unnecessary.[65]

In deciding to put up the money for a Broadway production of *Oscar Wilde,* Marshall's silent American partner Gilbert Miller knew from a bad experience that the American stage was not as safe from censorship as the English producer supposed. The *Daily News* revealed that:

> Although Gilbert Miller has a financial interest in the successful *Oscar Wilde,* it is reported that he is being meticulously careful about allowing his name to be officially mentioned. Mr. Miller thought, before the play was produced, that there may be some hue and cry as there was years ago when he produced *The Captive* which was ultimately closed by the courts.[66]

Gilbert Miller's fears proved unfounded. Except for a rather humorous incident, nothing was heard during the play's run from the individuals and pressure groups who provoked the police raid on *The Captive.* Only the United States Navy took exception to *Oscar Wilde,* over a single reference that made some service-connected men uncomfortable. "Quip Out" reported the *World Telegram:*

> A second look at *Oscar Wilde* revealed that the one loud gaffaw in the script has been deleted. In the trial scene, a stable boy, one of Oscar Wilde's protégés turned witness for the prosecution, testified opening night that he had given up the friendship of his strange benefactor and joined the navy.
>
> Some Navy League or other requested the trim. It was made,

though playwright Sewell Stokes cannot understand why it offended "intellectual" New Yorkers, since it concerns the British Navy and thirty years ago.[67]

Walter Winchell reported, "The first night audience may have witnessed theatrical history, at any rate, all of them were spellbound by a fine document, consummately interpreted by a masterful cast. A typically blasé first-night carriage trade attendance voted it about ten curtain calls."[68]

The *New Yorker* hailed *Oscar Wilde,* which opened at the Fulton October 19, 1938, as an "astonishingly successful attempt to bring the fanciest of all literary figures to life. Heartily recommended, especially for Robert Morley's impressive performance."[69] The same magazine's first-night critic, Wolcott Gibbs, added, "By sticking respectfully to their sources, the authors, Leslie and Sewell Stokes, have succeeded in showing us a traditional wit who is actually witty and a psychopath who is pitiable, but neither is comic or embarrassing."[70]

"There is no smutty leering," John Anderson assured his readers, "nor any attempt to capitalize on the abnormality of a perverted genius."[71]

"A very sad story," the *Christian Science Monitor* reported. "The authors treat it and Wilde with the greatest gentleness, asking their hearers to pity above all."[72] With the single exception of Richard Lockridge, who dismissed *Oscar Wilde* as "almost overpoweringly unimportant,"[73] the British production was enthusiastically welcomed by the critics of New York's eight dailies and played 274 performances[74] on Broadway prior to a successful eight-week engagement in Los Angeles.

While *Oscar Wilde* was one of a number of hit dramatic shows of the 1938–39 New York theatrical season, Robert Morley's acting was the single most impressive performance seen on Broadway during that period. The critics for the New York dailies and Gibbs of the *New Yorker* voted Morley the season's best actor.[75] Five of the first-nighters used the adjective "brilliant" to describe the Englishman's impersonation.

John Mason Brown reported, "Both actor and play came in on gumshoes, but on the following morning the air was filled with the critics' hats." One reviewer said, "For all I know, the audience at the

Fulton Theater may still be cheering Robert Morley."[76]

"Such an ovation as Mr. Morley received has not been heard this season," Brown noted.[77] The *Post* reviewer left us this appraisal of Morley's work:

> His assignment is not an easy one. It is fraught with uncommmon dangers. One false step, one gesture that went too far, and the very precarious subject of homosexuality with which the Stokeses deal would become objectionable. But Mr. Morley avoids every pitfall into which a less sensitive actor might have ben led.
> ...His is no static creation depending upon its uncanny resemblance to Wilde's photographs ... he suggests Wilde in the full arrogance of his wit, in the collapse of his self-confidence, and the pathetic stupor of his final days in Paris.[78]

Oscar Wilde brought overnight stardom to another actor. In 1940, Laird Cregar played Wilde at the El Capitan Theater in Hollywood. "The first-night audience went commendably ga-ga over the performance," reported the *Herald-Tribune*.[79] As a result, Cregar was signed to a studio contract and zoomed to motion picture stardom. In London, Francis Sullivan also did the title role in a revival at another private playhouse, the Arts Theater,[80] just days after the play proved such a box office sensation on Broadway.

Three years after *Oscar Wilde* completed its financially lucrative Broadway run, Gilbert Miller ran into trouble because of his connection with the play, but not from the police or pressure groups. *Variety* reported:

> Frank Harris's widow was awarded $57,767.36 as a result of the infringement of copyright by the 1938 hit play *Oscar Wilde* which ran 40 weeks in New York and eight in Los Angeles ... estimated profits were around $75,000 ... since the author and Marshall ... are not in this country, it looks as if he [Gilbert Miller] is left holding the bag."[81]

Recalling the press's hysteria of the last decade over Mae West's Broadway shows, one can only wonder at the reception accorded the Stokeses' drama. The change is apparent in the variety of reactions of the New York drama critics.

Sidney Whipple of the *World-Telegram* confessed:

> Plays dealing with deviations from normal relationships between humans generally leave me either in a state of anger or nausea. This one doesn't, first because it is excellently written, second because it shows a

shrewd appreciation of the psychology involved in the case, third because it is neither sly nor vicious.[82]

Richard Watts admitted,

> Theatrical exhibits on such a theme are generally embarrassing to watch, [but] even its detractors could hardly call it an immoral play, since the central character certainly suffers bitterly for his sins even though he doesn't repent them.[83]

Burns Mantle wrote,

> I question the wisdom of doing the play at all, but I admit freely that it has been well done. Wilde, to Morley, and to the dramatists who have written of him, Leslie and Sewell Stokes, is an unfortuante genius against whom the cards are stacked. Not by man, but by Nature."[84]

Two of the most prestigious critics were still using language that had been in more widespread use in reviews of *The Captive* and *The Drag*. Brooks Atkinson, of the *Times,* in two separate critiques of *Oscar Wilde* referred contemptuously to the playwright's courtroom ordeal as "unsavory,"[85] a "malodorous scandal,"[86] and a "ghastly case.'"[87] Atkinson called Wilde's homosexuality a "disease,"[88] "squalid,"[89] and "pathological infirmities."[90] Describing the Stokeses' drama as enjoying "the fetid odor of one of the world's most pitiful dramas,"[91] Atkinson held — as his colleague Richard Watts, Jr. pointed out — "that a play about Wilde should not be presented because it can only bring additional contempt and opprobrium upon an unhappy man of genius who suffered enough in his time."[92]

George Jean Nathan did an about-face on the appropriateness of gay themes and characterizations as subject matter for dramatization. Differing with Atkinson on the issue, Nathan still shared with the *Times'* reviewer similar sentiments concerning gay men:

> Leslie and Sewell Stokes's *Oscar Wilde,* another English importation, aroused a degree of moral mortification in certain quarters because it treated, naturally and obviously enough, with homosexuals.
> To write a play about Oscar and leave out homosexuality would plainly be like writing a play about Florence Nightingale and putting it in. But, aside from the moral aspect of the thing, the point, argued the sensitive ones, is that the spectacle of male phoebes is offensive, distasteful and disgusting.
> This seems to me to be defective criticism. That the sons of swish

may not *in facie curiae* constitute an endearing picture, it takes no heated argument with the bartender to prove. But in a world drama that has freely presented almost every other form of abnormal and perverted humanity, most often without objection, they may — if treated honestly and without cheap sensationalism — be allowed their clinical place. In *Oscar Wilde* they are treated thus frankly, honestly and with no attempt to cheap sensationalism, and it is the rankest kind of hypocrisy to protest against their presentation. If they are, as the moralists insist, offensive, distasteful and disgusting, that is the moralists' business. But it has nothing to do with their dramatic validity or the validity of the playwrights' effort and purpose.[93]

However mortified the aforementioned moralists may have been, they were strangely mute throughout *Oscar Wilde's* extensive, highly praised and publicized Broadway engagement.

Notes

1. George Jean Nathan, undated, untitled magazine article from unknown publication in *Oscar Wilde* file, Lincoln Center.
2 Sidney B. Whipple, "Ethel Barrymore Triumphs in Matriarch Role At Hudson," *New York World-Telegram,* 24 March 1938.
3. Ibee., "Whiteoaks," *Variety,* 30 March 1938.
4. Burns Mantle, ed., *The Best Plays of 1937-38* (New York: Dodd, Mead & Company, 1938), p. 434.
5. *Ibid.*
6. Arthur Pollock, "The Theater," *Brooklyn Daily Eagle,* 24 March 1938.
7. Richard Watts, Jr., "The Theaters," *New York Herald Tribune,* 24 March 1938.
8. *Variety,* 30 March 1938.
9. *New York World-Telegram,* 24 March 1938.
10. Mazo do La Roache, *Whiteoaks* (London: MacMillian and Co., Limited, 1936), pp. 66–67.
11. *Ibid.,* p. 42.
12. Burns Mantle, ed. *The Best Plays of 1938–39* (New York: Dodd, Mead & Company), p. 411.
13. John Anderson, "'The Good' Presented At Windsor Theater," *New York Journal American,* 6 October 1938.
14. *The Best Plays of 1938–39,* p. 411.
15. *Ibid.*
16. Brooks Atkinson, "The Play," *New York Times,* 6 October 1938.
17. Chester Erskin, *The Good,* (Typewritten copy), Lincoln Center, p. I–38.
18. *Ibid.*
19. "The Good," *Variety,* 12 October 1935.
20. *The Good,* p. I–38.
21. *Ibid.,* p. I–41.
22. *Ibid.,* p. I–42.
23. *Ibid.,* p. I–43.
24. Walter Winchell, "The Good," *New York Daily Mirror,* 7 October 1938.
25. *The Good,* p. 2–38.

26. *Ibid.*, p. 3–6.
27. John Cambridge, "'The Good' At the Windsor Saved By Competent Acting," *Daily Worker,* 7 October 1938.
28. *New York Times,* 6 October 1938.
29. Sidney B. Whipple, "Miss Starr, Jarvis Rice Play Difficult Roles," *New York World Telegram,* 6 October 1938.
30. *Ibid.*
31. Richard Plant, "The Men With The Pink Triangles," *Christopher Street,* February 1977, p. 6.
32. *Ibid.*
33. *Ibid.*
34. John Anderson, "'Waltz In Goose Step,' Trip Up On Theme," *New York Journal-American,* 2 November 1938.
35. John Mason Brown, "Two On The Aisle," *New York Post,* 2 November 1938.
36. Oliver H. P. Garrett, *Waltz In Goose Step* (Typewritten copy), Lincoln Center, pp. 1–9.
37. *Ibid.*
38. Richard Watts, Jr., "The Theaters," *New York Herald Tribune,* 2 November 1938.
39. *Ibid.*
40. *New York Journal-American,* 2 November 1938.
41. *Waltz In Goose Step,* pp. 2–12.
42. Burns Mantle, "'Waltz In Goose Step' Leaves Nazi Problem Where It Was," *New York Daily News,* 2 November 1938.
43. "Waltz In Goose Step," *Variety,* 9 November 1938.
44. William Shirer, *The Rise and Fall of the Third Reich* (New York: Simon and Schuster, 1960), p. 47.
45. *Waltz In Goose Step,* pp. 3–28.
46. *Variety,* 9 November 1938.
47. *Ibid.*
48. *Christopher Street,* February 1977, p. 6.
49. Walter Winchell, "Waltz In Goose Step," *New York Daily Mirror,* 2 November 1938.
50. Burns Mantle, ed., *The Best Plays of 1938–39* (New York: Dodd, Mead & Company, 1939), p. 423.
51. "Theatre," *London News Review,* 12 November 1936, p. 28.
52. Lord Alfred Douglas, "A Preface To Oscar Wilde," *New York Post,* 10 October 1938.
53. Sewell Stokes, "Writing of 'Wilde,'" *New York Times,* 20 November 1938.
54. "London's 'Wilde' Drama Stars Robert Morley," *New York Journal-American,* 9 October 1938.
55. Katherine Roberts, "Least Effort," *Colliers,* 17 December 1938, p. 11.
56. "Gate Theatre," *London Times,* 30 September 1936.
57. "'Oscar Wilde' At Gate Theatre," *London Daily Telegraph,* 30 September 1936.
58. Richard Manely, "These Brothers Pull As A Team Even When Yoke Spans Oceans," *New York Herald Tribune,* 4 December 1938.
59. Sewell and Leslie Stokes, *Oscar Wilde* (Typewritten copy), Lincoln Center, p. 1-3-27.
60. *Ibid.*, p. 2-1-14.
61. *Ibid.*, p. 2-1-18.
62. *Ibid.*, p. 3-1-7.
63. *Ibid.*, p. 3-2-20.
64. Lord Alfred Douglas, "Lord Alfred Douglas Praises Play As Truthful To His Friend," *New York Herald Tribune,* 9 April 1939.
65. Lucius Beebe, "Stage Asides," *New York Herald Tribune,* 25 September 1938.
66. "Shumlin Gets Wilde Play; WPA Rushes Sillar Drama," *New York Daily News,* 16 October 1938.
67. "Quip Out," *New York World Telegram,* 19 November 1938.
68. Walter Winchell, "Robert Morley Star," *New York Daily Mirror,* 11 October 1938.

69. "Goings On About Town," *New Yorker,* 22 October 1938, p. 2.

70. Wolcott Gibbs, "The Theaters," *New Yorker,* 22 October 1938, p. 34.

71. John Anderson, "Robert Morley Stars in 'Oscar Wilde,' " *New York Journal-American,* 11 October 1938.

72. Arthur Pollock, "The Stage is Very Much Alive," *Christian Science Monitor,* 18 October 1938.

73. Richard Lockridge, "The New Play," *New York Sun,* 11 October 1938.

74. Burns Mantle, ed., *The Best Plays of 1938-39* (New York: Dodd, Mead & Company, 1939), p. 413.

75. "Name Morley as Season's Best Actor," *New York Daily News,* 19 January 1939.

76. "Cheers Greeted Robert Morley As 'Oscar Wilde,'" *New York Post,* 23 November 1938.

77. John Mason Brown, "Two On The Aisle," *New York Post,* 28 October 1938.

78. *Ibid.*

79. "Wilde Finally Discovered," *New York Herald Tribune,* 28 April 1940.

80. "Arts Theatre," *London Times,* 26 October 1938.

81. "Confirms Award On 'Oscar Wilde' Life," *Variety,* 18 November 1942.

82. Sidney B. Whipple, "Play On Oscar Wilde Sparkles With Wit," *New York World-Telegram,* 11 October 1938.

83. Richard Watts, Jr., "The Theaters," *New York Herald Tribune,* 11 October 1938.

84. Burns Mantle, "'Oscar Wilde' A Sympathetic Retelling Of An Old Scandal," *New York Daily News,* 11 October 1938.

85. Brooks Atkinson, "The Play," *New York Times,* 11 October 1938.

86. Brooks Atkinson, "Language's Lord," *New York Times,* 16 October 1938.

87. *Ibid.*

88. *Ibid.*

89. *Ibid.*

90. *New York Times,* 11 October 1938.

91. *Ibid.*

92. Richard Watts, Jr., "The Theater: Applause and Cheers," *New York Herald Tribune,* 23 October 1938.

93. George Jean Nathan, undated, untitled, magazine article from unknown publication in *Oscar Wilde* file, Lincoln Center.

14

Aphrodites on Broadway:
Therapist to Gays Who Hurt Women

The state of the legitimate theater during World War II, rather than the enforcement of the homophobic penal code, accounts for the fact that only three shows with gay characters were seen on Broadway from 1939 to 1945. Theatrical productions had been drastically reduced between the start of the Depression and the start of the Second World War. While there were as many as 264 productions in the all-time best theatrical season (1927–28)[1], only 72 shows were seen in the 1940–41 season.[2] There was simply little or no place for gay roles in the sort of plays produced when the country was at war.

Wartime audiences flocked to escapist musicals such as *Oklahoma!* and to family comedies such as *Life with Father,* seen in 3,224 performances on Broadway[3]. There were a number of serious dramas concerning either Allied service personnel on duty abroad or individuals caught up in the political and emotional upheavals that wracked Nazi-occupied Europe. Since identifiable lesbians and gay men are excluded from serving in the armed forces, they were not visible as characters in World War II dramas about Allied personnel. The single exception was *Proof Through the Night* about army nurses.

Although there are no discernible gay roles in the dramatic literature produced during the period of the Second World War, most of it was authored by closeted gay British and American playwrights.

When Thornton Wilder,[4] Tennessee Williams,[5] Emlyn Williams,[6] Noel Coward,[7] and Terence Rattigan[8] wrote *Skin of Our Teeth, The Glass Menagerie, The Corn Is Green, Blithe Spirit* and *O Mistress Mine!* respectively, none contained characters that identified these playwrights' lifestyles, at least as far as the public could ascertain.

"During the whole period of almost half a century during which I was a Broadway producer, I suppose homosexual playwrights were on safer, surer ground writing about heterosexuals, at least personally if not artistically," Herman Shumlin said in discussing Emlyn Williams, whose play *The Corn Is Green* he had directed in 1940. Shumlin continued:

> I remember a conversation I had with Edith Evans who was annoyed at homosexual playwrights for being evasive when they did dramatize material that was obviously a homosexual consideration. "Why can't they come right out with it?" Miss Evans said. She was particularly piqued with Williams, whom she knew, for having been actually dishonest, she felt, in writing a play called *Accolade* that had failed in a 1950 production in London probably because it did not ring true. It was still very fascinating. About this novelist, happily married with a family, as Williams was, who got mixed up with girls on occasions when he periodically left his family for a weekend.
>
> Williams wanted me to do it since my production of his *Corn Is Green* worked out so well. Like Miss Evans, I, too, sensed that the play was actually about a homosexual father's dilemma, especially in a very moving scene during which the man tries to explain to his son what he was all about. Williams didn't want to risk being identified by the public with homosexual material that could reflect on his private life any more than the other homosexual playwrights did. It would have been the end of him not only as a playwright but as a performer.[9]

Some critics and theatergoers also thought they recognized gay characters "passing as straights" in other plays by British and American dramamtists, popular contemporaries of Emlyn Williams. According to critic Kenneth Tynan, "In the plays of Terence Rattigan an obvious homosexual theme was transformed into a heterosexual one to placate the Lord Chamberlain."[10] In his introduction to *Gay Plays: The First Collection,* editor William M. Hoffman writes:

> Gay theatergoers interpreted two of John Van Druten's comedies of the forties and fifties, *The Voice of the Turtle* and *Bell, Book and Candle,* as hidden gay plays. They saw the first as a disguised pickup situation involving a "straight" soldier, and the second, which is set in

an imaginary witch-cult in New York, as a parable of gay underground life.[11]

There really may have been such a thing as a gay witch cult, at least among some campy chorus boys. Kathleen Mulqueen saw one of their routines in the 1920s when she was a star of a musical comedy playing in a Chicago theater:

> I was doing a show with an obnoxious leading man who was hated by everyone in the company. "We'll put the bitches' curse on him," one of the chorus boys told me. One night after the performance, the inge-nue and I were invited to join the boys backstage after the theater was empty. By candlelight they danced and carried on in outrageous drag. The stage manager walked in on us and in a fury broke it up with the warning that the chorus boys better not camp it up again.[12]

There was nothing but camp about the role Danny Kaye portrayed in Moss Hart's *Lady in the Dark*. Kaye was the first performer to appear on the Broadway stage in the 1940s doing a gay impersonation. The comedian, little-known at the time, played a swish-stereotypical "fag" role in the enormously popular Kurt Weill, Ira Gershwin musical starring Gertrude Lawrence. Kaye played Russell Paxton, an effeminate magazine photographer in the 1941 musical written and directed by Hart. Just a fragment of Russell Paxton's outrageous "screaming queen" dialogue gives one some idea of what audiences and critics found so humorous:

> *Russell.* Girls, he's God like! I've taken pictures of beautiful men, but this is the *end!* He's got a face that would melt in your mouth...[13]

Russell Paxton in *Lady in the Dark* differed little from countless other comic "faggot" characters seen for more than half a century in burlesque and vaudeville skits in this country, and in music hall entertainments in Britain. George Jean Nathan was outraged because the so-called "moralists" did not appear to be disturbed by caricatures such as Russell Paxton, but petitioned the law to stop performances of plays with serious gay character studies. Citing *Laffing Room Only,* a musical revue by and starring Ole Olsen and Chic Johnson in 1944, Nathan wanted to know why License Commissioner Paul Moss had not closed that show. The critic wrote, "There is a homosexual episode that should properly be offensive to him, yet ... he has done nothing about it."[14]

Another comic talent who rose to superstardom on the American stage — as Danny Kaye did in motion pictures — played the only suspect lesbian role seen on Broadway during World War II. Carol Channing, who went on to portray the oversized Kewpie doll in the musical version of *Gentlemen Prefer Blondes* and the matchmaking widow in *Hello Dolly,* was seen as a butch lesbian called Steve, described by the author as "a large, raw-boned muscular girl who carries herself like a man."[15]

"This is the play that has been causing considerable excitement in Hollywood the last several weeks," Burns Mantle informed readers of the *Daily News.* "*Cry Havoc* was its original title and it is on its way to a picture production, having been bought by Metro-Goldwyn-Mayer."[16] When the studio did film *Cry Havoc* with an all-star cast, no lesbian nurse appeared in the motion picture version.

The Broadway production of *Cry Havoc,* retitled *Proof Through the Night* for New York theatergoers, was by no means the success it had been in its Hollywood premiere. Negative and lukewarm reviews ended its Broadway engagement eleven performances after it opened on Christmas Day, 1942, at the Shubert Theater.[17] *Proof Through the Night* was staged by its author, Allan R. Kenward, and produced by Lee Shubert. Since Shubert did not read the scripts he produced, he probably had no idea that one of the group of nurses in the Hollywood hit play was a celibate lesbian. Only a few of the New York reviewers mentioned the character. "Carol Channing, in spite of some stagy directions, manages to give the hulking, confused Steve some real humanity," the *Journal American* reported.[18] "A pathetic girl," noted the *World-Telegram,* "who doesn't know she is abnormal until the cause of her tenderness and solicitude is brutally hurled at her by Miss Locke in a later regretted outburst of hysteria."[19]

In the second act, Steve, in the scene referred to by the *World-Telegram,* attempts to comfort another nurse, Grace, who has been hurt:

> *Steve (stroking her head).* You've got a fever, honey. Now just relax and let Steve take care of you.
> *Grace.* Take your big hands off me ... You can't paw me like you do Connie.
> Steve (Believes her sicker than she really is). Easy, easy, honey ... Come on now, let's get those clothes off ... I'll help you.

Grace (Struggling). Take your hands off me, I tell you. Go maul your Connie.
Steve (Realizing Grace means trouble). What's bothering you, honey?
Grace. Honey hell — take your paws off me. *(She pushes Steve off balance and the girl falls to the floor.)* Always wantin' to put your arms around people . . . Callin' 'em "Honey" and strokin' their hair . . . Why don't you go out there and fight with the rest of the men, . . . you . . . you Freak!

(Steve is stunned. After a moment she gets up stiffly, looking into Grace's face. Unable to believe what she's heard. Slowly the meaning of the accusation hits her. . .)[20]

After Steve goes, Grace tells another nurse to run after her to say that she didn't know what she was saying. When Grace does see Steve in a later scene, she apologizes:

Steve (Interrupting again). Do the other girls say those things about me?
Grace. Of course not, Steve, it doesn't make any sense.
Steve. Pat does, doesn't she?
Grace. Honestly Steve, it was my leg, and you were there just when I didn't want anything more to touch me.
Steve. Do they really call me a . . . a . . .
Grace. Please stop talking like that, the whole thing's ridiculous.
Steve (Moving as though to leave). You shouldn't have said what you did. . .[21]

Steve cannot forget Grace's attack on her and continues to worry about her sexual identity. She talks to an older nurse:

Steve. Is there anything wrong with me, Smitty? Am I different from them, Smitty? *(Smitty hesitates and Steve mistakes her pause for embarrassment)* Tell me honest, Smitty, I gotta find out. I'm so confused.
Smitty. If there was anything wrong with you . . . anything you'd be ashamed of, you'd know it. You'd know it here, Steve . . . *(Touches her heart)* . . . long before anybody else.
Steve. But I don't, Smitty. I've never even thought. . .
Smitty (Interrupting). And you mustn't. Right now you're confused . . . hurt . . . Cancers grow from that kind of hurt, Steve — It's a word that hit you below the belt . . . Shake it off while it's still a word, Steve, because accepting it makes it real and gives it a chance to grow. . .[22]

Steve never does come to terms with herself sexually during the course of the dramatic action. Before the climax of *Proof Through the Night,* the unhappy woman is killed attempting to reason with an armed nurse who had been in communication with the Japanese enemy.

An interesting but muddled drama appeared on Broadway in 1943 that seemed to fault the American Jewish community for its traditional rejection of the gay minority. Rose Franken's *Outrageous Fortune* also appeared to contain a dramatized plea for gay tolerance. At the same time, the playwright reiterated the traditional Judeo-Christian concept that lesbians and gay men were deserving of social and personal contempt since most are moral weaklings, who should mend their ways. "By virtue of a facile style," Wolcott Gibbs wrote in the *New Yorker,* "the author occasionally makes it seem as if she is really saying something about homosexuality and intolerance, but I'm afraid that in the end you just get the idea she is against them."[23]

George Freedley of the *Morning Telegraph* reported:

> *Outrageous Fortune* is the story of a wealthy Jewish family which lives on the nearby shore in a handsome house which is afflicted with anti-Semitism and homosexuality, neither of which the author seems to understand completely, or if she does, she can't communicate it to an audience.[24]

Robert Garland observed of Franken's drama, "The initial worry is anti-Semitism, while the final worry is homosexuality. Just as if the one had anything to do with the other."[25] To resolve both conflicts the playwright brings a very unusual woman into the Harrises' summer home who, during the weekend, also has to deal with a marital estrangement. Rose Franken, a popular novelist who had had two Broadway hits (*Another Language* and *Claudia*), provoked Burton Rascoe of the *World-Telegram* to protest that in dealing with matters sexual, "her solutions (such as they are) are more glib and more questionable than those any pseudo-Freudian quack would dare offer."[26]

Crystal Grainger, the playwright's *raisonneur,* is a handsome, internationally renowned celebrity of uncertain age, "a 'celebrity.'" as Wilella Waldorf noted in the *Post,* "[with] a somewhat vague distinction having to do chiefly with the fact that she seems to have had a prodigious number of lovers in her time, and once attended a first-night accompanied by her colored maid."[27]

One character enthuses in the play, "Oh, she just happens to be the most talked of woman in America," to which another adds, ironically, "Why stop with America?"[28] The author permits none of the characters in *Outrageous Fortune* to identify this celebrity's claim to fame. "Crystal Grainger is famous not because of what she does, but because of what she is—"[29] comments a young lady. Not even the young man who introduces Crystal to the rest of the characters knows why she is so internationally acclaimed:

> *Barry.* I don't know what you are. I don't know anything about you. Nobody does really. You're an enigma. *(His voice deepens almost to tragedy.)* But I wish I did know the secret of you, Crystal. I wish to God I could be involved with you. . . [30]

Crystal's enigmatic character, like the play itself, confused and annoyed some critics. She does not always make sense nor is she philosophically consistent. Throughout *Outrageous Fortune,* there are clues to Crystal's obvious symbolic identity. When she comes downstairs dressed for dinner and ready to work her sensuous magic on stodgy Bert and shy, sexually insecure Barry, the author describes her stunning entrance. Like a goddess, "Crystal *appears on stairs, statuesque as a Grecian figure in a white gown draped in large simple lines.*"[31]

"You seem to love everybody," Bert remarks to the love goddess in mortal guise. "That's my reputation—"[32] Crystal replies lightly.

Of all the critics writing for the New York dailies, Louis Kronenberger of *PM* was harshest in appraising Franken's work:

> She not only confuses, she falsifies. Her people talk elaborate foderol, but never shed any light. Her wise lady, in particular, is a *trial* and an absurdity, really wise women don't come to strange houses and spend the weekend playing god.[33]

Crystal Grainger and her black maid, Cynthia, are brought to spend a summer weekend at the Harrises' New Jersey beach house by a handsome, twenty-six-year-old bachelor, Crystal's neighbor in Greenwich Village. Sensitive, artistic Barry Hamilton, a far-from-successful violinist, is suspected of being gay by two other characters in the play, and even comes to suspect himself.

Crystal is not the only older female confidante-companion in bachelor Barry's life. His hostess, Madeleine Harris, a middle-aged, middle-class Jewish mother of teenagers, has managed to invite him into her home by hiring him as her daughter's violin teacher. Madeleine's husband, Bert, accepts his wife's "protégé" because he does not feel threatened by this relationship.

Bert Harris is a very successful stockbroker from a conservative, working-class Jewish family. He is stodgy, insular and suspicious of gentiles. During the weekend with Harris and his family, Crystal Grainger serves not only as a practical psychotherapist, but as a sexual therapist. In the first act the glamorous gentile completely captivates both Bert and his sweet old mother. Bert falls in love for the first time in his life resolving his neglected wife's emotional and sexual frustration. Madeleine is no longer afraid she will become either mad or sexually promiscuous:

> *Madeleine.* ... I want to be married to a man ... a full man with the capacity to love me — even if he had to love another woman first to learn the art of love.[34]

While she is defusing Bert's racial suspicions and resolving his marital maladjustment, Crystal works at straightening out not only his sexually active gay brother, Julian, but also closeted, continent Barry. Because Julian does not comprehend Aphrodite's intolerance of any amorous activity other than that which with her divinity is identified, Crystal cannot reach the young composer. Barry, however, is made "a real man" overnight by a brief liaison with Crystal. She miraculously cures him of the need to have any more platonic relationships with women her age. He is suddenly interested in Kitty, a young woman who badgered Barry because she suspected effeminacy in him.

Crystal comes to Barry's aid seconds after he has had a traumatic encounter. Sexually aggressive Julian has made an unwelcomed pass at him. Shaken by the incident, Barry talks candidly to Crystal about his sexual insecurities while she sits on a love seat. "Why should these things happen to me?" he asks the wise lady:

> *Crystal (unemotionally).* No mystery about it. You were born with a few too many F cells in your body.
> *Barry (passionately).* I didn't ask to be made that way!
> *Crystal.* Do any of us? Did Bert ask to be born a Jew? Or Cynthia, a negress — Or me? — What I am? It's the thing that brings us together, I wouldn't be surprised. We all have to beat our stars.
> *Barry.* What happens if we don't?
> *Crystal.* Julian. — And maybe Madeleine?[35]

Barry admits that he is not a virgin. Once he made love to an older woman who had been his violin teacher:

Barry. ... Years later, I met her again, right after my mother died. I was lonesome, I guess—...
Crystal (broodingly). There was no one in your life you really loved—
Barry. My father.
Crystal. And no one else — ever?
Barry (with increasing difficulty). Yes — a boy who lived on our block. In one of those big private houses. He went to France the second summer I knew him. My mother found a letter I was writing to him. She thought it was to a girl. — I never finished the letter. I never wanted to see him again. *(With suppressed intensity)* And I hated my mother for what she did to me. She made me ashamed for no reason. She frightened me about myself.

Crystal. Be glad. If you didn't feel the pain of conflict, you'd be like all the poor young men, who wouldn't help themselves if they could. Boys of twenty and twenty-five without a ground tone in their voices, poor darlings. There's hope for all of them — while they suffer. — There's even hope for Julian now.[36]

Crystal is ready to help Barry escape the gay underworld:

Barry (in humility). I told Madeleine tonight that it took a certain greatness to be your lover — I wish I had that greatness.
Crystal. You have. *(She bends to lay her cheek against his head for a fleeting instant,* Barry, *motionless, watches her as she moves across the room to the stairs. He rises slowly to follow her, as*
THE CURTAIN FALLS[37]

The third and last act of *Outrageous Fortune* concerns, for the most part, Crystal's failure to help Julian. Despite her reputation for loving everybody, the visiting lady does not like Julian, rejecting his idolizing overtures to her when they first met. Crystal knows Julian has a young lover, a lyricist, with whom he is collaborating on a musical. His engagement to Kitty is a platonic arrangement to which she had agreed for their mutual social and financial convenience. Crystal's contempt for Julian grows when he breaks his engagement to Kitty, driving her to attempt suicide. A vicious cad, the composer spreads the rumor that Barry had made the sexual overture.

Julian's affair with a younger man is known by his distressed and jealous fiancée. Even his old, tolerant *yiddishe* mother recognizes that, "I don't know what it is in Julian, but I know he cannot make a woman happy.''[38] Julian's problem is in dealing with his brother, Bert, the naïve, rigid and conventional Jewish family man. Their relationship climaxes in a heated exchange when guilt-ridden but defiant Julian tells Bert that he is moving away from the East Coast:

Bert (in stunned realization). You're going with that boy — Russell Train—
Julian (defiantly). So what? We're doing a musical—
Bert (stunned). God—
Julian. I shouldn't have to come back in the first place. I hate like hell doing this to you. *(Picks up his hat).*
Bert (heavily). It's not what you've done to me. It's what you've done to yourself. To your race.
Julian (harshly). I've got no obligations to my race. What's it ever done for me except to be a millstone around my neck—[39]

During his final conversation with Crystal in the last scene of *Outrageous Fortune,* Bert claims that he understands his wife's passing, romantic but platonic infatuation with a handsome, attentive young man:

Crystal. I'm glad you understand her. Try to understand Barry, too. He's a poor lost lad, looking for the mother he never had in the woman he wants to love.[40]

Bert cannot accept his brother's sexual preference. Crystal tries to reason with him:

Crystal. ...Have courage to realize that your goodness holds the seeds of all the Barrys and the Julians in the world.
Bert (numb). Julian?
Crystal. A part of you has always known about Julian for a long time. A part of you is responsible for Julian.
Bert (rousing to violently) [sic]. That isn't true! He's my own brother but I'd rather see him dead than the thing that he's become. He's betrayed his race at a time when we need all our strength and honor!
Crystal. He's betrayed himself. That's the real pity of it. He needs you, Bert, and your answer to his need is your salvation.
Bert. I tell you, I'd rather see him dead.
Crystal (austerely). If he were ill or crippled, would you turn against him?[41]

With Crystal's guidance, Bert and Barry are now ready to respond to the love of Madeleine and Kitty who have suffered so much from want of masculine affection in *Outrageous Fortune.* The mysterious lady is unable to reach Julian because he has rejected the love of women. In the final moments of the play, Crystal slips into the next room to expire. The lady who gave her heart to so many dies of heart failure.

In her autobiography, *When All Is Said and Done,* Rose Franken wrote, "Because I had something to say that I felt needed saying during those early war years, I started to write *Outrageous Fortune.*"[42] Reviewers, almost without exception, however, both in Boston and New York, employed the words "confused," "confusing," or "muddled" in reacting to Franken's work. The playwright replied in an interview almost a month after the play's premiere:

> I haven't gotten over being astonished when some of the critics said the play was confusing. If I've chosen to let the public do its own chewing on the theme, instead of handing out a predigested package, neatly labeled, does it matter, as long as our audiences are entertained and absorbed? ... It's all there. Once you're born, it's settled what your handicaps are going to be. Maybe you're a Jew, maybe you have too many F cells in your body. The only question is: what are you going to do with yourself as you are? "It doesn't hurt us to be hurt," says the old grandmother in the play."[43]

The character in the play with too many F cells went to bed with a female, as she suggested, to "beat his stars." Bert overcame his outrageous fortune of being born Jewish, according to the Jewish-born author, by overcoming his distrust of gentiles even if he could not reject traditional Jewish homophobia. In her recommendation that American minorities assimilate by rejecting their racial heritage or their sexual preference, Franken seemed to have no solution, however, for blacks, since Crystal's maid Cynthia is afforded no opportunity to "pass for white."

Producer John Golden rejected the script because he could not understand the characters. Gilbert Miller, who produced *Outrageous Fortune,* announced its closing after reading the adverse review in the Boston dailies. Franken recalled, "The Boston intellects agreed with John Golden that they didn't know what I was talking about in my latest play."[44] Only L.A. Sloper of the *Christian Science Monitor* dissented, hailing it as "a brilliant, subtle, moving drama."[45]

Outrageous Fortune went on to Broadway when the author-director's husband, William Brown Meloney, took over the production from Miller. It opened at the Forty-eighth Street Theater on November 3, 1943. Veteran stage and screen star Elsie Ferguson, "who at the peak of her stardom was generally regarded as America's most beautiful actress,"[46] came out of a fourteen-year voluntary retirement to play Crystal. The New York premiere sold out as the curious flocked to see the sixty-year-old star's return to the Broadway stage. Franken recalled that on opening night, "the play came across without a flaw in the performance, and the applause at the final curtain was deafening. Nevertheless, the reviews the next morning were not unanimously enthusiastic.[47]

Burns Mantle reported that, "The press reception of *Outrageous Fortune* was surprisingly friendly. Even those reviewers who could not generously approve of it admitted its interest-exciting qualities and the excellence of the performance given it."[48] Mantle thought so well of Franken's controversial drama, that he included a synopsis in *The Best Plays of the 1943-44 Season*.[49] Seventeen years earlier Mantle had refused to include *The Captive* in his annual yearbook.

Outrageous Fortune, which the author called "a good play, although a little ahead of its time,"[50] impressed Richard P. Cooke of the *Wall Street Journal* for this very reason:

> Miss Franken has tackled, among others, two of society's most troublesome subjects: The place of the Jew in his environment, and that of the abnormal male. She succeeds in treating these problems, which most people discuss in whispers, if at all, with good taste and aplomb. She does not offer a solution, or contribute a great deal that is original, but she says it rather originally.[51]

Among the playwright's critical detractors, Burton Rascoe contended that she "has bitten off more than she can chew,"[52] while Robert Garland complained that Franken, "bit off more than I could chew..."[53] Lewis Nichols of the *Times* called *Outrageous Fortune,* "confused and complex," because the author "touches upon middle-age, normal love, profane love between members of the two sexes, homosexuality, the tradition of the family, fear, sickness and anti-Semitism."[54] Critic Louis Kronenberger was particularly brutal in evaluating Franken's talents and intelligence: "Such as they are, Mrs. Franken's real gifts lie in a far more housefrauish direction, when, for example, she talks about food, she makes sense."[55]

Wolcott Gibbs reported in the November 13, 1943 issue of the

New Yorker, "Broadway is enjoying one of the greatest booms in history."[56] Gibbs cited four plays reviewed negatively by the critics, *Outrageous Fortune* among them, that were box office hits.[57] "Her play," Burton Rascoe predicted on opening night, "will be violently denounced, violently upheld, liked and discussed with heat — which will attest to its vitality and to its interest as sheer entertainment."[58] *Variety* reported that, "After premiere, *Fortune* jumped to capacity, and surprised even Broadway."[59] "For ten weeks," Burns Mantle recorded, "arguments for and against the drama's statements and conclusions were freely spoken. When by that time a paying response on the part of the public had not developed, *Outrageous Fortune* was withdrawn."[60]

The New York critics were as unanimous in their raves for Elsie Ferguson as they were divided as to the meaning and the worth of her starring vehicle. Incredibly enough, Crystal Grainger was as puzzling to the actress who portrayed her as she was to critics and audiences. Ferguson confided to an interviewer before the play's New York opening:

> I really don't know what it's all about, but I shall manage I guess. I've never been really baffled by a play yet ... Rose Franken is of a mind that one of the best advertisements for a show is an audience that is slightly baffled when it leaves the theater.[61]

The playwright still remained close-mouthed about Crystal's identity, the most puzzling aspect of her drama when she recalled its production in her memoirs.[62] In her autobiography, Franken, explaining how she went about casting the show, wrote that she selected an ex–prize fighter to play "the sensitive homosexual."[63] Yet Barry is not gay in the play, only a "borderline case,"[64] with "a few too many F cells."[65]

Dean Norton, the ex–prize fighter and baseball player, who played the thankless part of Barry, failed to impress the critics. "After all," George Freedley explained, "a character can be too much praised in a play.[66] An actor named Brent Sargent, on the other hand, was singled out by many of the reviewers for his impressive performance as the defiant, promiscuous and caddish Julian. "Brent Sargent making his Broadway debut," Robert Garland wrote, "handled the trying and tricky role of the boy who meets boys with taste and skill."[67] Ward Morehouse observed that Sargent's was, "one of the most forceful performances you'll see in many months of playgoing."[68]

Julian Harris, Rose Franken's guilt-ridden yet defiant American Jew, was the only unmistakably and admittedly gay male character seen in a serious drama produced on the Broadway stage in the 1940s. *Outrageous Fortune* was also the only Broadway play of that decade that addressed itself to the status of the gay American male. "As a drama of ideas, it belongs in the kindergarten,"[69] scoffed critic Wolcott Gibbs. The author countered that it was "a little ahead of its time."[70] Indeed, its subject matter, as the reviewer for the *Wall Street Journal* reminds us, was still discussed "in whispers, if at all,"[71] as late as 1943.

"The novel upon which *Outrageous Fortune* was based," Franken revealed for the first time almost three decades after her play was produced on Broadway, "was suppressed, withdrawn from circulation, after it was published in 1935. That's how far ahead of its time I was with the subject of homosexuality."[72]

Franken bristled at the observation that *Outrageous Fortune* contained a pioneer plea for tolerance of the gay male. The author protested indignantly:

> I intended no such thing! I was not sympathetic to homosexuals back then, and I'm still not — only to those who want to change. Only those will I tolerate. I was sympathetic to women who unhappily became involved with them. That's what my novel, *Twice Born,* was about: three such women. I've never revealed that before, but *Outrageous Fortune* was the dramatization of my novel which was suppressed in the mid-thirties when the subject of homosexuality was hardly mentionable in normal conversation.
>
> Read *Twice Born* and you'll understand how I feel about homosexuals. The men are in the novel, but they became more important in my stage version, especially that awful pervert Julian. And I did not mean to equate Jews and blacks with homosexuals in the play. My family was partly Jewish, and I always considered it to be advantageous, a very special thing to be part of a minority. But the homosexuals aren't. They are sick and their liberation movement, like the women's, almost makes me sick. I never needed to be liberated by anyone! Neither do the homosexuals — they just need to change their ways.[73]

In her eighty-fifth year, Rose Franken does not recall including a plea by both Crystal and old Mrs. Harris for tolerance of gay men in *Outrageous Fortune.* "The only plea I wanted to make was that they straighten themselves out," the author reiterated, "and stop hurting women who fall for them."[74]

Notes

1. Harold Clurman, "What Was Broadway's All-Time Best Season?" *New York Times,* 16 March 1980.
2. Brooks Atkinson, *Broadway* (New York: MacMillian Company, 1970), p. 44.
3. *Ibid.,* p. 394.
4. Karl Maves, "Samuel M. Steward," *Advocate,* 24 August 1977.
5. Mel Gussow, "Tennessee Williams On Art and Sex," *New York Times,* 3 November 1975.
6. Interview with Herman Shumlin, New York City, 3 March 1979.
7. Cole Lesley, *Remembered Laughter, The Life of Noel Coward* (New York: Alfred A. Knopf, 1976), p. 93.
8. Charles Faber, "On Stage and Screen: Anne Baxter Is Back From Outback," *Advocate,* 6 March 1980.
9. Interview with Herman Shumlin, 6 March 1979.
10. Kenneth Tynan, Interview on the Dick Cavett Television Show, Channel 13, WNET-TV, New York City, 13 August 1980.
11. William M. Hoffman, ed., *Gay Plays: The First Collection* (New York: Avon Books, 1979), p. xxii.
12. Interview with Kathleen Mulqueen, New Hall, California, 1 January 1984.
13. Burns Mantle, ed., *The Best Plays of 1941–42* (New York: Dodd, Mead & Company, 1942), p. 141.
14. George Jean Nathan, "George Jean Nathan's Theatre Week," *New York Journal-American,* 12 March 1945.
15. Allan R. Kenward, *Proof Through The Night* (Typewritten copy), Lincoln Center, p. I-i-5.
16. Burns Mantle, "'Proof Thro' The Night' Is A Vivid Drama Of Woman In War," *New York Daily News,* 26 December 1942.
17. Burns Mantle, ed., *The Best Plays of 1942–43* (New York: Dodd, Mead & Company, 1943), p. 454.
18. John Anderson, "Kenward War Play At Morosco," *New York Journal-American,* 26 December 1942.
19. Burton Rascoe, "Theater," *New York World Telegram,* 26 December 1942.
20. Allan R. Kenward, *Proof Through The Night,* (Typewritten copy), Lincoln Center, pp. 4–5.
21. *Ibid.,* pp. 2–8.
22. *Ibid.,* pp. 2–14.
23. Wolcott Gibbs, "The Theatre," *New Yorker,* 13 November 1943, p. 36.
24. George Freedley, "Stage Today: New Franken Play Is Confused Piece," *New York Telegraph,* 5 November 1943.
25. Robert Garland, "Rose Franken Play Bows On Broadway," *New York Journal-American,* 4 November 1943.
26. Burton Rascoe, "Theater," *New York World Telegram,* 4 November 1943.
27. Wilella Waldorf, "Two On The Aisle," *New York Post,* 4 November 1943.
28. Rose Franken, *Outrageous Fortune* (New York: Samuel French, 1944), p. 39.
29. *Ibid.,* p. 86.
30. *Ibid.,* p. 55.
31. *Ibid.,* p. 64.
32. *Ibid.,* p. 104.
33. Louis Kronenberger, "'Outrageous Fortune' Very Fancy BUT VERY FOOLISH," *New York Newspaper PM,* 4 November 1943.
34. *Outrageous Fortune,* p. 182.
35. *Ibid.,* pp. 145–146.
36. *Ibid.,* p. 148.
37. *Ibid.,* p. 149.

38. *Ibid.,* p. 158.
39. *Ibid.,* p. 189.
40. *Ibid.,* p. 194.
41. *Ibid.,* pp. 194–195.
42. Rose Franken, *When All Is Said And Done* (Garden City, New York: Doubleday & Company, Inc., 1963), p. 277.
43. Helen Ormsbee, "Rose Franken Says Playwriting Like Piecrust Needs Light Hand," *New York Herald Tribune,* 28 November 1943.
44. *When All Is Said And Done,* p. 297.
45. L. A. Sloper, "Outrageous Fortune." *Boston Christian Science Monitor,* 19 October 1943.
46. Ibee., "Outrageous Fortune," *Variety,* 10 November 1943.
47. *When All Is Said And Done,* p. 305.
48. Burns Mantle, ed., *The Best Plays of 1943–44* (New York: Dodd, Mead & Company, 1944), p. 8.
49. *Ibid.,* pp. 198–235.
50. *When All Is Said And Done,* p. 305.
51. Richard P. Cooke, "The Theater," *Wall Street Journal,* 4 November 1943.
52. *New York World-Telegram,* 4 November 1943.
53. *New York Journal-American,* 4 November 1943.
54. Lewis Nichols, "The Play," *New York Times,* 4 November 1943.
55. *New York Newspaper PM,* 4 November 1943.
56. Wolcott Gibbs, "The Theater," *New Yorker,* 13 November 1943.
57. *Ibid.,* p. 36.
58. *New York World Telegram,* 4 November 1943.
59. *When All Is Said And Done,* p. 302.
60. *The Best Plays of 1943–44,* p. 8.
61. Lucius Beebe, "Stage Asides: If We Recall 'Such A Little Queen,'" *New York Herald Tribune,* 31 October 1943.
62. *When All Is Said And Done,* pp. 277–308.
63. *Ibid.,* p. 286.
64. *Outrageous Fortune,* p. 146.
65. *Ibid.,* p. 167.
66. George Freedley, "Stage Today: New Franken Play Is Confused Piece," *New York Morning Telegraph,* 5 November 1943.
67. *New York Journal-American,* 4 November 1943.
68. Ward Morehouse, "The New Play," *New York Post,* 4 November 1943.
69. Wolcott Gibbs, "The Theatre," *New Yorker,* 13 November 1943, p. 36.
70. *When All Is Said And Done,* p. 22.
71. *Wall Street Journal,* 4 November 1943.
72. Telephone interview with Rose Franken, 15 January 1980.
73. *Ibid.*
74. *Ibid.*

15

1945 Theatrical Cause Célèbre:
"The Little Flower
and Defective Genital Organs"

Eighteen years after the Wales Padlock bill became law, the statute was finally challenged. The resulting public clamor became a theatrical *cause célèbre*. The controversy centered around License Commissioner Paul Moss, a political appointee, who would have become Broadway's first censoring 'Lord Chamberlain' had the Dunnigan Bill succeeded. Although deprived of that position, Moss exercised his clout as Commissioner in 1945 when he closed *Trio*. *Trio* had been running for two months at the Belasco Theater in clear violation of the New York State Penal Code. When the Commissioner of Licenses, who had never seen the show, abruptly terminated its engagement, there was an immediate outcry from stars, stagehands, producers and playwrights, as well as from such supporters as the American Civil Liberties Union.

Trio's closing in 1945, and the aftermath, made those who had provoked it so uncomfortable that never again did any individual or pressure group instigate legal or political action to shut down a Broadway show because of gay roles. Both Mayor LaGuardia and his License Commissioner were not only criticized, but they were roundly ridiculed by the press and other politicians. Nevertheless, the censorship law remained on the books until 1967.

Legitimate theater mogul Lee Shubert instigated the crisis by insisting that Moss approve of the drama with a lesbian role before booking it, though the License Commissioner was not legally empowered to do so. The Protestant minister, whom Moss claimed to have accommodated by closing *Trio,* was at least devious if not downright dishonest in his complaint to the Mayor.[1] Both Shubert and the minister were faulted for their involvement in the case. LaGuardia ultimately chastised Moss for unilaterally closing a show, although the Mayor probably initiated the action.[2] In retreating, the Mayor even proposed a penal code amendment that Actors' Equity predicted would "spare the theater a reign of terror through the illegal and irresponsible action of a city official."[3]

"A United Theater Defeats Official Censorship,"[4] announced *Equity* magazine in February 1945, but the victory did not help those involved in the production and performance of the ill-fated show. Public performances of the lesbian love drama were still in clear violation of Section 1140-A of the criminal code. Nor was the support by theater people, drama critics, and civil rights activists of a drama with a lesbian antagonist sufficient to abet the continuing emergence of gay characterizations on the American stage.

The fate of *Trio* and the financial loss suffered served to remind producer, playwrights, and financial backers[5] that censorship was still possible under the Wales Law. Until Lee Shubert brought that fact to the public's attention, the Wales Law had been ignored since the success of *The Green Bay Tree* in 1933 — with a single exception. Lee Shubert's fear, of not only losing a theater license, but of being sent to prison for breaking the law, appears to have had a weighty role in the hiatus during the post-World War II period of gay-genre dramas. In 1942 the Shubert brothers leased one of their theaters to the producer of *Wine, Women and Song,* a revue consisting of classic vaudeville and burlesque acts. Despite his heart condition, the producer of the revue was sentenced to a six-month penitentiary term.[6] This was the only court case in which the Wales Padlock Law was cited in revoking the license to operate a theater for a period of a year.

Until 1956, when the government ordered the breakup of the Shubert monopoly, the corporation controlled the majority of legitimate theaters in the United States. The Wales Padlock Law was not rescinded during Lee Shubert's lifetime. Only after his death in the early '50s did producers begin to present plays with gay themes and characters, ignoring the law that had so intimidated Shubert. In his biography of the Shubert brothers, Jerry Stagg wrote, "The *New York Times* remarked that there seemed to be two kinds of censorship in the theater: one was the Wales Act, on the statute books, and the second was a Shubert fist."[7]

Perhaps because no mention was ever made of its gay motif in the advertisements, *Outrageous Fortune* was never threatened by the law. Two years later when ads for *Trio* identified the drama's subject matter, they provoked a controversy that climaxed with the termination of the show. When Fiorello H. LaGuardia was Mayor of New York City, it did not pay to advertise a show that was breaking the law, especially when the ads themselves were prohibited by New York's Criminal Code.

Two of the three lesbian characters seen in Broadway productions during the 1940s were even more personally unattractive than vindictive Julian Harris in *Outrageous Fortune.* The pathetic, affectionate and confused nurse played by Carol Channing in *Proof Through the Night,* with, as one critic noted, "real humanity,"[8] stood in striking contrast to the two other lesbian portraitures seen during the decade that began with the Second World War. Jean-Paul Sartre's lesbian character in *No Exit* stole a man's wife and drove her to suicide. *Trio* contained an evil and corrupt female Svengali.

Dorothy Baker was aided by her husband, Howard, in dramatizing her novel, *Trio,* which, critic John Chapman noted, "won prizes in California from sobersided judges as the work of a native daughter."[9] The stage version of *Trio* was never published, but the play is structured very much like the novel. Divided into three parts with only two settings, the novel has very few characters. The reviewers' references to the drama's plot and characterizations match those in the rather brief novel. The book gives us a very good idea of the contents of the controversial play that was performed trouble-free in Philadelphia, Boston and Los Angeles.

The reviewer for *Women's Wear Daily* provided this synopsis of *Trio*'s very simple plot:

> The story concerns a young girl student at the university who belongs body and soul to an older woman, a sophisticated and fascinating French woman endowed with charm and intellect. A young boy falls in love with the girl and hopes to marry her, but when he realizes the abnormal attachment the two women have formed for each other, his reaction is instantaneous and natural. He is repulsed and horrified, and turns his wrath upon

the girl. A few hours later, however, he reconsiders and returns to take the girl away from the woman and to eventual security and happiness.[10]

Producer Lee Sabinson hired Bretaigne Windust, director of the comedy hits *Life With Father* and *Arsenic and Old Lace,* to stage *Trio.* While there was nothing very funny about the drama, the authors did provide audiences with a single amusing moment. "The premiere afforded one solid laugh," reported the *Daily Mirror,* "'I came to college to get an education,' avowed the prof's victim, 'and I got it!' The first nighters howled."[11]

Czech-born actress Lydia St. Clair — seen previously on Broadway in 1940 in *Flight to the West* — played the lesbian villainess. Richard Widmark and Lois Wheeler, who had made favorable impressions in their Broadway debuts, were cast by Windust as the tough-fibered young man and the professor's so-called protégée. *Cue* magazine reported:

> When he and the girl fall in love the scene becomes rich with conflicts and excitements that make for audience interest. Having this much in hand, unfortunately, the authors haven't always chosen to make the most of it. Actually, you are more interested in Pauline Maury herself, than in the resolving struggle. She is a powerful, ambitious, ruthless and shockingly opportunistic woman, and Lydia St. Clair brings to the role a brilliant falseness, as fascinating as it is unpleasant. Turning, twisting, moving with a nervous tension from bullying to charm all within the same moment, she makes the other characters pale and frail in comparison. Richard Widmark and Lois Wheeler as the man and girl are never quite believable, possibly because their characterizations aren't to begin with.[12]

The authors' homophobic bias is obvious. When the brash young photographer criticizes a surrealistic painting because it "attempts to attain excitement before reality,"[13] critic Burton Rascoe believed it summed up the playwrights' moral since the picture symbolized the lesbian.[14] In the novel, the photographer says to the girl, "Did you ever hear of a fairy that wasn't artistic? The main thing wrong with the arts is that they attract so many degenerates."[15]

A Philadelphia drama critic described the Bakers' characterization of a degenerate educator:

> Pauline Maury ... is sick of an old and classic sickness, ... a thoroughly detestable figure, slightly overlaid with horror, and ripe for the loathing of any audience. For Pauline not only falls heir to the normal

contempt of the sexually healthy for the sexually ill, she is a thoroughly despicable human being aside from her allegiance to the third estate of sex. She is a snob, a plagiarist, a complete egomaniac and a corrupter of youth.[16]

The play begins with a cocktail party given by the French-born professor in her home to celebrate the critical success of a recently published book she has plagiarized. Critic Frank S. Leyendecker observed that this "sideline to the main theme, dealing with plagiarism is probably necessary to blacken the older woman's character in the eyes of the more narrow-minded play-goers ... After her protectress has been exposed as a plagiarist, ... the girl escapes from the unhealthy atmosphere of lesbianism forever."[17] That escape is made possible only with the help of the brash young man. Pauline Maury once put her student into a sanitarium after an unsuccessful attempt to run away. In the end, the professor prepares to kill herself in, according to the *Times,* "a rather gaudy, anti-climactic scene."[18]

The Shuberts leased producer Lee Sabinson their Locust Street Theater for *Trio's* preview engagement in Philadelphia. Since that city had no state or municipal theatrical prohibition against gay themes or characterizations, there was no problem with the law. The only complaints came from two of the city's reviewers. The *Evening Bulletin* dismissed it as bland, and recommended drastic cutting.[19] The *Philadelphia Record* complained about one of the dullest first acts in the reviewer's memory, but he liked the rest of the play.[20] The *Daily News* called *Trio* "highly literate, intelligently performed and completely absorbing,"[21] and the *Inquirer* gave it a rave review:

> *Trio* is not a play for any tot of 16 to take her simple-minded old grandmother to see. Dealing with pathological perversion, it isn't, indeed, a drama for the typical playgoer in quest of hearty, wholesome humor, or idle, if normal and natural, entertainment.
>
> Yet the superb and sensitive direction of Bretaigne Windust, the flawless and intense acting of the three all-important principals hitherto unfamiliar here, and the compelling craftsmanship of the drama of decadence defeated which Dorothy and Howard Baker have transferred save for an altered ending, gave singular fascination to the first performance anywhere of *Trio* at the Locust last night, making it an unforgettable event in the theater.[22]

The *New York Times* reported: "No complaint had been received during the last ten days of the attraction's Philadelphia try-out. Every reviewer there," the paper quoted producer Lee Sabinson as saying, "commented on the delicacy and sensitiveness with which the play treated its subject."[23]

When a complaint about *Trio* did materialize, it came from Lee Shubert. He had promised Sabinson Broadway's Cort Theater before he discovered the subject of the Bakers' drama. It was License Commissioner Paul Moss who had revoked the license of Shubert's Ambassador Theater for a whole year after a jury found the producer of *Wine, Women and Song* guilty of presenting an illegal burlesque show. Shubert did not want his Cort Theater padlocked because of *Trio*. "Mr. Shubert told us yesterday," theatrical columnist Sam Zolotow reported, "he would not permit *Trio*, which deals with lesbianism, to open at this house on Wednesday, as advertised, unless License Commissioner Paul Moss gives the play a clean bill of health."[24]

Saying he "was not a censor, but merely handled licenses,"[27] Moss declined at first to become embroiled in such a controversy. Lee Shubert, not Moss, was attacked initially for attempting to make of the License Commissioner a one-man stage censor. The *Times* reported, "A petition, authored by Will Geer and John McGovern, protesting Mr. Shubert's action as censorous, began circulating yesterday among performers in current Broadway shows for the purpose of presenting it to council of Actors Equity Association."[26]

Critic Jesse Zunser of *Cue* reminded readers of the Shuberts' theatrical monopoly:

> Mr. Shubert is quite right with his legal rights to refuse a lease of his theaters to whomsoever he pleases. But Mr. Shubert owns or controls 80% of the legitimate theaters on Broadway. Such a monopoly verges on developing into a public utility — and as such, there also grows upon those in control a definite responsibility to see that that power — wittingly or unwittingly — is not abused.[27]

George Jean Nathan came to Shubert's defense, pointing out that he was afraid not only of having one of his theaters padlocked, but of "the chance of being thrown into the hoosegow."[28] The New York City Committee of the American Civil Liberties Union, on the other hand, urged Shubert to reconsider:

> Such a position invites censorship, a practice which you undoubtedly deplore. Your refusal is all the more significant in view of your eminent

and predominant status in New York Theater, and your action here makes it increasingly difficult for the public to see plays uncensored.[29]

In an attempt to extricate himself from his poorly received plea to Moss, the theater mogul turned to the press for help. "Shubert suggested Sabinson invite the N.Y. drama critics to Philly," reported *PM,* "to see if the play would endanger his Cort license."[30] Seven critics took Sabinson up on Shubert's suggestion[31]; in the meantime, *Trio,* unable to move onto Broadway as planned, switched from the Locust to the Walnut Street Theater in Philadelphia, also owned by the Shuberts. "Broadway last week found itself unable to see a play which Philadelphia sat through for several weeks," Lewis Nichols of the *Times* commented, "apparently without coming to any harm."

> On a couple of frenzied excursions to Philadelphia a good many reviewers saw *Trio,* and it was their consensus that, regardless of its merits as a play, the drama could not be charged with being offensive, suggestive or objectionable. It was, as its sponsors said from the beginning, a serious and honest work.[32]

Burton Rascoe of the *World-Telegram* was very suspicious: "this all seems like a gag to me; I can't believe it; it looks like a publicity stunt to whip up public interest in a nice, quiet, very moralistic play."[33] Despite such reactions from the press, no Broadway playhouse was made available. Finally, producer Sabinson was able to get the Belasco, one of the few theaters along Broadway not owned by the Shuberts.

During the uproar over *Trio,* Dorothy and Howard Baker released this statement:

> The booking troubles that *Trio* has run into have started the misleading and damaging rumor that *Trio* is a drama about Lesbianism. This report falls short of the truth. We, the authors, would have had no interest in dramatizing anything so special, so chaotic, or so finally uninteresting as Lesbianism, and the attachment between the two women in our play is a very small part of a much larger pattern of psychological domination.[34]

Mrs. Baker elaborated on the matter in another interview. According to *PM,* the novelist said:

> Janet Logan, the girl in *Trio* — it's a little of the silver-cord thing — she broke the knot and that's all to the good. I think she'd be a better person for having known these things and having had the will to break free and the nerve to stand on her own feet. Against someone who'd done everything for her and made her know it.[35]

After *Trio* opened on Broadway, one critic commended the playwrights for their dishonesty in describing their drama. Maurice Stoller wrote:

Last night's admission by the heroine to her newfound male sweetheart that she had had "an affair" and "lived with" the other woman left no doubts. Nevertheless, the authors' game was a justifiable game of deceit, inasmuch as it helped bring to the local boards a truly terrific psychological drama.[36]

Trio began its two-month engagement at the Belasco Theater on December 29, 1944.[37] Sabinson declared:

The proscribing of *Trio* is but an indication of the inherent dangers in self-assumed censorship. There were many of us who condemned the book burning in Germany as barbarism. Now, as we fight fascism abroad, we find undeniable signs of it in the Shubert attempt to utilize his rights as a landlord to prevent the performance of any play, whatever its values may be. It is for the people to decide whether or not they are interested in any play.[38]

Critic Howard Barnes wrote, "Praise be that *Trio* has opened at the Belasco Theater ... [I]t would have been shocking had Lee Shubert's premonition of censorial wrath kept this Lee Sabinson production from the local boards."[39] Burton Rascoe gave this report of the first-nighters' reaction:

When the final curtain went down on *Trio* last night, bedlam broke out in the audience and resounded up and down 44th St. for half an hour. There were shrieks and yells of approval. Many of a claque had apparently brought wooden clappers, so noisy was the din ... I looked for them to tear down the marquee and do a snake dance up the street in frenzied triumph.

I have no doubt that some of the "ovation" had something to do with the play and its merits and the histrionism of Mlle. St. Clair,... but, for the most part, I think this demonstration was the natural reaction of Americans against any threat of official censorship — against any form of regimentation.[40]

Equity reported that in *Trio*'s Philadelphia tryout, "the critics gave it a mixed reception ... in New York again the reviews were neither wholly favorable, nor completely unfavorable. It settled down to a profitable, but by no means sensational business."[41]

"The most exciting event of the current season," according to the *Morning Telegraph*,[42] elicited less than exciting reviews, even among the minority of critics who most appreciated it. "This piece is an engrossing drama and it has some powerful moments," wrote Ward Morehouse of the *Sun*.[43] Louis Kronenberger of *PM* called it, "an honest and serious drama,"[44] and Jesse Zunser of *Cue* found that "while not a good play, this is certainly an absorbing one."[45] According to the *World-Telegram*, "the play is unpleasant but it is tense, dramatic and moral."[46] The *Times* concluded that, "*Trio* is straight-forward and unsensational; it just isn't a very good play."[47] Arthur Pollock dismissed it as being "hollow and artificial."[48] Jack O'Brien called it "almost interminably dull in its effort to avoid any blatant consideration of the unhealthy love affair it traces."[59] "It hasn't any message," complained John Chapman of the *Daily News*, "and it hasn't any moral."[50]

Almost every play with a gay motif produced after *The Captive* and *The Green Bay Tree* was inevitably compared to those shows. "An undistinguished restatement of *The Captive* theme," contended Robert Coleman of the *Daily Mirror*. "We hope it doesn't start a move toward censorship of the theater, as did *The Captive* and other plays of its era."[51] "A honest and sensitive account of elliptical human relationships, which does not compare with *The Captive*," wrote Howard Barnes.[52] Wilella Waldorf concurred: "Compared to such works as *The Captive*, and *The Children's Hour*, and *The Green Bay Tree*, *Trio* is a minor dramatic effort."[53]

By 1944, only one drama critic objected in writing to seeing a play with a lesbian character. The staff correspondent for the *Christian Science Monitor* complained:

> Just why anyone should feel the urge to present a stage story dealing with feminine degeneration is a mystery. The legitimate theater has deservedly attained a high repute in providing entertainment within the boundaries of good taste, and *Trio* most certainly strays boldly beyond these standard limits.[54]

Audiences, like the critics, had also grown somewhat more tolerant. "Had this piece treated of Lesbianism for salaciousness sake," commented the reviewer for *Stage Today*, "it would have failed to shock today's sophisticated audiences in the sense that *The Captive* shocked Broadway some years back."[55] According to *About Town* magazine, "Audiences were amazed that all the unnecessary fuss had been stirred up about a drama which is totally lacking in sensationalism."[56]

"It is incredible that the theme of *Trio* should ever have been questioned," Eleanor Monroe wrote in *Women's Wear Daily.*[57] "Moral to the point of being contrived," Howard Barnes declared in the *Herald Tribune.*[58] *Cue* magazine assured the public:

> By no stretch of the imagination can *Trio* be considered "immoral." Certainly, it is not as immoral, let's say, as *The Voice of the Turtle* — which, for all its delightful wit and hilarious humors, does play around with well bred adultery.[59]

George Jean Nathan (who had called *The Captive* "the most subjective, corruptive and potentially evil-fraught play ever shown in the American theater"[60]), referred to *Trio* as "a fine play."[61]

One week before *Trio* was scheduled to close after a disappointingly brief two-month run, License Commissioner Paul Moss refused to renew the liceense of the Belasco Theater, which was up for renewal, unless the engagement of the Bakers' drama was terminated immediately. The *Times* reported:

> The Commissioner is said to have taken the action following complaints from the Rev. John Sutherland Bonnell, pastor of the Fifth Avenue Presbyterian Church. Last night Dr. Bonnell admitted having sent the complaint to Mayor LaGuardia...
>
> Dr. Bonnell declared the regarded *Trio* as "most offensive because it deals primarily with an abnormal perversion and therefore is especially dangerous to the public morals and especially in the case of the young."[62]

Insisting that he had a right to censor plays, Moss — who had been appointed Licenser of Theaters by LaGuardia in 1934 — concluded that *Trio* was, "in the words of the complaint, 'lewd and lascivious.'"[63] The *Herald Tribune* reported:

> Moss pointed to section 1140-A of the penal code of the state of New York which prohibits obscene and indecent plays as misdemeanors and also provides penalties for advertisements relating to such plays. He contended that its sponsors had advertised it "as a play dealing with Lesbianism and the unnatural friendship between two women."[64]

"You have seen what Mr. Moss thinks is a lewd and obscene exhibition. If you disagree with him, write, telegraph or telephone the Mayor in protest,"[65] producer Lee Sabinson said in a curtain speech to a capacity audience at the close of the final performance of *Trio* on the night of February 24, 1945. Mayor LaGuardia was besieged with protests, not only from members of *Trio*'s final audience, but from thousands of people in and out of show business who deeply resented the censoring of a Broadway show.

The shutting down of the show received as much press coverage in the New York dailies as the closing of *The Captive* eighteen years earlier. John Chapman of the *Daily News* made this comment:

> Now the play has become a cause célèbre. It must be this way, too, for the liberalization of the New York stage is worth fighting for. But *Trio*, as a drama, isn't worth all this fuss. I think if it had been let alone it would have died all by itself pretty soon; it was curiosity, rather than its dramatic splendors, which kept it going.[66]

Moss's refusal to renew the Belasco license until *Trio* had been evicted provoked immediate, widespread and highly publicized protests from people in show business and their supporters. Special emergency meetings and mass rallies were held to devise a strategy for dealing with the License Commissioner's attempt at censorship.

Margaret Webster, the actress-director, followed the example of playwright Elmer Rice by resigning from the City Center's Board of Directors rather than serve with Moss there. A group of prominent producers and playwrights (Herman Shumlin, Howard Lindsay and Russell Crouse chief among them) joined the head of Actors Equity, the President of the League of New York Theaters, the American Civil Liberties Union and the Critics Circle in their insistence that "the theater is entitled to the same freedom allowed the press."[67] The A.F. of L. International Board of Associated Actors and Artists of America adopted a resolution addressed to LaGuardia which concluded:

> We respectfully appeal to you as Mayor that you do not allow any of New York City's public officials to set themselves above the courts and proper legal procedures by exercising unwarranted dictatorial authority which is one of the things that the United Nations and our American men and women in service are fighting to eliminate throughout the world.[78]

Mayor LaGuardia was criticized for supporting Moss's action.[69] In some quarters it was believed that the License Commissioner was simply fronting for the Mayor. By so staunchly supporting Moss, a columnist for *PM* suggested that, "The Mayor has shown his hand. All along, however, one might have guessed that though the voice was the voice of Paul Moss the hand was the hand of LaGuardia."[70] The *Daily News* also reported: "Burns Mantle Tags LaG. As Real Censor; Warns of Dangers."[71]

LaGuardia was ridiculed by members of the press such as Wilella Waldorf of the *Post:*

> Mayor LaGuardia has cut a very sorry figure in the controversy so far. His reply to Russell Crouse of the Author's League was a childish attempt to camouflage the issue that could hardly have deluded anybody but a Hearst editorial writer.[72]

In defense of the closing of *Trio* when many other Broadway shows were far more daring in their treatment of sex, albeit wholly heterosexual in nature, LaGuardia provoked this editorial reaction from *PM:*

> As for absurdity, the Mayor's comments on lesbianism (which he is too delicate to mention by name) betray some mighty strange ideas. He seems to think that lesbianism requires (what he isn't tco delicate to mention by name) "defective genital organs" — and that it is a "habit," like sleeping on your right side, and not a condition like suffering from insomnia.[73]

State Senator Fred G. Morritt, Democrat of Brooklyn, offered a bill in Albany that would permit a producer to get injunctive relief against the closing of a show pending a speedy court trial. The liberal politician, at the same time, released a statement "which paraphrased the well-known verse from the *Mikado* as follows:

> The Little Flower that bloomed in the spring, tra, la.
> Has something to do with the case.
> He's forced to take under his wing, tra, la,
>   A most unattractive old thing (The License Commissioner) with a
> caricature of a face (censorship).[74]

While the New York drama critics were unanimously outraged at the curtailing of *Trio's* engagement, some were consequently at odds with their more conservative publishers and editors whose views were made known on their editorial pages. For example, William Randolph Hearst's *Journal American* used capital letters in an editorial to declare that *Trio* was closed "BECAUSE IT WAS A BAWDY SHOW, WHICH NOBODY CAN DENY."[75] When George Jean Nathan, employed at that time by Hearst, called the License Commissioner "Führer Moss" in a column, his editor placed a statement above it declaring that, "The views expressed in the following article are those of Mr. Nathan and not of this newspaper."[76] In that column the critic pointed out:

While it is true that *Trio* does deal with such a perversion, the Führer along with his complainants, overlooks the clear fact that it deals with it in terms of acute disgust, leads one of the parties there violently to condemn the other, and leads this other in turn to suicide as the only way out. Just how, accordingly, it could be especially dangerous in encouraging immorality in the public, young or old, is not easy to determine. If the subject were handled sympathetically, things conceivably might be different, but it is handled in such a way as to make it thoroughly odious and contemptible.[77]

"We are sure that Mr. Moss is actuated by excellent motives," an editorial in the *New York Times* pronounced in defense of Section 1140-A of the New York State Penal Code. However, the *Times* still suggested that future stage censorship should be handled by a board: "A more dignified process than the impulse of one official."[79] Lewis Nichols, the *Times'* drama critic who covered the *Trio* controversy, differed with the publication's editorial writers. In an attack on the Wales Law, the reviewer concluded, "The state legislature did not spread the net of the Wales Law to catch such efforts as *Trio,* and the misfortune this time is that under a strict reading of the "Padlock Clause" there is no distinction between dignity and disgrace."[80]

LaGuardia and Moss drew their most vigorous support in the press from two Catholic newspapers. Both indicated their advocacy of the License Commissioner's actions and roundly criticized the protesting groups of theatrical organizations.[81] The *Tablet* declared that the banned play "had no more right to existence, than a disease-breeding sewer on Broadway."[82] According to the *Catholic News,* "Right-thinking moral persons with their traditional American as well as Christian convictions on morality have no intention of allowing the anti-moral, pagan minority to dictate to the law on the point."[83]

Two weeks after *Trio* was closed, Mayor LaGuardia finally bowed to demands from his critics that he meet at City Hall with representatives of eighteen different organizations which had become involved in the stage censorship furor. As a result, the Mayor agreed that the Commissioner of Licenses should, in the future, be able to close a show only after the producer was convicted in court. "He did express a desire to speed that trial," *Equity* reported, "to deprive any producer of the possibility of reaping a financial harvest during a long drawn-out trial, and with this the theater was in agreement."[84]

Paul Moss and Fiorello LaGuardia were not the only principals to suffer public reprimands. The Reverend Dr. John Sutherland Bonnell, of the Fifth Avenue Presbyterian Church, was caught by drama critic Wolcott Gibbs of the *New Yorker* being dishonest in drafting the petition to the Mayor that instigated the ban. Otis L. Guernsey, another reviewer, first checked when he became suspicious of the resolution signed by sixteen Protestant clergymen. "When this department phoned one of the ministers at random last week," reported Guernsey, "he admitted that he had never seen *Trio*."[85] Wolcott Gibbs contacted all sixteen ministers writing that "it appears that only one, the Reverend Dr. John Sutherland Bonnell, . . . had bothered to see the darn thing."[86] Gibbs also learned that six of the clergymen were from New Jersey and Long Island. One minister from Brooklyn told Gibbs:

> I haven't seen *Trio,* but Bonnell saw it. I was particularly interested in the fact that one or two people Bonnell knew had very definite Lesbian tendencies — he probably ran into them in his advisory work — well, the play had a deleterious effect on them. Of course, nobody wants censorship, but it's a question, actually, of the protection of the people.[87]

Fiorello H. LaGuardia's term of office expired the same year that *Trio* was closed and Paul Moss lost his job as Commissioner of Licenses with the change in the municipal adminstration. The Wales Padlock Amendment remained the law in New York State for more than two decades after the *Trio cause célèbre,* but never was tested again; however, it was never forgotten by Lee Shubert, the individual who had instigated the skirmish. The "Shubert fist,"[88] as the *New York Times* had called it, remained raised against any gay plays in any of their Broadway theaters until after Lee Shubert's death in 1953.

For more than a year after the closing of *Trio,* no play appeared on Broadway with a character identified by the critics as being gay. Then late in the 1946–47 season George Abbott produced *The Dancer* by Milton Lewis and Julian Funt. Burns Mantle gave a brief plot outline of the play about:

> . . . a famed ballet dancer whose mind gave way. Living under the protection of a wealthy dilettante, the dancer devoted his off time to murdering village prostitutes, puzzling the local gendarmerie greatly. Pursued by his wife, who wants his supposedly hidden fortune, and his daughter, who would like to be sure that his madness is not hereditary, the dancer's life is not a happy one. The law finally catches up with him.[89]

Almost without exception the critics noted the relationship between the mad ballet dancer and his patron as, in the words of the *Times,* "something odd."[90] Howard Barnes in the *Herald Tribune* was more precise, calling the deranged killer, "A homicidal homosexual," and his patron protector "an old fruit."[91]

Following a cool reception, Abbott's production of *The Dancer* closed after six performances.[92] "There Are More Broken Backs Than Chilled Spines in *The Dancer,*"[93] reported John Chapman, referring to the former ballet star's periodic visits to the local brothel to break the backs of prostitutes.

Two theatrical seasons after *Trio's* engagement was cut short, *No Exit* opened on Broadway without stirring any controversy. Paul Bowles' adaptation of Jean-Paul Sartre's *Huis Clos,* premiered in New York on November 26, 1946. "For more than two years," reported the *Post,* "Paris playgoers have been flocking to see it."[94] Sartre's dramatic concept of hell and damnation excited few Broadway theatergoers or critics, and none of the "moralists." "It lasted a month," Brooks Atkinson recalled, "before the production was consigned to that hell that receives all stage failures."[95]

Jean-Paul Sartre's long one-act philosophical fantasy concerns a man and two women — "three characters lifted from newspaper scandals,"[96] who have been condemned to spend eternity in one another's company. "Hell is just ... other people,"[97] Cradeau, the man, declares. He was a coward and a deserter. Estelle killed her baby, and Inez seduced a young wife, and destroyed two lives in the process. "Sensuality, cowardice and perversion, each provides its own punishment," the *Christian Science Monitor* observed.[98]

At one point in the play, Estelle, frustrated by the man's rejection of her, spits in the face of the lesbian. Inez is particularly unsympathetic as she explains what she is all about:

Inez. Well, I was what they call back there, one of *those* women, *already* damned, you know?...[99]

Inez tells of living with her cousin and his wife and of poisoning the wife's mind against the helpless man. The cousin is killed in a trolley accident after the two women left him:

Inez. ...I'm really bad. I mean I need to see other people suffer to exist at all. A torch. A torch in their hearts. When I'm alone I go out. For six months I flamed in her heart, burned in her heart. Then she got up one

Annabella, a film star Hollywood imported from France, played at being an evil lesbian and Ruth Ford, at left, a woman she tries to seduce in No Exit, *which flopped in 1946. The playwright, French philosopher Jean-Paul Sartre, condemned both characters, the lesbian and the woman who killed her own baby, to an afterlife, the drama's setting, in which "Hell is just ... other people."*

night and turned the gas on. I didn't hear her. She got back into bed beside me. That's all.[100]

Inez has only a few scenes during which she admires Estelle, so her impact on the drama is no match for that of the lesbian seductress in *Trio*; nevertheless, both the French-born actress Annabella, who played Inez, and director John Huston were faulted for the pallid characterization of Inez. The *Morning Telegraph* complained:

> John Huston has staged the play with a careful eye on the censors, but in doing so has robbed the play of much of the vigor which a freer production would have granted. Both in Paris and London the physical aspects of the play were granted more leeway and the pivotal role of Inez ran rampant. Frankly, if Monsieur Sartre's play is to have the vitality which is inherent, then prudery must have no part. It is essential to have an untrammelled theater if one is to have a free theater at all. A stage trimmed by the church's prudery, or by politicians intimidated by back-stage pressure, can never have a healthy theater development. The business of *Trio* must not

be repeated or we might as well reinstitute the Inquisition, with no disrespect intended toward liberal opinion in any church. . .

Annabella makes the Lesbian a sleek and tailored soul who is rather too feminine, lacking some of the masculinity the role requires. Nonetheless, she handles the love scenes with Ruth Ford with sufficient explicitness to hold an audience.[101]

From 1950 to 1975, when the appearance of the gay minority in plays was unimpeded by legal harassment — despite Section 1140-A of the penal code — there were very few productions on the New York stage with lesbian roles. However, gay male characterizations presented during the same period numbered no less than 153.[102] In his study, "The Theme of Homosexuality in Selected Theatrical Events Produced in the United States between 1969 and 1974," Dr. Stephen Shapiro wrote:

> Very few of the plays which were included in this study concern themselves with female homosexuality . . . This situation corresponds to society's general apathy with regard to female homosexuality as compared to male homosexuality. It is doubtful that the presence of a lesbian in a play would be more repugnant to an audience than the presence of a male homosexual. Therefore, it appears that the paucity of plays which deal with female homosexuals is a result of a general unconcern toward lesbianism. Also, in spite of the efforts of the women's liberation movement, the theater is still predominantly controlled by men. A majority of those who purchase tickets are male, and most of the plays are still written by men, this fact is reflected in the homosexually oriented theatrical productions through a preponderance of scripts which concern male homosexuals rather than lesbians.[103]

Only two of the twenty-four plays Dr. Gene Touchet examines in his study, "American Drama and the Emergence of Social Homophilia, 1952-1972,"[104] have lesbian roles: Frank Marcus' *The Killing of Sister George,* and Jonathan Katz's gay agitprop, an unpublished script called *Coming Out!*

Although no known lesbian has ever written a play about a lesbian for the Broadway stage, Carson McCullers did successfully dramatize her novel *Member of the Wedding* in 1948, and Edward Albee adapted her *Ballad of the Sad Café* in 1963. Both plays had asexual portraits of females with dispositions not unlike McCullers's own.[105] When Broadway audiences have seen identifiable lesbian roles, they have always been that of aggressive characters enamored of younger, seemingly heterosexual women. Most often these creations were written by playwrights not identified with a gay lifestyle. When William M. Hoffman selected eight gay plays for an anthology published in 1979, the editor chose only three about lesbians. In his introduction to *Gay Plays: The First Collection,* Hoffman explained:

> . . . This imbalance reflects the fact that there are very few plays about lesbians. This is probably so because the people most likely to write about them are women, and female playwrights, gay and straight, are rare. Until recently playwriting was an almost all-male profession. A bias against women in this field is still strong. Since being a female playwright can count as one strike against them to begin with, lesbians are understandably leery of provoking a second strike by writing about their own group. Also, since many lesbians identify themselves as feminists first, they often put their energies into material that concerns the straight majority of women.[106]

Until Tennessee Williams appeared in the mid-forties, gay male playwrights generally avoided writing about their own lifestyles. By his own admission[107] Williams was so terrified of rejection that in his earlier work gay characters, important either to the theme or to the plot, die before the curtain rises. In 1948, Williams broached the subject of gay sexual proclivity in *A Streetcar Named Desire,* but he did so with caution. Even eleven years later, after the author was internationally acclaimed, he still worried about writing another play in which the gay character is dead before the play gets started. "I thought I would be tarred and feathered and ridden out of the New York theater," Williams wrote after the off-Broadway opening of *Suddenly Last Summer,* "with no future haven except in translation for theaters abroad."[108]

In *A Streetcar Named Desire,* Blanche speaks in one moving scene of rejecting her adolescent husband after inadvertently discovering him with a male lover. "He came to me for help. I didn't know that,"[109] guilt-ridden Blanche confesses. Williams's first offstage gay creation was a suicidal bridegroom. "In 1947, novels were depicting homosexual 'men,'" Georges-Michel Sarotte wrote, "but the theatergoing public was not prepared to accept such a character on the stage — or even in the wings."[110]

Professor Sarotte's appraisal of the gay absence on the American stage in the forties, in "Male Homosexuality in the American Novel and Theater from Herman Melville to James Baldwin," is less than accurate. First and foremost, it was Lee Shubert and other theater-owners who, understandably, did not wish to accept the financial and personal risk involved. Broadway audiences had flocked to see *Oscar Wilde* in 1938, but by 1940, not only were theater-owners and producers afraid of gay plays, but so were gay playwrights. Gore Vidal's *The City and the Pillar,* published in 1948, was the first major American novel "to represent openly and on a full scale homosexual experience and the homosexual subculture in contemporary society."[111] Twenty years passed before Mart Crowley dared the same thing on stage with *Boys in the Band.*

Tennessee Williams waited until 1953 before including a gay character in a revised version of *Camino Real:* "at a time," Professor Sarotte contends, "when the public was prepared for a 'pervert' on stage — five years after the Kinsey Report and during an avalanche of homosexual novels.[112] Not until 1972 did Williams write a play, *Small Craft Warnings,* that included a character who survived with a gay lifestyle, something the closeted gay characters could not do in *A Streetcar Named Desire, Cat on a Hot Tin Roof* and *Suddenly Last Summer.*

Only four audiences saw performances of *The Rats of Norway,* the last Broadway production of the 1940s which included one unmistakably gay, but closeted character. Keith Winter's play concerns two heterosexual romantic involvements among members of a faculty in an English boys' boarding school. Playgoers had trouble relating the rather provocative title to the text. The playbills of both the original London production and the belated Broadway version of *The Rats of Norway* contained this explanation:

> In the play, the story centers around two pairs of lovers, one young and romantic, the other mature and passionate. Both are seeking blindly and with increasing desperation for a perfection of love which the very violence of their search prevents them from finding. So, like *The Rats of Norway,* they finally drown their spiritual selves in their quest for the impossible.[113]

The two contrasting couples destroy themselves through the demands they make on each other. Engaged and respectable, young Stephen Beringer and Tillie are not sexually intimate. The older couple, Hugh Sebastian and Jane, are having an adulterous affair behind her husband's back. The tension of the school year and the lovers' personalities render both couples incompatible.

The two women in *The Rats of Norway* are so superior, they make their men uncomfortable. The men are more relaxed with one another in a seemingly casual, platonic relationship. Hugh Sebastian, an alcoholic war veteran with a heart condition, tells his young friend:

Sebastian. It's an odd thing, Beringer, they're far better than us. I couldn't live without Jane, and yet as far as contentment goes I'm far happier with you.
Stephan. Yes, we're far happier being unbetter...[114]

Jane, the headmaster's wife, recognizes the rapport between her alcoholic lover and the younger teacher. When Sebastian dies in her bed before the final curtain, she turns to Stephan (who is helping her remove the body from her boudoir):

Jane. You loved him too, didn't you?
Stephan. Yes.
Jane. More than Tilly?
Stephan. Yes.
Jane. It's a pity we couldn't be happy.[115]

Stephan and Sebastian's relationship, at least as the roles were interpreted by the American actors, made them sexually suspect in the minds of a number of the New York critics. There could not have been any question about the sexual make-up of at least one secondary character. Chetwood, one of the younger members of the faculty, is unmistakenly a closeted gay. Described by the author as "a slim, effeminate-looking youth with a sullen and rather silly sort of beauty which fails only to impress,"[116] Chetwood becomes annoyed when other members of the school's staff notice his facial powder and tease him.

Produced by Gladys Cooper and Raymond Massey, who co-starred as the adulterous couple, *The Rats of Norway* was first seen at the Playhouse, Charing Cross, in the spring of 1933. "It received good press and ran six months," Massey wrote in his memoirs, *A Hundred Different Lives.* Remembering it as "a first-rate drama," concerning "two ill-starred, contrasted love affairs," Massey makes no mention of the men's sexual attraction to one another.[118] None of Laurence Olivier's biographers refer to the role of the younger instructor, which he originated, as being gay. One author refers to it briefly as being that of "an idealistic young schoolmaster corrupted by his elders."[119] He does not identify either the corruption or the corrupters.

Fifteen years after its successful London engagement, *The Rats of Norway* opened at Broadway's Booth Theater on April 15, 1948. Produced and directed by a twenty-three-year-old self-styled, theatrical genius, James S. Elliot, the American version featured John Ireland — who went on to film stardom — as the alcoholic veteran. The cast of players was far less accomplished than the London company. After a single tryout performance at the San Gabriel Playhouse in California, the play met with a uniformly hostile reception from the New York drama critics.

"The biggest bore of the season,"[120] Robert Coleman announced in the *Daily Mirror.* "One of the most frightful performances a cast of professional grownups has given in my time,"[121] Ward Morehouse warned his readers. Described as talky and static, *The Rats of Norway* lasted four performances.[122]

The Broadway critics were almost as unanimous in their suspicions about the nature of Sebastian and Stephan's friendship as they were on the worth of Winters's dramaturgy and Elliot's presentation. Brooks Atkinson made a brief, undefined reference to "sexual abnormalities,"[123] but his colleagues were far more explicit. Richard Watts, Jr., wrote in the *Post:*

> It may have been my imagination which made me suspect that the two young men were more interested in each other than in either of the women, but, anyway, none of the romances came out well.[124]

Wolcott Gibbs reported in the *New Yorker:*

> Since there seemed to be no more than an outside chance that Hugh and Stephan really like each other *much* better than they did their respective ladies, it was, as you can see, a remarkably disorderly situation all around.[125]

"There is a slightly off-center young man," Howard Barnes observed, "who cannot make his mind up whether he loves the female piano teacher or the lush [Sebastian]."[126]

The man from the *World-Telegraph* reported:

> ...at the time I left the performance I was beginning to think that some of the other instructors were falling in love with the other instructors. Even the two ladies of the cast were beginning to act effeminate.[127]

Variety reported that the "author appears to have coddled the title, which has nothing to do with the story, unless he thinks the characters, several having homosexual inclinations, are rats.[128] That is exactly what W. David Sievers thought of the characters in *The Rats of Norway.* In *Freud on Broadway,* he made this observation:

> ...Winter's analogy drawn from the lemmings who swim out to their

death toward an island that has long since sunk beneath the sea. The sunken island is homosexuality, and although the young instructor tries valiantly to reciprocate the love of a young girl, it is a man to whom he is irresistibly drawn — a man who has fought and lost his own battle against his desire for the wife of the headmaster.[129]

Notes

1. Wolcott Gibbs, "The Theatre," *New Yorker,* 10 March 1945, p. 40.
2. "Critical and Amusements," *New York Newspaper PM,* 2 March 1945.
3. "A United Theatre Defeats Official Censorship," *Equity,* February 1947, p. 7.
4. *Ibid.,* p. 5.
5. "Sues For $1,000,000 In Closing of 'Trio,'" *New York Times,* 3 March 1945.
6. "Producer Of Show Is Sent To Jail," *New York Times,* 18 December 1942.
7. Jerry Stagg, *The Brothers Shubert* (New York: Random House, 1968), p. 353.
8. John Anderson, "Kenward War Play Opens At Morosco," *New York Journal-American,* 26 December 1942.
9. John Chapman, "'Trio' Marks Time As Shubert Stands On Landlord Rights," *New York Daily News,* 8 November 1944.
10. Eleanor Monroe, "Belasco," *Women's Wear Daily,* 2 January 1945.
11. Robert Coleman, "'The Captive' Theme Restated by 'Trio'" *New York Daily Mirror,* 30 December 1944.
12. "Trio," *Cue,* 6 January 1945, p. 21.
13. Burton Rascoe, "'Trio' Is Good But Fails Buildup As Sensational," *New York World-Telegram,* 30 December 1944.
14. *Ibid.*
15. Dorothy Baker, *Trio,* (New York: Houghton Mifflin Company, 1943), p. 163.
16. Edwin H. Schloss, "'Trio' Bows In At Locust Street Theatre," *Philadelphia Record,* 26 October 1944.
17. Frank S. Leyendecker, "Theatre," *About Town,* 19 January 1945.
18. Lewis Nichols, "Trio," *New York Times,* 30 December 1944.
19. Fragment of review from the *Philadelphia Evening Bulletin,* 26 October 1944, in *Trio* file, Lincoln Center.
20. *Philadelphia Record,* 26 October 1944.
21. Jerry Gaghan, "'Trio' In Locust Debut. Sabinson Play Scores," *Philadelphia Daily News,* 26 October 1944.
22. Linton Martin, "'Trio' Makes Its Debut On Locust Stage," *Philadelphia Inquirer,* 26 October 1944.
23. Sam Zolotow, "Shubert Refuses Theatre To 'Trio,'"*New York Times,* 6 November 1944.
24. *Ibid.*
25. Abe Laufe, *The Wicked Stage* (New York: Frederick Ungar Publishing Co., 1978), p. 105.
26. "Barring of 'Trio' Arouses Players," *New York Times,* 11 November 1944.
27. Jesse Zunser, "New Plays: Furor Over 'Trio,'" *Cue,* 18 November 1944, p. 21.
28. George Jean Nathan, "George Jean Nathan's Theatre Week," *New York Journal-American,* 12 March 1945.
29. Sam Zolotow, "Violet To Close Saturday Night," *New York Times,* 8 November 1944.
30. "Broadway Report," *New York Newspaper PM,* 6 November 1944.
31. Arthur Pollock,"Theater," *Brooklyn Eagle,* 13 November 1944.
32. *New York Times,* 19 November 1944.

33. *New York World-Telegram,* 30 December 1944.
34. Dorothy and Howard Baker, "'Trio' Clarified by Authors," press release by Samuel J. Friedman, dated 8 November 1944, in *Trio* file, Lincoln Center.
35. "'Critical Amusements,' PM Visits: The Two Who Wrote Trio,'" *New York Newspaper PM,* 24 September 1944.
36. Maurice Stoller, "Stage Today," *New York Morning Telegraph,* 1 January 1945.
37. Burns Mantle, ed., *The Best Plays of 1944–45* (New York: Dodd, Mead & Company, 1945), pp. 407–408.
38. *Brooklyn Eagle,* 13 November 1944.
39. Howard Barnes, "The Theaters," *New York Herald Tribune,* 30 December 1944.
40. *New York World-Telegram,* 30 December 1944.
41. *Equity,* February 1945, p. 6.
42. *New York Morning Telegraph,* 1 January 1945.
43. Ward Morehouse, "The New Play," *New York Sun,* 30 December 1944.
44. Louis Kronenberger, "Critical and Amusements," *New York Newspaper PM,* 30 December 1944.
45. Jesse Zunser, "Trio," *Cue,* 6 January 1945, p. 21.
46. *New York World-Telegram,* 30 December 1944.
47. *New York Times,* 30 December 1944.
48. *Brooklyn Eagle,* 30 December 1944.
49. Jack O'Brien, "The Theaters," *AP News Features,* 11 November 1944.
50. John Chapman, "'Trio,' Finally Arrives and Proves Talky But Strangely Fascinating," *New York Daily News,* 30 December 1944.
51. *New York Daily Mirror,* 30 December 1944.
52. *New York Herald Tribune,* 30 December 1944.
53. Wilella Waldorf, "Two On The Aisle," *New York Post,* 30 December 1944.
54. "Broadway: Trio Is Play On Sordid Theme," *Boston Christian Science Monitor,* 30 December 1944.
55. "Trio," *Stage Today,* 1 January 1945, n.p.
56. Frank Leyendecker, "Theater," *About Town,* 19 January 1945.
57. Eleanor Monroe, "Belasco," *Women's Wear Daily,* 19 January 1945.
58. *New York Herald Tribune,* 30 December 1944.
59. *Cue,* 18 November 1944, p. 21.
60. George Jean Nathan, "Theatre," *American Mercury,* March 1927, p. 373.
61. George Jean Nathan, "George Jean Nathan's Theatre Week," *New York Journal-American,* 8 January 1945.
62. "'Trio' To Close Tonight," *New York Times,* 24 February 1945.
63. Lewis Nichols, "On Censorship," *New York Times,* 4 March 1945.
64. "Moss Insists He Has Right To Censor Plays," *New York Herald Tribune,* 23 March 1945.
65. "Moss Shuts 'Trio' And Warns Others," *New York Times,* 25 February 1945.
66. John Chapman, "Moss Keeps Things Humming In Theatre By Making Mistakes," *New York Daily News,* 27 February 1945.
67. "Moss 'Trio' Closing To Get Court Test," *New York Times,* 1 March 1945.
68. *Equity,* February 1945, p. 7.
69. "Mayor Backs Moss In Closing of 'Trio,'" *New York Times,* 2 March 1945.
70. "Critical and Amusements," *New York Newspaper PM,* 2 March 1945.
71. Burns Mantle, "Burns Mantle Tags LaG. As Real Censor, Warns of Dangers," *New York Daily News,* 5 March 1945.
72. Wilella Waldorf, "Two On The Aisle," *New York Post,* 10 March 1945.
73. "An Editorial, 'The Mayor and Trio,'" *New York Newspaper PM,* 2 March 1945.
74. "Mayor Approves Plan To Curb Moss," *New York Times,* 8 March 1945.
75. "A Question of Morality," (editorial), *New York Journal American,* 16 March 1945.
76. George Jean Nathan, "George Jean Nathan's Theatre Week," *New York Journal-American,* 12 March 1945.

77. *Ibid.*

78. "Mr. Moss and 'Trio,'" *New York Times,* 22 February 1945.

79. *Ibid.*

80. *New York Times,* 30 December 1944.

81. "Sues For $1,000,000 In Closing of 'Trio,'" *New York Times,* 3 March 1945.

82. *Ibid.*

83. *New York Journal-American,* 16 March 1945.

84. *Equity Magazine,* February 1945, p. 5.

85. Otis L. Guernsey, Jr., "The Playbill: A Gentleman By The Name of Moss," *New York Herald Tribune,* 4 March 1945.

86. *New Yorker,* 10 March 1945, p. 40.

87. *Ibid.*

88. *The Brothers Shubert,* p. 353.

89. Burns Mantle, *The Best Plays of 1945-46* (New York: Dodd, Mead & Company, 1946), pp. 7-8.

90. Lewis Nichols, "Melodrama of Abnormal," *New York Times,* 6 June 1946.

91. Howard Barnes, "Ballet Plus Murder," *New York Herald-Tribune,* 6 June 1946.

92. *The Best Plays of 1945-46,* p. 414.

93. John Chapman, "There Are More Broken Backs Than Chilled Spines In 'The Dancer,'" *New York Daily News,* 6 June 1946.

94. Richard Watts, Jr., "Two On The Aisle," *New York Post,* 27 November 1946.

95. Brooks Atkinson, *Broadway* (New York: The MacMillan Company, 1970), p. 404.

96. Ruby Cohn, introduction, Jean-Paul Sartre, *No Exit* (New York: Random House, Inc., 1967), p. vii.

97. Jean-Paul Sartre, *No Exit,* trans. Paul Bowles (New York: Samuel French Inc., 1945), p. 52.

98. Thelma Rantillo, "'No Exit' From France," *Boston Christian Science Monitor,* 27 November 1946.

99. *No Exit,* p. 29.

100. *Ibid.,* pp. 30-31.

101. George Freedley, "The Stage Today," *New York Morning Telegraph,* 28 November 1946.

102. Donald Lee Loeffler, *An Analysis of the Treatment of the Homosexual Character in Dramas Produced in the New York Theatre from 1950 to 1968* (New York: Arno Press, 1975), pp. 43-47 and pp. 47A-47D.

103. Stephen R. Shapiro, "The Theme of Homosexuality In Selected Theatrical Events Produced In The United States Between 1969 and 1974," (unpublished doctoral dissertation, University of California, Santa Barbara, 1976), p. 188.

104. Gene R. Touchet, "American Drama and the Emergence of Social Homophilia, 1952-1972," (Unpublished doctoral dissertation, University of Florida, 1974).

105. Virgina Spencer Carr, *The Lonely Hunter: A Biography of Carson McCullers* (Garden City, New York: Doubleday and Company, Inc., 1975).

106. William M. Hoffman, ed., *Gay Plays, The First Collection* (New York: Avon Books, 1979), p. x.

107. Georges-Michel Sarotte, *Like A Brother, Like A Lover* (Garden City, New York: Anchor Press/ Doubleday, 1978), p. 118.

108. *Ibid.*

109. Tennessee Williams, *The Theatre of Tennessee Williams* (A New Directions Book, 1971), p. 354.

110. *Like A Brother, Like A Lover,* p. 110.

111. Steven Marcus, "A Second Look At Sodom," *New York Herald Tribune,* 20 June 1965.

112. Like A Brother, Like A Lover, p. 110.

113. *The Rats of Norway Playbill,* The Playhouse, Charing Cross, London, 6 April 1933.

114. Keith Winter, *The Rats of Norway* (London: William Heinemann Ltd., 1933), p. 80.

115. *Ibid.,* p.104.
116. *Ibid.,* p. 16.
117. *Ibid.,* p. 3.
118. Raymond Massey, *A Hundred Different Lives* (Boston: Little, Brown and Company, 1979), p. 160.
119. John Cottrell, *Laurence Olivier* (Englewood Cliffs, New Jersey: Prentice Hall, Inc., 1975), p. 79.
120. Robert Coleman, "Rats of Norway," *New York Daily Mirror,* 16 April 1948.
121. Ward Morehouse, "The New Play," *New York Sun,* 16 April 1948.
122. Burns Mantle, ed., *The Best Plays of 1947–48* (New York: Dodd, Mead & Company, 1948).
123. Brooks Atkinson, "The Theatre," *New York Times,* 16 April 1948.
124. Richard Watts, Jr., "Theater," *New York Post,* 16 April 1948.
125. Wolcott Gibbs, "The Theatre: 'Passion in Dotheboys,'" *New Yorker,* 24 April 1948, p. 50.
126. Howard Barnes, "The Theaters," *New York Herald Tribune,* 16 April 1948.
127. William Hawkins, "'The Rats of Norway,' Limns The Lemmings," *New York World Telegram,* 16 April 1948.
128. Ibee., "Plays On Broadway," *Variety,* 21 April 1948.
129. W. David Sievers, *Freud On Broadway* (New York: Cooper Square Publishers, Inc., 1970), p. 412.

16

The First Drama in Any Language to Pit Homophobia Against Homophilia

During the first half of the 1950s lesbian and gay male characterizations finally emerged without fear of legal prohibition on Broadway. At the same time, thousands of gay people were subject to surveillance and attack by American governmental agencies.[1] Surprisingly enough, there were no repercussions from the public, the police or the politicians when showman Billy Rose produced Ruth and Augustus Goetz's free adaptation of André Gide's novel, *The Immoralist.* In a decade of gay oppression, police officers did not storm onstage to stop a show in which a gay apologist, the playwrights' *raisonneur,* defines immorality as sexual dishonesty. No one subpoenaed Billy Rose to answer charges that his production threatened the nation's security, despite the Republican Party warning that gays were "as dangerous as reds."[2]

In his anti-Communist crusade, Senator Joseph McCarthy linked lesbians and gay men to the country's fear of communism. "Conducted in the name of national security," one gay historian noted, "this campaign resulted in the expulsion of numbers of homosexuals from public employment."[3] At McCarthy's instigation the State Department and various branches of the Armed Forces began witch hunts which resulted in thousands of suspected lesbians and gay men being branded as security risks and summarily being dismissed from their government jobs.[4] "Perverts Called Government Peril," reported the *New York Times,* on

Hollywood film star Louis Jourdan made his Broadway debut playing a gay Frenchman married to a frustrated alcoholic, portrayed by stage star Geraldine Page, in the 1954 landmark production of The Immoralist, *based on Andre Gide's novel. David J. Stewart played the Frenchman's Arab confidante, the first homophilic gay character in American drama.*

April 19, 1950. "Gabrielson, G.O.P. Chief, Says They Are As Dangerous As Reds."[5]

    The anti-Communist purges of the Cold War touched both Hollywood and Broadway as early as 1947. Motion picture personalities testified before the House Un-American Activities Committee that "Communists Taint the Film Industry."[6] In the same *Times* article, the motion picture critic for *Esquire* magazine testified that:

> "Broadway is practically dominated by communists.". . . He asserted that forty-four plays out of 100 produced on Broadway between 1936 and 1946 furthered the Communist Party line and that thirty-two others favored that line.[7]

    Plays with gay themes and roles were rare on the American stage during World War II and its aftermath, and gay characters were never seen in motion pictures. Consequently, Washington investigators were unable to cite films or shows supportive of a tolerant stance on behalf of "subversive-prone" gays. In 1954 Washington watchdogs of public patriotism were far too preoccupied inciting communist and gay witch-hunts within the federal government to pay heed to a Broadway play called *The Immoralist.*

Both William Randolph Hearst and Lee Shubert, who had played major roles in keeping plays with gay characters off the New York stage, died in the early 1950s. John S. Sumner retired at the beginning of the decade as the unofficial guardian of public morals. The Society for the Prevention of Vice expired with Sumner's retirement. No other politician, religious leader or public personality appeared eager to continue the cause of Sumner, Hearst, LaGuardia and Shubert. The demise of Comstockery during the first half of the decade also marked the debut of gay activism. The Mattachine Society convened the first assembly of gay people in America in 1953. A year later the first lesbian organization, the Daughters of Bilitis, was formed. However, there was no connection between the emerging homophile movement and the final chapter of the gay emergence in the American theater.

Before the landmark production of *The Immoralist* appeared on Broadway, there had been revivals, earlier in the 1950s, of two famous plays with gay motifs and six productions of new plays with secondary gay, or suspiciously gay characters. The revivals, *The Green Bay Tree,* and *The Children's Hour,* had been performed unmolested some twenty years before and were not in legal jeopardy. The gay characters in the half-dozen new plays were secondary ones. Some were never identified in print as being gay. It was *The Immoralist* that served as an indicator of the growing tolerance within the establishment, at least in New York City.

The two silly, effeminate males in the comedy hit *Season in the Sun,* gave Broadway theatergoers their first look at gays in the 1950s. They contrasted dramatically with the two sober, masculine men of *The Immoralist.* Critics described the gay protagonist of *The Immoralist* as a "well-bred, intellectual young homosexual,"[8] and his Arab confidant as "a gentle deeply philosophical deviate."[9] The gay couple in *Season in the Sun* were identified as "two men who should have been women,"[10] "two amusing effeminates,"[11] and "two ... queens (a type which flourishes on Fire Island like Eel-grass)."[12]

It was not the dialogue that identified the male couple on a Fire Island vacation as effeminate. The dialogue in *Season in the Sun* is mundane, asexual and offers no clues to the men's sexual identity. But

Burgess Meredith, who directed Wolcott Gibbs's comedy, had only to read the author's character description to understand how he wanted the roles performed. "They would have no trouble at all," the critic-turned-playwright wrote, "flying in and out of windows."[13]

The first sight of gay characters in the fifties, dressed identically and gesturing with limp wrists, amused Wolcott Gibbs' colleagues. However, Joseph T. Shipley of the *New Leader* protested:

> Those who enjoy laughing *at* others, instead of with them, will find ample opportunity in *Season in the Sun*. Homosexuals are apparently still regarded in some quarters as funny *per se,* and two of them flutter across the stage a few times for no purpose other than to solicit a thoughtless laugh.[14]

Joseph Schildkraut had no intention of being laughed at when he agreed to star in the 1951 Broadway revival of *The Green Bay Tree*. The stage and film star explained:

> I've always wanted to play Dulcimer, but diametrically opposite to what he was played in the first production. We do not see Dulcimer as an active homosexual. It's a possessiveness. He needs youth, charm and companionship. It's a neurotic necessity, never must the audience feel he has ever touched the boy.[15]

The Green Bay Tree had been revived with decidedly gay Dulcimers in 1946 for four performances at the Equity Library Theater, and for very limited engagements in 1947 and 1950 by off-Broadway groups.[16] Schildkraut and director Shephard Traube's decision to play the elegant bachelor "straight" seemed to some critics, as *Variety* noted, "to be one of the major weaknesses of the production."[17] "They [the star and his director] have blunted the play and caused it to lose much of its edge," the *Morning Telegraph* reported. "Mr. Dulcimer is not at his evil best, and the sinister base essential to the completeness of the play is gone."[18] The *Post* observed:

> All the atmosphere of quiet, almost unspoken terror is gone from it now. Apparently Shephard Traube, who produced it, and Joseph Schildkraut, who now acts the leading role, shied away from the ominous note of the homosexual and tried to substitute for it a considerably healthier menace of a desire for luxury. I can understand their discomfort over that suggestion of the epicene, but, if they felt that way they shouldn't have produced *The Green Bay Tree*. As it is, they have produced a drama that isn't about much of anything.[19]

Despite Schildkraut's determination not to portray the role as an overt gay, a reviewer reported that the veteran star "plays Dulcimer with too obvious homosexual mannerism."[20] The critic from the *Journal American* also reacted to Schildkraut's performance as if he were playing at being a lecherous old gay who uses his wealth to seduce a luxury-loving young man to his perverted lifestyle. After seeing the opening-night performance on February 2, 1951, at the John Golden Theater, the reviewer complained:

> After all, there are people like this in the world and I suppose a consideration of their problems falls within the scope of the theater. My objection is the simple old fashioned one of being slightly revolted by the spectacle of corruption in triumph.[21]

Joseph Schildkraut was seen in only twenty performances in *The Green Bay Tree*'s 1951 revival.[22] A year later, Lillian Hellman likewise blunted the effectiveness of *The Children's Hour* in her staging of a Broadway revival of that play co-starring Hollywood film star Patricia Neal and Kim Hunter. "By having Patricia Neal play Martha in so mannish a fashion," George Freedley of the *Morning Telegraph* protested, "Miss Hellman telegraphs her punches."[23] Walter Kerr also objected to Neal's work, which he found "markedly mannish from the outset, a suggestion which tends to cloud the issue before it can be joined."[24] George Jean Nathan concurred with Kerr, objecting to "Patricia Neal's physical aspect with its wayward suggestion of he-ness rebelliously plants what should gradually come out later."[25] Another dissatisfied reviewer wrote:

> I do not believe a stride and a hair-do comprise the whole of characterization ... there was a stride, there was a Cornellesque hair-do and there was a voice which seemed deliberately pitched into low tones.[26]

"This is a somber play about a subject termed 'difficult' in polite society." George Freedley reported of the off-Broadway Equity Library Theater production of *The Children's Hour* in 1945.[27] Critics and theatergoers were far less squeamish about seeing a lesbian character seven years later, according to the reviewer for *Women's Wear Daily:*

> Gossip about sexual aberrations, actual and implied, has become more prevalent in our depraved plays of 1952 than it ever was in 1934. The implied Lesbianism between the teachers and the nasty gossip-mongering by the patrician grandmother of the malicious little girl seem completely topical and valid today.[28]

Hellman, who had been blacklisted during the McCarthy purge, was unable to find work as a Hollywood screenwriter during those years. "In need of some income," Professor Richard Moody wrote in his study of her dramaturgy, "and prepared to raise her voice against the outrages of HUAC [the House Un-American Activities Committee] and McCarthy, [producer Kermit] Bloomgarden persuaded her to revive *The Children's Hour.* "[29] "In 1952, the play was successfully revived," according to another Hellman's biographer, "then it spoke to audiences about the events of those times — the ruin of careers and lives by the 'McCarthy' technique of the smear, the blacklist and 'The Big Lie.' "[30]

Critic Eric Bentley faulted the revival for failing to generate more indignation at Martha's suicide. After she shoots herself, Karen quickly reconciles with their nemesis, Mrs. Tilford, as if Martha's confession has changed the gravity of the initial charges. In 1954 Bentley wrote in indignation:

> The material from which *A Children's Hour [sic]* is made suggests two stories. The first is a story of heterosexual teachers accused of Lesbianism! The enemy is a society which punishes the innocent. The second story is a story of Lesbian teachers accused of Lesbianism, the enemy is a society which punishes Lesbians. Now, since either of these stories could make an acceptable indignant play, one could scarcely be surprised if a playwright tried to tell them both at once. This is quite what Miss Hellman does. She spends the greater part of the evening on the first story. In fact the indignation she arouses in us has but one source — our impression that the charge of Lesbianism is unfounded, an impression reinforced by everyone's holy horror whenever the subject comes up. Then, in the last few minutes, we learn that one of the teachers is a Lesbian. But it is too late for Miss Hellman to tell story two and spell out its moral. The "guilty" teacher kills herself, and the curtain comes down. Taking the play as a technical exercise, we could praise this ending as clever, or damn it as clumsy, but if we are interested in Miss Hellman's indignation, and especially if during the evening she induced us to share it, we are bound to feel cheated.
>
> We are told that the play has been revived because of the current red scare. Now suppose it had been about teachers accused of communism, that for over two hours we had been asked to boil with indignation at the wrongness of the accusation, only to find, toward the close of Act Three, that one of the pair did harbor communist sympathies? ... Admittedly, the audience at the Coronet was not concerned with the moral ambiguities I find inherent in *The Children's Hour.* As far as I could observe, they were being delightedly shocked at two phenomenons: Lesbians and wickedness in a child.[31]

The revival of *The Children's Hour* is listed as a failure in *The Best Plays of 1952-53,* even though it had 189 performances.[32] No other drama with a gay character has been seen in as many Broadway performances, 877 in all.[33] Only the comedy *Torch Song Trilogy* has had a longer run, with 2,120 performances (after a lengthy off-Broadway engagement). The musical *La Cage Aux Folles* may match *Torch Song Trilogy's* record. The second most frequently seen Broadway drama with a gay character, *Tea and Sympathy,* played 712 performances.[34] The author, Robert Anderson, wanted to make the point that sissies do not always turn out gay any more than tomboys always turn out to be lesbians. Anderson's comfortable theme worked well with the American public. *Tea and Sympathy* was a great hit on Broadway. It was seen in countless stage productions all over the country, and became a motion picture in 1956.

Tea and Sympathy bears a striking resemblance to an earlier British play. Also set in a boys' boarding school, John Van Druten's *Young Woodley,* produced in 1925, had been banned from the public stage in London. It concerned a romantic, but sexually unconsummated relationship between a teenage boy and the wife of a headmaster. Twenty years later that same concept was seen in *Tea and Sympathy.* Anderson added a sexual seduction, a closeted gay homophobe, and — as the *Daily News* reported — the prime consideration of "homosexuality — or the suspicion thereof."[35] Britain's Lord Chamberlain banned Anderson's drama, but the New York production encountered no censorship problems. It opened at the Ethel Barrymore Theater on September 30, 1953 to unanimous rave reviews.

The climactic scene in *Tea and Sympathy* has the respectable, sympathetic headmaster's wife give herself to an effeminate teenager. Tom suspects that he is gay. His father, the headmaster, and some of his classmates entertain the same suspicion. Since the final curtain comes down on the seduction, there is really no way of knowing whether or not the sexual therapy will prove as effective as the same remedy was in *Outrageous Fortune,* where the "borderline" bachelor is "cured" by sleeping with Crystal. In *Tea and Sympathy,* Laura had not achieved the same success when she married a gay bachelor, Bill Reynolds, years before.

As Laura's husband, Bill — who is also the headmaster — remains gay in orientation, though closeted and continent. Bill protects himself from suspicion by his marriage, a brusque, macho manner and a particularly vicious homophobic stance. Bill Reynolds hates the sight of Tom Lee. "A man knows a queer when he sees one,"[36] the masculine misogynist tells his wife. Bill is most comfortable in the company of other males, particularly teenagers, while engaging in outdoor, athletic activities. If the schoolmaster's repression is not apparent to the audience before the last act of *Tea and Sympathy,* the playwright makes certain that it will be in an attack upon Bill by Laura:

> *Laura (quietly, almost afraid to say it).* Did it ever occur to you that you persecute in Tom, that boy up there, you persecute in him the thing you fear in yourself? (Bill *looks at her for a long moment of hatred. She has hit close to the truth he has never let himself be conscious of. There is a moment when he might hurt her, but then he draws away, still staring at her. He backs away, slowly, and then turns to the door.)* Bill!
> *Bill (not looking at her).* I hope you will be gone when I come back from dinner.
> *Laura.* I will be ... Oh, Bill, I'm sorry. I shouldn't have said that ... it was cruel. This was the weakness you cried out for me to save you from, wasn't it...[37]

Two years before *Tea and Sympathy* began its long engagement, Herman Melville's *Billy Budd,* adapted for the stage by two college professors, Louis O. Cox and Robert Chapman, opened. It was seen in 105 performances.[38]

Herman Melville offers no explanation in *Billy Budd* — his last, posthumously published novel — for the hatred which impels Claggart, master-at-arms aboard *H.M.S. Indomitable,* to persecute the young, handsome, good-natured sailor, Billy Budd. None of the New York dailies suggested that the petty officer's false witness was sexually motivated. Yet that conclusion seems indisputable to Dr. W. David Sievers, the author of *Freud on Broadway:*

> The unmistakable hint of homosexuality comes when Claggart, who had been comfortable with the knowledge that all men hate him, is baffled by Billy's friendliness. "Do you — like me, Billy Budd?" he asks searchingly, and when Billy picks up the whip Claggart had dropped, Claggart stares at Billy and then exclaims, "No, no! Charm me, too, would you! Get away," Claggart has no choice but to destroy Billy.[39]

The master-at-arms in *Billy Budd* and the housemaster in *Tea and Sympathy* were not the only unstable or treacherous gay male characters seen on Broadway. The ghoulish Nazi Von Laidi in *Waltz in Goose Step* betrays his gay comrades in order to escape suspicion. The Cockney male hustler in *Oscar Wilde* testifies as a witness for the prosecution when the playwright is tried on sodomy charges. Villainous Claggart and vindictive Bill Reynolds are the first dramatic representations of gay males persecuting other males either for their physical attractiveness, or for their discernible effeminacy.

Broadway audiences saw four other plays — besides *Season in the Sun, Billy Budd,* and *Tea and Sympathy* — with secondary gay characters produced in the fifties. Three were written by well-known authors: Tennessee Williams, George S. Kaufman and Dorothy Parker. The three plays failed to impress the critics or attract theatergoers. The fourth new play, *End As a Man* by Calder Willingham, was such a success in an off-Broadway theater that it was moved to Broadway's Vanderbilt Theater. It had a moderately successful run of 105 Broadway performances beginning on October 22, 1952.[40]

End As a Man merits little mention in any consideration of the emergence of gay characters in American theatrical productions. The minor character suspected of being gay by some critics was not so identified by the playwright. Willingham wrote of Perrin McKee, a teenage sadist and voyeur, "his manner can hardly be described as altogether masculine. However, he is really more creepy and weird than effeminate."[41]

In an ugly scene in *End As a Man* a teenage bully named Jocko threatens another student at a military academy. McKee's behavior, and the author's description, were clues to his sexual disposition:

(McKee *wets his lips eagerly, eyes wide open — literally jumping up and down with nervous excitement and eagerness. Gleeful, joyous, he can hardly contain himself . . . He is like a maniac child with the prospect of going to the zoo. His tone is effeminate, very much like a young lady.)* Beat him! Beat him terribly Jockoo! O-h-h-h . . . Beat him savagely . . . Beat him, beat him, beat him, ooooh Jocko with a *coat* hanger . . . Oh yes. Yes! Hit him. Now hit him! Hit him hard. Don't show any mercy on him. . .[42]

It is not clear that McKee is a gay sadist just because the author refers to him as being effeminate in tone, "very much like a young lady."[43] There is no question that the first covert gay character Tennessee Williams created in his plays was a gay masochist. Williams borrowed Baron de Charlus from Marcel Proust's novels, *A la recherche du temps perdu.* He placed the notorious gay aristocrat into his surrealistic play *Camino Real.* It was seen in sixty performances at the National Theater after it opened on March 19, 1953.

"A strong homophobic statement is embodied in the character of Baron de Charlus," Dr. Gene R. Touchet noted in his dissertation. "The Baron, a man of morbid desires, is dedicated to the pleasures of the body. But he is inflicted with a deep sense of guilt because of his homosexuality."[45] Novelist and playwright Gore Vidal, once an intimate of Williams', wrote of the admittedly gay dramatist:

> He was — and is — guilt-ridden, and although he tells us that he believes in no afterlife, he is still too much the puritan not to believe in sin. At some deep level Tennessee truly believes that the homosexualist is wrong and that the heterosexualist is right.[46]

In *Camino Real,* Williams' guilt-ridden character appears along with an assortment of other troubled characters such as Casanova, Lord Byron, and Marguerite Gautier. Proust's creation appears in the first scene in front of a tacky hotel run by A. Ratt. According to the playwright:

> The Baron de Charlus is an elderly foppish sybarite . . . On his trail is a wild-looking young man of startling beauty called *Lobo. Charlus* is aware of the follower and, during his conversation with *A. Ratt,* he takes out a pocket mirror to inspect him while pretending to comb his hair and point his moustache...
> *A. Ratt.* Vacancy here! A bed at the "Ritz Men Only!" A little white ship to sail the dangerous night in...
> *The Baron.* Ah, bonsoir, Mr. Ratt.
> *A. Ratt.* Cruising?
> *The Baron.* No, just — walking!
> *A. Ratt.* That's all you need to do.
> *The Baron* I sometimes find it suffices. You have a vacancy, do you?
> *A. Ratt.* For you?
> *The Baron.* And a possible guest. You know the requirements. An iron bed with no mattress and a considerable length of stout knotted rope. No! Chains this evening, metal chains, I've been very bad, I have a lot to atone for...[47]

Dr. Touchet explains that "the Baron goes off to seek a man to inflict his penance." "Almost immediately we hear a 'strangulated outcry.' The homophobic statement of the play is complete when the Baron, dead, is pushed across the stage and out of the play."[48]

Rather than turning to a sadistic street hustler to expiate his "sinful" attraction to his gender, another guilt-ridden gay character, created by George F. Kaufman and his wife Leueen MacGrath for *The Small Hours,* turns to a psychiatrist. Judges of the period in America often ordered lesbians and gay men to seek psychiatric help. In *The Small Hours* such help is provided during a prison stay.

The Kaufman's *The Small Hours,* which lasted only twenty performances,[49] concerns the not-too-bright wife of a successsful publisher whose life is full of domestic traumas. These include her son's imprisonment on a narcotic charge for smoking marijuana. After his release, he explains to his mother what drove him to it:

> *Peter.* ... You know what's the matter with me, don't you? You know why I've been such a stinker, and why I took dope, and why I can't get on with anybody. (Laura *just waits.*) I don't know how else to say this. No matter how I say it, it's going to upset and shock you. I wish I could have shielded you from this, but my own need for help is too great. I'm a latent homosexual, that's what's wrong with me. (Laura *still does not speak, there is the merest tightening of her hand.*) In my defense I have to tell you that I fought against it in every way I knew how. It was a difficult fight and it was a lonely fight because it wasn't anything I could discuss, especially not with you and father. But these past months I've been having some talks — a man that I think can help me. He's a doctor I met in prison, and we've been going ahead with it since I came out. Right now I'm going through a tough phase, and when it gets tough I'm tempted to drop the whole thing. I'm really not telling you this to distress you, but because I need your help.
> *Laura.* You know you have it, don't you, my darling? (He *bends over and kisses her,* She *gives a little half cry, holds him tight for a moment* He *goes.*)[50]

Another mother was less sympathetic to her son. The young man is accused of pederasty He denies the charges Yet he goes to the park to watch boys at play, and applies for a teaching position in a private boys' school. This character, the first suspect pederast portrait on the American stage, appears in *Ladies of the Corridor,* written by Dorothy Parker with Arnaud d'Usseau. The playwrights, as Richard Watts, Jr., of the *Post* reported, "have looked with pity and terror into the lives of quiet desperation led by some lonely and aging widows in a gloomy New York hotel."[51] Watts' colleagues had mixed reactions. They praised the performers, but were unenthusiastic about the play itself. *Ladies of the Corridor* began a brief forty-five-day engagement at the Longacre Theater on October 21, 1953.[52]

Grace Nichols, a hotel resident confined to a wheelchair, is cared for by her subservient son, Charles. "Look carefully at him and he is beautiful,"[53] the authors wrote, describing the role played by handsome Shepperd Strudwick. Charles has announced to his mother that he wants to return to teaching. He plans to find a professional attendant to look after her. He has not worked since losing his last teaching post. The parents of one of his students accused him of seducing their son. "I paid that preposterous sum and we left town," Grace recalls.[54] The school has been closed for years and no record exists that might spoil Charles' chances of being hired. Mr. Whittaker has interviewed him for a position at a private school for boys in New York City. Mrs. Nichols objects to Charles' leaving her to the care of someone else citing "the obligations of a human being."[55]:

Charles (goes to her). Grace, what are you talking about?
Mrs. Nichols. I'm talking about the most important thing of all — duty. Mr. Whittaker has a tremendous duty to those children. Those little boys are in his charge. He dare not expose them to—
Charles (sitting in chair). To what?
Mrs. Nichols. Need we go into that?
Charles. Are you tellng me that you feel you have a duty?
Mrs. Nichols. Yes, Charles, I am.
Charles. To whom?
Mrs. Nichols. To those little children, Charles. As I get nearer the grave I realize that I must do what is right. Painful though it may be to me, and mine. If you're not going to tell Dr. Whittaker the truth, then I must!
Charles. But it wasn't the truth! It was a vicious lie!
Mrs. Nichols. Appearances, Charles, appearances.
Charles (jumps up). And what were the appearances?
Mrs. Nichols. You kept the boy after school.
Charles. I wanted to help him with his composition. (Pacing L. and back to C.)
Mrs. Nichols. But it was appearances. They were damaging. He was such a pretty little boy.[56]

His mother threatens to write to any prospective employer. Charles is trapped. The fact that the only employment he will consider is teaching at a school of young boys, calls his professed innocence into question. Mrs. Nichols, while seemingly vindictive and selfish, may actually be protecting Charles and herself from a second financially devastating and humiliating scandal.

Before the appearance of "the first American play to present an avowed homophile,"[57] as Dr. Touchet characterizes the Arab apologist in *The Immoralist,* the other plays with gay characters produced in the first half of the 1950s offered theatergoers a sorry, unsavory lot. Broadway audiences saw a couple of flitty Fire Island effeminates, a persecuting homophobe, a slandering closeted villain, one masochist, one suspected sadist, a convicted drug-user and a suspected child molester. Because the majority of these roles were minor ones, however, the reviewers made little of their sexual predilections. In addition, none of these plays were primarily concerned with the social or personal conflict of the gay male.

In *Tea and Sympathy* suspicions of gay inclinations figured prominently in the drama's plot. However, the sensitive, persecuted young man was heterosexual. His problems reflected those experienced by some heterosexuals, a dramatic predicament not unfamiliar to Continental playgoers in the first half of the twentieth century. "In the theater homosexuality is always a false accusation," André Gide observed in 1950, "never a fact of life."[59] Four years later, Ruth and Augustus Goetz dramatized Gide's internationally acclaimed and denounced novel, *The Immoralist.* American theatergoers saw a protagonist whose gay predilection becomes the most important aspect of his life. *Variety* recognized the giant step in the development of gay characterizations on the American stage:

> A generation ago Mae West crudely exploited homosexuality in *The Pleasure Men [sic].* Other plays dealing with the subject have been *The Captive, The Green Bay Tree,* and *Trio.* More recently there has been *Tea and Sympathy,*... compared to the Gide Story, the story of *Tea and Sympathy* is a pretty valentine which leaves most people feeling a sentimental glow that courageous clean-mindedness has triumphed over nasty rumor. Gide is not dealing with rumor, this hero is guilty as charged.[59]

The protagonist, if not the hero, of the Goetzes' *The Immoralist* is a fine-looking French bachelor, son of an affluent archaeologist. Michel's own work in archaeology has gained him a reputation more illustrious than his father's. Act One begins in 1900 at their country home in Normandy after the father's funeral. Michel learns that Bocage, the estate manager, has been appointed his legal guardian. The father's will stipulates that, "The propriety of my son's behavior shall be the sole condition of his enjoying his inheritance."[60] Michel is insulted, enraged and deeply hurt by this demeaning stipulation.

Both Michel and Bocage know why the old man died suspicious.
The son has devoted his whole life to proving that he is not gay. The old
man, however, never forgot an experience, humiliating to them both.
Michel had been expelled from a boarding school for boys:

> *Michel (in torment).* I was eleven years old! I had a problem . . . and when
> you are eleven years old you are not very good at problems. And I solved
> mine vilely — I know that!
> *Bocage.* If it had been anything else — like stealing or lying — the school
> would not have expelled you. But this was a sin of the flesh, an offense
> against yourself and the other boy — it frightened your father! He never
> forgot it.
> *Michel. He* never forgot it! Do you think I did? That morning as the
> teachers packed my boxes, they threw my clothing in as if it were infected.
> Then they walked me through the courtyard at the recess so that everybody
> could watch me leave. I was alone on the earth. At that moment they cut
> me away from other human beings. I was never able to make my way back
> . . . not even to my father. . .[61]

Michel decides to leave his Normandy country home immediately,
feeling himself a failure. Marcelline, a pretty young neighbor who has
been in love with Michel since they were children, wants to go with him.
Despite her brother's objections, Marcelline asks Michel to marry her.
The first scene ends as Michel, driven into the arms of the adoring young
woman whom he calls, "My only friend,"[62] accepts Marcelline's pro-
posal. They plan to be married immediately so that Michel can continue
his archaeologicial research.

It is clear in the next scene that the marriage is a failure. They are
living in Biskra in the Sahara Desert of Algeria. Michel is ailing with un-
diagnosed tuberculosis. The two-month-old marriage is unconsummated. While Marcelline is tormented by this unnatural situation,
Michel, satistfied with their platonic relationship, professes his love for
her. Attempting to prove himself, he takes his bride in his arms, but the
physical exertion brings on another of his coughing spells. Michel's
hemorrhaging terrifies Marcelline. She screams for help as the curtain
descends on the first act.

In Act Two, Michel returns from a week's stay in the hospital to
find that Marcelline has hired an Arab houseboy to help her during his
recovery. The audacious boy — Bachir, a blackmailing petty thief who
prostitutes himself to gay tourists — immediately recognizes Michel's
proclivity. The first chance he gets he mentions to his master an orchard

outside of the city in which a man named Moktir "lives without women — only boys and men are out there. Beautiful men."[63] Michel is annoyed at Bachir's presumptuousness and will hear no more.

Bachir will not be put off. "Then maybe I amuse you, sir," he tells Michel, "I dance for you..."[64] The boy does so, picking up Marcelline's sewing scissors to use as castanets. When she comes into the room interrupting the boy's seductive dance, Bachir leaves with Marcelline's scissors. Michel has seen the handsome young thief steal them. He says nothing, however, when his wife notices that they are missing.

Two weeks later, Michel is sitting one evening on the terrace, when an Arab seeks him out and shows him a small piece of stone sculpture that was unearthed. Michel invites the man to join him for coffee. He learns, much to his amazement, that the Arab has not only read his books but has taught at the University of Fez:

> *Michel (astonished).* It is a great University! Why did you leave?
> *Arab.* One must choose, sir. Of the thousand forms of life each of us can know but one. I came here because I chose to live without shame.
> *Michel.* Shame of what?
> *Arab.* I am Moktir, the shepherd.
> *Michel.* From the orchards?
> *Arab.* Yes.
> *Michel.* I have heard of you. I want nothing from you. *(Michel rises, to down right of terrace.)*
> *Arab.* You didn't begin by insulting me. I am no different now than when I entered here.
> *Michel.* You are to me! I didn't know who you were!
> *Arab.* You don't know now. I have given up more freedom than you will ever have in order not to lie to you, or to anyone, and above all not to myself.
> *Michel.* Everything I have been taught tells me that what you are is wrong.
> *Arab.* Wrong! How can a man of science use such a word! My instincts are a part of nature.
> *Michel.* That is not true!
> *Arab.* How can you judge what is true for me? I must do that for myself. For me only the present exists.[65]

Michel asks Moktir to leave before Marcelline returns. Offended by a fellow scholar, the Arab starts to exit. Suddenly disturbed at his impulsive, rude behavior, Michel stops him and apologizes. The two men shake hands. Michel promises to come and visit the orchard. He gives

Moktir a book written by Aristippus, the Greek philosopher of Cyrene who taught him that pleasure is the only rational aim oᶠ 'ife:

> *Moktir (looks at it).* Aristippus! Thank you. *(He goes out the gate then turns.)* There is a line here I have never forgotten. *(He quotes)* The art of life lies in taking pleasures as they pass, and the keenest pleasures are not intellectual — nor are they always moral. . .[66]

Michel watches his guest depart.

Bored with life in the Sahara and by Michel, Marcelline has begun to drink. He, on the other hand, finds himself at ease for the first time. He is recovering from his tuberculosis and, together with his wife, has been going for daily visits to the orchard. Marcelline finds no satisfaction in their outings. "When I sit with you and Moktir," she says, "I feel completely unnecessary."[67] Before racing off to bed, the virgin wife says, "I could live with you anywhere, without comfort, without children — but I cannot live with your denial of me. It makes me feel half-dead!"[68]

Bachir enters to find Michel in a bad humor. Within minutes the audacious houseboy is fired. Bachir insinuates that his employer is very interested in the orchards:

> *Bachir.* . . . The first time I saw you with Madame — the day you took this house — I knew you were— *(Michel reaches out for Bachir's throat. Bachir grabs his hands)*
> *Michel.* How dare you? *(He grabs him)*
> *Bachir.* Don't! I will not tell her! I promise you! *(Michel flings him to the ground)*
> *Michel.* Get out!
> *Bachir.* It is no secret— *(He stands up)* Maybe not even to her— *(He exits quickly away from the house. His laughter can be heard in the distance)* It is no secret!. . .[69]

Offended and enraged by the houseboy's mockery, Michel goes to the wife's bed to prove his heterosexual capabilities as the curtain descends.

In the next scene, some months later, Marcelline comes home from the wine shop drunk. Michel is so wrapped up in his writing and his friendship with Moktir that he has not been aware of his wife's alcoholism. Moktir is visiting Michel when the hysterical, incoherent young woman must be helped to bed:

Moktir (Comes onto the terrace). You have not deceived her! You have deceived yourself!

Michel. I have to help her! *(Moktir starts out)* Don't go! Help me, Moktir!

Moktir. It is dishonor to live two lives! I return to my own life. I deceive no one. I corrupt no one. Do you think that because I am what I am I have no morality? Do you think that because you have come to our life, you will be able to live without any?

Michel. I must help her!

Moktir. Your power to help is not great. You hide behind her. The only way you could help her is to spare her what is coming — you should bear that alone!

Michel. No! No! I will not be alone! I cannot lose her! I cannot live as you do!

Moktir (Gravely). You harm us all. . .[70]

Michel goes to his drunken wife :

Michel. I have to tell you the truth. I have to tell you everything. You will not understand it, just as I cannot. But if you know about me, you will not destroy yourself anymore.

Marcelline (Puts her feet on the ground to rise). I am drunk. Thank God, I am drunk.

Michel (Comes to her and takes her by the arms). I am everything you fear I am.

Marcelline (Almost screams). How dare you tell me the truth? How dare you?[71]

Michel wants Marcelline to save herself by leaving him. He will go on living in Biskra:

Marcelline. What will I say? What will I tell people?

Michel. Don't spare me! Tell the truth. See that no one ever makes our mistake again!

Marcelline (Pleading). I don't care about the others. I just care about you and me.

Michel. Listen to me, Marcie! You must go home hating me! For your own sake you must see me as I am.

Marcelline (Pulls away from him). Don't .. don't   don't ... *(She pulls away from him — exits to terrace)*

Michel (Following her). You must understand me! *(Marcelline is trying to escape the words, but he follows her — she sits down and covers her ears)* I will say it everywhere! I will write it! I will speak it!

Marcelline. Don't, Michel ... don't!

Michel (Against her loud protests takes her hands from her ears so that she can hear him). I will never be silent again! Whoever hears of me, will hear that before anything! If there is an ounce of energy within me, I will say what I am like! This one thing I can do! I can speak out! *(He raises his head in defiance as the curtain comes down)*[72]

As Marcelline prepares to leave Biskra, she learns she is pregnant. She will not allow the doctor to tell her husband. In a final conversation with Bachir, Marcelline learns that he plans to blackmail Michel if he remains in Algeria:

Marcelline. Poor Michel.
Bachir. He will have it everywhere, Madame. It might as well be Bachir who profits—...[73]

Six weeks later, Michel appears at the house in Normandy. He tells Bocage, his guardian, that misery drove him home:

Michel. I have scavenged through the back streets of every town I passed through — There is no loneliness like that! I have been exploited by those who are like me, and shunned by those who are not.
Bocage (Not wanting to hear). My God, Michel—
Michel. And for that freedom I left Marcelline...[74]

Robert, his brother-in-law, threatens to ruin Michel if he ever claims Marcelline's unborn child. This is the first Michel hears of the pregnancy. Aware of her loneliness, he wants to stay with Marcelline:

Marcelline. How could we be together? Think of the things we can never say to one another, the questions we can never ask ... What kind of a life would that be?
Michel. There is no assurance I can give you. I will no more lie to you than you to me. Our life together might destory us both ... but it might not. There are many kinds of marriages, Marcie, and people sacrifice many things to hold on to them.[75]

Bocage pleads Michel's case:

Bocage. ...Oh, Miss, let him stay. Let him stay and face these people down. In time they will listen to him. And if not to him, then to his books.
Marcelline. No one will listen! That is a solution for those who come after we are gone — It won't solve our lives.[76]

Bocage warns Marcelline, "If you send him away now, there is only one life he can go back to—":

Marcelline. Is Bocage right? Is that the only life you face?
Michel. I wish it were not — but there is no place on earth where those who

are like me will not seek me out. Only here in this house where I was raised, can I shut them out.[77]

After Marcelline agrees, Michel makes her a promise before the final curtain falls:

Michel. I promise one thing: whatever life we may have here we will live it in dignity.[78]

Only a little more than a third of André Gide's novel is set in Algeria. The Goetzes freely devised almost all of the plot and most of the characterizations. The novel's protagonist does not openly consort with gay Arabs. He does not reveal his sexual predilection to anyone. He neither separates from, nor reconciles with his wife. In the novel, Marcelline's death conveniently resolves Michel's dilemma.

Additional elements, suggested by Gide's own biography, were woven into the dramatization. Only in the denouement, in which Michel chooses celibacy over social ostracism and sexual vulnerability, do the Goetzes depart from the facts of Gide's own unconsummated marriage. His biographer, Klaus Mann, noted that Madeleine Gide "did not mind his erratic habits, or at any rate did not prevent him from indulging in them. Gide, the husband, roved throughout the world — no less un-bound than did Gide, the bachelor."[79]

Eric Bentley faulted the Goetzes for the way in which they resolved Michel's dilemma:

The question has been: what can a homosexual husband do — assum-ing that his wife loves him and that he needs her affection? The answer proffered in the last scene of the play is that he can do without homosex-uality! Or can he? This is modern drama. We can end, if we like, with a question mark. What the Goetzes don't seem to have realized is that this is not to ask a question but to beg one — and that, the main question of their play ... The goal the Goetzes were making for was the open presentation of homosexuality and the open advocacy of a humane attitude to it. Up to now, as Gide told them in an interview, homosexuality in the theater has been an accusation ... Its standard form at present is, in fact, the *unjust* accusation, for our public has reached the point where it will allow the sub-ject of homosexuality to come up, provided that the stigma is removed before the end of the evening. Our public's motto is: tolerance — provided there is nothing to tolerate ... In short, the Goetzes stuck on a final scene [that] is last minute conformism.[80]

The goal that the Goetzes had set was "the open presentation of

homosexuality and the open advocacy of a humane attitude to it."[81]
Twenty-five years after *The Immoralist* played on Broadway, Ruth
Goodman Goetz revealed that the play had been written as a gesture of
outrage. A well-known English actor-director whom they admired was
gay. He had been forced to live an uncomfortable, covert lifestyle considered so depraved and revolting, that any reference to it was unthink-
able. "We decided, for the sake of this fine, superior human being and
others like him," Mrs. Goetz recalled, "we were going to drag the subject out into the open, out on the stage to which we had access since we
were writing for the theater."[82]

Mrs. Goetz traced the genesis of *The Immoralist* back to when she
had noticed a slender volume at the Alfred A. Knopf Publishing Company in New York City:

> It was Gide's classic novel, written, would you believe it, before the
> turn of the century, and translated into English by Dorothy Bussy. I had
> read some of Gide's notebooks in France, but had never heard of *The
> Immoralist*. I was very impressed, returned it to the shelf, and then
> remembered it years later during a conversation with Gus, my husband,
> when we were in England in 1950 for the London production of our
> Broadway hit, *The Heiress*. During the rehearsals we became painfully
> aware that the English director was simply incompetent. We went to our
> producer, the late Binky Beaumont — a darling person — and told him
> that the director did not know what he was doing. He said he'd get in
> touch immediately with his friend, who was starring in a show, about com-
> ing in as a replacement. The next day he took over. I can't tell you how
> impressed Gus and I were watching that man work. He was so sensitive, so
> considerate, so intelligent — the way he handled the actors. And he had
> such insight into our script. He could recognize what we, the writers, had
> had in the back of our minds when we were in the process of putting some-
> thing down on paper. Of course, he made the play work beautifully and it
> went on to be a sensational hit in London.
>
> We were so appreciative, Gus and I. After the first tryout perform-
> ance in Brighton, we were walking back to our hotel on the promenade
> along the beach. "What a shame," I said, "that this man, this talented,
> intelligent, kind human being has to live as he does — half-hidden from
> the rest of us and always on the defensive, careful and guarded about a
> whole part of his life." Of course, we knew he was homosexual, and
> Binky, too. "Nobody even dares to talk about the subject openly," Gus
> replied; "I don't think anyone has even written about what they have to
> go through, have they?" "Yes," I said. "André Gide has."
>
> My husband had never heard of *The Immoralist*. I went out the next

day and bought a copy for him. As soon as he finished reading it, we both knew that it was going to be our next project. We had to do it, for him, our director, whom we respected so and admired. We wanted to get the subject out, where it belonged, so that he and people like him wouldn't have to go on living half-hidden from the rest of the world.

Eighteen months later when we finally finished the play, we sent it to him before anyone else had read it. He wrote to say that he hated it. That it was awful and dirty, the whole subject matter. Poor Gus was devastated, I remember, at that reaction from the man for whom we had written it. Now, in 1980, I can better understand, looking back, why this stage star reacted as he did. He must have felt very threatened, of course, that the play might very well bring the subject out of the closet.[83]

The Goetzes went to see André Gide in Paris before returning to New York to start writing the play. The elderly author told the American couple:

Take my play and do for it what you did for *Washington Square* [on which *The Heiress* was based]. I will abide by any form you give me in the theater. And when your play comes to be done in France, I ask only that I may be permitted to translate it.[84]

The Goetzes worked two years on their adaptation. Gide died before they had finished their first draft.

"Why did we feel that we could dare handle a subject, and do justice to it, when even in the 1950s most people felt uncomfortable about it if the subject ever came up in conversation?" Ruth Goetz asked:

To begin with I had known homosexuals all my life. My father was a theatrical producer and I was raised and educated in Manhattan. I worked with them when I grew up. They never offended me and I never felt hostile to them. Lesbians never seemed threatening to me, a bit perplexing perhaps, because I could never never figure out what they could possibly do. Somehow it was easier to understand what the men might be up to. It never occurred to me to pass judgment on them.

As a happily married couple, and well known as such, Gus and I were hardly suspect of a subject matter that might have seemed personally or professionally threatening to some other playwrights. Then, too, we were understandably more sensitive to the plight of minorities. I was Jewish and Gus was raised as a Catholic. While neither of us were really touched by any prejudice, because of our fortunate families' circumstances, we were aware of Catholics and Jews who had been.[85]

The Goetzes spent ten torturous months searching for a producer.

The play was turned down by every major producer in the theater. "As a last resort, we sent it to Billy Rose," Mrs. Goetz recalled:

> Billy Rose wanted to be cultured. I honestly think that was the real reason that he decided to do our play so he'd be identified with something that to his way of thinking was cultured or intellectual.
>
> We asked Herman Shumlin to direct — which it turned out was almost our undoing! Herman had been one of the producers to turn the play down, but in rejecting it, he wrote that it was a beautiful script. He didn't dare do it, take a chance on such a daring show, if I remember correctly, because at that time he had money problems of some sort — as a producer.
>
> After Louis Jourdan and Geraldine Page were set as our stars, Herman brought us this blond, unknown kid, James Dean, that he insisted should play the Arab houseboy despite our misgivings about his Nordic physical appearance. Herman was right, it turned out, as we began to realize during rehearsals; Jimmy was sensational in the role.
>
> We also found out during rehearsals that Herman was distorting the theme of our play. He decided to sentimentalize the wife's situation so that the husband seemed the villain. We had written *The Immoralist* with compassion for the homosexual's predicament in such a situation. "But audiences will sympathize with the wife," Herman insisted. "They can't relate to a homosexual husband!" We concluded that Herman couldn't. Then he gave us trouble with a scene in our original script in which Michel goes to see Moktir in the orchard. Herman was so uncomfortable with it he wanted it cut. He didn't know how to handle the two boys tossing a ball in the background. We were afraid he was going to have them play it swishy or with limp wrists. To make matters worse, Herman okayed a God-awful set that made the orchard look like one of those post-cards of an oasis tinted in harsh colors. The set was junked and the scene cut. Moktir came to see Michel at his home in the rewriting we had to do.
>
> When Herman persisted in spoiling everything we had worked for with his sentimental staging, we went to Billy. He took in a rehearsal, fired Herman and replaced him with Daniel Mann. We felt badly because we were fond of Herman, but he was simply too far out of his element to deal fairly with homosexual characters.
>
> It was too late to put the orchard scene back into the play during our try-out engagement in Philadelphia where we got rave reviews even though we shocked them even without the boys in the orchard. We went onto Broadway still minus the scene Herman had been unable to deal with. So the New York critics and audiences never had to.[86]

When Billy Rose's production of *The Immoralist* opened in 1954, critic Louis Kronenberger called it "perhaps the most serious and outspoken treatment of homosexuality that Broadway had seen."[87] Only one of the critics was discomforted by the subject matter. John Chapman of the *Daily News* wrote of the performers, "I was embarrassed for them last evening. And for me, too."[88] Brooks Atkinson hailed *The Immoralist* as "an admirable piece of work. The tragedy is austere, crushing and genuine." He referred to Michel's boarding school incident as an "abominable crime," and to André Gide's gay orientation as "his misfortune."[89] Robert Coleman, of the *Daily Mirror,* was more tolerant in his reaction to the Goetzes' work:

> *The Immoralist* has to do with the plight of the homosexual, often scorned and shunned by the moral and usually blackmailed and exploited by the corrupt. Gide wrote at a time when the law had not taken cognizance of the fact that such unfortunates are victims of errant genes.
>
> Though most of us now take a more understanding view, the statutes still do not provide sufficient protection for them. They have no status in our civilization. They doubtless have to pay a terrible price for nature's quirks. If *The Immoralist* does nothing else, it may awaken us to a sober consideration of the subject.[90]

Thomas R. Dash of *Women's Wear Daily* wrote:

> Here we behold an ill-starred sex deviationist, who does not want to be considered a social pariah, who wants to pursue his chosen task with dignity and honor. What should our attitude be? Should society be intolerant, should we treat these cases as clinical specimens, or as ordinary human beings, should we treat them with sympathy as we would treat a person with some physical malady?[91]

The man from *Variety* commented:

> Gide does not explain, nobody could, how it is that certain men become fixated upon their own sex and cannot love women. He does make piteously clear the suffering which being "different" inflicts upon the individual. The sneers of the holier-than-thous, the black-mailings of tramp-nances are only passing sidelights. The terrible hurt laid bare in this play is deeper than mere social ostracism.[92]

The Goetzes' drama failed to move Noel Coward. *"The Immoralist,* a gloomy little number whipped up from André Gide's turgid preoccupation with the same theme, bored me to death when it wasn't giving me the giggles."[93] Coward also dismissed *Tea and Sympathy,* as "a mixture of naïveté and dishonesty ... treated unruly and lasciviously."[94]

The mixed reviews somewhat blunted the box office impact of co-star Louis Jourdan, a strikingly handsome and popular movie star, and Geraldine Page, who had been hailed by the critics as a new Broadway star the previous season. Herman Shumlin's prediction that audiences would not relate to a sympathetic gay protagonist was also a factor in the disappointing three-month engagement. Still, according to Dr. W. David Sievers, "its respectable sum of ninety-six performances indicates the psychological maturity of the Broadway Theater by the mid-fifties."[95]

John McLain of the *Journal American* felt that the Goetzes lack of candor hurt their work. "The writing seems to skirt the fringes of the issue, rather than facing up to the facts that have become fairly pedestrian in our present world."[96] The word "homosexual" is not used in the play and Michel's confession is not explicit. Reginald Cockburn, a veteran theatergoer, recalls, "The night I saw the show, as we were leaving the theater, a man walking ahead with his wife turned to her and said, 'What was his problem? He have cancer?' "[97]

The critics who were disappointed with *The Immoralist* claimed it lacked an emotional wallop. This may be attributed to a structural defect in the plot. The play moves to its denouement before the couple's marital conflict climaxes. "It is like sitting on a dynamite charge that never explodes," Robert Coleman complained.[98] "A grave drama about abnormality seemed to me pretty dull theatergoing," concurred Richard Watts, Jr., in the *Post*.[99] Walter Kerr wrote, "Ruth and Augustus Goetz have brought a quiet, patient candor to the subject of homosexuality. But a quiet, patient candor is not precisely an exhilarating theatrical vein."[100] John McLain reported, "Here is a girl who insists upon marrying a guy who is not really a guy, and what happened thereafter failed to capture me."[101]

Despite its financial failure and mixed critical reception, *The Immoralist* was selected as one of the best plays of the 1953–54 season:

> The Goetzes combined understanding with detachment; they equally eschewed prissiness and sensationalism, and the result is an honest and clear-sighted study, a soberly effective formulation. If there is a vital weakness, it is too thorough-going a "study" to come altogether to life on the stage. If it is as accurate, it is also at times as inexpressive as a blueprint. Everyone seems a little too articulate, everything a little too explicit; there is a certain sense of figures carefully placed in the moral landscape. In

terms of story, we should be kept guessing more at the beginning, while in terms of theme we should be left guessing less at the end. But what, all in all, seems noteworthy is how much the play achieved rather than fell short of.[102]

Dr. Touchet observed, "*The Immoralist* had the potential to be a strong homophilic play. But it is not. In spite of some advocated homophilia, the protagonist finally denounces his homosexuality and takes steps to live his life as a homophobe."[103] Touchet concluded, "In spite of these faults, *The Immoralist* is a landmark work, for it is one of the first dramas to pit homophilia against homophobia."[104] Moktir, the Arab shepherd, is "the first homophilic homosexual in American drama in the 1950s. He is the first character to refute homophobic motives and to present a valid homosexual identity."[105]

Touchet's doctoral study was limited to the decades between 1952 and 1972. He does not mention the first homophilic characters in American drama. Those landmark characters were the high school student and young choirmaster in Chester Erskin's 1938 failure, *The Good.* Howard refused to deny his gay sexual orientation and Mr. Duncan refused to speak of their relationship as "wrong," but only "different."[106] They ran off to live together as lovers. The following theatrical season Oscar Wilde's defense of "the love that dare not speak its name,"[107] was heard in the Broadway hit.

Both *The Good* and *Oscar Wilde* were illegal. The New York state law prohibiting gay characters, however, was being blatantly ignored by the end of the 1930s. After the closing of *Trio* in 1945, producers and playwrights were reminded that the Wales Padlock Law was still on the books. In 1954, when Billy Rose produced *The Immoralist,* the Goetzes' play could have been closed. Aware of that possibility the Goetzes said, "What Gide wrote in a great burst of bravery 50 years ago, takes a great amount of bravery, it seems, to produce in 1954."[108]

In 1980, Ruth Goetz wondered aloud:

When was Jean-Paul Sartre's *No Exit* produced? Yes, the year after LaGuardia had *Trio* closed. I think that was the end to the whole censorship threat, but we really didn't know that for sure until our play was produced. *No Exit* just had that lesbian in it; *The Immoralist* was, as we intended it to be, the first sympathetic dramatic consideration of the homosexual's predicament. We got it out in the open, out of the closet and onto the stage.[109]

The Immoralist and *No Exit* differed greatly. The Goetzes' work, "An Outstanding Example of Theatrical Courage,"[110] according to critic Whitney Bolton, presented two gay lifestyles: one unashamedly open and active; the other, continent but intellectually, professionally, and personally open and active. Jean-Paul Sartre's piece is an existential, dramatic, three-character dialogue, in which one character happens to be a lesbian. Sartre damned Inez to hell, so it is hardly surprising that no voices of protest were raised. However, Goetzes' compassionate treatment of Michel and Moktir did not result in protest either.

Censorship was not on their minds when they wrote the play:

> We had been working on it for some time when the subject first came up. Gus mentioned to a friend that we were adapting Gide's novel. "It's against the law," he reminded us. Of course, I knew about the Padlock Law. My father had taken me to see *The Captive* when I was in my teens. He felt sorry for the producer, Gilbert Miller, when the show was closed by the police. I remembered the *Trio* closing, too; still Gus and I never gave it a second thought as we continued working on *The Immoralist*.

> Whatever qualms any producers may have expected with the law or censorship of some kind had they put it on, Billy Rose had absolutely none. I never heard that possibility mentioned even once all during rehearsals or during the run of the play. Not a single word! Stage censorship was a dead issue by the mid-fifties. Had it not been, *The Immoralist* would certainly have provoked considerable activity and hostility.[111]

In 1963 when *The Immoralist,* starring newcomer Frank Langella, was revived with great success off-Broadway, some critics mentioned scenes in the revival that had been cut from the Broadway original because of problems with censors. Judith Crist of the *Herald Tribune* covered the revival at Bouwerie Lane Theater where it was seen in 210 performances.[112] "With the changed moral climate," Crist reported, "at least of our theater in the past nine years, Mr. and Mrs. Goetz have reportedly made their play more frank and more pointed in dealing with homosexuality."[113] Augustus Goetz had died in 1957 and his widow had made only minor changes in the dialogue. The orchard scene with the two Arab boys tossing a ball in the background was seen for the first time by New York audiences in the revival. Ironically enough, the scene had been cut from the original production not by any censor, but by Herman Shumlin, the most active opponent of stage censorship in the history of American theater.

Notes

1. Sal J. Licata, "The Emerging Gay Presence," *Los Angeles Advocate,* 26 July 1978.

2. "Perverts Called Government Peril," *New York Times,* 19 April 1950.

3. *Los Angeles Advocate,* 26 July 1978.

4. Jonathan Katz, *Gay American History* (New York: Thomas Y. Cromwell Company, 1976), pp. 91–104.

5. *New York Times,* 19 April 1950.

6. Anthony Leviero, "Menjou Testifies Communists Taint Film Industry," *New York Times,* 22 October 1947.

7. *Ibid.*

8. Whitney Bolton, "Stage Review: 'The Immoralist' Outstanding Example of Theatrical Courage," *New York Morning Telegraph,* 10 February 1954.

9. Brooks Atkinson, "'The Immoralist' By Ruth and Augustus Goetz, Made From Andre Gide's Novel," *New York Times,* 9 February 1954.

10. John McClain, "'Season In the Sun:' Full of Wonderful and Painful Laughs," *New York Journal-American,* 29 September 1950.

11. John Chapman, "'Season In The Sun' Is Humor At Its Best, and Beautifully Acted," *New York Daily News,* 29 September 1950.

12. Whitney Bolton, "'Season In the Sun' Nice Piece of Funny Writing," *New York Morning Telegraph,* 30 September 1950.

13. Wolcott Gibbs, *Season In The Sun* (New York: Random House, 1950), p. 27.

14. Joseph T. Shipley, "On Stage," *New Leader,* 14 October 1950.

15. Joseph Schildkraut, "A New Conception of 'The Green Bay Tree,'" *New York Post,* 31 January 1951.

16. Robert Garland, "'The Green Bay Tree' By Off-Broadway Group," *New York Journal-American,* 17 July 1947; Robert Garland "'Green Bay Tree' Impressively Staged at Mews Playhouse," *New York Journal-American,* 17 July 1942; "Green Bay Tree," Equity-Library Theatre, no publication, 1950, and "Green Bay Tree," Triangle Players of West Side Y.M.C.A." both on file in "The Green Bay Tree" file, Lincoln Center.

17. "The Green Bay Tree," *Variety,* 7 February 1951.

18. Whitney Bolton, "'The Green Bay Tree,' Revived With Character Alterations," *New York Morning Telegram,* 3 February 1951.

19. Richard Watts, Jr. "Decline Of 'The Green Bay Tree,'" *New York Post,* 2 February 1951.

20. Joseph T. Shipley, "On Stage: Two Revivals Disappointing," *Cue,* 12 February 1951, p. 26.

21. John McClain, "A Strong Though Rather Soiled Play," *New York Journal-American,* 2 February 1951.

22. John Chapman, ed., *The Burns Mantle Best Plays of 1950–51* (New York: Dodd, Mead & Company, 1951), p. 346.

23. George Freedley, "On Stage — and Off," *New York Morning Telegraph,* 26 December 1952.

24. Walter Kerr, "The Theatres: 'The Children's Hour,'" *New York Herald Tribune,* 19 December 1952.

25. George Jean Nathan, "George Jean Nathan's Theatre," *New York Journal-American,* 11 January 1952.

26. Whitney Bolton, "Stage: 'Children's Hour' Still Taut, Powerful Drama," *New York Morning Telegraph,* 20 December 1952.

27. George Freedley, "The Stage Today," *New York Morning Telegraph,* 29 May 1945.

28. Thomas R. Dash, "'The Children's Hour,'" *Women's Wear Daily,* 19 December 1952.

29. Richard Moody, *Lillian Hellman, Playwright* (New York: Pegasus, 1972), p. 238.

30. Doris V. Falk, *Lillian Hellman* (New York: Frederick Ungar Publishing Co., 1978), p. 8.

31. Eric Bentley, "Lillian Hellman's Indignation," *The Dramatic Event* (New York: Horizon Press, 1954), pp. 74–75.

32. Louis Kronenberger, ed., *The Best Plays of 1952–53* (New York: Dodd, Mead & Company, 1953), p. 313.

33. *Lillian Hellman, Playwright*, p. 38.

34. Louis Kronenberger, ed., *Best Plays of 1953–54* (New York: Dodd, Mead & Company, 1954), p. 401.

35. John Chapman, " 'Tea and Sympathy' A Beautiful Play. Deborah Kerr Magnificent," *New York Daily News,* 1 October 1953.

36. Robert Anderson, *Tea and Sympathy* (New York: Random House, 1953), p. 48.

37. *Ibid.,* pp. 176–177.

38. John Chapman, ed., *The Burns Mantle Yearbook of Best Plays of 1948–49* (Garden City, New York: Dodd, Mead & Company, 1949), p. 349.

39. W. David Sievers, *Freud On Broadway* (New York: Cooper Square Publishers, Inc., 1970), p. 409.

40. Louis Kronenberger, ed., *The Burns Mantle Yearbook of The Best Plays of 1952–53* (New York: Dodd, Mead & Company, 1953), p. 339.

41. Calder Willingham, *End As A Man* (New York: Samuel French, Inc., 1953), 1-2-11.

42. *Ibid.,* p. 2-2-24.

43. *Ibid.*

44. *The Burns Mantle Yearbook of the Best Plays of 1952–53,* p. 295.

45. Gene R. Touchet, "American Drama and the Emergence of Social Homophilia, 1952–1972" (unpublished doctoral dissertation, University of Florida, 1974), p. 6.

46. Gore Vidal, *Matters of Fact and Fiction* (New York: Random House, 1973), p. 138.

47. Tennessee Williams, *Three Plays by Tennessee Williams* (New York: A New Directions Book, 1959), p. 202.

48. "American Drama and the Emergence of Social Homophilia, 1952–1972," p. 7.

49. *The Burns Mantle Best Plays of 1950–51,* p. 236.

50. George S. Kaufman and Leueen MacGrath, *The Small Hours* (typewritten copy), Lincoln Center, 2-31.

51. Richard Watts, Jr., "Two On The Aisle," *New York Past,* 22 October 1953.

52. *The Best Plays of 1953–54,* p. 311.

53. Dorothy Parker and Arnaud d'Usseau, *Ladies Of The Corridor* (typewritten copy), Lincoln Center, p. 1-1-13.

54. Dorothy Parker and Arnaud d'Usseau, *Ladies Of The Corridor* (New York: Samuel French, Inc., 1945), p. 82.

55. *Ibid.,* p. 83.

56. *Ibid.,* p. 84.

57. "American Drama and The Emergence of Social Homophilia, 1952–1972," p. 16.

58. Ruth and Augustus Goetz, "Genesis of A Play From An Andre Gide Novel," *New York Times,* 31 January 1954.

59. "Play On Broadway," *Variety,* 10 February 1954.

60. Ruth and Augustus Goetz, *The Immoralist* (New York: Dramatists Play Service, Inc., 1954), p. 31.

61. *Ibid.,* p. 32.

62. *Ibid.,* p. 36.

63. *Ibid.,* p. 61.

64. *Ibid.,* p. 64.

65. *Ibid.,* pp. 72–73.

66. *Ibid.,* p. 76.

67. *Ibid.,* p. 78.

68. *Ibid.,* p. 81.

69. *Ibid.,* pp. 83–84.

70. *Ibid.*, pp. 90–91.
71. *Ibid.*, pp. 91–92.
72. *Ibid.*, pp. 92–93.
73. *Ibid.*, p. 104.
74. *Ibid.*, p. 116.
75. *Ibid.*, p. 120.
76. *Ibid.*
77. *Ibid.*
78. *Ibid.*, p. 121.
79. Klaus Mann, *Andre Gide* (New York: Farrar, Straus & Giroux, Inc., 1943), p. 101.
80. Eric Bentley, *The Dramatic Event* (Boston: Beacon Press, 1954), pp. 206–207.
81. *Ibid.*
82. Interview with Ruth Goodman Goetz, New York City, 12 January 1980.
83. *Ibid.*
84. *New York Times,* 31 January 1954.
85. Interview with Ruth Goodman Goetz, 12 January 1980.
86. *Ibid.*
87. *The Best Plays of 1953–54,* p. 10.
88. John Chapman, "'The Immoralist' Sure Enough Is," *New York Daily News,* 9 February 1954.
89. Brooks Atkinson, "'The Immoralist' by Ruth and Augustus Goetz, Made From Andre Gide's Novel," *New York Times,* 9 February 1954.
90. Robert Coleman, "'The Immoralist' Treats Hard Subject With Sympathy," *New York Daily News,* 9 February 1954.
91. Thomas R. Dash, "The Immoralist," *New York's Women's Wear Daily,* 9 February 1954.
92. *Variety,* 10 February 1954.
93. Cole Lesley, *Remembered Laughter, The Life of Noel Coward* (New York: Alfred A. Knopf, 1976), p. 325.
94. *Ibid.*
95. *Freud On Broadway,* p. 413.
96. John McLain, "Fails To Stir Emotional Reaction," *New York Journal-American,* 9 February 1954.
97. Interview with Reginald Cockburn, New York City, 11 January 1980.
98. *New York Daily Mirror,* 9 February 1954.
99. Richard Watts, Jr., "A Grave Drama About Abnormality," *New York Post,* 9 February 1954.
100. Walter Kerr, "The Immoralist," *New York Herald Tribune,* 9 February 1954.
101. *New York Journal-American,* 9 February 1954.
102. *The Best Plays of 1953–54,* p. 10.
103. "American Drama and the Emergence of Social Homophilia, 1952–1972," pp. 17–18.
104. *Ibid.*, p. 28.
105. *Ibid.*, p. 19.
106. Chester Erskin, *The Good* (typewritten copy), Lincoln Center, p. 42.
107. Sewell and Leslie Stokes, *Oscar Wilde* (typewritten copy), Lincoln Center, pp. 2-2-25 & 26.
108. Vernon Scott, "Curtain Cues," *New York Post,* 29 January 1954.
109. Interview with Ruth Goodman Goetz, 12 January 1980.
110. *New York Morning Telegraph,* 10 February 1954.
111. Interview with Ruth Goodman Goetz, 12 January 1980.
112. Henry Hewes, ed., *The Best Plays of 1963–64* (New York: Dodd, Mead & Company, 1964), p. 351.
113. Judith Crist, "'The Immoralist' Antiquely Good," *New York Herald Tribune,* 8 November 1963.

17

An Ugly Chapter in the History of the American Theater and of the New York Times

It was not the best of times, in the estimation of other American play-wrights, to follow the example of *The Immoralist*. While not a single voice was raised in protest over the sympathetic treatment of the illegal gay characterizations, the red and gay witch-hunts spawned by Senator Joseph McCarthy continued unchecked well into the 1950s. The Goetzes began their adaptation of André Gide's novel before McCarthy's demagoguery began to intimidate the nation's artists, liberals and intel-lectuals. By the time they had finished the play, the authors had great difficulty finding a producer, despite their previous commercial success, *Washington Square*.

After the production of *The Immoralist,* only five plays with unmistakably gay male roles were seen on Broadway during the 1950s. Meyer Levin proposed a gay infatuation as a possible motive for a gratu-itous murder in his production of *Compulsion.* Levin's characterization of two cold-blooded teenage killers resembled those of the famed Leopold-Loeb murder case. Such unsympathetic roles could hardly unsettle even the most homophobic theatergoers. Michael Gazzo added a gay secondary character to his shocking, successful drama of drug addiction, *A Hatful of Rain.* Strictly for laughs that came infrequently, Herman Wouk included two gay males in his comedy, *Nature's Way.* One tries to lure the protagonist away from his pregnant bride in

Wouk's unsuccessful play. A minor character declares that he is a "homosexual" in Maxwell Anderson's hit, *The Bad Seed.* Finally, another gay minor role appeared in N. Richard Nash's flop, *The Girls of Summer.*

Even after Senator McCarthy's political censure and downfall, Tennessee Williams admitted that he was still afraid of including a gay character in any of his plays, even if that character were dead before the start of the dramatic action.[1] Williams did so in *A Streetcar Named Desire* in 1947, and twice more in both *Cat on a Hot Tin Roof,* and *Suddenly Last Summer.* Because off-Broadway audiences are generally more sophisticated and more tolerant of avant-garde productions than Broadway theatergoers, Williams premiered *Suddenly Last Summer* in a small playhouse. The playwright was worried about critical reaction to a deceased gay character in that one-act drama. Coupled with *Suddenly Last Summer* under the title *The Garden District,* was another of Williams' one-acts, *Something Unspoken.* It concerned the closeted lesbian relationship of a Southern dowager and her private secretary. Williams was so evasive in handling lesbian characters that only one of the reviewers recognized the sexual implication of the title *Something Unspoken.*[2]

Edward Albee was introduced to New York theatergoers with a production of *Zoo Story* at the Provincetown Playhouse, another off-Broadway theater. Albee was just as elusive as Williams in handling gay characters. It was not apparent to critics why the troubled protagonist of *Zoo Story* commits suicide. Many thought he was a disturbed beatnik. The desperation and social alienation felt by the young man in *Zoo Story* had been experienced by many closeted gay Americans. They were being vilified, hunted down and discharged from both private and public employment as possible security risks. Although Arthur Miller's *A View from the Bridge* is not concerned with gay characters, it did dramatize the devastating effects of a gay accusation made in a homophobic society. The protagonist of this play, which was produced in 1955, attempts to discredit a heterosexual romantic rival with the false charge that he is gay. Miller was particularly sensitive to the political climate since he himself was suspected during the red witch-hunt.

The climate of opinion in which Senator McCarthy thrived lingered long after his downfall, at least on Broadway. Just as there had been talk of a Communist conspiracy to undermine America's security, there was talk, early in the 1960s, of a gay complot to demean women and families in the American drama. Rumors that three of the four most esteemed American playwrights were gay reached the ears of the drama critics writing for the New York dailies. None of this triumvirate had written a Broadway play with an overt gay protagonist. Certain critics set their homophobic sights on these closeted playwrights, hoping to disqualify their work as disguised, degenerate distortions of heterosexual relations. One theater historian has called this hunt for gay dramatists "an ugly chapter" in the "history of homophobia among the critics."[3]

Despite its editorial abhorrence of McCarthyism, it is hardly surprising that the New York Times supported its drama critic's use of similar tactics to identify and disqualify any gay dramatist's writing. The 'Good Gray Lady' of publishing was even more homophobic when Howard Taubman was her employee than she has since continued to be under the Ochs-Sultzberger family. Only a single, briefly annotated article by Allan Pierce in Christopher Street magazine has ever documented that "ugly chapter" in the history, not only of the American theater, but of the New York Times as well.

According to Pierce, the New York drama critics, with few exceptions, have reacted to lesbian and gay male characters with no more tolerance than the reviewers for the Times:

> ...[A]n examination of fifty years of reviews of plays with gay themes or characters, or that reviewers considered to be gay allegories, reveals that the critics have generally been abrasive to the healthy homosexual sensibility. Rather than fostering mass enlightenment, theater critics have by and large acted as narrow-minded, prejudiced fag-haters and baiters.[4]

In the homophobic tradition of Brooks Atkinson, George Jean Nathan and Burns Mantle, Howard Taubman of the Times became, according to gay theater historian William H. Hoffman, "a pioneer homophobe."[5] In a 1961 Sunday feature article, Taubman announced:

> It is time to speak openly and candidly of the increasing influence and incidence of homosexuality on the New York stage — and, indeed, in the other arts as well.
> The subject is too important to be left forever to the sly whispers and malicious gossips...
> The infiltration of homosexual attitudes occurs in the theater at many levels...
> The insidious results of the unspoken taboo is that sincere, searching

writers feel they must state a homosexual theme in heterosexual situations. They convince themselves that what they wish to say will get through anyhow. But dissembling is unhealthy. The audience senses rot at the drama's core.

The taboos are not what they used to be. Homosexuality is not a forbidden topic.[6]

"What seemed to worry Taubman especially," wrote Allan Pierce, "was that homosexual playwrights, in submission to the public's preference for 'normality,' were writing plays about heterosexuals, but in a homosexual way."[7]

The "rot" Taubman suspected was, of course, a gay sensibility. The *Times* drama critic concluded that "The work of some talented writers seems tainted ... [with] furtive, leering insinuations that have contaminated some of our arts."[8]

Two years after his original warning about the contamination of American drama, Taubman wrote a second article for the Sunday *Times,* elaborating upon his hypothesis. Entitled "Modern Primer: Helpful Hints to Tell Appearances Vs. Truth,"[9] Taubman informed readers that, "since this column is a public service of sorts,... possibly we can come up with helpful hints on how to scan the intimations and symbols of homosexuality in our theater."[10] The critic drew up a list of unpleasant or frustrating dramatic situations relating to conflicts between the sexes which, if found in a play, might indicate that the author was gay.

As a result of the clues provided by Taubman, a gay witch-hunt — limited, however, to a vicious word-of-mouth guessing game — got under way in the 1960s. Allan Pierce observed:

> Fear that an unidentified gay playwright would lure the public into "renouncing heterosexuality" and participating in "disgusting, sinful acts" became widespread, coinciding with the straight man on the street's dread of being "seduced."...
>
> Playwrights who were suspected of being gay were watched, major authors whose work was especially misrepresented critically included Edward Albee, Tennessee Williams, and William Inge.[11]

Following Taubman's lead, Martin Gottfried of *Women's Wear Daily* called Edward Albee's *Who's Afraid of Virginia Woolf?* "perhaps the most successful homosexual play ever produced on Broadway, if its sexual core had been evident to more people it probably never would have run — even though it is perfect theater (although basically dishonest)."[12]

In 1966, another drama critic for the *Times,* Stanley Kauffmann, declared that "three of the most successful American playwrights of the last twenty years are (reputed) homosexuals."[13] The drama critic insisted on the unmasking of gay playwrights so they could write about their own kind rather than about heterosexual relationships; Kauffman wanted to avoid 'distortion.' "Only this one neurosis," Kauffman wrote in 1966, "homosexuality, is taboo in the main traffic of our stage."[14] The *Times* reviewer pleaded, "I do not argue for increased homosexual influences in our theater. It is precisely because I, like many others, am weary of *disguised* homosexual influences that I raise the matter."[15]

Kauffmann's article claimed that the "vindictiveness" of gay playwrights who "hate those who make them hate themselves" caused them to "distort marriage and femininity."[16] He pleased some readers who wrote to the editor. Many letters complimented Kauffmann. However, one reader protested, "Are Jews only to write about Jews?"[17] In a follow-up article Kauffmann wrote in his own defense:

> I mean simply (to repeat) that homosexual dramatists need the same liberty that heterosexuals now have. If this is too much for us to contemplate, then at least let us drop all the cant about homosexual "influences" and distortion; because we are only complaining of the results of our own attitudes.[18]

In an article two years later, for the *New York Times,* Rosalyn Regelson reported:

> Some drama critics have been accusing certain major playwrights of an arrogant homosexual imperialism toward the normal world. Plays like *A Streetcar Named Desire* and *Who's Afraid of Virginia Woolf?* which have moved large audiences over the world, have been treated as esoteric missiles in guerrilla attacks by the "homosexual underground." Among the critics waging a counterattack have been Howard Taubman, Stanley Kauffmann, John Simon, Philip Roth and also Elizabeth Hardwick, who calls for a return to "a masculine theater."[19]

Along with those critics cited, Allan Pierce has added to the list of homophobes: Brooks Atkinson, Clive Barnes and Mel Gussow, all of the *Times;* John Chapman and Douglas Watt of the *Daily News;* George Oppenheimer of *Newsday;* and Leo Miskin of the *Morning*

Telegraph.[20] "Chapman walked out in the middle of one gay play in 1967," Pierce reported, "and reviewed no more plays the whole season that smacked of homosexuality."[21] Watt described one gay character as "somewhat queer (even for a queer),"[22] in a 1976 review.

The witch-hunt for gay playwrights that lasted throughout the 1960s concluded with a defense of one major American playwright by William Goldman in his book, *The Season: A Candid Look at Broadway.* Goldman confided to readers that, "Arthur Miller is the only major playwright since World War II who had not been associated with homosexuality. He is also the only Jew."[23]

"Whether it's changing for the better these days is open to question," wrote gay theater historian Richard Hall in an appraisal of the homophobic bias of drama critics. "John Simon, Douglas Watt and Mel Gussow," Hall reminded, "continue their vitriolic ways unchecked."[24] In 1975, Simon disparaged gays in the audience of a play,[25] just as police spies had made similar reports on audiences viewing *The Captive, The Drag* and *Pleasure Man* back in the 1920s. In January 1979 Richard Eder of the *New York Times,* reviewing Tennessee Williams' new play, *A Lovely Sunday for Creve Coeur* with an all-female cast, suggested that "perhaps these characters are not women, but men transformed into women."[26]

When Clive Barnes reviewed *The Boys in the Band* in 1968 for the *New York Times,* he referred to the gay male characters as "queers," "fairy-queens," and "fags," without using quotation marks.[27] By 1979, the drama critic was using quotation marks for the word "queer" in reviewing Martin Sherman's *Bent.* Douglas Watt, of the *Daily News,* claimed that was the way the characters "refer to themselves."[28] Walter Kerr of the *Times* also used quotation marks when he, too, made reference to "queers"[29] in two critiques of *Bent.* Like all writers employed by the *Times,* Kerr generally uses "homosexuals" to identify gay males since it is the policy of that publication to continue to call both lesbians and gay men "homosexuals." "After *ten* years of struggle to educate the media, you'd think they'd say it right!" television critic Cindy Stein protested in Boston's *Gay Community News* in 1980. "You'd think that the words we have chosen to call ourselves, lesbians and gay men, could have been adopted instead."[30]

The efforts of drama critics for the *Times* to disqualify the work of Tennessee Williams, Edward Albee and William Inge failed.

Broadway's most successful and renowned authors continued to write plays reflecting the concerns and lifestyles of the majority of American theatergoers. Taubman and Kauffman could not believe a gay playwright was capable of creating, with psychological verisimilitude, realistic roles outside of their own sexual context. There is no reason to believe that mass audiences were any more sophisticated or any less homophobic during the same period. Had any of the playwrights heeded Taubman and Kauffman's advice and written about gay lifestyles in the 1960s, the subject matter would have hung about their necks like an albatross, or a halter, "Don't put your head in a noose,"[31] W. Somerset Maugham had warned other gay playwrights.

Twenty-two years after the shadow of that noose fell across the work of suspected dramatists, their plays still remain under suspicion. Edward Albee has always resented any assumption about his sexual orientation as impertinent and irrelevant; Tennessee Williams, on the other hand, finally identified himself as being gay in 1975. In either case, it has made little difference to those reviewers following Howard Taubman's lead. "Critics are forever discovering homosexual references in my plays where they don't exist," Albee complained in 1983. "The critics were always doing that to poor Tennessee Williams, you know. He kept protesting, 'The women in my plays are women, and the men are men,' but still they insist it wasn't so."[32]

Broadway audiences had not seen a gay protagonist in twelve years when Stanley Kauffmann wrote, "Only this one neurosis, homosexuality, is taboo in the main traffic of our stage."[33] Just four years later, in 1968, the critic for the *Christian Science Monitor* complained, "Perhaps it is a commentary in the malaise of our times that homosexuality is no longer a novelty in the theater."[34] An international sexual revolution was underway by the end of the 1960s that brought about radical changes in the theatrical fare on both sides of the Atlantic. Eight American playwrights, besides Albee and Inge, included supporting gay roles in plays produced on Broadway in the sixties. Half a dozen British playwrights not only did the same; they also offered Broadway audiences gay protagonists. Unintimidated by the *New York Times'* witch-hunt for gay playwrights, British dramatists began writing plays with gay protagonists before Parliament had liberalized the Theatre Licensing Act that had curtailed freedom of expression on the British stage for more than two centuries.

One of the plays that unsettled the critic for the *Christian Science Monitor* was the 1966 British import *Staircase,* a drama concerning the longtime relationship of two aging, troubled gay males. "Charles Dyer's *Staircase* seems to me," declared Walter Kerr, "the simplest and most honest treatment of homosexuality I have come across in the theater."[35] Dyer's drama also impressed another critic, Martin Gottfried, who hailed it as "the first play that I have seen deal sensitively and adroitly with homosexuality."[36]. Not all reviewers agreed. John Chapman, the most rabid homophobe within the critics' circle, walked out on the play. Chapman informed readers that according to the author's brief biography in the program, he was happily married with three children. "I was glad to hear this," Chapman wrote, "otherwise, I might have tossed and turned all the rest of the night, worrying about him."[37]

It is interesting that when plays with gay protagonists have been produced on Broadway, the program often made clear that the author was married and had fathered children. During the first half-century, gay men and lesbians were most often portrayed as suicides, seducers, murderers, drug addicts, traitors, transvestites and bizarre grotesques. Howard Taubman detected no "rot at the drama's core" in these plays, yet most were authored by straight writers. Stanley Kauffmann made no protest that the vindictiveness of John Osborne's homophobia was obvious in the protagonist in his 1969 Broadway production, *A Patriot for Me.* Only one critic was distressed by the portrayal of a "bull dyke" lesbian in the 1966 British import, *The Killing of Sister George,* written by Frank Marcus, a married man and father of three. Joseph Le Sueur of the *Village Voice* asked:

> Have we really come a long way from the *Children's Hour* which presented lesbianism as a disease no woman should be unfortunate enough to have, to the present work's nasty and uncompassionate treatment of it as a joke? . . . I advise lesbians to stay away from it. Life is cruel enough.[38]

During the start of the sexual revolution of the late 1960s, two sensational plays concerning very different gay lifestyles appeared in off-Broadway playhouses. Neither drama was written by a married man with children. *Fortune and Men's Eyes,* by Canadian ex-convict John Herbert, was a shocking disclosure of the pecking order among prisoners, both gay and straight, who turn to one another, often brutally, for sexual satisfaction. *The Boys in the Band,* by Mart Crowley, concerned a clique of guilt-ridden, self-mocking gay friends who torment themselves and one another at a bizarre birthday party. Both productions initially attracted predominantly gay audiences. Crowley's tragicomedy eventually came to the attention of straight theatergoers. *The Boys in the Band* was seen in over a thousand performances[39] before it was made into a motion picture. The play was still running in an off-Broadway theater when riots at the Stonewall started a revolution which demanded an end to discrimination. *The Boys in the Band* was re-evaluated in the ensuing process of raising gay consciousness. Even by many who initially found it amusing and entertaining, Crowley's dramatic guilt-trip was eventually damned as another negative, stereotypical portrait of the gay community.

"The play is by far the frankest treatment of homosexuality I have ever seen on the stage,"[40] declared Clive Barnes of the *New York Times.* The production of *The Boys in the Band* was just what Barnes' critical predecessors had been insisting upon: a dramatization by an author, apparently gay, reflecting "the rot" of his lifestyle rather than one in which he would — in the words of Stanley Kauffmann — "distort marriage and femininity."[41] The bitchery of *The Boys in the Band* seemed to critic Barnes to be truer and more typical of gay relationships than he had found it it to be of straight relationships in *Who's Afraid of Virginia Woolf?* Barnes wrote:

> A couple of years ago, my colleague Stanley Kauffmann, in a perceptive but widely misunderstood essay, pleaded for a more honest homosexual drama, one where homosexual experience was not translated into false pseudoheterosexual terms. This I think *The Boys in the Band,* with all its faults, achieves.[42]

"Homosexual drama will be old hat in five years,"[43] predicted actor Cliff Gorman who appeared in *The Boys in the Band.* That prediction was so accurate that no less than twenty plays with gay characters were seen on Broadway, and another twenty-six off-Broadway, from 1968 to 1973.[44] During the decade that followed, eighty-four plays with either gay characters or gay themes were seen on New York stages.[45] Few of these shows had lesbian roles, but gay male roles became not only old hat but almost a staple of the American drama during this period.

While the number of plays with gay male roles and gay themes produced in Broadway, off-Broadway, and off-off-Broadway theaters since 1968 is impressive, few of these shows had gay protagonists. Fewer became critical or commercial successes. None caused the sensation that greeted *The Captive, The Drag, Trio,* or even *The Boys in the Band.* Concerning the popularity of *The Boys in the Band* with straight theater-goers, actor Cliff Gorman said, "They think because it's about homo-sexuals, it's a freak show."[46] In 1933 critic Burns Mantle described the experience of seeing a play with gay characters as "an adventure com-bining the pleasures of the theater with the inspection of a kind of human zoo."[47] By the 1970s, the gay protagonists of hit Broadway shows were, with allusory exceptions, little or no different from straight male roles in the way the playwrights characterized them or performers played them. There were no freaks in *Bentley, The Dresser, Gemini,* or *The Fifth of July.* Neither were there any smash hits with gay themes like *The Captive* in the twenties.

Certain die-hard homophobic critics — such as Stanley Kauffmann and John Simon — seemed more comfortable at the sight of a freakish gay stage portrait in 1982 than they appeared to have been with non-stereotypical gay roles in the 1970s. There were few characters to be seen on the New York stage quite as outlandish as the drag queen in *Torch Song Trilogy* who, in the very first scene, sits preening at his dressing table while delivering a monologue about his raunchy sex life. Kauffmann and Simon joined other critics in unanimous praise for the show when it opened in a Greenwich Village playhouse. After being moved uptown to a Broadway theater, *Torch Song Trilogy* won the Antoinette Perry Award as the best play of 1982. Its author, Harvey Fierstein, also won a Tony for his perfor-mance as the female-impersonating entertainer.

Stanley Kauffmann's positive reaction to *Torch Song Trilogy* in 1982 helps one understand his 1966 plea for a more tolerant theater in which a gay playwright could dramatize, as female impersonator Harvey Fierstein had done, his or her own lifestyle without fear of cen-sor or scorn. Kauffmann wrote of the vehicle the drag-queen entertainer had fashioned:

> It is seriously revealing, not just in the informational sense, ("So *that's* what 'they' are really like") although that's true, too; Fierstein treats his characters as any serious author does, to dramatize as much as he can of their mystery.[48]

Kauffmann could sit back in his aisle seat amused by the out-rageous antics of a cross-dresser in *Torch Song Trilogy* confident, too, that he understood and could cope with what he saw on the stage. There was no real mystery in a character who behaved as Kauffmann would like to think all gay men "are really like." Watching other shows, the veteran critic was most often nonplussed in trying to evaluate the work of playwrights reputed to be gay, but not campy cross-dressers who did not restrict their dramaturgy to their own limited sexual lifestyles.

John Simon protested that another Broadway hit, *La Cage aux Folles,* had gone too far in sentimentalizing the way "'they' are really like." Simon wrote: "For homosexuals, this, even more than *Torch Song Trilogy,* is the Broadway legitimization of their modus vivendi, all the way from respectably bourgeois to outrageously transvestite, via a budget of $5 million." Dismissing *La Cage aux Folles* as a sentimental misrepresentation of its subject matter, Simon was contemptuous of "the sanctimonious piety with which the show is being hailed in standing ovations, critical hosannas, bourgeois self-congratulation, and homosexual ecstasies..."[49]

Like John Simon, Stanley Kauffmann, too, objected that the first musical to center on a male love story should be "a sentimental show that extols the values of love, honor, and fidelity of home and family."[51] One can only surmise that Kauffman had either walked out on or slept through the third act of *Torch Song Trilogy.* He did not protest that comedy's conclusion in which the transvestite sets up a family unit which included his gay mate and their adopted gay son. A similar set-up at the beginning of *La Cage aux Folles* provoked the critic. Kauffmann reprimanded librettist Harvey Fierstein for telling the audience, over and over, that:

> ...basically we're all alike, that the homosexual has triumphed by finding the courage to proclaim what he is, and that he is just one more human being, interchangeable with anyone else on the block, except for the way he makes love. This isn't equality; this is mush. This is to say that blacks are no different from whites, Jews from Gentiles, women from men, when the real value of these groups is in their differences. The test of any sane society is its ability to welcome those differences, to grow by them, not to push them all into a cross-cultural Waring blender.[51]

Since it is the gay transvestite entertainers in *La Cage aux Folles* who delight in their differences, one might wonder whether the veteran critic had dozed throughout most of *La Cage aux Folles.* But even a napping reviewer would have bolted up in his seat when the transvestite entertainer defiantly bellows "I am what I am." Kauffmann's distortion of the musical does not really deserve serious consideration, except as another telling clue to the rationale behind the gay witch-hunt he helped foster.

Kauffmann had announced his willingness in 1966 to welcome the work of gay playwrights so long as they confined their considerations to their own lifestyles. By so doing, the critic posited, such authors would no longer be able to "distort marriage and femininity."[52] No wonder then that he was so befuddled by *La Cage aux Folles*. The biggest musical hit of the 1983–84 theatrical season celebrates both marriage and femininity, but within a family unit composed of a female impersonator, his gay mate and the latter's straight son.

Outraged at the distortions of traditional concepts inviolable to him, the conservative sexagenarian made another plea in print relating to gay characters in the drama. Kauffmann insisted upon a stricter definition of individuals in a heterogeneous society: a definition based upon their gender, race, creed, and sexual orientation. Within that more definitive frame of reference, Kauffmann could more assuredly disqualify any theatrical re-evaluation or reconsideration of "sane" society's status quo.

Like the "Good Gray Lady" who had once employed him, Stanley Kauffmann insists upon identifications to distinguish the chosen from the rejected. "Homosexuals" must be reminded of their proper place within the traditional social order by a demeaning nomenclature with negative and restrictive connotations. With rare exception, "homosexuals" met with sorry ends in the dramas that introduced such characters to Broadway theatergoers over a period of almost three decades. The female-impersonating protagonist in the 1983 production of *La Cage aux Folles* may be an effeminate cross-dresser, a minority member even within a minority, but he could hardly have been conceived as a "homosexual." It is a gay male character who brings audiences to their feet with Jerry Herman's lyrics, "I am what I am," an anthem in celebration of his individuality in a musical celebrating "love, honor and fidelity of home and family." Lesbians and gay men have come to incorporate such values within their own distinctive lifestyles just as any other men and women might be doing on the same block.

Notes

1. Georges-Michel Sarotte, *Like A Brother, Like A Lover* (Garden City, New York: Anchor Press/Doubleday, 1978), p. 118.
2. Whitney Bolton, "Williams Twin Bill At York Theater," *Morning Telegraph,* 9 January 1953.
3. Richard Hall, "Richard Rehse, All About 'Out and About,'" *Advocate,* 11 January 1979.
4. Allan Pierce, "Homophobia and the Critics," *Christopher Street,* June 1978, p. 44.
5. William M. Hoffman, *Gay Plays, The First Collection* (introduction), (New York: Avon Books, 1979), p. xxv.
6. Howard Taubman, "Not What It Seems: Homosexual Motif Gets Heterosexual Guise," *New York Times,* 5 November 1961.
7. *Christopher Street,* June 1978, p. 41.
8. *New York Times,* 5 November 1961.
9. Howard Taubman, "Modern Primer: Helpful Hints to Tell Appearances vs. Truth," *New York Times,* 28 April 1963.
10. *Ibid.*
11. *Christopher Street,* June 1978, p.41
12. *Ibid.*
13. Stanley Kauffmann, "Homosexual Drama and Its Disguises," *New York Times,* 21 January 1966.
14. *Ibid.*
15. *Ibid.*
16. *Ibid.*
17. "Drama Mailbag: 'Arguing About Homosexuality,'" *New York Times,* 6 February 1966.
18. Stanley Kauffmann, "On the Acceptability of the Homosexual," *New York Times,* 6 February 1966.
19. Rosalyn Regelson, "Up the Camp Staircase," *New York Times,* 3 March 1968.
20. *Christopher Street,* June 1978, p. 40.
21. *Ibid.,* p. 41.
22. Douglas Watt, "Kate In Loonie Land," *New York Daily News,* 4 February 1976.
23. William Goldman, *The Season: A Candid Look At Broadway* (New York: Harcourt, Brace & World, 1969), p. 238.
24. *Advocate,* 11 January 1979.
25. *Christopher Street,* June 1978, p. 44.
26. Richard Eder, "'Creve Coeur' New Drama by Tennessee Williams," *New York Times,* 22 January 1979.
27. Clive Barnes, "Theater: 'Boys in the Band' Opens Off Broadway," *New York Times,* 15 April 1968.
28. Douglas Watt, "Entertainment: 'Bent' is Shocking But Not Moving," *New York Daily News,* 3 December 1979.
29. Walter Kerr, "'Bent,' Starring Richard Gere," *New York Times,* 3 December 1979; and "For The Serious Theatergoer," *New York Times,* 16 December 1979.
30. Cindy Stein, "Television: Queers In America's Living Room," *Boston Community News,* 5 January 1980.
31. Robin Maugham, *Somerset and All The Maughams* (New York: The American Library, 1966), p. 20.
32. Michiko Kakutan, "The Legacy of Tennessee Williams," *New York Times,* 6 March 1983.
33. *New York Times,* 21 January 1966.
34. Alan N. Bunce, "The Tragicomic 'Boys in the Band,'" *Christian Science Monitor,* 17 August 1968.

35. Walter Kerr, "Kerr On Staircase 'Honest Human,'" *New York Times,* 21 January 1968.

36. Martin Gottfried, "Theater," *Women's Wear Daily,* 11 January 1968.

37. John Chapman, "Did You Ever See Such Brave Old Twists as Those in 'Staircase?'" *New York Times,* 11 January 1968.

38. Joseph Le Seur, "Anglotrivia," *Village Voice,* 13 October 1966.

39. Otis L. Guensey,Jr., ed., *The Best Plays of 1970–71* (New York: Dodd, Mead & Company,1971).

40. *New York Times,* 15 April 1968.

41. *New York Times,* 21 January 1966.

42. *New York Times,* 15 April, 1968.

43. Judy Klenesrud, "You Don't Have To Be One To Play One," *New York Times,* 29 September 1968.

44. Donald Lee Loeffler, *An Analysis of the Treatment of the Homosexual Character in Drama Produced in the New York Theater from 1960 to 1968* (New York: Arno Press, 1975), pp. 47A–47D.

45. Author's computation.

46. *New York Times,,* 29 September 1968.

47. Burns Mantle, "'Green Bay Tree' Highly Emotional," *New York Daily News,* 21 October 1933.

48. Stanley Kauffmann, "Torch Song Trilogy," *Saturday Review,* March 1982.

49. John Simon, "Guys as Dolls," *New York,* 5 September 1983.

50. "Broadway Out Of the Closet," *Time,* 29 August 1983, p. 65.

51. Stanley Kauffmann, "Designated Hit," *Saturday Review,* November-December 1983, p. 49.

INDEX

335

A wide variety of books with gay and lesbian
themes are available from Alyson Publications.
For a catalog, or to be placed on our mailing list,
please write to:
Alyson Publications
40 Plympton Street
Boston, Mass. 02118.